W9-ACD-809

# Henry James and Impressionism

To Juanita

Henry James and Impressionism

by

James J. Kirschke

The Whitston Publishing Company
Troy, New York
1981

*Acknowledgments*

I should like to thank the Pierpont Morgan Library for extending publication rights to quote from: Henry James. Als. 28 August 1878 to W.E. Henley.

I should also like to thank the following publishers for permission to reprint materials which have appeared originally in their publications: to Little, Brown and Company for permission to quote from *Renoir, My Father* by Jean Renoir (pp. 221-222); to Prentice-Hall, Inc., for permission to quote from Winslow Homer, cited in John McCoubrey, ed. *American Art. 1700-1960: Sources and Documents* (pp. 155-156); to University of Michigan Press for permission to quote from Thomas Walton's Introduction to Emile Zola's *The Masterpiece,* 1957 edition (p. 6); to Harvard University Press for permission to quote from John Lincoln Sweeney, ed. *The Painter's Eye* (pp. 173 and pp. 174-175); to New York University Press for permission to quote from Henry James. *Parisian Sketches* (pp. 111-112); to the University Press of Virginia for permission to quote from Viola Hopkins Winner. *Henry James and the Visual Arts* (p. 90 and p. 92).

Portions of Chapter Four have appeared, in somewhat revised form, in "Henry James's Use of Impressionist Painting Techniques in *The Sacred Fount* and *The Ambassadors." Studies in the Twentieth Century.* 13 (Spring 1974), 83-116.

*Preface*

The painters of the Impressionist movement[1] are frequently acknowledged to be the first of the Modernists in the plastic arts. Similarly, many people consider Henry James to be the first of the Modernist writers of fiction in English. Although critics have frequently alluded to the Impressionist nature of much of James's fiction, and often compared this fiction to the work of the Impressionist painters, previous discussions of this complex and intriguing subject have been vague, fragmentary, or confusing. Considering the apparent importance of Impressionism as a key to understanding the Modernist Movement in the arts, it seems surprising that the only book-length study in English of Impressionist fiction in the light of Impressionist art is little more than an exploratory monograph.[2]

The purpose of *Henry James and Impressionism,* then, will be to trace possible Impressionist influences upon Henry James. I will begin by tracing Impressionist techniques in the visual and plastic arts. In Chapter Two I will consider the possible Continental literary sources for James's Impressionism. Chapter Three deals with possible sources for James's Impressionism from the literature in English. My final chapter, Chapter Four, contains two parts: Part One deals with James's theory of fiction. In this part of Chapter Four, I outline James's theory of fiction and show how, on all but one or two points, this theory accords with the Impressionist techniques that I have outlined in Chapter One. The second part of Chapter Four deals entirely with the fiction. In this portion of the James chapter, I select representative works from the beginning of the author's career through the fiction of

the so-called Major Phase. I then examine these works and demonstrate the manner in which James steadily adds to his store of Impressionist techniques from the writing of his third story, "A Landscape Painter" (1866), through the three novels of the later period.
As an example of the later period, I choose to discuss at length only
*The Ambassadors*—although many of my remarks concerning this
novel are applicable also to *The Wings of the Dove* and *The Golden
Bowl.*

In *Henry James and Impressionism,* then, I hope to provide a new
and important way of viewing the fiction of James and to present
the first extended treatment in English of Impressionism in literature and the visual and plastic arts. Henry James was first and foremost a writer of fiction. But he also remained alert to the artistic
currents of his age. During the latter third of the nineteenth century—the period in which James developed his talents as a writer—
the Impressionist style predominated in all of the arts. Since James
was so alert to contemporary styles in art (on many aspects of which
he commented voluminously in his critical writings), he would seem
to have been one of the most likely authors to have been influenced
by Impressionist methods.

The art that partakes of "the Impressionist style" attends, above
all, to the "world of fine gradations and subtly linked conditions,"
as Walter Pater has said, "shifting intricately as we ourselves change."
When Pater mentioned that the artistic experience refines itself to
the "single sharp impression," he was acknowledging that the nineteenth century was among the most visual periods of Western culture. I shall, then, begin my consideration of the Impressionist
style with an analysis of Impressionism in painting. Painting is not
literature, and literature is not painting, but it does not follow that
therefore the two have nothing of significance in common. Part
of my intention in the chapter that follows is to indicate what is
significant in Impressionist painting which may have had a fundamental influence upon the fiction of Henry James.

*Notes*

[1]I refer here to the movement, covering the last third of the nineteenth century, originating for the most part in France, and including among its leaders the following artists: Manet, Pissarro, Monet, Renoir, Sisley, Whistler, Cézanne, Van Gogh, Degas, Bazille, Gauguin, Morisot, and Cassatt.

[2]I refer here to Maria E. Kronegger's *Literary Impressionism.* College and University Press, 1973. The actual text of *Literary Impressionism* is only eighty-nine pages. The remainder of the book consists of black and white plates and roughly two dozen pages of notes.

To my knowledge, the only other book-length treatment of Impressionism in literature and the visual arts is Richard Hamann's *Der Impressionismus in Leben und Kunst* (Marbourg, 1908). Hamann's book is woefully inadequate. Ruth Moser's *L'Impressionnisme français* (Geneva: Droz, 1952) is somewhat better, but Moser's study, a published version of her Geneva Master's thesis, leaves much uncovered—as does Hugo Sommerhalder's twenty-seven page *Zum Begriff des literarischen Impressionismus* (Zurich: Polygraphischer Verlag, 1961).

While my book was being produced, I received review copies of Charles R. Anderson's *Person, Place and Thing in Henry James's Novels* (Duke University Press, 1978). Anderson's book deals with Impressionism in *The Ambassadors* (pp. 220-276) and with Henry James as an Impressionist writer (pp. 277-284).

# Contents

*Chapter One*

*Impressionism in the Visual and Plastic Arts*

In a brief monograph, entitled "The Impressionism of Henry James," E. E. Hale has suggested that John La Farge (1835-1910) may have been an influence on the young James, who met the painter at William Morris Hunt's studio in Newport, around 1859. In the late 1850's, the James family abandoned Europe in favor of Newport, in order to give William the opportunity to study with William Morris Hunt, who had recently settled there. Henry also studied informally with Hunt. Not offically a pupil, Henry worked in a room apart from the others—who included John La Farge and his brother William.

La Farge, an American pupil of Thomas Couture (1815-1879)[1] (who, as I shall indicate later, was one of the two teachers who exercised the greatest influence upon the training of the leading group of original French Impressionists), was supposedly intoxicated by light.[2] And La Farge reported to his biographer, Royal Cortissoz, that even in these early days Henry was possessed of "the painter's eye"[3] (whence the title of J.J. Sweeney's collection).

As early as 1859, or before the first major Impressionist performances by Monet, La Farge had moreover shown in his theoretical comments on art and, occasionally, in his paintings themselves, a cast of mind that can best be described as Impressionist.[4] He speaks, for instance, of his first landscapes "being studies out of the window to give the effect and appearance of looking out of the window, and not being in the same light as the landscape. And also to indicate very exactly the time of day and the exact condition of the light in the sky."[5] A quotation such as this, along with a La Farge landscape such as "The Last Valley," which James praised in his 1872 review, "Art,"[5a] leads one to the conclusion that if La Farge was not a thoroughly Impressionist painter, he was at least of a largely similar temperament and, on occasion, worked in the Impressionist vein years before the term "Impressionism" was recognized as a properly descriptive term in the arts.

Perhaps even more to the point, for our concerns, is what James had to say about La Farge. In James's *Autobiography,* he remarks that La Farge's influence was fundamental, because the painter helped James to see that "even with canvas and brush whisked out of my grasp I still needn't feel disinherited" and that "the arts were after all essentially one."[6]   And in a letter from Venice to John La Farge, which James was to incorporate into "Travelling Companions" (1870), he wrote that he wished that John were in Venice with him.  Here one "needs a companion and intellectual sympathy" to help him "dispose" of "more impressions than I know what to do with."[7]

Given Henry James's early testimony to the artistic and personal example of John La Farge, one of the leading forerunners of Impressionism in painting, it would not be surprising if James were influenced by the Impressionist aspects of La Farge's style.  But what is the Impressionist style in Henry James?  And what is an Impressionist style in literature?  In order to answer these questions, we must first answer the question "What is the Impressionist style in painting?"  Before we consider this question, however, it would perhaps be worthwhile to examine the roots of Impressionism in painting, to see how the Impressionist group was formed, and to make a few general observations about its chief contributors.

### The Genesis of the Movement in Painting

At about the same time that Henry James was beginning his literary career, the group that we now know as the Impressionists, under the title *Société anonyme des artistes, peintres, sculptures, graveurs,* held their first exhibition. Over one-hundred-sixty works of art were shown at this exhibit, which was held in the Paris studio of Nadar, the photographer, a friend of the Impressionists, on April 15, 1874. Caprice evidently dictated the naming of the group: according to John Rewald, the leading authority on the movement, Monet told Renoir's brother, Edmond (who was editing the first catalogue for the group) to call an untitled painting of the port of Le Havre that Monet entered into the exhibit simply "Impression."[8]

The Société, which was established by Claude Monet (1840-1926), Auguste Renoir (1841-1919), Edgar Degas (1834-1917), and Camille Pissarro (1839-1899), flourished during the 1870's. Many of its members were French, although the group's membership was international and never lacking in fluidity. At one time or another it included Sisley, Jongkind, Van Gogh, and many others who were not French by birth or citizenship. Moreover, the various Impressionist exhibits had a variety of contributors. Of the eight Impressionist exhibitions held between 1874 and 1886, for example, among the fifty or sixty artists who showed their work at one time or another, only Pissarro entered canvases on every occasion.

Of the thirty artists listed in the catalogue for the initial Impressionist exhibition, many had also exhibited at the *Salon des Refusés* (1863) and, during the 1860's, helped to form what is now referred to as "the Batignolles Group," several of whose members were the actual creators of Impressionism in painting. The key figures associated with the movement were on friendly terms for much of the decade prior to the 1874 exhibition at Nadar's studio. Manet and Degas met at the Louvre in 1862, the same year that Monet was discharged from the French cavalry and returned to paint with Boudin and Jongkind at Le Havre. Later that year, Monet went to Paris where he met Renoir and Sisley who were then sharing the studio of Frédéric Bazille.

In the first half of the '60's, Monet painted in a style that was principally influenced by Manet and that used broad areas of strong colors, but by around 1867 (or shortly after the first of many gatherings at the Café Guerbois), he began to paint in a manner that eventually became known as the Impressionist style. He began to insist that open-air scenes must be painted on the spot and not in the studio, and he proceeded to alter his style according to this belief.  In 1869 Monet was joined by Renoir and Pissarro, and the three painted a series of views at a site called La Grenouillière, where they attempted to capture on canvas the fleeting effects of light on the trees and water at this bend in the Seine.

After the Franco-Prussian War of 1870, in which the young Bazille was killed, Monet renewed his friendship with Renoir and Sisley in Paris.  In the early 1870's Monet, Renoir, and Pissarro carried the idea of painting light and colored reflections even farther. They began to use purer colors than before and developed the discovery, hinted at by Delacroix, but only fully explored by the Impressionists themselves, that shadowed surfaces are not merely darker than the same surfaces in full light, but that they are actually different in color.  Such technical discoveries were among those which have helped to make the Impressionist style so well known today.  The discussion which follows will analyze the Impressionist style in painting by closely examining some of its major techniques.

## Impressionist Techniques in Painting

In essence, the Impressionst style consists of six major techniques.  And they are as follows:  1, rendering the direct and fleeting impression; 2, painting in the open air with emphasis upon seizing the effects of light and color; 3, moving around a subject and painting it from several different angles; 4, using broken brushwork which requires viewing from a distance; 5, juxtaposing colors to establish artistic effects; 6, presenting scenes in a hazy atmosphere.

Among the Impressionist techniques in painting,[9] perhaps foremost is the dictum that the artist must render the Impression that objects make on the eye.[10] Claude Monet, considered by many to be the most talented Impressionist painter, told an American pupil that he wished "he had been born blind so that he would have begun to paint (after he gained the ability to see) without knowing what the objects were that he saw before him."[11] And Monet's interest in capturing the personal and direct visual sensation is seen to good advantage in his "Boats at Argenteuil" (1874, Durand-Ruel Collection, Paris). Théodore Duret, emphasizing Monet's choice of water in its momentary appearance as his subject of predilection, indicated that Monet's originality lay in his rendering of "les aspects fugitifs que les accidents de l'atmosphère donnent (au passage)"[11a]. An interest in seizing instantaneous visual effects runs throughout the work of the leading Impressionists, and perhaps accounts for Marc de Montifaud's use of the term "école des yeux" to describe the group.

As Jacques Barzun has noted in *Classic, Romantic, and Modern*, the Impressionists increasingly refined this "retinal doctrine" until, eventually, they were able to see "that complementary colors heighten each other's intensity when set close together."[12] The visual experience of the world depends inevitably upon light, and the actual light of day became the vital principle for the Impressionist painters.[13] We see this principle at work in a painting such as Mary Cassatt's "The Poppy Field" (ca. 1874-1880) where the light lends a sense of joy to the colors of the sky and to the poppies themselves. Monet uses similar effects in "Sailboats at Argenteuil" (ca. 1872, Musée du Louvre) and "Impression, Sunrise" (1872)— a pair of paintings which combine a lyric touch with the immediacy of an open-air impression that seems almost scientifically exact.[14]

A number of the leading Impressionists, such as Monet, Sisley, and Pissarro, insisted that the landscape painter must not only record a particular view, but that he must record it at only one particular moment of the day and in the particular light present then.[15] Monet, himself a rapid worker who painted the same lake forty-eight times, executed two great series of canvases to establish his point: one of haystacks and one of the facade of Rouen Cathedral (several versions of which are in the Louvre and elsewhere). He moreover pursued the painting of multiple views of a subject into the '90's when he did many versions of the "Garden at Giverny."[16]

Phoebe Pool has remarked that the Impressionist painters considered "light and the exchange of colored reflections as the unifying elements of a picture,"[17] instead of relying upon the traditional method of construction based on drawing, outline or sharp contrasts of light and shade.[18]   Louis Duranty seems to capture well the essence of the effect which this new type of construction managed to convey: "(l'effect) de rendre la marche, le mouvement, la trépidation et l'entrecroisement des passants, comme on a essayé de rendre le tremblement des feuilles, le frissonnement de l'eau et la vibration de l'air inondé de lumière...."[19]   In similar fashion, Gustave Geffroy wrote of "the perpetual growth" of an Impressionist painting.[20] And there is a sense of rhythmic movement in a painting such as Monet's "Rue Montorgueil Decked with Flags" (Musée des Beaux Arts, Rouen, 1878), inspired by the peace celebration of June 30, 1878.[21]   In this painting, by use of emphatic brush strokes, which call for distant viewing and which punctuate the canvas, the artist has imparted a sense of rhythmic movement to the tricolored French flags.   The typically Impressionist use of broken brushwork moreover requires that the viewer maintain a distance from the canvas in order to fully appreciate the technique.   And at least part of the effect of this technique is to disengage the scene from the artist's feelings.   In this way, the atmosphere emerges from afar, and gradually.[22]

Arnold Hauser has noted that "nothing is more typical of an impressionist painting than that it must be looked at from a certain distance and that it describes things with the omissions inevitable in them when seen from a distance"[23]—a remark which leads us to another characteristic of the Impressionists; namely, their propensity to exclude minute details and to eschew elaborate finish.[24]   Many of the Impressionists and their major forerunners were thus able to get at the heart of the landscape, as Corot (1796-1875) had done with his "The Sèvres Road."

Analogously, Manet once said that "conciseness in art is a necessity and an elegance.... . Always move in the direction of conciseness."[25]   And he followed this dictum in many of his best indoor scenes.   In the "Bar at the Folies Bergère," for instance, with the exception of the barmaid, the figures are suggested rather than defined.   Using only a few bold strokes, Manet presents ladies in colorful costumes, girls with opera glasses and bearded men in stovepipe hats.  With his rapid technique, he is able to capture the mood of an evening's diversion.[26]

This rapid brush-work was one of the elements of the Impressionist painters' techniques which Louis Duranty chose to cite when he elevated their work above that done by the Academic and official practitioners of the day:

> It matters little whether the public understands or not.  What matters is that artists do, and that one can show them [sic] sketches and preparatory studies in which the painter's mind, his theme and his ability with the brush are frequently expressed more rapidly and in a more concentrated form than in the finished work, so that one gets a truer idea of the grace and vigor of his style and his powers of clear and accurate observation.[27]

The Impressionists also developed the notion that shadow is a counterpart to light, for light necessarily influences and changes the colors of those areas remaining in shadow.[28]  Monet and Pissarro, for instance, showed in their work  a perpetual interest in the effect of light and shadow, and of light into shadow, in portraying the landscape motif.  As Théodore Duret has phrased it in "The Impressionist Painters" (1878), "when winter comes, the Impressionist paints snow.  He sees that the shadows on the snow are blue in sunlight; unhesitatingly, he paints blue shadows."[29]

In his *History of Impressionism,* John Rewald has observed that the Impressionist painters realized "that so-called local color was actually a pure convention and that every object presents to the eye a scheme of color derived from its surroundings and from atmospheric conditions."[30]  Growing out of these observations of a landscape that possesses its proper color scheme is the Impressionist penchant for comparing color values.  In this respect we recall Bazille, who wrote in his Notebook, while doing preparatory sketches for the bathers in "Scene d'Eté" (1869):  "I must not forget to compare the color-value of bright water with that of sunlit grass."[31]  This practice seemingly led the Impressionists to portray landscapes that provide an impression of shimmering light.

Another element in the Impressionist style is the presentation of a scene in "atmospheric perspective."  Manet provides a good example of this in his "Bar at the Folies-Bergère" (1881-82, Courtauld Institute Galleries), his last large-scale painting. When we look at this painting, it seems at first that the barmaid is about to serve the viewer, since she is looking straight ahead. But her customer is apparently the top-hatted gentleman, with a goatee, who is seen in the mirror behind the young woman's reflection at the upper left of the canvas. In order for the painting to reflect "reality," the barmaid would have to be standing almost sideways to catch such a reflection, but Manet has her facing forward, and thereby provides us with a much more startling "impression." In doing so, Manet seems to have been following Delacroix's comments on the subject of the part that the mind plays in the perception of the world:

> even when we look at nature, our imagination constructs a picture. We do not see the blades of grass in a landscape, nor minute blemishes in the skin of a charming face ... the mind itself has a special task to perform without our knowledge; it does not take into account all that the eye offers, but connects the impressions it receives with others that have gone before.[32]

This passage, in turn, calls to mind the reflections of the chemist Chevreul, whose writings deeply impressed Seurat. In his *De l'ab-straction* (1864) Chevreul wrote:

> When it is a question of representing the view of a landscape or a group of figures participating in some action, whether public or private ... the paint-er to be truthful can represent only a moment in a landscape in which light and shadow vary continually, he is obliged to choose *this moment* from among others; henceforth this moment should be considered a *ver-itable abstraction of the moments making up the duration* ... .[33]

Illustrative of this idea in painting is Degas' "Woman with Chry-santhemums" (probably 1865, Metropolitan Museum of Art). It is seemingly not a posed picture, since the painter leaves the impression that the woman might almost have sat down at the table by chance. Yet everything in the scene is very carefully arranged, even to the carelessly placed gloves and the crystal water pitcher. In effect, although the bouquet, the lady, and the table all contribute to the total "impression," it would be very difficult to say which is the most important element in this audacious composition.

Another technique used by the Impressionists is broken brush-work. This style of brushwork makes for a painting that provides little articulation. The comparative absence of articulation forces the viewer to "put the painting together" himself. Stephen Spender, in *The Struggle of the Modern*, states the matter thus:

> Already with the French Impressionists, this double aspect of the mod-ern—that the thing observed is changed, and the observer also is changed in his manner of perceiving—begins to appear. Impressionism is not only a 'more scientific' way of looking at nature in an age of science. It also suggests the way in which the eye, conscious of the mechanism of vision, sees light. But to be conscious of the way the eye sees and to represent this as well as the thing seen is to make art partly out of the mechanics of seeing.

Spender goes on to note that "the mode of perceiving itself becomes an object of perception, and is included as part of the thing per-ceived."[34]

Synge was mostly right, then, when he wrote in the "Preface" to *The Playboy of the Western World* that "all art is a collabora-tion"—a claim that the Impressionists affirm in their painting. They do so in several ways. In a painting such as Degas' "Carriage at the Races" (1871-1872, Museum of Fine Arts, Boston), for example, the abrupt cutting-off of the carriages in the foreground and on the left edge of the composition not only enhances the feeling of action, but also implies that the composition is only a fragment. From the viewer's standpoint, the painting has the effect of a quick, sidelong glance, especially like that provided by a moving observer. The artist thus seems not only to invite the viewer to supply the missing elements to the scene, but also to create a sense of motion seldom induced by the academic paintings that were done during the Impres-sionist era.[35]

The Impressionist painters furthermore demanded the partic-ipation of the viewer, insofar as their brushwork made for objects whose boundaries are blurred and whose contours are seldom drawn.[36] In the Impressionist technique, colors were generally not mixed and blended on the palette before being applied to the canvas. The colors were, rather, synthesized by the viewer who at first sees only small daubs, spots and smears of closely juxtaposed hues.

More specifically, as Rudolf Arnheim notes:

> the technique of the impressionist in the nineteenth century radically ignored the perceptual distinction of object values and illumination values by presenting any surface as a sequence of graded nuances and leaving to the eye the task of separating the properties of the object from those of illumination. [37]

It is, of course, difficult to say which painters first made these kinds of demands upon the viewer. Certainly Turner—whose art in some ways forms a prelude to such Impressionist masters as Monet, Sisley, and Pissarro—is one of the first to come to mind. In viewing a Turner painting such as "Interior at Petworth" (painted 1830-37, Tate Gallery, London), for example, at first glimpse all is a chaos of color. But gradually one discerns what seem to be a piano, a white dog, a piece of gold brocade thrown over the divan, and the reflection of a statue in the mirror.

One finds something of this quality of indistinctness, too, in Monet's "Impression, Sunrise" (1872, Musée Marmottan, Paris), the painting which Leroy had ridiculed in his attack in *Le Charivari*. Yet I think that one much more readily gets a sense of the setting of this painting than one does with Turner, who truly forces the viewer to become "a creative eye."[38] Turner further anticipates Sisley, for example, in "Rain, Steam, Speed" (National Gallery, London, 1844) with the haunting atmosphere that the English artist herein so boldly conveys.

In his letters to his son, Camille Pissarro indicated that he and Monet had at least learned something about Turner's technique in the visits to the National Gallery which they had made on their several months' stay in London during 1870-1.[39] But it was Corot, whose pupil Pissarro claims to have been, who perhaps most directly anticipated the Impressionists in demanding the viewer's attention and participation. We can note these kinds of demands, especially, in a painting such as "Avignon from the West" (National Gallery, London, 1836) with its extremely sensitive changes of tone.

The last aspect of Impressionist painting to be considered may well be the most important; namely, the desire expressed to get onto the canvas the fleeting impression of the moment—"la recherche d'une saisie de l'instant fugitif."[40] To illustrate, one day upon finding Monet idle, Courbet asked the reason. Monet promptly replied that he was "waiting for the sun."[41] In a letter to Gustave Geffroy, Monet further remarked [regarding his work on a series of different "effects" (i.e., haystacks)]: "what I am seeking [to convey is]: 'instantaneity,' above all, the envelopment of the same light spread over everywhere."[42]

This desire of the Impressionist, which does service to the primacy of the moment of change and chance, seems to imply the domination of *l'instant fugitif* over the solid qualities of life in general and of the external world in particular. In his dissertation on Impressionism as a literary style, William A. Harms has characterized the Impressionist vision as being one which comprehends human experience in terms of "phenomenological mutability."[43] Monet, for instance, often seems to have wished to capture the fleeting aspects of the world in his open-air work.[44] The young Guy de Maupassant, who followed Monet to Etretat in his search for out-door impressions, wrote of Monet that

> He was no longer in truth a painter, but a hunter. He went out, followed by a child who carried his canvases, five or six canvases representing the same subject at different hours of the day and with different effects. He took them up and put them aside in turn, according to the changes in the sky. And the painter, facing his subject, lay in wait for the sunshine or for the cloud that passed, and disdainful of error or propriety, painted them rapidly on his canvas. I have seen him thus seize a glittering play of light on the white cliff and fix it with a flow of yellow tones which rendered in a strangely surprising way the effect of that unseizable and blinding brilliance. Another time he took the rain beating on the sea in his hands and dashed it on the canvas.[45]

It is often true that many of the Impressionists convey through their depiction of water imagery something of the impermanence and insubstantiality of the visible world [an effect that Monet, for example, effectively rendered in his "Garden at Giverny" (Art Institute, Chicago, 1899)]. But something of the same effect, too, is generally conveyed in the Impressionists' portrayal of human figures. In Berthe Morisot's "Young Woman in a Party Dress" (Museum of Impressionism, The Louvre, 1879), for instance, everything about the woman's appearance suggests the passing moment—the pow-dered face, the expectant look, the luminescent skin, the revealing dress. When this painting was shown at the Salon des Impression-nistes, Rue des Pyramides, in 1880 (at the group's fifth exhibition), a critic remarked: "There are five or six lunatics there, one of them a woman." This woman herself confessed that her ambition "is limited to the desire *to set down something as it passes, oh, some-thing, the least of things.*"46

This Impressionist emphasis upon "the moment" thus implies "the prevalence of a relation to things the property of which is to be non-commital as well as changeable,"47 a complex of feelings that is well expressed in a painting such as Edouard Manet's "Concert at the Tuileries" (1862), wherein the quick sweep of the brush-work lends to the gaiety of the scene a sense of its very transience. This mood reflects a singularly Modernist sense in the work of the Impres-sionists. Stephen Spender comments on the unique Modern-ness of this aspect of Impressionist art when he writes (again in *The Struggle of the Modern*):

> The Moderns are therefore those who start off by thinking that human nature has changed: or if not human nature, then the relationship of the individual to the environment, forever being metamorphosized by science, which has altered so completely that there is an affective illusion of change which in fact causes human beings to behave as though they were different. This change, recorded by the seismographic senses of the artist, has also to change all the relations within the arrangements of words or marks on canvas which make a poem or make a painting.48

And it follows that an art which accords with such a vision will stress not only the fleeting perceptions of the world, will see in man not only the measure of all things, but will pursue the basis for truth in the "here and now" of the individual.49 In his study, *The Mortal No: Death and Modern Imagination*, Frederick J. Hoffman ties much of the concern with time in Modern literature to the large-scale breakup of belief in immortality. As Hoffman phrases it:

"... a man expecting and believing in eternity will be less concerned with his temporal experiences, will see them less in depth than as a move toward eternity."[50]　Conversely, a Modern age, whose people seem for the most part unconvinced of immortality, will show a great deal more interest in the fluctuating moments of time.

Before saying a few words about the breaking-up of the Impressionist movement in painting, I would like to touch upon the kinds of subjects that the Impressionists dealt with in their paintings. Albert Boime has indicated the extent to which the development of independent artists such as Delacroix and Corot can be understood only in its relationship to current "Academic" technique, as presented by the artists who were rewarded by the officials and, even more, by traditional teachers such as Couture and Gleyre outside the *Académie* who nevertheless availed themselves of many of the techniques and most of the curriculum that was used within the Academy.　Boime has also indicated the extent to which such Impressionist notables as Monet, Renoir, Sisley, Manet, Bazille, Pissarro, and Seurat were influenced by their studies under Charles Gleyre (1806-1874) and Couture.[51]

Yet there can be no doubt that the Impressionists, for the most part, made a conscious break from the powerful Paris Salon.　The paintings favored by the Salon, for instance, were dramatic, religious, and historical scenes.　The Impressionists, with their use of *plein-air* principles, almost never did such scenes.[52]

The subjects that the Impressionists portrayed are dancers, cabaret singers, musicians, barmaids, jockeys, café waiters, harvesters or fellow painters at their work.　Often, they simply painted people doing "nothing," enjoying themselves at concerts and dances in the park or picnicking or rowing on a holiday.[53]　In contrast to the most renowned painters who worked before them, the Impressionists treated mundane, everyday, non-dramatic, non-message subjects.　In thus selecting mundane subjects for treatment, they not only broke with artistic tradition, but they also, I think, helped pave the way for the art-for-art's sake phenomenon which gained momentum as the nineteenth century drew to a close.

In keeping with the sense of disengagement which their brush-work induces, the Impressionists were little inclined to deal with issues of great social concern. And this reluctance is found even in the work of Pissarro, an anarchist who read Kropotkin and admired Blanqui.. Monet's "Sailboats at Argenteuil" (Musée du Louvre) was probably painted in 1873, the year that the Franco-Prussian war was finally disposed of for the French people. At this time the country's economic condition was comparatively poor; recovery was halting. Yet of the war of 1870 and its aftermath, nothing can be seen in this canvas. As with so much Impressionist art, the whole painting exhales light and air. In its spontaneous execution it gives a strong feeling of harmony and lends to the viewer a sense of freedom and openness.

In their ability to capture the accurate momentary impression, the painters of the Impressionist movement have, then, broken with most of their predecessors, for whom "subject" was of such primary importance. In his cathedral studies and in his painting of the "Doges' Palace" Monet, for instance, largely ignored the artistic qualities of the buildings that serve as his ostensible subjects. Bazille, moreover, once significantly told his family that "the subject doesn't matter so long as I am doing something as interesting as painting."[54] Likewise, in a Monet painting such as "Quai du Louvre, Paris" (ca. 1880, Coll. Haags Gemeentemuseum), the artist shows that he has just chosen "a corner of nature" with nothing special in the subject; he has just depicted a certain point of the Seine in Paris.[55] In the same regard we can contrast, for instance, a French Realist painting—such as Gustave Courbet's (1819-1877) "Burial at Ornans" or "The Stone Breakers"—with virtually any landscape by Pissarro. The former canvas achieves its effect largely through the discursive treatment of subject. With Pissarro, however, there is a substantial quality to the homes, trees, and other individual objects on the canvas; but they also give up their identity to the whole landscape of which they are a part.

### The Breaking-Up of the Original Impressionist Group
### and the Redirection of its Members

As early as 1882, profound differences of opinion came to be felt among most of the original Impressionist painters.[56]    At the beginning of that year the likeable Gustave Caillebotte was unsuccessful in his several attempts to organize his Impressionist friends for a common exhibition.    Realizing his failure, he placed his hopes on Durand-Ruel, who had to bring all of his considerable diplomacy to bear in order to organize a collective exhibit at all.    Degas, through his various political intrigues and financial irresponsibility, had contributed much to the break-up of the group.    Moreover, the 1882 failure of the Union des Générale des Banques brought upon the public a not unsurprising unwillingness to buy the art of the Impressionists.    Durand-Ruel was surely very hard hit by this crisis and seems to have been driven nearly bankrupt by the spring of 1884. By 1883, he had altogether abandoned any idea of holding a common Impressionist exhibition and had applied himself—not altogether sucessfully—to forming separate exhibitions of Monet, Renoir, Pissarro, and Sisley.    By this time, however, several of the old-timers among the Impressionists (of the above four, for instance, certainly all but Sisley) had begun to question the value of the aesthetic course that they had chosen.    Renoir, for example, became disenchanted with Impressionism in the early 1880's and moved in the direction of a more Classical technique, shown to perhaps best advantage in his large "Baigneuses" in the Philadelphia Museum of Art.    And during this period even Pissarro made similar experiments with the brush.    Then, too, from the beginning of the 'eighties, the never-overly-propinquitous Degas began to paint in a style that increasingly diverged from that of his Impressionist contemporaries.

The Impressionist painters continued to paint into the first years of the twentieth century, but by the early 1880's they had ceased to show their paintings as a group, and their position as the antennae of the art field was taken by other artists who had profited by the Impressionist lessons, but who afterwards modified, or even rejected, the Impressionists' artistic principles. The term "Impressionist" soon came to be applied to analogous techniques in the other arts, including music, sculpture, and architecture. Impressionist painting spread to England, the United States, and other countries. And some painters even today are using Impressionist techniques, often in combination with other stylistic methods.

Numbered among those who modified and eventually rejected the Impressionist principles were three especially talented artists: Gauguin, Cézanne, and Van Gogh. Gauguin, for instance, had exhibited with the Impressionists on five separate occasions, beginning in 1876.[57]

In 1874, Paul Cézanne (1839-1906) was working quite closely with Pissarro.[58]   For several years, he absorbed the new Impressionist technique and exhibited at that shocking inaugural exhibit of 1874.   While Cézanne never seems to have identified himself as closely with Impressionism as did Gauguin and Van Gogh, nevertheless his manner of using form and color—especially during the '70's—places his style beyond Realism and into Impressionism.   In viewing Cézanne's "The Bridge at Maincy" (ca. 1879-80, Museum of Impressionism, The Louvre), for instance, we are drawn into a world of luscious and penetrable beauty.   The deft use of greens, the gorgeous white stone arching into the wooden footbridge, and the dazzling reflection of the green in the still water beneath the bridge all lend to an effect similar to that which Baudelaire described in his introduction to the translation of the stories of Poe, the *Nouvelles Histoires Extraordinaires,* when he referred to the emotion induced by certain works of art "which would like to seize on this earth a revealed paradise."   In its general lack of finish,[59] Cézanne's technique is also similar to that of the Impressionists.

Like Gauguin and Cézanne, Vincent Van Gogh (1853-1890) shows a number of affinites with the Impressionist painters and followed some of the same masters in developing his fundamental techniques.   At the time that he came to Paris in 1886, for instance, Van Gogh professed great admiration for the work of Corot, Daubigny and, especially, Millet.[60]   In Paris, where Van Gogh spent the years 1886-7, the artist viewed Impressionist paintings that seemingly induced him to abandon the somber style that he had learned from such Dutch painters as Israels, and to adopt a brilliant palette.   Virtually all of the canvases done at Asnières are filled with light in a manner reminiscent of the Impressionists' outdoor work.  Moreover, as late as 1888, Van Gogh and Gauguin were still calling themselves Impressionists, although by this time, surely, their paintings no longer properly fit such a description.[61]

While Van Gogh was truly indebted in many ways to the Impressionists and to some of their leading forerunners, his association with other contemporary schools of painting seems to have been less significant to him than his love of literature.  Indicative, perhaps, of his relative lack of interest in the work of other leading painters of his day is that he was not to pay his first (and last) visit to the studio of Seurat until a few hours before he took the train to the south of France, accompanied by Theo, in late February, 1888.[62]  Van Gogh, whose appetite for contemporary literature was insatiable, was influenced in his decision to go to Arles by his reading of Zola and Daudet—a pair of writers who were, as we shall see, intimately associated with the Flaubert *cénacle.*

By the mid-'80's, then, it is clear that a redirection became visible in the French art world.  A younger generation—many of whom had had little personal association with the members of the Impressionist group—by introducing a more "scientific control," along with a renewed interest in formal and spatial organization, began to work changes upon the Impressionist method.  Pissarro, one of the older spokesmen for this new group, succinctly stated its aims in a letter to Durand-Ruel (written from Eragny, November 6, 1886): "We seek modern synthesis by scientific means, based on the theory of colors discovered by M. Chevreul, and following the experiments of O.N. Rood. . . As for the execution, we consider it of no account; it has only the slightest importance:  art has nothing to do with it. According to us, the sole originality consists in the character of the design and the vision peculiar to each artist ...".[63]

The inventor of this new style—variously referred to as Neo-Impressionism, *pointillisme,* or "Divisionism" (the term which the practitioners themselves preferred)—was Georges Seurat (1859-1891). Seurat, who died before he reached his thirty-second birthday, did not leave many finished works behind him, but he did make several revolutionary discoveries while attempting to lead a group that would challenge the strong influence of the Impressionists.[64]

At the outset of his brief career, however, Seurat used many of the methods of the Impressionist painters. He started with the Impressionist's use of strong, pure colors and the Impressionist "discovery" of colored shadows. His "Gardener" (ca. 1882), for instance, is a tiny canvas, the size of a cigar box, which uses dappled sunlight in a manner analogous to that used by Renoir in many of his nudes done in the Impressionist style. Early in Seurat's career, the painter believed that in any group of objects on which light falls there are three kinds of color: the local color, or the color which the object would have under white light; the color that it receives from the course of light; and a third color due to the fact that one color juxtaposed with another induces its complementary in it.[65]

Using this knowledge, which he gleaned largely from the Impressionists, Seurat carried even farther than the original French Impressionists the technique of composing by color and light, rather than by line. In "The Water Can" (1883, Collection of Mr. and Mrs. Paul Mellon, Upperville, Va.), for instance, or "Barbizon Forest" (1883, Collection of Mr. and Mrs. Alexander M. Lewyt, N.Y.), Seurat forms his outline not by line but by gradations—a halo of light and a proliferation of color spots.

Seurat also aligned himself with the distinctively Modernist aspect of the Impressionists that led them to prefer technique to subject. In the style that Seurat used for the preliminary outdoor studies that he did upon his return from military service, for example, the artist held his brush against the surface of the canvas, so that the bristles were kept at a right angle to the brush handle. He then made his strokes with the flat part of the brush, rather than with the tip. The result of this technique was a patchwork of strokes, brushed in at right angles, each of which resulted from the imprint of the length and structure of the bristles. It might therefore be rightly said that the technique itself became the primary element in these early *plein-air* studies, in which Seurat apparently attempted to seize the flickering outdoor light effects which he observed.[66]

These affinities with Impressionism notwithstanding, the best known of Seurat's canvases are more precisely termed pointillist.[67]

In "A Sunday Afternoon at the Grande Jatte" (1885), one of many versions of the same subject, we can see the artist's *pointillisme* at its most fully developed. In this and in the other versions of the scene, there is a stiff, mechanical quality to the performance—a "woodenness" to the figures and the landscape which seems deliberately alien to the best of the Impessionist outdoor work. Moreover, while the Impressionists tended to apply their brushwork in loose touches and comma strokes of unmixed color (a technique which also tends to leave to the eye of the beholder the task of synthesis), Seurat, in his post-Impressionist phase (from roughly 1885 until his death in 1891),[68] condensed the small, flaky spots into solid units—thereby, in a sense, destroying the fluid effect which Renoir, Monet and their followers seemingly wished to produce.

In protesting through his art against the style of the Impressionists, Seurat gathered a circle of artists and writers that frequented the editorial offices of the *Revue Indépendante,* which was begun by Felix Fénéon in collaboration with Charles Angrand and Gustave Kahn. In addition to Seurat and the above-mentioned figures, "the Independents," as they were often called, attracted such notables as Pissarro, Paul Signac, and Dubois-Pillet.[69]

Of the painters among Seurat's group of friends at the review, Paul Signac (1863-1935) stands out as having been the most literate (excepting, of course, the genius Seurat himself). Signac was also a passionate sailor and, much to his widowed mother's consternation, had inscribed the names of Manet-Zola-Wagner on the stern of his first boat.[70]

In his early phase, Signac's work mirrored Seurat's in the use that the artist made of the work of his Impressionist forerunners. Concerning the two canvases that he entered at the Salon des Artistes Indépendants exhibition (1884), for instance, Paul Signac wrote that they were "painted only with the colors of the prism placed on the canvas in little comma strokes, following the Impressionist mode and under the influence of my chosen masters:   Claude Monet and Guillaumin, whom I was not to know until later, but always without mixing the pigments on the palette."[71]  Even in a canvas done several years later (but still prior to Signac's becoming a systematic Divisionist), such as "Boulevard de Clichy in Paris" (1886, The Minnesota Institute of Arts), the artist's freedom of technique and comma-shaped brushstroke align him much more closely with the Impressionist group than with that of Seurat and his followers.[72]

### The British and American Impressionists

In the preceding section of Chapter One, then, I have touched upon the major painters associated with Impressionism in France. Painting by those who had learned the lessons of Impressionism was not, however, limited to the European mainland, since British and American artists were increasingly becoming aware of the lessons of the masters of French Impressionism. And Henry James knew a great deal about the theory and practice of some of these British and American artists.

In 1875, the young Henry James, who had already begun to spend most of his time abroad, commented upon the work of a number of young Realist painters in his review of some paintings at the National Academy of Design's annual exhibition. Among those about whom James's comments were less than acerbic was the American Winslow Homer. Although Homer (1836-1910) had studied in Paris, he does not seem to have known very much about the work of the French Impressionists. Yet, as with John La Farge, Homer's comments often closely parallel those of the Impressionists and express a vision that is really quite similar to that of the French artists. Unlike La Farge, however, Homer seems to have developed his opinions concerning the *plein-air* effect independent of the French Impressionists. Of the popular official artist Bouguereau, for instance, Homer remarks (to G.W. Sheldon, a nineteenth-century historian of American art) in 1882:

> I wouldn't go across the street to see Bouguereau. His pictures look false; he does not get the truth of that which he wishes to represent; his light is not out-door light [... .] I prefer every time ... a picture composed and painted out-door [... .] Very much of the work now done in studios should

be done in the open air [... .] I tell you it is impossible to paint out-door figure in studio-light with any degree of certainty. Outdoors you have the sky overhead giving one light; then the reflected light from whatever reflects; then the direct light of the sun; so that, in the blending and suffusing of these several luminations, there is no such thing as a line to be seen anywhere.[73]

And Homer's vivid treatment of sky and open air in an early painting, such as "Long Branch, New Jersey" (1869, Museum of Fine Arts, Boston) was no less freely handled than comparable subjects by Monet that were being done around the same time.[74]

Still other American artists, not strictly considered Impressionists, nevertheless contributed something toward building an atmosphere conducive to the acceptance of the Impressionist aesthetic in America. In "A Painter on Painting," for example (an article based on an interview with the Realist painter, George Inness), when the unidentified interviewer asks, "What is it that a painter tries to do?" Inness rejoins:

> Simply to reproduce in other minds *the* impressions which a scene has made upon him. A work of art does not appeal to the intellect. It does not appeal to the moral sense. Its aim is not to instruct, not to edify, but to awake [sic] an emotion.[75]

Inness could not be labelled an Impressionist in the strictest sense of the word, yet he did know the work of such Impressionist forerunners as Corot, Troyon, Daubigny, and Rousseau. In an Inness painting such as "June" (1882, Brooklyn Museum), for example, the American artist shows the influence of Corot with the simple, broad brush-work and the cool blue-greens and soft greens that fade into rosy browns. The undulating planes, too, are not unlike those that are found in many landscapes by Corot.

French Impressionism, *per se,* was not introduced to the American public until 1886, the year that Durand-Ruel made the first showing of his collection in New York City. Even at this late date, however, the reception afforded the French artists by the American public was far from magnanimous. While a handful of forward-looking collectors, such as the wealthy H.O. Havemeyer, friend of Mary Cassatt, and some of the members of the press, showed evidence of having been in sympathy with the Impressionists' aims, the show attracted a considerable amount of adverse criticism. The painters who exhibited in the Durand-Ruel show in New York were called "insolent in the crudity and rudeness of their work." Their show was labelled "a collection of monstrosities of composition, color and drawing which would not be tolerated in any well regulated barber shop." And the nudes of Degas, which had proved so inspirational to Van Gogh, were characterized by an American expert as "nothing but a peeping Tom behind the *coulisses* [wings of the stage], and among the dressing-rooms of the ballet dancers, noting only travesties on fallen, debased womanhood, most disgusting and offensive."[76]

Their considerably less than whole-hearted American reception notwithstanding, the Impressionists did manage to exert a considerable influence upon American culture. The Impressionist style affected American art, and particularly American painting, from the late 19th century until well after the First World War. The 'eighties and 'nineties, for example, saw the development of an American school of Impressionism, centered in New York City.[77] And toward the end of the century, a number of the more prominent American Impressionists, including John H. Twachtman, Theodore Robinson, Childe Hassam (1859-1935), and J. Alden Weir (1852-1919), banded together as "Ten American Painters" and held the first official exhibition of United States Impressionists. While Theodore Robinson (1852-1896) was the only American to study with Monet (Robinson worked under Monet's tutelage for a brief time during the 1880's), many of the American artists studied in France before attaining a reputation in their native country.

A few of the paintings done by "The Ten" are truly worthy of the Impressionist style as it was passed down from the French masters. Robinson's "Willows" (ca. 1891, Brooklyn Museum), for example, with its shimmering light and colored shadows, represents a beautiful "offspring" of the brush of the Monet of the Argenteuil period. And John H. Twachtman (1852-1903), in "Sailing in the Mist" (Pennsylvania Academy of the Fine Arts), with the little symphony of blues and whites that the canvas renders to the eye, reveals the delicate American Impressionist style at its best. But all too often the paintings of Weir, Twachtman, Robinson, Hassam, and the

less notable members of the Ten are really, as John W. McCoubrey
has observed, specimens of "a pale, belated impressionism."[78]

And much the same criticism can be made of another group that
learned from the French Impressionists; namely, the "colorless
Impressionists"[79] of the New English Art Club.  The Club, which
was founded in 1886, contained two prominent members who
received considerable critical attention—Philip Wilson Steer (1860-
1943) and Walter Richard Sickert (1860-1942).  Both achieved
notoriety by employing, by and large, what can only be described as
a kind of "watered-down" impressionism.[80]

That the Club's brand of Impressionism met with some success
might seem surprising, especially since Impressionism was not really
new to the England of the 'nineties.  Several of George Moore's
Impressionist works were published in the '80's, and the Whistler-
Ruskin trial of 1877 brought many ideas associated with Impressionism in art to the attention of the British public.  Nevertheless,
as Holbrook Jackson has observed, the appearance of the Impressionist painters in England was an event which aroused an interest
probably comparable to the first performances of Wagner's operas
in that country.[81]  The canvases of Philip W. Steer, done in his early
career after a period spent studying in Paris (1882-4), show evidence
of his having absorbed some of the lessons of the French Impressionists.  Especially in the paintings executed at Walberswick in the
'90's, Steer demonstrates a vitality and sparkle that align him with
the French Impressionist masters.  Steer's best work in the Impressionist vein was "Girl on a Pier, Walberswick" (1886), a canvas that
he painted just after returning from his sojourn in Paris.

Sickert, Steer's influential partner in the Club, seems to have
learned a great deal from Degas during the Englishman's Parisian
stay.[82]   Sickert was also somewhat of a bibliophile and admired
Balzac, the Goncourts and Delacroix, among others.  And while he
did not especially care for the fiction of Henry James, the painter
was a good friend and correspondent of Miss Ethel Sands who was,
in turn, a friend of the Master.[83]

One other member of the New English Art Club whose work was

known by Henry James was John Singer Sargent (1856-1925). Sargent did Impressionist sketches for the Club, and these sketches helped him to earn a place in the *avant-garde*.[84]  Sargent helped to form that large group of talented nineteenth-century American expatriates (a group which included Whistler, Mary Cassatt and Henry James) who were drawn to the charms of European civilization and who made such impressive contributions to European arts and letters.  In his published criticism James refers to Sargent on numerous occasions. And the Master warmly acknowledged Sargent's artistic contribution in his especially generous appraisals of the artist's work.[85]  James also "sat" for a Sargent drawing that was included in the summer, 1895 issue of *The Yellow Book,* and later posed for an ill-fated portrait by Sargent that was placed in the National Gallery (London).[86]

In this chapter, then, I have considered in detail the major techniques and the main subjects of the Impressionist painters, as well as those of their leading forerunners and imitators.  In the chapter that follows, I shall examine the Impressionist aspects of the styles of some of the Continental authors who wrote during the latter third of the nineteenth century.

*Notes*

[1]See John La Farge. *Considerations on Painting.* New York: Macmillan, 1896 (p. 201).

[2]Royal Cortissoz. *John La Farge: A Memoir and A Study.* New York and Boston: Houghton Mifflin, 1911 (p. 146).

[3]Cortissoz. *La Farge* (p. 117).

[4]Malraux has observed that "the relations between theory and practice in every kind of art often give scope to irony. Artists build theories round what they would like to do, but they do what they can," *The Voices of Silence* [Paris, 1951]. trans. Stuart Gilbert. New York: Doubleday, 1956 (p. 117). This comment is applicable to some extent to La Farge. He was, however, demonstrably possessed of a very sound knowledge of the ground out of which the major Impressionists grew. His collection entitled *The Higher Life in Art* (New York: McClure Co., 1908), for instance, contains lectures on such major Impressionist forerunners as Delacroix, Millet, Rousseau, Daubigny, and Corot.

On William Morris Hunt, who introduced James to La Farge, see Henry James. *Autobiography.* Criterion Books, 1956 (p. 286). James thought that La Farge was the "embodiment of the gospel of esthetics." *Autobiography* (p. 290). For similarly adulatory comments, see *Autobiography* (pp. 287, 289, 291, and 296).

[5]Cited by Cortissoz in E.E. Hale. "The Impressionism of Henry James," *Faculty Papers of Union College*, Vol. 2, No. 1 (Jan., 1931), p. 115.

[5a]James. "Art [French Pictures in Boston]". *Atlantic Monthly*, XXIX (January 1872), 115-118. La Farge worked on this canvas from 1859 to 1870. On La Farge's connections with Impressionism, see Richard J. Boyle. *American Impressionism.* New York Graphic Society, 1974 (pp. 80-83).

[6]James. *Autobiography.* Criterion Books, 1956 (p. 294).

[7]James. *Letters.* Vol. 1, ed. Edel. Belknap Press of Harvard Univ. Press, 1974 (p. 134).

[8]John Rewald. *History of Impressionism.* Museum of Modern Art, 1961 (p. 316). Rewald, however, quotes Manet's friend, Antonin Proust, who said that Manet had been using the word "impression" to describe the quality of his painting for more than a decade prior to his 1867 one-man show at the Paris World's Fair. Rewald. *History.* 1961 (p. 212). On the genesis of the term Impressionism in art, see also Teddy Brunius. *Mutual Aid in the Arts.* Uppsala, Sweden: Almqvist and Wiksells, 1972 (pp. 100-101) and Albert Boime. *The Academy and French Painting in the Nineteenth Century.* London: Phaidon, 1971 (pp. 166-167; and pp. 170-172).

[9]The Impressionists exhibited the greatest similarity of technique in the period during the 'seventies when they gathered at Monet's home in Argenteuil and painted in front of the same motifs. Even Renoir and Monet, however, did not use Impressionist techniques exclusively. As late as 1880 Monet, for example, was doing an occasional canvas after the Realist manner. See, for instance, "Flowers in a Vase" (1880, Collection of Mrs. William Coxe Wright), which utilizes a Realistic technique not unlike that of the Manet of the early '60's. And Renoir shows evidence of a break with Impressionism through much of the early 1880's, during which time he returned to a Classical style.

The Impressionists had a number of precursors. Boudin, Jongkind, Corot, Millet, Delacroix, Constable, Turner, Ford Madox Brown, Winslow Homer, and John La Farge were all, in some manner, forerunners of the Impressionist painters. Although it is important to emphasize that the Impressionists borrowed many of their techniques from the tradition (and the knowledge of their use of the tradition informs one of the best, and one of the earliest, appraisals of their technique—by Louis Duranty (1833-1880) in his *La Nouvelle Peinture: A propos du groupe d'artistes qui exposent dans les Galeries Durand-Ruel* (1876), ed. Marcel Guerin. Paris: Librairie Floury, 1946 (see, for instance, p. 38), it was the *combination* of techniques that the Impressionists used which was revolutionary and which set them apart as artistic innovators.

I wish to acknowledge here my debt to Professor John W. McCoubrey of the University of Pennsylvania and to Mr. Thomas Folds, Dean of Education at the Metropolitan Museum of Art, both of whom have directed me to some important art historical sources and helped me to think out several matters of importance with respect to the Impressionist style in painting.

10For more on the importance of rendering what the eye sees in the work of the Impressionists, cf. Théodore Duret. *Les Peintres Impressionnistes.* Paris: Librairie Parisienne, 1878, rpt. in T. Duret. *Histoire des Peintres Impressionnistes,* 3rd ed. Paris: H. Floury, 1922 (p. 175). William A. Harms seems to have captured well the Impressionist aim with this comment: "Impressionistic [I would have said 'Impressionist'] painting is an art of reproducing instantaneous sense-perception, a point of view which is rooted in the sheer delight of visual effects." *Impressionism as a Literary Style,* Indiana Univ. Dissertation, 1971 (p. 10).

11Monet's comment is quoted in Kenneth Clark. *Landscape Painting.* Charles Scribner's Sons, 1950 (p. 94). On the recovery of human sight, see Patrick Trevor-Roper. *The World through Blunted Sight: An Inquiry into the Influence of Defective Vision on Art and Character.* Bobbs-Merrill, 1970 (pp. 158-161). The seeming delight with which the Impressionist has painted open-air scenes is not, of course, without precedent. Turner and (with considerably less vivacity) Constable have both excelled in their different ways in rendering a sense of weather and of atmosphere.

Lilla Perry has quoted Monet as having said: "When you go out to paint, try to forget what objects you have before you, a tree, a house, a field or whatever. Merely think here is a little square of blue, here an oblong of pink, here a streak of yellow, and paint it just as it looks to you, the exact color and shape, until it gives your own naïve impression of the scene before you." Cited in Lilla Cabot Perry, "Reminiscences of Claude Monet from 1889 to 1909," *The American Magazine of Art,* Vol. XVIII (March 1927), 120.

11aThéodore Duret [1878] cited in Steven Z. Levine. *Monet and His Critics.* Garland, 1976 (p. 33).

12Jacques Barzun. *Classic, Romantic, and Modern.* Garden City, New York: Doubleday, Anchor paperback, 1961 (p. 112). Such a technique of juxtaposing complementary colors J. Carson Webster has termed "divided color" (in contrast to the term "retinal fusion"). And Webster makes the following important distinction:

> [in] ... Impressionism in general, retinal fusion seems to have no place ... , but that does not mean that divided color is useless. It is important in that it allows a color, no matter how contrasting, to be introduced into an area of another color while still maintaining its own hue. Retinal fusion, as well as pigment mixing, would defeat this end. Thus the divided color is not a means to resultant colors; it is a means for recording colors in intimate association, in interpretation, as it were, within a given area, while allowing each to be seen for what it is.

Webster judges that "what takes place when touches of one color, or when touches of two colors are set side by side, is not retinal fusion, but rather a kind of mental (not visual) averaging, for the area involved, of the colors or their values." J. Carson Webster. "The Techniques of Impressionism: A Reappraisal." *College Art Journal.* 4 ( 4, 1944), pp. 20-21.

This Impressionist means of "recording colors in intimate association" is another method whereby the Impressionist painters force the viewer to "put the painting together himself." See my discussion on pp. 12 ff., especially the quotation from Stephen Spender, including footnote 35.

[13]This notion—that the artist must paint light—was not newly discovered by the Impressionists, for this feeling was anticipated by Uvedale Price as early as 1801: "I can imagine a man of the future, who may be born without the sense of feeling, being able to see nothing but white light variously modified." *Dialogue on the Distinct Characters of the Picturesque and Beautiful.* Quoted in *Principles of Art.* New York: Oxford Univ. Press [1938], 1967 (p. 145n.), by R.G. Collingwood, to whom I owe this suggestion.

[14]Monet and his followers probably learned something about *plein-air* techniques from Eugène Boudin (1824-1898) and C.F. Daubigny (1817-1878). Daubigny, who worked out-of-doors a great deal, seemed to have influenced the Impressionists in a painting such as "Gobelle's Mill at Optevoz" (ca. 1857, William L. Elkins Collection) wherein he manages to capture the sparkle of natural light on water. And we recall here that James himself noted that in his early days he was introduced to Daubigny by Hunt.

Monet was to some extent guided in his *plein-air* work by Boudin, who first painted outdoors with the young Monet at Le Havre in 1858. In his writings, James fails to mention Boudin, but he refers to Daubigny in *A Small Boy and Others* (see p. 193).

Other possible sources for the Impressionists' open-air work are legion. Constable, for instance, did outdoor sketches that show him to be a precursor of Boudin, although the two men did not seem to have known each other's work. In this vein, Morse Peckham makes a forceful (if not altogether convincing) case for naming John Constable as the founder of Modernist painting, as well as a strong influence upon Monet and Pissarro, in "Constable and Wordsworth," *College Art Journal,* XII (Spring 1953), 196-209; rpt. *The Triumph of Romanticism: Collected Essays.* Columbia, S.C.: Univ. of South Carolina Press, 1970; and in *Beyond the Tragic Vision: The Quest for Identity in the Nineteenth Century.* New York: George Braziller, 1962 (p. 136, in particular). Among other British painters prior to the Impressionists, Ford

Madox Brown, the grandfather of Ford Madox Ford, was already, in his quiet way, painting out-of-doors during the early 1850's.

James also, of course, knew Constable's work, and referred to it on at least two occasions in his criticism. See "The Old Masters at Burlington House." *The Nation,* XXIV (Feb. 1, 1877). pp. 71-72 and "The Picture Season in London." *The Galaxy,* XXIV (August 1877), pp. 149-161 (both pieces are reprinted in Henry James. *The Painter's Eye, Notes and Essays on the Pictorial Arts.* London: Rupert Hart-Davis, 1956. See p. 72 and p. 160).

Henry James likewise knew the painting of Ford Madox Brown (1821-1893), whose work James refers to in a pair of essays entitled "London," both of which appeared in *Harper's Weekly* in 1897 [at just about the time that James first met Brown's grandson, Ford Madox Ford (then Hueffer)]. For James's published references to Brown, see *Harper's Weekly,* XLI (Feb. 20, 1897), 183 and XLI (June 5, 1897), 562-563.

15 *The History of Impressionism,* p. 196. See also Rewald for studies done by Sisley and Monet upon "the changes in coloring aspect and form" (p. 239) which the change of seasons brings about in the same motif. See Rewald, too, for the Impressionist artist's observations of the sea (p. 196). For further remarks on this subject, consult Arnheim, *Art and Visual Perception* (Berkeley, Calif., 1965), p. 269. Bazille's notebook in G. Poulain, *Bazille et ses Amis* (Paris: La Renaissance du Livre, 1932), "I must not forget to compare the color-value of bright water with that of sunlit grass" (p. 153).

16 As with most artistic techniques used by the Impressionists, this was not an original notion. The idea of painting the same motif in different weather, from different angles and at different times of the year was to some extent anticipated by Valenciennes—the founder of 19th-century historic landscape— who painted a single motif from nearly identical viewpoints at different hours of the day. On the probable influence of Valenciennes upon Monet and Corot, cf. Boime. *Academy,* pp. 62-3.

Another possible source for this technique is the work of the 19th-century Japanese landscape painters. In 1856, the etcher Braquemond made a chance discovery of Japanese woodcuts in a Paris shop. He then showed them to the Goncourts, Baudelaire, Manet and Degas (and probably also to Whistler). Van Gogh, moreover, wrote to his brother Theo (from Arles in 1888) that "one likes Japanese painting ... . One has felt its influence—all the Impressionists have that in common" [cited in Rewald. *Post-Impressionism.* 2nd ed., Museum of Modern Art, 1962. (p. 76)]. The Impressionists seemed to have been initially attracted to Japanese art by its delicate use of color and by its technique of circling around a subject. Manet, Whistler, Degas and Van Gogh admired the work of Hokusai and Hiroshige, and seemingly learned something from these Japanese artists.

Katsushika Hokusai (1760-1849) made numerous drawings of Mount Fuji which were then turned into woodblocks and printed in color ("Thirty-Six Views of Mount Fuji" 1829, for example) and in ink ("One Hundred Views of Mount Fuji"). Ando Hiroshige (1797-1858) in like fashion did "Fifty-three Stages on the Tokaido" (eastern sea highway), 1833. On the profound stylistic changes which independent French painting underwent from 1860 onward as a result of the "discovery" of Japanese prints, cf. Rewald. *History of Impressionism,* 1946. p. 176; Mark Roskill. *Van Gogh, Gauguin and the Impressionist Circle.* Thames and Hudson, 1971, *passim.* On Van Gogh and Japanese art, specifically, cf. also Rewald. *Post-Impressionism,* 1962. pp. 72-3. See also Colta Feller Ives. *The Great Wave: The Influence of Japanese Woodcuts on French Prints.* Museum of Modern Art, 1974. Chapter One, especially.

Moreover, it is no accident that the great *plein-air* artists of the nineteenth century turned for inspiration to the Dutch painters of the seventeenth, for the Dutchmen seemed to have been the first to teach that nature in all its varied aspects has a grand and intimate appeal, capable of being portrayed outside the boundaries of the Classical motif. It is good to keep in mind, however, that these artists seldom worked out-of-doors. The practice of painting in the open air became common only during the nineteenth century (on the subject of *plein-airism* in Dutch painting, see Jakob Rosenberg, Seymour Slive and E.H. ter Kuile. *Dutch Art and Architecture: 1600 to 1800.* Penguin, 1972 (pp. 240 and 246, in particular), but Rubens painted scenes around his home in Antwerp—almost certainly *en plein air.* In his writings, Monet makes voluminous references to Rubens (who is likewise mentioned more than any other painter in the *Journals* of Delacroix).

I cannot say for sure if James knew the work of Valenciennes or the Japanese artists mentioned above, but he surely did know well most of the important Dutch and Flemish painters of the seventeenth century whose work he alludes to often in his published criticism. James refers to Rubens, for example, on at least a dozen occasions, from June, 1872 (see *Atlantic Monthly,* XXIX. pp. 757-763—p. 757, in particular) to *The Middle Years.* Scribner's, 1917 (see p. 569 and p. 599), which was published a year after James died.

James was also very familiar with Delacroix's work (1798-1863). James's first published reference to him appeared in "Contemporary French Painters: An Essay." *North American Review,* CVI (April 1868), 716-723 (See p. 721, in particular). And James made significant references to Delacroix's painting on more than a half dozen other occasions.

[17] A technique perhaps largely learned from Delacroix. For James's essential opinion of the latter, see "The Letters of Delacroix" (1880) in *The Painter's Eye* (pp. 183-201).

[18] Phoebe Pool. *Impressionism.* Praeger, 1967 (p. 7).

[19] "They [the Impressionists] have tried to render the walk, the movement, the tremor and the intermingling of passersby, just as they have tried to render the trembling of leaves, the shivering of water, and the vibration of air inundated with light ... " (in Linda Nochlin. *Impressionism and Post-Impressionism: Sources and Documents.* Prentice-Hall, 1966 (p. 7). Duranty, incidentally, is the one who introduced Zola to Manet.

[20] Gustave Geffroy. *Histoire de l'Impressionnisme—la Vie artistique.* 3rd series. Paris: Dentu, 1894.

[21] In using the term "rhythmic" to refer to a painting, I am of course aware that there has been controversy over the term as being descriptive of performances in the visual and plastic arts. An argument for the use of the term "rhythm" in all of the arts has been put forward by Theodore M. Greene in *The Arts and the Art of Criticism.* Princeton University Press, 1940. See especially pp. 221-226. See also John Dewey. *Art As Experience.* Minton, Balch and Co., 1934. 175ff., 218ff. Rudolf Arnheim has moreover argued convincingly that although paintings exist "all at once," the eye takes in a painting sequentially. See *Art and Visual Perception.* University of California Press, 1971.

Arguments against the use of "rhythm" as a descriptive term in the plastic arts are to be found in Fritz Medicus. "Das Problem einer vergleichende Geschichte der Kunste," in *Philosophie der Literaturwissenschaft,* ed. E. Ermatinger. Berlin: Junker and Dümhaupt, 1930 (pp. 195ff). Oscar Wilde likewise dealt with this subject, but in a less systematic way.

[22] See Wylie Sypher. *Rococco to Cubism in Art and Literature.* Random House, 1960 (p. 180).

[23] Arnold Hauser. *A Social History of Art.* Vol. 4 (1951) rpt. Vintage Books, 1958 (p. 171).

[24] A characteristic also of the painting of Delacroix.

[25]Manet cited in Paul Jamot and Georges Wildenstein. *Manet*. Paris: Les Beaux-Arts, 1932. Vol. 1 (p. 71).

*The Shorter Oxford Dictionary* (1964) gives the following definition of an Impressionist: "A painter who endeavors to express the general impression produced by a scene or object, to the exclusion of minute details or elaborate finish; also, a writer who practices a similar method" (Common usage by 1881, from French impression*niste*, 1876).

[26]The Impressionists more than likely learned something about this technique from Delacroix. In 1853 Delacroix, for instance, wrote: "When we finish a picture, we always spoil it a little. The final touches which are supposed to draw the parts together detract from its freshness," *Journal de Eugène Delacroix*, ed. Andre Joubin, Vol. II. Paris: 1932 (p. 17). In the *Journal*, the conflict arising from an obsession with the unfinished and the need to translate it into a finished work of art is one of the main subjects discussed.

Baudelaire was also much concerned with the "sketch-finish" question. See, for example, *Curiosités esthétiques*, ed. Henri Guillemin. Paris: Calmann-Lévy, n.d. (p. 70).

[27]Louis Duranty. *La nouvelle peinture*, ed. Marcel Guérin. Paris: 1946 (p. 50), translation mine. The difference in aesthetic satisfaction rendered by the sketch as opposed to that of the finished work was perhaps first clearly expressed by Giorgio Vasari. *Le vite*, ed. Gaetano Milanesi, 9 vols. Florence: 1878-1885. Vol. 2, pp. 170-171, and Vol. 5, p. 568.

[28]John Rewald. *The History of Impressionism*. New York: 1946, p. 178, and D.S. MacColl. *Nineteenth Century Art*. James Maclehose and Sons, 1902 (p. 163).

[29]Cited in Nochlin. *Impressionism and Post-Impressionism*, p. 9. This concern, of course, was not unique to the Impressionists. In his *Notebooks* da Vinci showed great interest in the influence of the contrasting color of objects set side by side. He furthermore wrote about colored shadows—a subject that Goethe likewise concerned himself with. Athanasius Kircher, in his *Ars magna lucis et umbrae* (*The Great Science of Light and Shadow*). Rome, 1646, called colors "the children of light and shadow." Goethe, of course, knew Kircher's treatise, and referred to it with approval in the chapter on "Colored Shadows" (Chapter VI) of his *Theory of Colors* (1810).

At least one major Impressionist forerunner, incidentally, took Goethe's work seriously. In *Colour in Turner: Poetry and Truth* (London: Praeger,

1969), John Gage has shown that Turner had read the translation of Goethe's *Farbenlehre* by his friend C.L. Eastlake very closely. On the problematic question of the influence of Goethe's *Theory of Color* on practicing painters, however, cf. Marilyn Torbruegge's "Goethe's Theory of Color and Practicing Artists," *The Germanic Review* XLIX: 3 (May 1974), 189-199.

[30]Rewald. *The History of Impressionism,* 1961 ed. (p. 196). For further remarks on this subject, cf. Arnheim. *Art and Visual Perception.* Berkeley, Calif.: Univ. of Calif. Press, 1965 (p. 269).

[31]Cited in G. Poulain. *Bazille et ses Amis.* Paris: 1932 (p. 153).

[32]As cited in René Huyghe. *Delacroix,* trans. Jonathan Griffin. New York: Abrams, 1963 (p. 172).

[33]Chevreul, *De l'abstraction.* Dijon, 1864, cited in Courthion. *Impressionism.* Abrams, 1972 (p. 184).

[34]Spender, *Struggle* (pp. 133-4). Spender, of course, is not the first scholar to write about this particular Impressionist technique. As early as 1922, in a collaborative study entitled *Foundations of Aesthetics.* 2nd ed. New York: International Publishers, 1929, C.K. Ogden, I.A. Richards and James Wood break ground by attempting to incorporate this theory into a systematic treatment of Aesthetics. The authors stated a belief that the beauty of a work of art is discovered when a state of synaesthetic balance is attained. And this balance represents an experience in the audience rather than a mysterious "thing" within the artistic performance itself. Without acknowledging a debt to Ogden, Richards, and Wood, R.G. Collingwood perhaps more engagingly pursues similar lines of thought in *Principles of Art* (1938). Collingwood, who seems to have had little esteem for the Impressionist painters, nevertheless helps to clarify the French painters' technique, which calls for the assistance of the viewer in putting the painting together. In the sections on "the audience as collaborator" and "the artist and the audience" in his chapter on "The Artist and the Community," Collingwood helps to elucidate this aspect of Impressionist art. Consult, in particular, p. 312 and p. 324, for concise statements on the kind of collaboration that Impressionist art seems to call for. Joyce perhaps had something of this idea of collaboration in mind when he wrote (speaking of a sucessful work of art), "Its soul, its whatness, leaps to us from the vestment of its appearance." *Stephen Hero.* New Directions, 1955 (p. 213).

Joyce's comment, which mirrors the seeming recognition of the Impressionist painters that "the look" of a work of art changes as the viewer himself does, had far-reaching philosophical implications. Such implications relate to the

Heraclitean "doctrine of sensible things"—the doctrine that stems from Heraclitus's statement: "You cannot step into the same river twice." On the partial significance of "the River Statement" of Heraclitus, see W.K.C. Guthrie. *A History of Greek Philosophy.* Vol. 1. Cambridge University Press, 1962 (pp. 450-452). Appendix, pp. 488 ff. H. Richard Niebuhr makes some interesting comments on the related question of the discovery of spatial and temporal relativity which Heraclitus's observation in part served to forecast. See Niebuhr *The Meaning of Revelation.* New York: Macmillan, 1948 (p. 7).

[35]In his use of this technique, Degas has seemingly drawn upon the art of photography. In *The Painter and the Photographer from Delacroix to Warhol* (Univ. of New Mexico Press, 1972), Van Deren Coke speculates that the "French Impressionists do not seem to have used photographs directly for portraits" (p. 55). But there is some evidence that Coke was not altogether right. In *Art and Photography,* Aaron Scharf has pointed out that a photographic album in the collection of André Jammes contains 197 stereoscopic photographs called *Vues instantanées de Paris.* "Taken probably between 1861 and 1865, these were put on sale by the photographer Hippolyte Jouvin. The cutting-off of figures, horses and carriages can be found very often throughout the series... . In some of them [i.e., the Jammes photographs], horses and carriages are cut off in much the same way as is Degas' vehicle in his pictures of a 'Carriage at the Races' (1873)." Aaron Scharf. *Art and Photography.* The Penguin Press [1968], 1969 (p. 154). On p. 155 Scharf presents further persuasive elaboration upon the probable indebtedness of Degas to the photographer's technique of "cutting-off." Scharf's speculations concerning Degas and photography, while not absolutely conclusive, are certainly not to be lightly dismissed.

Some broad discriminations can be made among the visual and plastic arts. In contrast to the other visual and plastic arts, such as sculpture, architecture, and the film (with its sound track and "narrative" action), the arts of painting and photography can be generally said to have a meaning that is specifically visual (though even here one must exercise caution, for the series of frescoes in Giotto's Arena Chapel, for example, certainly show a sense of well worked out character development—and just as certainly "tell a story." Then, too, some of the serial photographs of Andy Warhol also achieve a "narrative effect" not unlike Giotto's—although the subject that the respective artists have chosen to depict are very different, indeed!)

Moreover, painting and photography are alike in being essentially restricted to the occupation of a two-dimensional surface, although here, too, there are exceptions. As F.A. Trapp has pointed out, a Van Gogh painting may sometimes have more "relief" than an Egyptian bas-relief sculpture. See, especially, Trapp's "On the Nature of Painting," in *Art and Philosophy: Reading in Aes-*

*thetics,* ed. W.E. Kennick.  New York: St. Martin's Press, 1964 (pp. 216-217).

The camera, of course, does not record physical objects, but only one aspect of such objects; namely, their effects in light at the moment of exposure to the lens.  In this sense, too, the canvas and the photograph are alike, since neither can be observed by being walked around or rotated in the way that an architectural structure or a sculptural work of art can be.  For a discussion of "photographic reality," see E.H. Gombrich. *Art and Illusion: A Study in the Psychology of Pictorial Representation.*  Princeton Univ. Press, 1960; Bollingen paperback, 1969 (pp. 34-36).

[36]Cf. Rudolf Arnheim.  *Art and Visual Perception.*  Univ. of Calif. Press, 1965, p. 269.

[37]Arnheim. *Art and Visual Perception.* 1965, pp. 251-2.

[38]Morse Peckham's term in *Beyond the Tragic Vision* (p. 224).

[39]But direct influence is difficult to establish.  Cf., e.g., Teddy Brunius. *Mutual Aid in the Arts,* p. 105 and Kenneth Clark. *Landscape Painting,* p. 93 and p. 95, wherein both authors set out some of the problems involved in trying to establish Turner's direct influence upon the Impressionist style in painting.

[40]Hans Platte. *Les Impressionnistes,* trans. Marianne Duval-Valentin. Paris: Arthaud, 1962 (p. 154).  See also Sypher. *Rococco* (p. 118).

[41]Rewald. *History of Impressionism,* 1961 ed. (p. 131).

[42]Cited by Nochlin. *Impressionism and Post-Impressionism: Sources and Documents* (p. 34); Lilla Cabot Perry told how Monet "always insisted on the great importance of a painter noticing when the effect changed, so as to get a true impression of a certain aspect of nature and not a composite picture, as too many paintings were, and are."  Lilla Cabot Perry, "Reminiscences of Claude Monet from 1889 to 1909," *The American Magazine of Art,* Vol. XVIII (March 1927) p. 121. Boime, *Academy.* has called this article to my attention.

[43]Harms. *Impressionism as a Literary Style* (p. 33).

[44]What was to become a cardinal point of Impressionism was perhaps first made by Boudin in the 1850's: "Everything painted directly and on the spot has a strength, vigour and vivacity of touch that can never be attained in the studio; three brush strokes from nature are worth more than two days' studio work at the easel."  William Gaunt. *Impressionism.*  London: Thames and

Hudson, 1970 (p. 11).  For a beautiful example of the results of *plein-air* work, see Monet's "Autumn at Argenteuil" (1873).

[45]Maupassant cited in Courthion. *Impressionism.* (p. 24).

[46]Berthe Morisot, one of the few women associated with the Impressionist movement, was encouraged in her early work by Corot.  She met Edouard Manet at The Louvre through Fantin-Latour.  She subsequently posed often for Manet before marrying his brother (who, in turn, became "the subject" for many of her paintings).

[47]Hauser. *Social,* Vol. IV (p. 179).

[48]Spender. *Struggle* (p. XIII).  For similar statements by the same author, see p. XII and p. 143.  W.H. Auden appears to be correct when he cites Poe as the first writer of fiction to devote his "attention to timeless passionate moments in a life."  W.H. Auden, *The Dyer's Hand.*  New York:  Random House, 1962 (p. 474).

The Impressionist, however, seemed to recognize that the movement of time speeds up, or slows down, according to the emotion of the person experiencing the moment.  Bergson's philosophical recognition (1892) of the important distinction between "time" and "duration" preceded Einstein's relativity theory by thirteen years.  Yet it was not until the French Impressionist movement was already history that Bergson had systematized what the French painters seem to have discovered in their art.  In delineating his theory of time (one which takes into account the fact that human time seems to pass more rapidly on some occasions, and more slowly on others), Bergson formulated and made accessible a development in the arts that had been first fully realized with Impressionism.

Ezra Pound was probably right when he wrote that artists are the "antennae of the race."  On the question of attitudes toward time, in particular, Alexander Smith was surely right when he observed that "men of letters forerun science like the morning star the dawn."  *Dreamthorp.*  London:  Strahan and Co., 1863. rpt. Oxford Univ. Press, 1914 (p. 127).

[49]I paraphrase Hauser. *Social,* Vol. IV (pp. 169-170).

[50]Hoffman, *The Mortal No: Death and the Modern Imagination.*  Princeton Univ. Press, 1964 (p. 4).

[51]For a consideration of this topic in its relationship to Monet, Sisley, Renoir, Bazille, and Manet, cf. Boime. *Academy.* (pp. 58-67); to Pissarro and

Seurat, cf. Boime. *Academy.* n. 119, p. 200; to Whistler, see E.R. and J. Pennell. *The Life of James McNeill Whistler,* rev. ed., London: J.B. Lippincott, 1911, pp. 35 and 385.

[52]Spengler is correct in remarking upon "the impossibility of achieving a genuinely religious painting on *plein-air* principles," Oswald Spengler, "Impressionism," cited in *The Decline of the West* (abridged), ed. Helmut Werner and Arthur Helps, trans. Charles F. Atkinson. New York: Modern Library, 1962, n. 5, p. 154.

[53]I paraphrase herein some of the observations of César Grana. *Fact and Symbol: Essays in the Sociology of Art.* New York: Oxford Univ. Press, 1971 (pp. 78-93). In these pages Grana also provides some interesting comments on the peculiarly Modernist Parisian-ness of the group.

In their freedom from subject the Impressionists may have gained some insights from a colorist such as Turner (1775-1851). In this regard, we recall Hazlitt's criticism of Turner: "pictures of nothing, and very like," "Round Table," *Examiner* (1816); cited by J.A. Finberg in *The Life of J.M.W. Turner, R.A.* Oxford: Clarendon Press, 1961 (p. 241). For more on this break from subject in Turner cf. Morse Peckham. *Beyond the Tragic Vision* (pp. 222-3).

[54]Bazille cited in Sypher. *Rococo* (p. 172). T.E. Hulme captured the idea well when he wrote: "in painting, where the old endeavored to tell a story, the modern attempts to fix an impression... ." *Further Speculations,* ed. Sam Hynes. University of Minnesota Press, 1955 (p. 72).

[55]As Renoir claimed, "There isn't a person, a landscape, or a subject that doesn't possess at least some interest—although sometimes it is more or less hidden... . Old Corot opened our eyes to the beauty of the Loing, which is a river like any other; and I am sure that the Japanese landscape is no more beautiful than other landscapes. But the point is that Japanese painters know how to bring out their hidden treasures," cited in Nochlin. *Impressionism and Post-Impressionism: Sources and Documents.* 1966 (p. 48).

[56]Cf., e.g., John Rewald. *History of Impressionism* (1946 ed.), pp. 355-87. Cf. also, e.g., Monet's comment regarding "certaines personnes" who were to participate in the planned exhibition of 1882, Monet letter to Durand-Ruel of 10 Feb., 1882, cited in L. Venturi, *Les Archives de l'Impressionnisme,* Vol. 1. Paris and New York: Durand-Ruel Editeurs, 1939 (p. 121). See also Sven Loevgren. *The Genesis of Modernism: Seurat, Gauguin, van Gogh, and French Symbolism in the 1880's* [1959]. Rev. ed. Indiana Univ. Press, 1971 (p. 8) and Levine. *Monet and His Critics.* 1976 (pp.50-51).

57On the middle three of these occasions Monet is said to have protested that he did not care to exhibit with the first dauber who happened to come along. Cited in Jaworska. *Pont-Aven*, 1972. p. 11.

58Cézanne, who met Pissarro on his first trip to Paris in 1861, claims to have been influenced by Pissarro. See, for example, Joachim Gasquet. *Cézanne*, 2nd ed. Paris: Les Editions Bernheim-Jeune, 1926.

59On Cézanne's difficulty in finishing a picture, cf., especially, John Rewald. *Paul Cézanne: A Biography*. Schocken Books, 1968 (p. 97).

60Between the fall of 1889 and the spring of 1890—very late in Van Gogh's brief career—the artist "did no fewer than 23 paintings" after the manner and subject of Millet. Rewald. *Post-Impressionism*, 1962 (p. 350).

61In Chapters V and VI of her *Pont-Aven*, W. Jaworska amply documents the break from Impressionism made by such of its former advocates as Gauguin, Van Gogh and Bernard in the late '80's when they were living and working in the regions of Pont-Aven and Le Pouldu. See Wladyslawa Jaworska. *Gauguin and the Pont-Aven School* [1971], trans. Patrick Evans. London: Thames and Hudson, 1972.

62On Van Gogh's near absence of knowledge concerning the leader of the Neo-Impressionist circle of painters, see Rewald. *Post-Impressionism*, 1962 (p. 76).

63Cited in Loevgren. *Genesis* (p. 216). For conclusive evidence that the writings of Chevreul, the internationally known scientist, helped form the basis for the color techniques of the famous Neo-Impressionists, Pissarro, Signac, and Seurat, cf. Marilyn K. Torbruegge. "Goethe's Theory of Color and Practicing Artists." *The Germanic Review* XLIX: 3 (May 1974). n. 36. Interestingly, thirty-four years before Signac approached Chevreul himself for an elucidation of his scientific system—the one that Seurat had used in developing his Neo-Impressionist theory of painting—Delacroix, whom Seurat much admired, had written to the scientist, asking if he might discuss with the famous Chevreul the science of color and question him regarding certain problems of artistic technique. But a constant sore throat prevented Delacroix from keeping their appointment. See Rewald. *Post-Impressionism*, 1962 (p. 82).

On the Neo-Impressionists' scientific theories of light, see especially the following: W.I. Homer. *Seurat and the Science of Painting*. Cambridge, Mass.: Harvard Univ. Press, 1964; Paul Signac, *D'Eugène Delacroix au néo-Impressionnisme* (first published in 1899 in the *Revue Blanche*). Paris: Françoise

Cachin, 1964; and Pissarro's letters to his son Lucien.  As to the Impressionists, their analysis of light may appear to be scientific but their approach was essentially intuitive.  See Boyle. *American* (p. 22).

[64]Degas always referred to Seurat as "the notary" because of his conservative mode of dress.  Seurat seemingly took to heart Flaubert's good words of counsel: "Be patient and orderly in your life, like a good bourgeois, so that you can be violent and original in your art."

[65]My discussion of light and color is greatly indebted to Anthony Blunt's essay on 19th-century French Painting in D.G. Charlton, ed. *France.* London: Methuen, 1972, pp. 473-484, in particular.

In addition to having cherished a great respect for the Goncourt brothers, Seurat was even more interested in Delacroix (from whose writings he took copious notes), in the ideas of Corot and, above all, in the writings of Charles Blanc and the scientific treatises of Chevreul, Sutter, and Rood.

[66]For more on Seurat's early technique, cf. Gustave Coquiot. *Georges Seurat.* Paris:  A. Michel, 1924, pp. 193 ff.  Pierre Courthion has made this accurate judgment about Seurat's "The Canoe" (1884, Private Collection, Paris):

> This is surely the most Impressionist picture in all of Seurat's work.  We might say that here, under the pretext of his title, the painter has tried to combine all that is transient:  the fragile craft gliding swiftly on the river, the wind in the leaves, the passage of time.  No other work gives such a feeling of the moment—and of a moment taken more or less at random, like a fragment detached from the whole.  Courthion. *Impressionism* (p. 182).

[67]Although, see Rewald.  *Post-Impressionism.* 1962, n. 50, p. 145, for Seurat and his associates' preference for the word "divisionism" as a term to express what they were doing.  *The Shorter Oxford* (1964) defines "Pointillism" as "a method invented by French Impressionist painters of producing luminous effects by crowding a surface with small spots of various colors, which are blended by the eye."

[68]The best pointillist work by Seurat that I have seen is his "Poseuses" (1888, Barnes Foundation, Merion, Pa.).  For an excellent comparison of Seurat's "Une Baignade" and Renoir's "Le Déjeuner des Canotiers" (painted at Bougival in 1881)—a comparison which highlights the essential dissimilarities between the Neo-Impressionists and the Impressionists—cf. Loevgren. *Genesis*, pp. 7-8 and p. 207, n. 9.

[69]Among the contributors to the first number of the *Revue*, incidentally, were Edmond de Goncourt, Zola, Huysmans, and Verlaine.

[70]Rewald. *Post-Impressionism.* 1962 (p. 49). Yet in his story, "La Trouvaille," in *Le Chat Noir,* 11 Feb. 1882, p. 4, Signac dealt ironically with Zola's work.

[71]Cited in Loevgren. *Genesis* (p. 5).

[72]While I would not exactly refer to this painting as a "color symphony" after the lyrical manner of a landscape by Monet or Renoir, nevertheless Signac's early skill as a colorist is seen in the treatment of the buildings and in the white and bluish tones of the snow.

[73]This quotation is an excerpt from a longer passage in John W. McCoubrey, ed. *American Art: 1700-1960: Sources and Documents.* Prentice-Hall, 1965 (pp. 155-156). Bracketed ellipses indicate passages that I have omitted; the unbracketed ellipsis indicates a passage omitted by the editor.

[74]I am thinking here, for example, of the Monet of "The Beach at Trouville" (ca. 1870), which clearly shows the influence of the Boudin to whom Renoir once referred as "the king of the skies." For James's highly qualified praise of Homer, see the 1875 essay in *The Painter's Eye* (pp. 71-72).

[75]"A Painter on Painting," *Harper's Monthly,* LVI (Feb. 1878), 458-561.

[76]Cited in Rewald. *Post-Impressionism.* pp. 19-20. For more on the response of the American press, critics, and public cf. Rewald. *History.* 1961 (p. 395); and K. Bidle. *Impressionism in American Literature,* Northern Illinois dissertation, 1969 (pp. 150-153).

[77]E.P. Richardson has remarked that, during this period, "it was almost impossible for an artist to gain a reputation or to secure an audience if he did not live in New York City." *History of American Painting.* New York: Crowell, 1956 (p. 307).

[78]McCoubrey. *American Tradition.* Braziller, 1967 (p. 31). Twachtman's "Arques-La-Bataille" (1885, Metropolitan Museum of Art) represents a fairly typical example of the paleness and often vague, unlocalized prettiness of American Impressionist painting.

[79]Quentin Bell uses this apt phrase to describe the work of such painters as Alfred East, Fred Brown, Wilson Steer, and B.W. Leader (in Bell's *Victorian*

*Artists.* Harvard Univ. Press, 1967; rpt. Basic Books, 1968)—all of whom were associated with the group. In addition to Walter R. Sickert (one of the co-founders, along with Steer) and Aubrey Beardsley, who was pleased to have been elected to the Club in 1893, this group made up the leading members of the New English Art Club.

[80]While the founding of the New English Art Club in 1886 signalled a change in English painting, the Club, in essence, merely transplanted the French Impressionist style.

[81]Holbrook Jackson. *The 1890s* [1913]. Capricorn Books, 1966 (p.207). In reckoning the popularity of the Impressionists in the England of the last decade of the 19th century, it is important to bear in mind that the advanced art which had during the nineteenth century was always an art which had flourished in Paris thirty years before. British painting, moreover, had traditionally been far less vigorous and less rooted in the life of the country than English literature. These factors perhaps help to account for some of the British acceptance of the Impressionism of the New English Art Club.

[82]On this subject see, for instance, William Gaunt. *A Concise History of English Painting* [1964]. rpt. London: Thames and Hudson, 1970 (pp. 203-4). For Sickert's other contacts with French painting, cf. R.H. Wilenski's chapter on this subject in his *English Painting* [1937]. rev. ed. Hale Cushman and Flint, 1954.

[83]It is not clear whether James and Sickert were actually friends. In *Sickert: The Painter and His Circle* (London: Elek, 1972), Marjorie Lilly makes the point that the two artists were on friendly terms, and that Sickert much admired James's conversational powers and dignity of presence. Yet Leon Edel reports that no letter from the novelist to the painter exists, and knows of no substantial reason to claim that a friendship existed between the two men. It also deserves mention that in his published criticism James nowhere, to my knowledge, alludes to the British painter's work.

[84]The *Art Journal,* for instance, referred to him as the "arch apostle" of the "dab and spot" school.

[85]See, for instance, "John S. Sargent" *Harper's New Monthly Magazine,* LXXV (Oct. 1887), 683-691; and the essays entitled "London" which appeared in *Harper's Weekly*, XLI (June 5, 1897, and June 26, 1897). For the former, see especially p. 563; for the latter, p. 640.

[86]This portrait met with a less than happy fate; it was mutilated by an irate woman, wielding an axe. James subsequently expressed considerable amusement at having been thus "impaired by the tomahawk of the savage." Cited in Edmund Gosse. *Aspects and Impressions.* Charles Scribner's, 1922 (p. 49).

*Chapter Two*

*Continental Influences on the Literary*
*Impressionism of Henry James*


Those who come to read a great deal of Henry James's work soon begin to realize that this most important of American writers was also probably the most literate. And of writers from the English-speaking world, few have been more absorbed than James with France and with French writers.[1]

One of the first of these French writers to make extended use of Impressionist techniques in his fiction, Gustave Flaubert (1821-1880) was a writer with whom Henry James was very familiar. James arrived in Paris in 1875, the year after the inaugural Impressionist exhibit, to write letters for the *New York Herald Tribune.* Shortly after he arrived, the thirty-two year old American author was introduced to Turgenev, who shortly thereafter took James to Flaubert's apartments, high up in the Rue du Fauborg St. Honoré. Here, at Flaubert's Sunday afternoon gatherings, James encountered Zola, Daudet, Edmond de Goncourt, the as yet unpublished Maupassant, and other figures from the Impressionist art world.[2] On the whole, James's sense of these gatherings seems to have been not unlike Lambert Strether's impressions of the conversations and the comings and goings in Paris during his stay in that "great good place":

> The strolls over Paris to see something or call somewhere were accordingly inevitable and natural, and the late sessions in the wondrous troisième, the lovely home, where men dropped in and the picture composed more suggestively through the haze of tabacco, of music more or less good and of talk more or less polyglot, were on a principle not to be distinguished from that of the mornings and the afternoons. . . . Strether had never in his life heard so many opinions on so many subjects.[3]

Of the members of "the Circle," James was especially impressed by his large and amiable host, whose writings he knew well. Henry James wrote about Flaubert on five different occasions, from 1874 to 1902 (his last contribution on the French author being an Introduction to a translation of *Madame Bovary* in "A Century of French Romance" series).[4]   In balancing these five essays, by no means all of which hold a consistently positive view of Flaubert, it nevertheless seems clear that to James, Flaubert seemed "the most characteristic and powerful representative of what has lately been most original in the evolution of the French imagination."[5]   James noted the extraordinary singleness of aim exhibited in Flaubert's letters, and observed that he felt that they "show us the artist not only disinterested, but absolutely dishumanized"; often, the Frenchman's "restless passion for form strikes us as leaving the subject out of account altogether."[6]   James saw what he thought to be a gulf between the "comparatively meager conscience" and the "absolutely large artistic consciousness."[7]

This absence of "conscience" was a feature which James often criticized in reviewing the work of Flaubert and his French colleagues—the ones whom James often held up for contrast with the British.  In his 1883 essay on Trollope, while praising English authors for their awareness of the conscience, James also admitted the superiority of the French in matters of technique:

> This has been from the beginning the good fortune of our English providers of fiction, as compared with the French.  They are inferior in audacity, in neatness, in acuteness, in intellectual vivacity, in the arrangement of material, in the art of characterizing visible things.  But they have been more at home in the moral world; as people say today, they know their way about the conscience.[8]

James also found Flaubert's grimness about his profession as objectionable as his serious outlook on the world.  "One has always a kind feeling for people who detest the contemporary tone if they have done something fine." James remarked in an 1893 essay on Flaubert, "but the baffling thing in Flaubert was the extent of his suffering and the inelasticity of his humour."[9]   Of course, James had little of Flaubert's evident difficulties with literary composition;

the American author enjoyed writing, and in pursuing his highly successful occupation for fifty prolific years felt little of Flaubert's sense of burden. Flaubert, on the other hand, labored incessantly over successive drafts of his work and complained often in the correspondence about "what a bitch of a thing prose is" ("Quelle chienne de chose que la prose").[10]

Notwithstanding these dissimilarities of temperament, a number of traits that James found in Flaubert may have served to attract him to the Frenchman's Impressionist method. Both, for example, were Ivory Tower artists. "The Ivory Tower tradition," as Maurice Beebe has shown, "exalts art above life and insists that the artist can make use of life only if he stands aloof."[11] "L'auteur, dans son oeuvre," Flaubert said, "doit être comme Dieu dans l'univers, présent partout, et visible nulle part," (a comment that Joyce elaborated upon in *A Portrait*). While in James's work we probably feel the author's presence more than we do in Flaubert's, the *attitude* of artistic aloofness that Flaubert described, James also found congenial.[12]

Flaubert and James were also temperamentally similar insofar as they both experienced youthful traumas which seemingly provided them with the excuses that they needed to maintain their solitude. For James this trauma took the form of the "horrid if secret hurt" that he supposedly sustained in 1861. For Flaubert the trauma was the one that he claims to have had in January, 1844, on the road near Pont l'Evêque. Here he evidently experienced some manner of "prise de conscience," in which he felt himself "carried off suddenly in a torrent of flames." In August, 1846, Flaubert wrote to Louise Colet:

> The 'I' now living only comtemplates the other, who is dead. I have had two very distinct existences. Eternal events have signaled the end of the first and the beginning of the second. ... My active, passionate, emotional life ... came to an end in my twenty-second year.

Not surprisingly, the authors who sustained such traumas—whether they be real or imaginary—found the "divided self" technique an apt method for portraying the sense of disengagement that they seemingly wished to render. In a passage in Flaubert's *The First Sentimental*

*Education* (1845), the passive, introspective, and egoistic Jules makes a comment that is revelatory not only of Flaubert, but also of virtually every major Impressionist writer:

> The soldier who is actually engaged in fighting is no more capable of grasping the action as a whole than the gambler is conscious of the poetry of gambling, or the libertine of the splendour of debauch, or the lover of love's beauty, or even perhaps the monk of the grandeur of religion. If every passion and every dominant idea in life is a circle in which we turn in order to discover its size and its circumference, we must not remain shut up in it but get outside it.[13]

In line with this attitude toward art and experience are James' and Flaubert's feelings about life and conclusions. "Life is an eternal problem," Flaubert wrote in 1857, "so is history and everything else. Fresh figures are always being added to the sum. How can you count the spokes of a turning wheel?" And in the same letter he proclaimed, "no great genius has come to final conclusions, no great book ever does so, because humanity itself is forever on the march and can arrive at no goal."[14] James later gave assent to Flaubert's views when he replied to a critic that nothing was ever his *last word* on any subject—whatever.

Flaubert wrote to Louise Colet in 1852 that "broad construction itself is becoming more and more impossible, with our limited and precise vocabulary and our vague, confused and fugitive ideas. All that we can do, then, is out of sheer virtuosity, to tighten the strings of the overstrummed guitar and become primarily virtuosi, seeing that simplicity in our age is an illusion."[15] The Goncourt brothers furthermore recorded that Flaubert said to them: "The story, the plot of a novel is of no interest to me. When I write a novel, I aim at rendering a color, a shade. For instance, in my Carthaginian novel [*Salammbô*], I want to try to do something purple. The rest, the characters and the plot, is mere detail."[16]

In another passage under the *Journal* entry for the same date, the Goncourt brothers record that Flaubert said, "What seems beautiful to me, what I should like to write, is a book about nothing, a book dependent upon nothing external, which would be held together by the strength of its style. ..."—an aim that James also often seemingly held.[17] Surely also Flaubert's concerns about style were not lost upon a James who spoke of the Frenchman as a writer whose form was unequalled and whose art was extraordinary.[18] Flaubert's painstaking process of creation actually seemed in part to confirm James's belief that "nothing counts ... in art but the excellent; nothing exists for appreciation, but the superlative."[19] And James's remarks about Flaubert's style seem but another way of declaring his own convictions. "Beauty comes with expression ... expression is creation ... it *makes* the reality, and only in the degree in which it is, exquisitely, expression."[20]

Twentieth-century students of prose style have pointed to Flaubert as one of the pioneer users of "Impressionist" stylistic methods. One of the most often cited of such methods is his use of the imperfect verb where the past definite might have been expected. As Maria E. Kronegger has pointed out, this use of the imperfect form of the verb in French provides a blurring effect in Flaubert's narrative descriptions. In *Literary Impressionism,* Kronegger draws many examples from the opening pages of *The Sentimental Education* to buttress her generalizations.[21]

James, who knew Flaubert and his writings, said that because of the Frenchman the novel had become one of the great art forms of European literature and the one that was possessed of the highest contemporary ideals.[22] And James even went so far as to provide Flaubert with the supreme compliment by calling him the "novelist's novelist."[23] Considering, then, how well James knew and admired Flaubert the artist, considering, too, the many similarities that the two writers had in their approaches to art, it would be surprising if James had not learned something about Impressionist techniques from Flaubert—especially since these techniques are found in abundance in several of Flaubert's most important works.

Gustave Flaubert seems one of the more likely authors to have shown traces of the contemporary art world in his fiction. Although he had an Ivory Tower side to his disposition, Flaubert was not unlike James in that he associated personally and professionally with many of the important figures of the Impressionist movement, including such notables as Duranty, Gautier, Gleyre, and Cézanne.

Flaubert, of course, felt the influence of the revival of interest in landscape painting that came about during the period from 1830 to 1850, the years when he was beginning to develop his talents. In his early travels to Italy, Flaubert frequently described pictures that he encountered on his journeys.[24] His interest in using landscapes in literature was likewise seemingly sharpened by his early travels through the southeastern Mediterranean countries. During his eighteen-month journey through these countries, Flaubert took copious notes on the landscapes that he encountered. Evident on many pages of these Notes (which were not published during his lifetime) was a sensitivity to outdoor work that foreshadowed Impressionist painting. On one occasion, for instance, Flaubert observed the tint that played over a landscape and remarked: "Axiome: c'est le ciel qui fait le paysage."[25] In a passage written at an earlier date, he moreover showed the kind of interest in the effects of light upon the landscape that we have come to associate with Impressionism. In *Par les champs et par les grèves* (1847) he described the effect of the light on the sand which appeared to make the sand undulate.[26] Similarly, at one point he goes so far as to describe the light as a moving force in the landscape: "L'air était d'une transparence bleuâtre, sa lumière enveloppant tout frappant tout, pénétrait jusque dans leurs pores les vieux bois gris de la barque, les fils épais de la voile, la peau des hommes grelottante de sueur ... ."[27] If we keep this Flaubertian and Impressionist attitude toward light in mind, Frédéric Moreau's allusion (in *The Sentimental Education,* 1869) to Mme. Arnoux as the "point lumineux où l'ensemble des choses convergeait" ("the luminous point towards which all things converged"),[28] perhaps not only gains additional force, but also emphasizes the continuity between the author's early landscape Notes, which prefigure Impressionist techniques in painting, and his novel, which he finished during the late 1860's, at a time when the Impressionist movement in painting was just beginning to flower.

In his early travels, Flaubert often observed that in bright sunlight a new view at first comprises mostly colors and shapes, and that sometimes only after one notes these is one able to determine what they are[29]—a discovery that predates by several decades similar ones by Monet and Cézanne. In his early Notes, Flaubert also demonstrated in advance the Impressionists' ability to analyze colors closely.[30]

After re-writing the material from his travels in the southeastern Mediterranean, Flaubert put the Notes aside, and with them, seemingly, any thought of publishing them. But he returned to the landscape motif to good effect in his two most successful novels, *Madame Bovary* and *The Sentimental Education.*

As Benjamin Bart has pointed out, in *Madame Bovary* (1857) landscape descriptions are used sparingly, and "are always subordinated to the character who is viewing them."[31] In the novel, an interesting example of Flaubert's subordination of the landscape to the character viewing it is found in a passage wherein Emma contemplates the Parisian landscape. If we view this passage in the light of Impressionist painting techniques, we can see in it an additional reason why the Impressionist Henry James might have found Emma Bovary to be "a two-penny lady." Here is the passage in which Emma contemplates Paris:

> Paris, city vaster than the ocean, glittered before Emma's eyes in a rosy-light. But the teeming life of the tumultuous place was divided into compartments, separated into distinct scenes. Emma was aware of only two or three, which shut out the sight of the others ... .[32]

In this passage, the authorial voice informs us that Emma is not capable of letting the scene blend and vibrate before her, and thereby suggests limitations that are not only perceptual, but spiritual as well. Since Flaubert shows Emma as being incapable of appreciating the way that objects are transformed by their surroundings, and since he indicates that she sees the Parisian landscape as a series of compartments, rather than as one unified and brilliant whole, Flaubert seemingly intends to show Emma Bovary as, to that extent, limited. As with so many characters in James's early fiction, Emma's aesthetic limitations also imply a moral flaw. But what is perhaps more important is that these aesthetic limitations are underlined by her inability to appreciate the "Impressionist qualities" of the Parisian scene. In light of James's Impressionist sensibility, we are not much surprised to learn that his verdict upon Emma is that she is "an extremely minor specimen, even of the possibilities of her own type, a two-penny lady, in truth, of an experience so limited that many of her chords, it is clear, can never have sounded at all."[33]   And in the essay that was reprinted in *Notes on Novelists,* James wrote that "Emma Bovary's poor adventures are a tragedy for the very reason that in a world unsuspecting, unassisting, unconsoling she has herself to distil the rich and rare."[34]

In *Madame Bovary* there are still other Impressionist techniques that Henry James may have learned from.  Relatively early in his career, for example, he acknowledged Flaubert's "refined, subtilized and erudite sense of the picturesque."[35]   A passage such as the following one from *Madame Bovary,* therefore, containing as it does so much of the Impressionists' attitude toward the beautiful moment, would undoubtedly have very much appealed to Henry James:

> The evening mist was rising among the bare poplars, blurring their outlines with a tinge of purple that was paler and more transparent than the sheerest gauze on their branches.[36]

Although, as we have seen, there are a few traces of Impressionism in *Madame Bovary,* only in *The Sentimental Education* does Flaubert make sustained use of techniques that I regard as Impressionist.[37] James's overall judgment of *Sentimental Education* was that it was a dead novel in comparison with *Madame Bovary.*  James thought that Flaubert erred in placing so much of the novel's weight upon Frédéric: "It was a mistake to propose to register in so mean a consciousness as that of such a hero, so large, so mixed a quantity of life as *L'Education Sentimentale* intends."[38]   James, in fact, felt that Mme. Arnoux was the only point of interest in this novel, which he referred to as "an ill-starred curiosity for a literary museum."  He felt that she was Flaubert's attempt to represent beauty as being other than sensual.  Yet James's generally negative opinions about the novel do not rule out the possibility that he was influenced by Flaubert in the latter's use of Impressionist techniques in the novel.  James himself has remarked of Flaubert that "he is, nonetheless, more interesting as a failure, however qualified, than as a success, however explained."[39]

Of the Impressionist techniques employed by Flaubert in *The*

*Sentimental Education,* perhaps most obvious is the way in which the juxtaposition of colors and objects—that Emma Bovary was incapable of appreciating—is so freely employed. Here, for example, is a descriptive passage from early in the novel:

> The sky behind the Tuileries took on the hue of its slate roof. The trees in the garden became two solid masses, tinged with purple at the top. The lamps were lit and the pale green expanse of the Seine broke into shot silver against the piles of the bridges.[40]

In the following passage, which could almost be a Parisian boulevard scene from Monet or Pissarro, not only do objects lend color and shadow to the figures that surround them, but Flaubert captures something of the brilliant movement in nature that the Impressionists also realized in their work:

> The setting sun, piercing the vapor, cast through the Arc de Triomphe an almost horizontal beam of reddish light, which glittered on the wheel hubs, the door handles, the butts of the shafts, and the rings of the axle-trees. The great avenue was like a river carrying on its current the bobbing manes of horses and the clothes and heads of men and women. On either side rose the trees, like two green walls, glistening after the rain. Above, patches of blue as soft as satin appeared here and there in the sky.[41]

In *American Literary Naturalism* Charles Child Walcutt has written that Impressionist writing "presents the mind of a character *receiving* impressions rather than judging, classifying ... [them] ."[42] And William A. Harms, in his dissertation on *Impressionism as a Literary Style,* has phrased Walcutt's ideas in a slightly different way when he remarked that the Impressionist style of writing "gives aesthetic evidence of an author's profound absorption in life as a diaphanous flow of internalized feelings."[43] Both of these observations about literary Impressionism are manifest in those passages in *The Sentimental Education* wherein Frédéric's mind continually returns to visions of Mme. Arnoux:

> On the flower-woman's trays, the blossoms opened only that she might choose them as she passed; the little satin slippers, edged with swan's down, in the shoemaker's window, seemed to await her feet; every road led to her

house; and the cabs waited in the squares only that they might speed her friends toward her. Paris depended on her person, and the great city, with all its voices, resounded like a vast orchestra about her.[44]

Flaubert very accurately, I think, describes the mind of a young man in love, and the impressions that we, as readers, receive, are the ones that Frédéric himself records. For this reason, what we see is influenced, to a great extent, by the way that Frédéric himself sees his world. In this emphasis upon the viewer as a creative eye, there is probably more than a little philosophical truth. Suzanne Langer, in *Philosophy in a New Key*, phrases the idea thus:

> 'Seeing' ... is not a passive process, by which meaningless impressions are stored up for the use of an organizing mind ... . 'Seeing' is itself a process of formulating; our understanding of the visible world begins in the eye.[45]

Flaubert, of course, was not the first writer to body forth the concept expressed by Langer. To the Shelley of "Lines Written Among the Euganean Hills," "all things exist as they are perceived." But in Shelley's verse this idea remains a philosophical posture; in Flaubert's novel the notion is presented effectively in the emotions of his character who impressionistically records the scene that we must, finally, formulate for ourselves.

If Henry James was impressed by Flaubert the artist, he was probably even more impressed by Ivan Turgenev, the artist and the man. In the Introduction to *Henry James: Letters* (Vol. 2, 1875-1883), Leon Edel has noted of James's relationship to the Flaubert cénacle:

> ... he can meet them on the ground of their own language—and with great fluency—while they know not a word of his. Perhaps this was why the cosmopolitan Ivan Turgenev, among his other qualities, had so potent an appeal for the cosmopolitan Henry James.[46]

James's admiration for Turgenev (1818-1883) was a life-long one. In the Preface to *The Portrait of a Lady*, written for the New York Edition of 1909, James wrote:

I have not lost the sense of the values for me, at any time, of the admirable Russian's testimony ... . Other echoes from the same source linger with me, I confess, as unfailingly—if it be not at all indeed one much embracing echo.[47]

That James was acquainted, from an early age, with Turgenev's work is indicated perhaps by an 1869 letter from William to Henry, in which William praises the style and artistry of the *Nouvelles moscovites* by "your old friend Turgenieff."[48] While James's first essay on Turgenev did not appear until 1874 in *The North American Review*,[49] yet as Barbara Wilkie Tedford has remarked, after the James had many opportunities "to become acquainted with Turgenev's tales, sketches, novels, and short plays. Other Americans began to discover the Russian author in the early 1870's, and James's essay of 1874 appeared during a crest in Turgenev's popularity with English-speaking readers."[50] Pieces by and about the Russian author appeared with some regularity in the *Revue des Deux Mondes*, from at least as early as October 1, 1851. Not surprisingly, the "salmon-colored" volumes of the influential *Revue* found their way into the James family library during James's early years of voracious reading.[51] In addition, T.S. Perry, one of James's best American friends from his youth, translated, between 1871 and 1881, a number of Turgenev's stories for *Galaxy* and *Lippincott* magazines. Perry was also *de facto* editor of *The North American Review* from 1873-74, and from this post he solicited James's first essay on Turgenev.[52]

There are Impressionist elements in Turgenev's work that appealed to the young Henry James who was alert to the possibilities of developing a distinctive artistic voice of his own. Henry James may, of course, have been drawn to Turgenev's work because the Russian author manifested some particular ways of conducting his fictional world that had supreme value for the American author. First of all, Turgenev was a master prose stylist.[53] And for Turgenev, as for James, the structure of plot was much subordinate to the development of character and manners.[54]

Then, too, unlike many of his contemporaries, Turgenev was a Russian novelist who knew how to be selective in his dialogue and action (another distinctively Impressionist literary technique). *A*

*Month in the Country* (1850), for instance, while not among the many
Turgenev works mentioned by James in his 1874 article on the
Russian author, was almost certainly known by Gustave Flaubert,
and may have influenced the French author in the selectivity of
viewpoint in *The Sentimental Education.*

James also found a temperamental kinship with Turgenev's brand
of realism: "We value most the 'realists' who have an ideal of deli-
cacy," James wrote in his 1874 essay on Turgenev, "and the elegiasts
who have an ideal of joy." And James felt that Turgenev achieved
this kind of balance with supreme success. In the same article James
remarked of the Russian author:

> In susceptibility to the sensuous impressions of life—the colours and odours
> and forms, and the myriad ineffable refinements and enticements of beau-
> ty—he equals, and even surpasses, the most accomplished representatives
> of the French School of story-telling; and yet he has, on the other hand,
> an apprehension of man's religious impulses, of the ascetic passion, the
> capacity of becoming dead to colours and odours and beauty, never
> dreamed of in the philosophy of Balzac and Flaubert.[55]

In this 1874 essay, too, James responded thus to Turgenev's *On the
Eve* (1859):

> The story is all in the portrait of the heroine, who is a heroine in the literal
> sense of the word; a young girl of a will so calmly ardent and intense that
> she needs nothing but opportunity to become one of the figures about
> whom admiring legend clusters ... . She passes before us toward her mys-
> terious end with the swift, keen movement of a feathered arrow.[56]

It is not difficult to see[57] how James's imagination might have been
led, from this early association of the victimized heroine, to give the
heroine of his first major Impressionist novel the name Isabel Archer.
While Isabel's name is perhaps a rebound from Turgenev's character,
as she is described by James, Isabel's situation is ironic in light of
James's reading of *On the Eve,* since her victimization is not at all
swift, but painfully slow. She is a victim, yes—but a victim who
*chooses* to be victimized—a situation that is not at all untypical in
Henry James, but which is somewhat less so in Turgenev. While James

does not allude to *On the Eve* in his lengthy 1874 essay on Turgenev, he does make significant reference to the novella in the essay on the Russian author that he contributed to the *Library of the World's Best Literature,* edited by Charles Dudley Warner in 1896.[58]  And in the letter to W.E. Henley, dated August 24, 1878 or 1879 that I have cited above (see footnote 48 to this chapter), James alludes to the Turgenev novella in such a way as to indicate that he has read it.

In his novels and novellas, Turgenev made considerable use of landscape descriptions—many of which resemble those that were later done on canvas by the Impressionist painters.  George Moore (in *Impressions and Opinions)* recognized in some of Turgenev's *Sportsman's Sketches* and *Strange Tales,* for instance, a "light, facile, and yet certain" execution that is similar to that of a landscape by Corot.[59] And Corot, of course, as we have seen in Chapter 1, was one of the major forerunners of the Impressionist painters in France.

Perhaps even more directly presaging the Impressionist style in literature is a Turgenev landscape such as the one that the Russian presents in the 1854 novella, "A Quiet Spot." Turgenev presents a description of a small birch forest near the home of Veretiev:

> The recently risen sun flooded all the grove with strong, though not brilliant light; everywhere dewdrops were glistening, here and there large drops suddenly caught fire and glowed; everything had a breath of freshness, of life, and that innocent exaltation of the first moments of the morn, when everything is already so liminous and still so soundless ... . The pure, light air was flooded with cooling breezes.[60]

This description of an outdoor scene in which the air is inundated with light anticipates much that can be found in the Impressionist *plein-air* work, and expresses the kind of visual beauty that we have come to associate especially with Monet and Renoir among the pioneer Impressionist painters.

In *Return to Yesterday,* one of Ford Madox Ford's books of memoirs, the author at one point attempted to account for the phenomenon of literary Impressionism by remarking that he learned the Impressionst technique from Joseph Conrad, and that Henry

James and Conrad had learned it from Turgenev. While the subject of artistic apparentation in the case of Impressionism is not quite so simple as Ford has indicated, there is undoubtedly at least some truth to his observation.    In taking account of Impressionist landscape touches in the fiction of Henry James, we cannot overlook the suggestions that he may have received from the masterful Russian stylist who had done much of his best work in the Impressionist vein before the budding American novelist had launched upon his very successful literary career.

There are some writers of whom we should care to know little, if the intrinsic merit of their work were the only thing concerned, but of whom we cannot know enough, because of the influence that they have exerted upon their contemporaries and upon the subsequent course of literary affairs.  Such are the characteristics of the next pair of writers whose work we shall consider.  In Edmond (1822-96) and Jules (1830-70) de Goncourt what is intrinsically of little importance becomes of great importance to historians of literature and of art; for the Goncourt brothers were very important figures in the stellar art world of Paris during the Impressionist era.  Like Pater, they were aesthetes—critics of art, collectors, connoisseurs—and they moved freely in the upper middle-class Parisian society that was their millieu.  One of their earliest books, the novel *Germinie Lacerteux* (1864), probably exerted a strong influence upon the naturalism of Zola.  And as has been indicated in the previous chapter, the brothers were influential in introducing Japanese art and culture to France.  Edmond's *La Maison d'un Artiste* (1881), moreover, provided additional stimulation to the already awakened interest in Japanese art and artefacts in the Paris of his day.   Their artist novel, *Manette Salomon,* had a very powerful influence upon the French fiction of their generation, and remains even today of supreme interest to anyone who wishes to investigate the genre of the "artist novel" in France.

The brothers developed their style during the 1860's, prior to the major development of Impressionist painting in the '70's and '80's. Jules de Goncourt, who died in 1870, left his brother Edmond (who was approximately the same age as Flaubert) to write four more novels and to found the Académie Goncourt in order to perpetuate their name.

Henry James wrote his first critical assessment of the work of the Goncourts when he was in his mid-thirties. And his essential feeling about their work does not seem to have changed over the years. James wrote that

> they represent the analysis of sensation raised to its highest powers, and that is apparently the most original thing that the younger French imaginative literature has achieved. But from them as from Gustave Flaubert the attentive reader receives an indispensible impression of perverted ingenuity and wasted power. The sense of the picturesque has somehow killed the spiritual sense; the moral side of the work is dry and thin.[61]

He felt, moreover, that they were unduly limited by their Parisianness: "If time with these writers terminates at about 1730," James wrote, "space comes to a stop at the limits of Paris."[62]

After pointing out the defects of the multi-volume Goncourt *Journal*, however, James remarked of its authors: "When we meet them on their own ground, that of the perception of feature and expression, that of translation of the pointed and published text of life they are altogether admirable."[63] But again James's final judgment on their work is a negative one, for he observes that their writing lacks space and air: "We end with the sensation of a closed room, of a want of ventilation."[64]

But there are a number of points on which James and the Goncourts would surely have agreed. The Goncourts, for instance, shared with Flaubert an announced contempt for novels with plots.[65] James, too, of course, was much fonder of character delineation than of plot development. Moreover, the Goncourts' comments *about* style, the Impressionist-minded James would have found agreeable: "... le style doit être, comme la sensation, musical et coloré; il doit réunir en lui, résumer tous les autres arts, et nous donner l'émotion et l'illusion de la vie et du mouvement."[66]

James was also no doubt attracted to the Goncourts' treatment of the conflict between the demands of marriage and the demands of artistic perfection—handled notably in *Charles Demailly* and in *Manette Salomon*—a theme that runs through many of the Impressionist novels in the Ivory Tower tradition. The Goncourts, like James, seem to have held this notion of marriage even in their personal lives. In their *Journal* entry for May 1, 1864, for instance, they wrote:

> In any household, it is the wife who dissolves the husband's integrity. In the name of material interests, she is the counsellor who urges every act of selfabasement, of meanness, of cowardice, every little compromise with conscience.[67]

In *Manette Salomon* the Goncourts depict this notion in the relationship between the painter Coriolis and the vicious, uneducated, and course-grained Manette, who "judged a man's worth and talent solely by the monetary value of his work. For her, money meant everything and proved everything. She labored incessantly to place the temptation of money in Coriolis' path."[68]

In his monograph on *The Painter in French Fiction,* Theodore R. Bowie referred to *Manette Salomon* as "the standard work" in the class of French fiction dealing with a painter "as a protagonist in a work completely devoted to him and his type."[69] And Bowie, after remarking upon the "self-conscious and cumulative" nature of French literature, notes that "it is interesting but not surprising to perceive the debt owed ... particularly to the Goncourts by many of the novelists who choose the subject of the painter."[70]

While *Manette Salomon* is not an Impressionist novel in the same sense as, for instance, *The Sentimental Education,* the novel shares with Impressionist painting a concern for nature. On several occasions Coriolis, for example, refers to the necessity for the artist to have "a capacity for being moved by Nature."[71]

*Manette Salomon* also reveals a great deal about the daily life of the painter in the Academies of the day. This day-to-day "record" tells us much about the exercises which helped the Impressionist painters to develop their own techniques. In the novel, for instance, we read that Anatole, who performed poorly in all of the other atelier exercises, generally astonished his master with his sketches. Anatole's sketches invariably revealed the kind of "personal attitude" that the Impressionist painters came to embrace as one of the strong points of their technique. In *Manette Salomon,* moreover, the students of Langibaut's atelier contributed to the special fund that enabled them to picnic now and then in the country, and there to sketch their models *en plein air.* This, too, of course, was one of the actual practices learned by the Impressionist painters when they were pupils in the studios of Couture and Gleyre (the latter, we recall, numbered among his pupils Bazille, Renoir, and Monet).[72]

James may have learned something of the above-mentioned aspects of Impressionist painting from *Manette Salomon.* But from the standpoint of the development of Impressionism in the arts, the novel is noteworthy for still more, for it presents a bold and vigorous statement in support of art-for-art's sake. This view is expounded, for example, by Coriolis in his letter (which comprises Chapter 12 of the novel) to the Bohemian painter Anatole Bazoche. The Impressionists' love of the beautiful and fleeting moment is moreover manifest in the hymn to beauty which is found in the penultimate chapter (CLIV):

> Le Beau, ah! oui, le Beau! ... s'y reconnaître dans le Beau! Dire c'est cela, le Beau, l'affirmer, le prouver, l'analyser, le définir! ... Le pourquoi du Beau? D'où il vient? ce qui le fait être? son essence? Le Beau! la splendeur du vrai ... .

From a literary standpoint, James, of course, did not hold Edmond and Jules de Goncourt in high esteem. Yet he may have gotten some ideas about Impressionism from his personal contacts with them (the brothers were good friends of Daudet, and through him of James himself), their fiction, their *Journal* (which James reviewed), and their other non-fictional prose on art. James, of course, knew the Goncourts' work very well, and wrote about it on numerous occasions.

Even so, artistic influence from the Goncourts to James need not have been entirely direct,[73] since Paul Bourget, whose criticism Henry James very much admired,[74] wrote about the Goncourts and pointed out what he saw to be parallels between their style and styles in

Impressionism in painting.[75]    Henry James first met Bourget in London in 1884.   This meeting occasioned a long and fruitful acquaintance which lasted for many years.[76]

As so often with lesser talents, Alphonse Daudet (1840-1897) mirrored much more faithfully the apparent mood and sentiments of his age than many of his contemporaries of much greater genius. Daudet, like many nineteenth-century authors, wrote a volume of fiction on the life of the artist [*Les Femmes d'Artistes* (1873)] which affords a glimpse of the lives of painters.   And much else in Daudet's work reflects contemporary literary concerns.   Although more selective with regard to detail than either the Goncourts or Zola, his work is very much in the Realist tradition of his day.   And yet his style was also poetic—"Avant tout," Zola said of Daudet, "c'est un poète."[77]

Quite early critical commentary has associated Daudet with Impressionism.   "L'essence du talent de M. Daudet étant dans la vivacité de l'impression première," Louis Desprey wrote in 1884, "il a soin de fixer la sensation ou l'idée dans tout leur fraîcheur ... .   Il traduit seulement dans un paysage ou dans un groupe l'aspect qui le frappe ... ." Desprey also observed that the originality of Daudet's style is in "la délicate originalité des images."[78]

In "L'Impressionnisme dans le roman," an 1879 article that first appeared in *Revue des Deux Mondes,* Ferdinand Brunetière was probably the first critic to publish an essay in which the term Impressionism is used in relationship to a writer of prose.   In his essay, Brunetière singled out Alphonse Daudet as "un impressionniste dans le roman."[79]

During the 1870's James himself began to appear in translation in the pages of the *Revue des Deux Mondes,* which we already know he read avidly from his early years.   For these reasons, it seems very likely that James saw Brunetière's article when it first appeared. Brunetière begins by trying to find a word to describe Daudet's writing.   He rejects the terms "classicism" and "romanticism" which he feels are outmoded.   He feels, too, that "realism" and "naturalism" do not accurately define Daudet, since these terms describe what the critic judges to be decadent trends.   Brunetière then provides several passages to illustrate what he feels to be the superior quality of Daudet's writing. The critic goes on to conclude that the magic of Daudet lies in his special ability to induce the reader to participate in the shaping of character and action. Of Daudet's novels Brunetière remarks, "if they are not well written, they are magnificently painted." Brunetière sees the subject thus: "Nous pourrons définir dé jà l'impressionnisme littéraire [comme] une transposition systématique des moyens d'expression d'un art, qui est l'art de peindre, dans le domaine d'un autre art, qui est l'art d'écrire."[80]  I shall return to this effect, as it is used by Daudet in a pair of his novels, but for now it is enough to point out that, as early as 1879, an important if controversial critic wrote a lengthy article in an influential journal (that from his youth James habitually read) wherein he used the term "Impressionist" to describe a writer with whom James was demonstrably familiar for a number of years.

In *Literary Reviews and Essays,* Henry James referred to Daudet as "the most charming story-teller of the day."[81]  James began to write criticism on Daudet's work as early as 1875, and continued to refer to him in print right up to the publication in 1913 and 1914 of *A Small Boy and Others* and *Notes of a Son and Brother.* Nor did James's personal respect for Daudet diminish with the years. As late as 1895, for example, during a very busy time professionally, James kindly hosted the Daudet family during their trip to England. And the Master at this time referred to Daudet as "that intensely sensitive and vibrating little Frenchman of genius."[82]  As with the Goncourts, James wrote his first reviews of Daudet's work while still a relatively young man. And he remained throughout his life familiar with Daudet's writing. Of Daudet James said:

> He is at the opposite pole ... from Flaubert, with whom a kind of grand, measured distance from his canvas ... was an ideal, and who seemed to attack his subject with a brush twenty feet long.[83]

James furthermore collaborated with the French author in translating Daudet's *Port of Tarascon* for an English audience.

Although James and Daudet were close friends and associates (James referred to the Frenchman as his "cher ami et confrère"), the Master did not hesitate to comment trenchantly upon Daudet's work.   In a letter from London (dated June 19, 1884), James for instance gave a strong warning to Daudet, after the French author had indulged in characterization from the outside:   "il n'y a rien de plus réel, de plus positif, de plus à peindre, qu'un caractère; c'est là qu'on trouve bien la couleur et la forme."[84]   James believed that character should be rendered and not described; he did not therefore hesitate to inform his French companion where he felt his friend had erred.   In a letter to Grace Norton, James nevertheless remarked that the French author's "talent was so great ... that I feel ... that the best of it will quite intensely remain."[85]   But he went on to qualify this judgment by saying that Daudet "was a queer combination of a great talent with an absence of the greater mind, as it were—the greater feeling."[86]

To James, however, the greatest lesson that the French had to teach was their demonstration of the supreme importance of style. And this was a lesson of which James the Impressionist might well have availed himself in the fiction of Alphonse Daudet.   Like James, Daudet often considered impressions to be of primary importance. In *Notes sur la Vie*, for instance, Daudet wrote:

> Fallait-il que je fusse poreux et pénétrable; des impressions, des sensations à remplir des tas de livres et toutes d'une intensité de rêve.[87]

The Impressionist elements of Daudet's style show to perhaps best advantage in his *Kings in Exile* (1879), a novel that Brunetière, in his piece in *Revue des Deux Mondes,* singled out for special praise. James also knew this novel and referred to it on three separate occasions, in essays that appeared from 1882 to 1897.   The following passage from *Kings in Exile* (1879) might be a description of a canvas by Monet or Renoir from the Argenteuil period which was contemporaneous with the appearance of Daudet's novel:

> Boats decked out with flags, full of oarsmen in smart red or blue jerseys, covered the lake in every direction, furrowing the surface with the silvery stroke of the oars, and the white foam of the sparkling little waves.[88]

And a longer passage combines elements of the paintings of Manet, Monet, and Renoir in its buoyant color and sweeping movement which lend to the scene a joyous sense of life:

> From the great avenues through which the carriage was slowly making its way, under the still sparse thickets, sprinkled violet with the early wild hyacinths, could be seen luncheons spread out on the ground, white plates dotted over the grass, open-mouthed baskets, and common thick glass from the neighboring wine-shop stuck among the green shoots like peonies; shawls and smock-frocks suspended on the boughs; men in shirt-sleeves, women without cloaks, reading, dozing, or sewing as they leant against the trees; bright glades flecked by skirts of cheap fabrics, flitting hither and thither in some game of battledore, blind-man's buff, or quadrilles improvised to the sound of an invisible band, the melody of which reached them in gusts.[89]

James himself not only read *Les Rois en Exil,* but commented upon it several times with great favor. "... I cannot open either *Le Nabab* or *Les Rois en Exile,*" James said,

> cannot rest my eyes on a page, without being charmed by the brilliancy of execution. It is difficult to give any idea ... of Daudet's style—a style which ... gathers up every patch of color, every colloquial note, that will help to illustrate, and moves equally, lightly, triumphantly along, like a clever woman in the costume of an eclectic age. There is nothing classic in this mode of expression; it is not the old-fashioned drawing in black and white. It never rests, never is satisfied, never leaves the idea sitting half-draped, like Patience on a monument; it is always ... trying to add a little more, to produce the effect which shall make the reader see with his eyes, or rather with those marvelous eyes of Alphonse Daudet.[90]

After discussing the merits of *Le Nabab,* James remarked, *"Les Rois en Exil,* however, has a greater perfection. It is simply more equal, and it contains much more of the beautiful."[91] Since Daudet's novel contains many Impressionist scenes such as the ones that I have quoted above, the Impressionist touches in the novel probably constituted at least one of the visual elements that Henry James found most appealing.

James was also familiar with another of Daudet's friends in the Flaubert circle, Émile Zola, the man who is often acknowledged to be the premier French Naturalist author of the nineteenth century. In

1880, James criticized Zola's work for being vulgar.[92]    James was also, perhaps, somewhat uneasy about Zola's political commitments. Meeting Zola on his first visit to London, James noted the impression that he had of the Frenchman "fairly bristling with the betrayal that nothing whatever had happened to him in life but to write *Les Rougon-Macquart."* James then commented thus upon Zola's fight for the rehabilitation of Captain Dreyfus: "The act of a man with a means of personal history to make up, the act of a spirit for which life, or for which at any rate freedom, had been too much postponed, treating itself at last to a luxury of experience."[93]

Yet, generally speaking, James had no small esteem for Zola the writer.   On several occasions in his letters, James criticized "the floods of tepid soap and water which under the name of novels are being vomited forth in England ... ."[94]   In contrast, in an 1879 letter to T.S. Perry, James wrote:   "Zola's naturalism is ugly and dirty, but he seems to me to be *doing something*—which surely (in the imaginative line) no one in England and the U. S. is, and no one else here."[95]   In another letter to Perry, dated February 16, 1881, James remarked that "Zola has his faults and his merits; and it doesn't seem to me important to talk of the faults.   The merits are rare, valuable and extremely solid."[96]   This fundamental assessment of Zola alters little over the years.   In an 1899 piece for *The North American Review,* James remarked of the author of the Rougon-Macquart novels:   "He would still be magnificent if he had nothing but his solidity ... .   He is a large enough figure to make us lose time in walking round him for the most convenient view."[97]   And in an article on Zola for *Atlantic Monthly,* James compared Zola to the grand sowers or reapers of Millet (who was, as we recall, one of the leading Impressionist fore-runners) who are depicted in dusky outline against the sky.[98]   And James's 1913 essay on Zola, printed in *Notes on Novelists,* represents the Master's final apparent attempt to hold up Zola's talents against the Frenchman's many detractors.

Émile Zola (1840-1902) was twenty years younger than the generation of Flaubert and of the Goncourts, and he seems to have learned a great deal from these older writers.   Like James, Zola also spent much time in the company of artists of all kinds and wrote often about the world of the artist.   Zola started writing art criticism in *Le Figaro* in 1866, and consistently, though not always effectively, praised the moderns—that is, the Impressionists—and execrated the fashionable painters of the day.

Cézanne and Zola were schoolmates at Aix. And Cézanne is commonly given credit for having first tutored Zola in the appreciation of painting by conducting him around the *Salon des Refusés* in 1863. In time, Zola seems to have become quite proud of his association with and knowledge of the Impressionist painters: "I not only supported the Impressionists," he said, "I translated them into literature, by the touches, notes, coloration, by the palette of many of my descriptions."[99] Zola began to "interpret the Impressionists to the Public" when he did his series of articles on the *Salons* of the 1860's and 1870's. In his *Salon de 1876*, Zola, for instance, emphasized the importance of color and light:

> La découverte de ceux d'ici [Impressionnistes] consiste proprement à avoir reconnu que la grande lumière *décolore* les tons, que le soleil reflété par les objets tend, à force de clarté, à les ramener à cette unité lumineuse qui fond ses sept rayons prismatiques en un seul éclat incolore, qui est la lumière. Ils décomposent et constituent la lumière, dans la clarté brillante du plein jour.[100]

Zola came into contact with the Impressionists mainly through Cézanne, who introduced the writer to Pissarro—who himself had been Cézanne's fellow student when the latter was attending the Académie Suisse in 1861. Subsequently Zola came into contact with Bazille and Monet, who in 1865 were sharing a studio occasionally visited by Cézanne and Pissarro. In 1866 Zola began to receive guests on Thursday evenings in the house that he set up with his future wife. And these weekly sessions were regularly attended by Pissarro and Bazille. Zola's popularity with the so-called "first wave" of Impressionists is attested to further by the fact that in early 1870 the ill-fated Bazille did a painting of his studio, where he pictured Zola chatting with Renoir.

Zola, who was a friend of Manet from 1866 until his death in 1902,[101] did his first article on the painter as part of his first *Salon* (in *L'Evénement*, 7 May 1866). The writer also did a lengthy piece on Manet for *Revue du XIX^e Siècle* [1 January 1867 (pp. 43-67)] which was reprinted in pamphlet form later the same year. Zola praised Manet's work, in general, for its clear and personal vision of nature, its penetration of reality—the clarity of light—"il voit blond" —and the simplicity of construction—"il voit par masses."[102] Manet subsequently expressed to Zola his gratefulness for these "remarkable" articles.[103] In 1868 Manet further extended his gratitude by painting a portrait of Zola (which now hangs in the Musée du Louvre).

On the whole, Zola can probably best be classified as a Naturalist with aspects of Impressionism in his work. Yet the force of his writing often derives from its pictorial quality; and much of this quality derives from techniques that Zola seemingly learned from the Impressionist painters whose names I have cited in the foregoing discussion. Zola's *L'Oeuvre* evokes, as no other novel has, the artistic life in Paris during the time when the Impressionists were beginning to make their important presence felt. Years before the appearance of *L'Oeuvre,* however, Zola had drawn an artist character who saw the world through an Impressionist painter's eyes.

On the whole, *Le Ventre de Paris* (1873)[104] is a naturalistic novel whose genesis can be partially traced to Zola's own strolls around the Halles market district of Paris. In this novel, Zola introduces the character, Claude Lantier, Florent's artist friend. Claude, son of the Gervaise of *L'Assommoir,* figures prominently in *L'Oeuvre* which tells how Lantier's struggle for fame resulted in madness and suicide.

That Zola perhaps conceived *The Fat and the Thin* in terms of a painting is indicated by the fact that for this (and for every novel that succeeded *The Fat and the Thin*), his first step was to draft what he called the ébauche, a term that he borrowed from the vocabulary of the contemporary painter.[105] And it cannot be gainsaid that Zola modelled young Lantier at least partially on some of the Impressionist painters who were the author's contemporaries. In "Émile Zola, Critique d'art," F.W.J. Hemmings suggested Jongkind as the probable model for Claude.[106] On the other hand, Lanoux and Mitterand suggested that Claude is based upon the Cézanne of Zola's early years.[107] To both of these claims there surely is a great deal of truth. Yet surely there is something also in Claude of the Monet who told Renoir that when the sun went down he felt that he would die: "He [i.e., Claude] wandered about the streets, wrapped in the gloomiest of thoughts, and waiting for the morning as a sort of resurrection. He used to say that he felt bright and cheerful in the morning, and horribly miserable in the evening."[108] And something of all three of the afore-mentioned painters can be discovered in a passage where Claude, staring at the bustle of activity in the Halles, "was quite charmed with all this uproar, and forgot everything to gaze at some effect of light, some group of blouses, or the picturesque unloading of a cart."[109]

By the time Zola's novel first began to appear, however, the author could also have drawn for such descriptions upon such literary sources as *L'Education Sentimentale* (1869), *Germinie Lacerteux* (1865), and *Manette Salomon* (1866)—all of which contain scenes that describe similar effects.[110] And the likelihood seems good that the same literary sources may have influenced Zola in the writing of his major portrait-of-the-artist novel, *L'Oeuvre*.

Zola began to write *L'Oeuvre* on May 12, 1885, and the book was finished on February 23, 1886. The novel appeared as a *feuilleton*, commencing December, 1885, in *Gil Blas*. From the time of its appearance in serial form, *L'Oeuvre* aroused a great deal of critical debate and literary commentary. The novel appeared in Paris during a period of considerable literary activity of a high order. And in painting, the Paris of the time was surely the undisputed mistress of the West. Even in such a time of high artistic excitement, people read and discussed Zola's novel with a keen interest that few works since then have seemingly provoked.[111]

*The Masterpiece* (1886) is a roman fleuve (a saga novel in an indefinite number of volumes)—the fourteenth of the twenty novels of the Rougon—Macquart family.[112] Much commentary has dealt with the *roman à clef* aspects of the novel. Some historians feel that the Claude Lantier of *The Masterpiece* was based upon Cézanne, and that Cézanne's alleged "break" with Zola, following the publication of the novel, served to confirm that Cézanne himself realized that the unsuccessful Lantier was meant to be his "real life" representative.[113] Characters in *L'Oeuvre* have also been identified with Monet and Manet.[114] As F.W.J. Hemmings and Sven Loevgren have shown [see, for instance, Hemmings. *Zola,* 2nd edition, 1966 (pp. 221-3) and Loevgren. *The Genesis of Modernism* (pp. 40-43)], many difficulites are involved in attempting to label this novel a *roman à clef.* In weighing the evidence, perhaps the closest that we can come to the truth is the statement made by Thomas Walton in the "Introduction" to his translation of *The Masterpiece:*

> The story of Claude Lantier, artist, Pierre Sandoz, author, and their literary and artistic friends is based on the story of Émile Zola and the friends of his youth, their struggles, successes, failures in the literary and artistic world of Paris.[115]

In *The Masterpiece* all of the painters are failures of one kind or another. But the hero, Lantier, is perhaps the biggest failure of all, since he is never even able to bring himself to finish the masterpiece that he so much desires to paint. This failure is what eventually drives him to suicide.[116]

Of the vast pictures of Parisian social life that Zola has placed throughout *The Masterpiece,* Thomas Walton has remarked, they "are the sort of pictures Claude Lantier wanted to paint and could not."[117]

Let us turn now to examine some of the Impressionist effects of these pictures, as they are presented in the novel. Here, for instance, is the first version of Claude's painting, "Open-Air"—the canvas that the public came to recognize as the leader of the school of that name in *The Masterpiece:*

> There was a long silence, during which both stood contemplating the painting. It was a big canvas, five metres by three, all planned out, though parts of it were still hardly developed beyond the rough stage. As a sketch it was remarkable for its vigour, its spontaneity and the lively warmth of its colour. It showed the sun pouring into a forest clearing, with a solid background of greenery and a dark path running off to the left and with a bright spot of light in the far distance. Lying on the grass in the foreground, among the lush vegetation of high summer, was the naked figure of a woman. One arm was folded beneath her head, thus bringing her breasts into prominence; her eyes were closed and she was smiling into space as

she basked in the golden sunlight.   In the background, two other nude women, one dark and one fair, were laughing and tumbling each other on the grass, making two lovely patches of flesh-colour against the green, while in the foreground, to make the necessary contrast the artist had seen fit to place a man's figure.   He wore a plain black velvet jacket, and was seated on the grass so that nothing could be seen but his back and his left hand upon which he was leaning.[118]

As others have pointed out, this picture bears a striking resemblance to Manet's "Déjeuner sur l'herbe."[119]   Elsewhere Impressionist effects are used to bolster Zola's repeated assertion in his critical writings that a work of art is a "corner of nature viewed through a temperament."   This principle is demonstrated in a cityscape, such as the following, which brings to mind many of Monet's best canvases, depicting the Paris that the Impressionists loved so well:

It was four o'clock, and the day was just beginning to wane in a golden haze of glorious sunshine.   To right and left, towards the Madeleine and the Corps Législatif, the lines of buildings stretched far into the distance, their rooftops cutting clean against the sky.   Between them the Tuileries gardens piled up wave upon wave of round-topped chestnut trees, while between the two green borders of its side alleys the Champs-Élysées climbed up and up, as far as eye could see, up to the gigantic gateway of the Arc de Triomphe, wide open on infinity.   The Avenue itself was filled with a double stream of traffic, rolling on like twin rivers, with eddies and waves of moving carriages tipped like foam with the sparkle of a lamp-glass or the glint of a polished panel down to the Place de la Concorde with its enormous pavements and roadways like big, broad lakes, crossed in every direction by the flash of wheels, peopled by black specks which were really human beings, and its two splashing fountains breathing coolness over all its feverish activity.[120]

And in Chapter 5, which describes in detail the public reaction to the "Salon des Refusés," we see Zola taking note of the contemporary gallery-goer's response to the Impressionists' use of the juxtaposition of colors, in which the colors of objects are transformed by that which surrounds them,

I say, what's this, washing day?   People blue, trees blue, he's blued up the whole thing, if you ask me!  The ones who did not laugh lost their tempers, taking the overall blueness, Claude's original way of rendering the effect of daylight, as an insult to their intelligence.[121]

Later in the novel, when Christine ventured to criticize Claude for painting a blue poplar, he "showed her on the spot the delicate blue cast of the leaves, and she had to agree with him that the tree really did look blue,"[122] a manner of seeing color *en plein-air* that accords with Impressionist technique.  In the chapter that deals with the painter's third-year submission to the Salon jury, we read that

> the really startling thing about the picture [i.e., Claude's] was its original treatment of light, breaking it down into its components after uncom- promising accuracy of observation, but deliberately contradicting all the habits of the eye by stressing blues, yellows, and reds in places where no one expected to see them.  In the background the Tuileries melted away into a golden mist; the pavements were blood red and the passers-by were merely indicated by a number of darker patches, swallowed up by the over-bright sunshine.[123]

Most of the elements of the Impressionist style are contained in this painting:  the use of light and color as means of conveying transient effects, the sense of the all-important individual observing eye, the use of the "actual," suffused light of day, and the suppression of detail in order to heighten the overall effect.

Still other elements in *The Masterpiece* lend the novel an affinity to Impressionism in the arts.  Claude, for instance, feels trapped by Christine, whom he sees as smothering his creative talents.  *The Masterpiece* is still another Impressionist novel in the *Sacred Fount* tradition—a fact that Zola underlines with dramatic intensity when Christine (whose name echoes Claudine, Monet's first wife) tells Claude: " 'Art is your master; it can wipe out the pair of us, and you'll offer up a prayer of gratitude?' " to which Claude rejoins: " 'Yes. Art *is* the master, *my* master, to dispose of me as it please.' "[124]

We later learn that Sandoz, the major literary figure in the book shares Claude's impersonal feeling about art, for he used to visit Christine "for the sake of little Jacques, his godson, and of poor, wretched Christine, whose passion amongst so much squalor moved him so deeply, *for he saw in her a woman in love he would have liked to portray in his books,*"[125] a reflexive comment that is also indicative of the attitude of the artist as he is portrayed in much of Modernist literature.

As I have pointed out, then, Zola had made extensive use of techniques from Impressionist painting in the two novels that we have considered above. Henry James almost certainly knew *The Fat and the Thin,* since he referred to this novel three times in a pair of essays, "Émile Zola," *Atlantic Monthly* (August 1903), and "New York Revisited," *Harper's Magazine* (February, March, May, 1905).[126] And James almost certainly knew *The Masterpiece.* Although he nowhere refers to this novel in his published criticism and notebooks, James probably read it, since the novel was, as I have indicated above, on everyone's lips from the time that it began to appear in serial format during the mid-'80's. That James may have been influenced by the Impressionist elements in both of these novels, therefore, seems altogether likely.

Guy de Maupassant (1850-1893), the last French author from the Flaubert circle whose work we shall consider, is a writer who was intimately connected with Flaubert and his group. Maupassant was the godson of Flaubert and also his disciple. Although roughly James's age, Maupassant did not launch his literary career until 1880, with the publication of his first story, "Boule de suif," which appeared in Zola's collection *Les Soirées de Médan.* Despite Maupassant's late start, however, he wrote some three hundred stories, most of which were published in the newspapers *Gil Blas* and *Le Gaulois* during the 1880's.[127] Since Maupassant's death from syphilis occurred after a period of insanity, the bulk of his professional work was completed during the 1880's (although volumes of his work continued to appear right up until his death). By the date that Maupassant first appeared in print, therefore, James had already established an impressive record of published work.

There are, however, a number of important and interesting affinities between James and Maupassant. Like the Impressionist writers at their best, Maupassant realized that, in handling character, it is never possible to *tout comprendre* (notwithstanding Flaubert's claims concerning Emma Bovary). And Maupassant, like James, had an able talent for developing, in a dramatic way, the insignificant events of every day life—events whose subsequent meanings often become of the utmost importance to us—in life, as in art. This sense is well expressed, for example, in the closing lines of Maupassant's "Un Soir":

> Certain encounters, certain inexplicable combinations of things—without appearing in the slightest degree exceptional—assuredly contain a greater quantity of life's secret quintessence than that dispersed through the ordinary run of events.

The Henry James who wrote "The Art of Fiction" would certainly not have found such an observation incommodious. In 1890, for example, after having outlined the subject of a short tale that was never written, James added, "The sketch, picture, vision—à la Maupassant."[128] Other examples from the *Notebooks* furthermore indicate that James admired Maupassant's conciseness. Thinking of "The Real Thing," for instance, James remarked: "This is a lesson—if I'm to do a good many. Something as admirably compact and selected as Maupassant."[129] James admiringly alluded to Maupassant's conciseness again in 1893 when in his *Notebooks* he praised Maupassant's brevity in *Pierre and Jean*.[130]

James wrote an article on Maupassant in the *Fortnightly Review* for March 1888.[131] In this article, Henry James alluded to thirty-four separate pieces by Maupassant. In subsequent critical discussions of Maupassant's work, James mentioned many more. Of all of Maupassant's works James cited *Pierre et Jean* most often—alluding to it seven times in the 1888 essay alone. He afforded unreserved praise for Maupassant's technical felicity—his gift of telling a story. James began the article by crediting "*le Roman*," the preface to *Pierre et Jean*, with having given him, in sensible form, his general ideas about the novel, and for having properly insisted upon the necessity for the writer to express himself in the form that best suits his temperament. But James seems to me to have been writing with tongue in cheek, for he surely could have learned the latter lesson from Zola's early criticism, which he probably knew (although in his notebooks and critical writings on Zola he referred almost exclusively to the

French author's fiction), where Zola on many occasions repeated virtually the same dictum. Even a cursory glance at James's "The Art of Fiction" (1884), moreover, serves to show how closely the theories that James set out therein were echoed three years later by Maupassant, in his Preface. Joseph Conrad likewise seems to have profited from James's essay—but he did so at least partially through the mediation of Maupassant's Preface, as we shall see in Chapter Three. Malcolm Cowley was probably right when he wrote that "a theme once brilliantly stated is likely to be echoed for a long time."

The important point for our immediate considerations, however, is that Henry James need not have read an essay by Maupassant in order to have realized what he seems to have known almost from the outset of his career; namely, that the novelist is an artist and can only hope to communicate the illusion of life. Never can he successfully manage to do what so many of the Naturalists and Realists wished to do in their art; for the writer can seldom successfully reproduce life in the manner of a scientist.

Just as before him James defined the novel as a *personal* impression of life, so too Maupassant maintained in his Preface that the novelist's only mission is the faithful reproduction of his own illusion. In his Preface, Maupassant discussed the problems and obligations of the novelist "qui prétend nous donner une image exacte de la vie." But in life, as Maupassant reminds us, "there is no difference of foreground and distance, and events are sometimes hurried on, and sometimes left to linger indefinitely ... ." Thus, he continues,

> The realist, if he is an artist, will endeavor not to show us a commonplace photograph of life, but to give us a presentment of it which shall be more complete, more striking, more cogent than reality itself. To tell everything is out of the question: It would require at least a volume for each day to enumerate the endless insignificant incidents which crowd our existence. A choice must be made—and this is the first blow to the theory of the whole truth. ... Whence I conclude that the talented Realists should rather call themselves illusionists ... .[132]

There is a great deal in this single essay by Maupassant that the literary Impressionist would assent to. But an even more interesting connection between Maupassant and Impressionism is that which is provided by his direct contacts with the world of the painters themselves. We have already noted that in the mid-'80's Maupassant accompanied Monet on his trip to Étretat where the younger literary man watched the accomplished Monet painting the same subject on different canvases, at different times of the day,[133] an experience that Maupassant recorded in "La Vie d'un paysagiste" (in *Gil Blas.* September 28, 1886). This piece, cast in the form of a letter, dated September of that year and written from Étretat (which was also one of James's favorite seashore resorts), recorded Monet's struggles to capture the right effect out-of-doors. These struggles, of course, may have influenced Maupassant, not only in his famous Preface, but also in the composition of *Pierre et Jean*, and in much of the work that followed it.

Another important Maupassant contact from the painting world was Vincent van Gogh. Van Gogh, who was a voracious reader, claimed among his favorite authors the Goncourts and Maupassant. In fact, in one of Van Gogh's still lifes, done in Paris in 1886, the painter, as a seeming tribute, represented the volumes of Maupassant's *Bel Ami* and the Goncourts' *Germinie Lacerteux.*[134] Van Gogh often mentioned Maupassant in his letters, and in December 1888 told his sister that he was attempting to paint a café terrace that was to him very reminiscent of Maupassant's description of a Parisian boulevard café in the opening pages of *Bel Ami.*[135]

Of perhaps even more direct concern to us, however, is the fact that in April, 1888, Vincent reported to Théo that he was reading *Pierre et Jean.* Van Gogh then asked his brother if he had read the Preface, in which Maupassant defended the right of the author to exaggerate:

> I am in the middle of *Pierre et Jean* by Guy de Maupassant. It is good. Have you read the preface where he declares the liberty of the artist to exaggerate, to create in his novel a world more beautiful, more simple, more consoling than ours, and goes on to explain what perhaps Flaubert meant when he said that 'Talent is long patience, and originality an effort

of will and of intense observation.'[136]

We see, then, that there are indications that Maupassant's Preface seems to have given Van Gogh an artistic creed which made it possible for the artist to combine the two sides of his nature: the side that craved violence and exaggeration and the side that desired the aesthetic ideal of perfection. Maupassant, writing three years after James's seminal essay on "The Art of Fiction" and ten years before the appearance of Conrad's Preface to *The Nigger of the "Narcissus,"* seems to have learned something from James and from Monet, the premier Impressionists in their respective arts, and used these lessons to provide an important inspiration—however brief—for another Impressionist genius—the ill-starred Vincent van Gogh.

Before turning to a consideration of some of the possible Impressionist literary influences from across the channel, we should perhaps briefly consider a pair of important and influential French writers who were not members of the Flaubert circle. In several ways, Charles Baudelaire (1821-67) may have exerted some effect upon Impressionism. Like the Impressionists, for instance, Baudelaire (probably through Poe) placed the most emphasis in his imaginative writings upon the fleeting moment.[137] At a time when the Impressionist movement had not yet come to flower, Baudelaire had accurately written about the fleeting sense of movement that one often encounters in Modernist art. As early as 1863, moreover, he declared that "a characteristic symptom of the spiritual condition of our century is that all of the arts tend, if not to act as a substitute for each other, at least to supplement each other, by lending each other new strength and new resources."[138]

The poet, who was also a critic and friend of painters such as Courbet, Delacroix, Manet, and Monet, made the following comments in one of his articles on Constantin Guys (which first appeared in *Le Figaro* in 1863, but which was written as early as 1859-60):

> By modernity I mean the transitory, the fleeting, the incidental, one half of art, whose other half is the eternal and immutable ... . You have no right to scorn or by-pass this transitory, fleeting element whose changes are so frequent ... for almost all our originality wants the stamp time leaves on

our impressions.[139]

The sense of the fleeting moment that Baudelaire ascribes to the Modernist spirit was rendered by many of the French writers of the Flaubert circle in the word pictures of external reality that can be found in their work. But we must look to Baudelaire, and to Mallarmé after him, in order to discover the important element that connects French Impressionist writing to the best of the Impressionist writing in the English-speaking world. And this connecting element is probably best termed "internalization."

Early in the century, for example, Baudelaire had already become disenchanted with the world of the camera. In his "Salon of 1859" he lamented the development of photography which he felt contributed much "to the impoverishment of the French artistic genius ... ."[140] He lamented the evidence that led him to believe that "each day art further dimishes its self-respect by bowing down before external reality; each day the painter becomes more and more given to painting not what he dreams but what he sees."[141]   And as early as 1846, the poet attacked Horace Vernet's predilection for detail: "Who knows better than he the correct number of buttons on each uniform, or the anatomy of a gaitor or a boot?"  In the same essay Baudelaire went on to criticize the painter with "a memory like an almanac."[142]

Baudelaire, who saw Imagination as "the queen of truth,"[143] said that the earlier artists sought spiritual reality outside themselves, "but it was only to be found within."[144]   In the "Salon of 1859," he observed that "if an assemblage of trees, mountains, water and houses, such as we call a landscape, is beautiful, it is not so of itself, but through me, through my own grace and favour, through the idea or the feeling which *I* attach to it."[145]   This is not a comment that would have been well accepted among the French writers of the Flaubert circle, but it would have been read with great approval by the best of the early Modernist writers from the English-speaking world.

This was a dictum that Stéphane Mallarmé (1842-1898) also seems to have followed, and one that James, too, seems to have embraced. Mallarmé, of course, was a personal friend of several of the Impressionist painters.  His personality inspired illuminating portraits of himself by Manet, Gauguin, and Whistler. He was so much drawn to the world of the painter, in fact, that he made many (generally unsuccessful) attempts to have his poems illustrated by his artist friends from the Impressionist school. Moreover, the poet translated into French Whistler's important and controversial statement, "Ten o'clock" (translated as "Le Ten O'Clock" in 1888).

In one of Mallarmé's own early statements of poetic intentions, the poet's italicized words may well stand as a capsule manifesto (if such a word can be used for this group) of the leading British and American Impressionist writers "J'invente une langue qui doit nécessairement jaillir d'une poétique très nouvelle, que je pourrais définir en ces deux mots: *Peindre, non la chose, mais l'effet qu'elle produit.*"[146]

In line with this internalizing tendency in Mallarmé and Baudelaire is the attitude that both poets (and many who have followed them) manifest toward "finish" in a work of art. As early as 1845, after remarking that Corot (who was, we recall, one of the leading Impressionist fore-runners) as a landscapist stands "at the head of the modern school" [*Mirror,* p. 29], Baudelaire proceeded to say that "a work of genius ... in which every element is well seen, well observed, well understood and well imagined, will always be very well executed when it is sufficiently so [And] ... there is a great difference between a work that is *complete* and a work that is *finished*; ... in general what is *complete* is not *finished,* and ... a thing that is highly *finished* need not be *complete* at all ... ."[147]

With Baudelaire's sage words in mind, I shall conclude my examination of the major Continental literary influences on Henry James's Impressionism. Now that we have looked at some of the major influences from the Continent, we are ready to consider some of the major British and American literary sources—the subject of the chapter that follows.

# Notes

[1]See, for instance, "Chronology of James's Life and Work with Special Reference to French Literature," Philip Grover. *Henry James and the French Imagination.* (Barnes and Noble, 1973), pp. 189-207. On the French aspects of James's character, see Bruce Lowery. *Marcel Proust et Henry James: Une Confrontation.* (Paris: Plon, 1964), p. 40. Lowery herein draws together the testimonies of Edmund Gosse, William James, Edith Wharton, and James himself, to underline the French aspects of James's character. See also Edmund Gosse. *Aspects and Impressions.* (London: Cassell, 1972), p. 41.

In 1866, James told his best friend, T.S. Perry (who was then on his Grand Tour of Europe) to bring back all the French books that he could, "so that I can beg, borrow and steal 'em." Henry James. *Letters,* ed. Leon Edel. (Harvard University Press, 1974), Vol. 1, p. 84.

[2]On James's relationship to the Flaubert circle, see especially Leon Edel. *Henry James: 1870-1881, The Conquest of London.* (Lippincott, 1962), pp. 214-21; and Edel and Ilse Dusoir Lind. "Introduction." *Henry James; Parisian Sketches:* Letters to the New York Tribune 1875-1876 (New York University press, 1957: Collier Books, 1961). See also Robert Baldick. *Dinner at Magny's* (Gollancz, 1971) which used fictional and non-fictional "evidence" to recreate the life of the Paris art world during the Impressionist era.

[3]Henry James. *The Ambassadors.* Vol. I (New York: Scribner's, 1909), p. 173.

[4]This essay was reprinted without revision as "Gustave Flaubert" in *Notes on Novelists.* (Scribner's 1914).

[5]Henry James. *French Poets and Novelists* (New York and London: Macmillan, 1878), p. 199.

[6]Henry James. "Gustave Flaubert" (1893). *Essays in London and Elsewhere.* London: James R. Osgood, McIlvaine and Co., 1893 (pp. 125 and 145).

[7]Henry James. "Gustave Flaubert" (1902). *The House of Fiction,* ed. Leon Edel. London: Hart-Davis, 1962 (p. 210).

[8]Henry James. "Anthony Trollope" (1883) in Leon Edel ed. *Henry James: The Future of the Novel* (New York: Vintage Books, 1956), p. 253. James's own complex (but not, it seems to me, critically inconsistent) views on the morality of art are summarized by Paul Maixner. "James on d'Annunzio—'A High Example of Exclusive Estheticism,' " *Criticism,* 13 (1971), 295-301, especially.

[9]Henry James. "Gustave Flaubert" (1893) in *Essays in London and Elsewhere* (London: James R. Osgood, McIlvaine and Co., 1893), p. 143.

[10]On Flaubert's slow and painful progress as a writer, see Émile Faguet. *Flaubert* (1899), trans. R.L. Devonshire (Boston: Houghton Mifflin, 1914), ch. 10, especially; and Antoine Albalet. *Le Travail du Style* (1903) 2nd ed. (Librairie Armand Colin, 1904), pp. 64-95.

[11]Maurice Beebe. *Ivory Towers and Sacred Founts.* (New York University Press, 1964), p. 13.

[12]On James's love of solitude, see *Notebooks,* ed. F.O. Matthiessen and Kenneth B. Murdock. (Oxford University Press, 1947), p. 43; and *The Letters of Henry James,* Vol. 1, ed. Percy Lubbock. (New York: Scribner's, 1920), p. 248 and p. 239. On the Ivory Tower aspects of James's personality see, in addition to Beebe's book, Lowery. *Marcel Proust et Henry James* (pp. 48-49) and Percy Lubbock, "Introduction" to *Letters of Henry James,* Vol. 1 (1920), p. xv.

Guy de Maupassant has analyzed Flaubert's contempt for the bourgeois in his *Étude sur Gustave Flaubert* rpt. in *Oeuvres complètes de Gustave Flaubert.* (Paris, 1885), Vol. VII. See especially p. 67 and p. 59.

Among most of the important Impressionist painters and writers there moreover existed a strong prejudice against marrying. "Si tu l'aimes et si elle est jolie . . . ton art est mort"—Delacroix's advice to a young painter in love seems to have been taken to heart by most of the major artistic figures associated with the Impressionist movement. In the chapter on "Society Life" in *Daily Life of French Artists in the Nineteenth Century* [(1968), trans. Hilary E. Paddon. London: George Allen & Unwin, 1972], Jacques Lethève provides a brief discussion of the artists' prejudice against marriage.

[13] Flaubert. *The First Sentimental Education* (1845), trans. Douglas Garman. (University of California Press, 1972). p. 226.

[14] Flaubert. Letter to Mlle. Leroyer de Chantepie (1857). *Letters*, ed. Richard Rumbold and trans. J.M. Cohen. Cited by R. Ellmann and Feidelson in *The Modern Tradition* (1965), p. 72.

[15] Flaubert. Letter to Louise Colet (1852). *Letters,* ed. Rumbold (1950), p. 73. For similar Flaubertian statements on the primacy of art over Life and of Style over Subject, see Francis Steegmuller. *The Selected Letters of Gustave Flaubert* (New York: Farrar, Straus and Young, 1953), p. 256; and Flaubert, "Style as Absolute," from Edmund and Jules de Goncourt. *Journal,* cited in Ellmann and Feidelson, eds. *The Modern Tradition* (1965), p. 217.

[16] 17 March 1861 entry. *Pages from the Goncourt Journal,* ed. and trans. Robert Baldick (Oxford University Press, 1962), p. 58.

[17] For evidence see his *Notebooks* and *Letters.* Although I should point out that James once remarked that "Style itself ... with all respects to Flaubert, never totally beguiles; since even when we are so queerly constituted as to be ninety-nine parts literary we are still a hundredth part something else." "Gustave Flaubert" (1902). *Notes on Novelists,* 1914 (p. 234).

[18] See Henry James. *Notes on Novelists,* p. 63 and p. 78.

[19] James, *The Future of the Novel* (1956), p. 118.

[20] Henry James. *The Future of the Novel* (1956), p. 154. It is, of course, very difficult to compare the styles of authors writing in different languages. And I do not intend to compare the so-called Impressionist elements of James's

style with similar elements of Flaubert's or any of the other continental authors whose work I consider. On general aspects of English and French style, however, see J.P. Vinay and J. Darbelnet. *Sylistique comparée de français et de l'anglais.* (Paris: Didier, 1959, rev. ed. 1967) *passim*; and B. Lowery. *Marcel Proust et Henry James*, p. 321. On the styles of these two authors, in particular, however, Lowery makes some valuable and suggestive remarks. See p. 323.

[21] In his *Style in French Prose: A Method of Analysis* (Oxford University Press, 1953), R.A. Sayce likewise terms this use of the imperfect form "Impressionist" (see p. 43). Although the frequent use of the imperfect is associated with the nineteenth century, it is not unique to this period in French literature, since Montaigne used the imperfect form of the verb to good effect in his *Essais.*

Another aspect of Flaubert's style that has been considered Impressionist is *"le style indirect libre."* This stylistic feature receives lengthy treatment in Thibaudet's *Gustave Flaubert.* (Paris: Gallimard, 1935), *passim;* and in Stephen Ullman. *Style in the French Novel* (1957) (Oxford: Blackwell, 1964), pp. 94-110.

[22] James's remarks to this effect can be found in *The Art of Fiction.* Interestingly, Walter Pater expressed virtually the same sentiments about Flaubert in his essay on "Style" (which first appeared in *Appreciations,* 1889); rpt. in *Prose of the Victorian Period,* ed. William E. Buckler. (Riverside edition, 1958), see especially pp. 564-569.

[23] Henry James. *Selected Literary Criticism,* ed. Morris Shapira. (London: Heinemann, 1963), p. 225. For Flaubert's influence on Modernist writers in England, see Mary Neale. *Flaubert en Angleterre.* (Bordeaux: Sobodi, 1966). Miss Neale summarizes her findings on p. 99.

[24] See, for example, Flaubert. *Notes,* Vol. 1 (1849-1851) (Paris: The Conard Edition), p. 24 and pp. 27 ff.

[25] Flaubert. *Notes,* Vol. 2. 1849-1851. Conard edition.

[26] Flaubert. *Par les champs et par les grèves.* (The Conard edition, 1847), p. 135.

[27] Flaubert. *Par les champs,* p. 116.

[28]Flaubert. *L'Education sentimentale* (Paris: Garnier, 1964), p. 9.

[29]See Benjamin F. Bart. *Flaubert's Landscape Descriptions.* (University of Michigan Press, 1956), p. 35. The foregoing discussion is heavily indebted to Bart's valuable monograph.

[30]See, for example, *Notes* 1, pp. 112-13; and p. 285. Conard edition. On Flaubert's use of color, see also Hans Guddorf. *Der Stil Flauberts.* Munster Dissertation, 1933.

[31]Bart. *Flaubert's Landscape Descriptions,* p. V.

[32]Flaubert. *Madame Bovary* (1859), trans. Francis Steegmuller. Modern Library, 1957, p. 65.

[33]Henry James. *The North American Review,* CLXIX (October 1899), 494.

[34]Henry James. *Notes on Novelists,* p. 76.

[35]Henry James. *French Poets and Novelists* (1884 ed.), p. 210.

[36]Flaubert. *Madame Bovary,* trans. Steegmuller, p. 125. Such a passage is probably the kind that James meant when he referred to Flaubert's "quest and multiplication of the image ... [as being] accordingly his high elegance." James. *Notes on Novelists,* p. 79.

On Madame Bovary's possible influence on James, see "Flaubert's Technique." Grover. *Henry James and the French Imagination,* pp. 75-91.

[37]In *Literary Impressionism* (College and University Press, 1973), Maria E. Kronegger cites a number of examples of what she sees to be Impressionism in *The Sentimental Education.* See Kronegger. Notes 18, 19, and 21; and pp. 135-136, note 24. I do not, however, find literary Impressionism where Kronegger does, since I define the term in a different fashion—one that accords more precisely with the techniques as derived from Impressionism in painting.

[38]Henry James. *The House of Fiction,* ed. Leon Edel (London: Hart-Davis, 1957), pp. 202-3. For a sensibly argued opposing view, see Benjamin F.

Bart. *Flaubert.* (Syracuse University Press, 1967), pp. 493-494.

[39]Henry James. *The House of Fiction,* p. 189.

[40]Flaubert. *The Sentimental Education* (1869), trans. Anthony Goldsmith. (New York: E.P. Dutton, Everyman's Library, 1941), p. 24.

[41]Flaubert. *The Sentimental Education,* p. 195. Here we see a brilliant example of what Frederick C. Green evidently meant when he observed that "Nature, static and evocative in Balzac, Flaubert endows with movement," *French Novelists from the Revolution to Proust* (1931) (New York: Frederick Ungar, 1964), p. 240.

[42]Charles C. Walcutt. *American Literary Naturalism* (University of Minnesota Press, 1956), p. 232.

[43]William A. Harms. *Impressionism as a Literary Style.* Dissertation, Indiana University, 1971, p. 35.

[44]Flaubert. *Sentimental Education,* p. 64.

[45]Suzanne Langer. *Philosophy in a New Key* (New York: Mentor, 1948) p. 73.

[46]Leon Edel. "Introduction." *Henry James: The Letters,* ed. Edel. Vol. 2. 1875-1883. (The Belknap Press of Harvard University Press, 1975), p. xii.

[47]See also Dale E. Peterson, *"One Much-Embracing Echo": Henry James's Response to Ivan Turgenev.* Dissertation, Yale University, 1971, especially p. 60.

[48]F.O. Matthiessen. *The James Family* (Oxford University Press, 1947), p. 548. In an unpublished letter of 1878 or 1879 to W.E. Henley, James furthemore indicates that he already posesses copies of all of Turgenev's works. See James letter to Henley dated August 24. A.L.S. 18, Henley Collection, Pierpont Morgan Library, New York.

[49]Henry James. "Ivan Turgeniew," *North American Review,* 118 (1874), 326-356. James uses here one of the several English spellings of the Russian author's name.

[50]Barbara Wilkie Tedford. *Henry James's Admiration of Turgenev, an Early Influence "Ineradicably Established."* Dissertation, University of Pittsburgh, 1970, p. 22.

[51]See, for example, James's comment on "the aid" supplied him by the *Revue. Notes of a Son and Brother* (1914), pp. 85-86 and p. 56.

[52]See Virginia Harlow. *Thomas Sargent Perry: A Biography.* (Duke University Press, 1950), pp. 37, 40, and 65.

It deserves mention here, however, that James probably read Turgenev first in French translation, and then in the later German and English editions. See Tedford, "Henry James's Admiration," p. 2.

[53]"One of the great prose stylists in Russian fiction ... " is F.J. Simmons's judgment, in the Introduction to *Fathers and Children* (New York: Rinehart, 1955), p. xv.

[54]See W.D. Howells. "The Editor's Study," *Harper's Monthly*, LXXIII (November 1886), 964.

[55]Henry James. *French Poets and Novelists*, p. 219.

[56]James. *Poets and Novelists*, pp. 224-25; 225-26.

[57]And several critics have already done so; notably Sylvia Bowman. "Les Heroines d'Henry James; *The Portrait of a Lady* et Ivan Tourgeniev dans A la Veille," *Études Anglaises*, XI (April-June, 1958), 136-149; and Peterson. "One Much-Embracing Echo," 1971, pp. 172-73. In his dissertation Peterson makes much the same point that Bowman makes in her article, but he neither cites her piece in his footnotes, nor lists it in his bibliography. G. Phelps in *The Russian Novel in England* devotes Chapter 5, "The Beautiful Genius" [James's description of Turgenev], to a general comparison of James and Turgenev. Phelps, too, deals with Turgenev's possible influence on *The Portrait*.

[58]See *Library of the World's Best Literature*, ed. Charles Dudley Warner (New York: R.S. Peale and J.A. Hill, 1896), pp. 15057-62. See especially the reference to "On the Eve," p. 15061.

In her dissertation, Barbara W. Tedford provides in Appendices A, B, and C titles available to James when he wrote his lengthy 1874 article on Turgenev. Although she provides titles available in English, French and German, she does not mention that her lists are by no means restrictive, since James knew Russian sufficiently well to have produced a prose translation of Turgenev's "Croquet at Windsor." This translation, done in rhyme and meter in five 8-line stanzas, appeared anonymously in the *Nation,* October 5, 1876. While James did have the benefit of being able to work also from a French translation of the poem that appeared in *Le Figaro,* Barbara W. Tedford judges that James's translation was "the only one to reach English-speaking readers in a widely circulated periodical." Tedford. Dissertation, 1970. p. 109.

[59]George Moore. *Impressions and Opinions.* Brentano's, n. d. p. 61. In this regard, see especially "A Gentleman of the Steppes"; "A Fear of the Steppes"; and "Toc Toc."

[60]Turgenev. "A Quiet Spot" (1854), trans. Harry Stevens in *The Vintage Turgenev,* Vol. 2 (New York: Knopf, 1950), pp. 308-09.

[61]Henry James. *Literary Reviews and Essays,* ed. Albert Mordell. (New York: Twayne, 1957), p. 162.

[62]James. *Literary Reviews and Essays,* p. 158.

[63]James. "The Journal of the Brothers De Goncourt" (1888) in *Essays in London and Elsewhere,* 1893 (p. 226).

[64]James. "Journal" 1888, *Essays in London,* p. 208.

[65]Strangely, though, in what are probably the Goncourts' two most successful novels, *Renée Mauperin* (1864) and *Germinie Lacerteux* (1865), the narratives are cast in the dramatic mould in which plot and situation are paramount.

[66]E. and J. de Goncourt. *Journal des Goncourt,* Vol. 3. Bibliothèque-Charpentier, 1891 (cited in Beverly J. Gibbs). "Impressionism as a Literary Movement." *Modern Language Journal,* XXXVI (1952), 175-183. See also the passage on style that Gibbs cites from Vol. 5 of the *Journal.*

67Edmond and Jules de Goncourt. *Journal,* édition définitive. Vol. 2 (Paris: Flammarion, 1936). Entry for May 1, 1864. Translation mine.

68Edmond and Jules de Goncourt. *Manette Salomon* (1866) (Paris: Flammarion, 1936), p. 437. Translation mine.

69Theodore R. Bowie. *The Painter in French Fiction.* (University of North Carolina Studies in the Romance Languages and Literatures, No. 15, 1950), p. 4.

70Bowie. *Painter in French Fiction,* p. 5. That this should be so is especially noteworthy, since the Goncourts were not even the first in their generation to work in this tradition. Ernest Feydeau, in his *Catherine d'Overmeire* (1860), largely relates the story of Marcel, a young Parisian painter. This novel must have been one of the first in the long series of *romans d'art* which helped to form a view of the Parisian artists' lives during the Impressionist era. And we recall that in *L'Education Sentimentale* Flaubert's hero started out by wanting to be a painter; and he hovers on the edges of the Parisian art world throughout the novel.

I do not know if James had read Feydeau's novel. But he surely knew *Manette Salomon,* for he alluded to the novel in "The Minor French Novelists," *The Galaxy,* XXI (February 1876), p. 230; and in the article in the *Journal* that I have cited above. This article originally appeared in *Fortnightly Review,* L (Oct. 1888), 501-520. James referred to *Manette Salomon* on three separate occasions in this piece. See p. 504, p. 506, and p. 509.

71E. & J. de Goncourt. *Manette Salomon* (1866) (Paris: Flammarion, 1936), pp. 261-66, *passim.*

72On the possible influence of the Academy on the *plein air* practices of the Impressionists, see Boime, *Academy,* p. 47 and p. 195.

73We recall here that the word *influence* originated as an astrological term signifying an emanation from the stars (into a person or thing) of any kind of divine or secret power or principle.

74See, for instance, James's letter to Urbain Mengin (1894) *Selected Letters,* ed. L. Edel, p. 218. In his criticism, James likewise made frequent mention of Bourget.

75See Paul Bourget. "Edmond et Jules De Goncourt" (1885), pp. 135-185 and Appendix M (1882), pp. 186-193 in *Essais de Psychologie Contemporaine,* Vol. 2 (Paris: Librairie Plon, 1947), see especially pp. 160-64. It should be noted, however, that Bourget does not use the term "Impressionism" as a label for the style of the Goncourts. On Impressionist aspects of the brothers' prose style, see Ruth Moser. *L'Impressionnisme Français: Peinture, Littérature, Musique.* (Geneva Thesis No. 140, 1952), pp. 128-131; and Stephen Ullman. "New Patterns of Sentence Structure in the Goncourts," *Style in the French Novel* (Cambridge University Press, 1957), pp. 121-145.

76See I.D. McFarlane. "A Literary Friendship: Henry James and Paul Bourget," *Cambridge Journal,* IV (December 1950), 144-161.

77Émile Zola. "Alphonse Daudet," *Les Romanciers Naturalistes* (Paris, 1910). Cited in Lyall Powers. *Henry James and the Naturalist Movement* (Michigan State University Press, 1971), p. 39.

78Louis Desprey. *L'Evolution Naturaliste* (Paris: Tresse, 1884). Cited in Beverly J. Gibbs. "Impressionism as a Literary Movement," *Modern Language Journal,* XXXVI (1952), 181.

79The article first appeared in *Revue des Deux Mondes,* 6 (November 15, 1879), 446-459; rpt. in *Le Roman Naturaliste* (Paris: Calmann Lévy, 1892), pp. 75-102. Fragments of this article were translated into English by Pauline C. Bouvé. "Impressionism in the Novel," *Gunton's Magazine,* XXVI (March 1904), 237-242. Eloise Knapp Hay sees Brunetière's essay as "a possible link, missing between Ford's 'maxims' and Conrad's unkind words about impressionism." See "Impressionism Limited." *Journal of Aesthetics and Art Criticism* (1976); rpt. *Joseph Conrad: A Commemoration,* ed. Norman Sherry. Barnes and Noble, 1976 (p. 55). I shall return to these two authors in Chapter 3.

80Brunetière. "L'Impressionnisme dans le roman" (1879), cited in *le Roman Naturaliste,* p. 94.

81Henry James. *Literary Reviews and Essays,* p. 183. James's unflagging personal opinion of Daudet is well stated in *Letters,* Vol. 1, ed. Lubbock (London: 1920), where he refers to Daudet's "remarkable personal charm,"

p. 103.

[82]Cited in John C. Major. "Henry James, Daudet, and Oxford," *Notes and Queries*. N.S. 13 (February 1966), 70.

[83]James.  Essay on Daudet in *Literature*, I (25 December 1897), cited in Delbaere-Garant.  *Henry James:  The Vision of France* (1970), p. 307.  On James's general debt to Daudet, see Delbaere-Garant.  *Vision*, p. 142.  Lyall Powers has dealt with James's debt to *L'Evangeliste* in the composition of *The Bostonians*.  See Powers, "James's Debt to Alphonse Daudet," *Comparative Literature*, XXIV (Spring 1972), 150-162.

[84]James letter to Daudet.  *Letters*, Vol. 1, ed. Percy Lubbock.  Scribner's, 1920 (p. 109).

[85]James letter to Grace Norton.  *Letters*, Vol. 1, ed. Lubbock, p. 277.

[86]James's letter to Grace Norton, p. 277.

[87]Cited in B.J. Gibbs.  "Impressionism," *MLJ*, p. 181.

[88]Alphonse Daudet.  *Kings in Exile* (1879), trans. Laura Ensor and E. Bartow.  (London:  J.M. Dent, 1902) p. 228.  *Kings in Exile* was dedicated to Edmond de Goncourt.

[89]Daudet. *Kings*, pp. 226-27.

[90]Henry James.  "Alphonse Daudet," *Century Magazine*, XXVI (August 1883), 507.

[91]James, "Daudet," p. 508.

[92]James.  "Review of Nana" in *The Parisian*, 26 (February 1880), rpt. *The House of Fiction*, p. 276.  James was of course not alone in his verdict on Zola.  On the mixed reaction to Zola in Victorian England, see Gilbert Phelps. *The Russian Novel in English Fiction* (London:  Hutchinson Library, 1956), pp. 26-34; on Zola's reception in America, see Herbert Edwards, "Zola and the American Critics," *American Literature*, IV (1932), 114-129; for an overall assessment of Zola's reception in England and America, see Angus Wilson. *Émile*

*Zola.* (Morrow, 1952). Appendix A, "Zola and His English and American Readers."

[93] Henry James. *The House of Fiction*, p. 224. In a letter to Robert Louis Stevenson, written from London during Zola's stay, James made a similar comment. See *Letters*, Vol. 1, ed. Lubbock, p. 215.

[94] James, *Letters*, p. 105.

[95] Virginia Harlow. *Thomas Sargent Perry*, p. 304.

[96] James, *Letters*, ed. Leon Edel, p. 341.

[97] Henry James. *The North American Review*, CLXIX (October 1899), 498.

[98] James. Article on Zola (1902) rpt. *The House of Fiction*, p. 222.

[99] Cited by Henri Hertz in Niess. *Zola, Cézanne, and Manet: A Study of L'Oeuvre.* (University of Michigan Press, 1968), p. 285, n. 32.

[100] Émile Zola. *Salons,* eds. F.W.J. Hemmings and R.J. Niess (Paris: Droz, 1959), p. 194. On Zola's *Salon* article of the '60's, see Hemmings and Niess, pp. 126-133.

[101] In "Zola, Manet, and the Impressionists" *PMLA.* LXXIII (l158), 407-410; 414-15, F.W.J. Hemmings presents a forceful argument against the "break" that supposedly occurred between Zola and Manet.

[102] Zola cited in Angus Willson. *Émile Zola: An Introductory Study of His Novels* (William Morrow, 1952), p. 17.

[103] See Manet letter in Paul Jamot and Georges Wildenstein. *Manet* (Paris: Les Beaux-arts, 1932), pp. 81-82.

[104] *Le Ventre de Paris* was first published serially in the journal *l'Etat,* in 61 installments from January 12 to March 17, 1873. In correcting the serial edition for book publication, Zola made only a few changes of a slight nature. See *Notes* by Armand Lanoux and Henri Mitterand in the Pléiade edition (1960-

67), Vol 1, pp. 1609-1640. In the Introduction to his translation of *Le Ventre de Paris* Ernest A. Vizetelly traces the germ of the novel to an article on violets that Zola probably wrote in 1866, the year that he began to publish articles in defense of the Impressionists. See Vizetelly. "Introduction." *Le Ventre de Paris* [translated as *The Fat and the Thin*. (F. Tennyson Neely, 1896)], pp. v-ix.

105For a summary of this technique as Zola used it, see Hemmings. *Zola*. 2nd ed. pp. 63-65. On the use of the ébauche in nineteenth-century painting, see Boime. *Academy*.

106Hemmings's essay is in *Émile Zola. Salons,* ed. Niess and Hemmings, 1959.

107See Lanoux and Mitterand. Notes on the Pléiade edition. Vol. 1, p. 1627.

108Zola. *The Fat and the Thin*, trans. Vizetelly, p. 23.

109Zola. *The Fat and the Thin*, p. 23.

110We recall that Zola was in some ways a disciple of Flaubert and the Goncourt brothers. And *L'Education Sentimentale* was Zola's favorite novel. See F.W.J. Hemmings, "Zola and L'Education Sentimentale" *Romanic Review,* 1 (1959), 35-40.

111The author himself took the writing of the novel quite seriously. Zola said in a letter to his friend Henri Ceard that *L'Oeuvre* is a novel "into which my memories and my heart have overflowed." Letter to Ceard, cited by Thomas Walton in the "Introduction" to his translation of *The Masterpiece*. (Elek [1950], 1957), p. 12. Hereafter references to *L'Oeuvre* will cite Walton's translation of 1957.

112In "natural history," Claude Lantier, the hero of *The Masterpiece*, is the brother of Etienne of *Germinal* (1885).

113See, for instance, John Rewald. *Cézanne, Sa vie, son oeuvre, son amitié pour Zola.* (Paris: Albin-Michel, 1939), p. 6. For an opposing view see, for instance, Gerstle Mack, who concluded that "*L'Oeuvre* had little connection with the cooling of the friendship between Zola and Cézanne. That the intimacy came to an end just about the time that *L'Oeuvre* was published was probably a mere coincidence." *Paul Cézanne* (London: Cape, 1936), p. 300.

114See, for example, Charles Merrill Mount. "New Materials on Claude Monet: The Discovery of a Heroine," *The Art Quarterly*, 25 (Winter 1962), especially p. 327; and Robert J. Niess. *Zola, Cézanne, and Manet: A Study of L'Oeuvre.* (University of Michigan Press, 1968), especially Chapter 6. Mount, however, fails to take account of a pair of fairly obvious models in the persons of Renoir and Jongkind. In *Mutual Aid in the Arts*, Teddy Brunius summarizes a great deal of the scholarship on the *roman à clef* aspects of *The Masterpiece.* See Brunius, p. 144, n. 2, especially.

115Thomas Walton. Introduction. *Masterpiece* (1886), trans. Walton. (University of Michigan Press [1950], 1957), p. 6.

116Among the literary sources for *The Masterpiece*, incidentally, some critics have pointed to Balzac's "Le Chef d'oeuvre inconnu" and to James's "The Madonna of the Future," *Atlantic Monthly* (March 1873), trans. "La Madone de l'avenir," in the *Revue des Deux Mondes* (April 1, 1875). See, for example, Robert J. Niess. *Zola, Cézanne, and Manet*, pp. 8-11. In "The Madonna" James admits his indebtedness to "Le Chef d'oeuvre inconnu" when, in typically reflexive fashion, he has one of the painters remark that if the painter Theobald's unknown masterpiece is ever seen, it will doubtless turn out to be no more than the painting "in that terrible little tale of Balzac."

As to differences between Zola and Balzac, Zola himself probably came closest to the mark when he wrote, in a kind of *aide-mémoire:* "Differences entre Balzac et moi"—that for his part his work would be "moins sociale que scientifique." Zola cited in F.W.J. Hemmings. *Emile Zola*, Oxford: Clarendon Press [1953], 2nd ed., 1966, p. 55. Zola's scientific inclinations are discussed by Sven Loevgren, "In Search of a Style," *Genesis.*

Another important source for *The Masterpiece* is *Manette Salomon.* On this subject, see Patrick Brady. "Les Sources littéraires de l'Oeuvre de Zola," *Revue de l'université de Bruxelles*, new series xvi (August-September, 1964).

117Thomas Walton, "Introduction," *The Masterpiece*, p. 11.

118Zola. *Masterpiece*, trans. Walton, p. 35.

[119]On "Impressionist pictures" in *L'Oeuvre*, see Henri Mitterand. Notes to the Pléiade edition, 1966, Vol. 4, p. 1457.

[120]Zola. *Masterpiece*, trans. Walton, p. 75.

[121]Zola. *Masterpiece*, trans. Walton, p. 128.

[122]Zola. *Masterpiece*, p. 156.

[123]Zola. *Masterpiece*, pp. 207-208.

[124]Zola. *Masterpiece*, p. 349.

[125]Italics mine.

[126]For the first essay, see p. 199 and p. 201, in particular; for the second, see p. 82.

[127]We recall, incidentally, that throughout his entire career Henry James refrained from using the newspapers as an outlet for his fiction.

[128]Henry James. *Notebooks*, p. 102.

[129]Henry James. *Notebooks*, p. 104. As early as 1875 (or shortly before James first met Maupassant at Flaubert's apartments), the American author spoke with admiration of "the French theory of centralization." Henry James. *French Poets and Novelists*, p. 93.

[130]See *Notebooks*, p. 135.

[131]"Guy De Maupassant," *Fortnightly Review*, XLIX (March 1888), 364-386.

[132]Maupassant. Preface to *Pierre et Jean*. Translation mine.

[133]See Rewald. *History*, p. 516.

[134]This painting is now in the Kroller-Muller Museum, Otterlo, as Loevgren. *Genesis*, p. 162, informs us. Of the Goncourts' novels, Van Gogh's other especial

favorite was *Manette Salomon.*

James referred to *Germine Lacerteux* on three separate occasions in his published writings. For his essential opinion of the novel, see "The Minor French Novelists," *The Galaxy,* XXI (February 1876), 219-233, 230, in particular. James also referred to *Manette Salomon* in the same article. See also James's article on the brothers' *Journal. Fortnightly Review,* L (October 1888), pp. 504, 506, and 509.

James's essential opinion of *Bel Ami* can be found in the *Fortnightly Review* article on Maupassant that I have cited above. See p. 381, in particular. To my knowledge, James nowhere in his published criticism or *Notebooks* refers to Van Gogh's work, although he surely knew it, as I shall illustrate at the outset of Chapter 4.

[135]For Van Gogh's work on this picture, see Loevgren. *Genesis,* pp. 175-179.

[136]Van Gogh cited in Loevgren, *Genesis,* p. 177.

[137]Henry James felt that Baudelaire was compromised by his having translated—i.e., having taken seriously—Poe's works. James judged that "an enthusiasm for Poe is the mark of a decidedly primitive stage of reflection." James. "Charles Baudelaire," *The Nation,* XXII (April 27, 1876), 280. This brief essay, which runs from pp. 279-281 of *The Nation,* contains James's essential pronouncements upon Baudelaire, although James referred in print to the French author on at least two other occasions: in *"Art,"* *Atlantic Monthly* XXIX (January 1872), 116; and in the essay on Sainte-Beuve, *North American Review,* CXXX (January 1880), 64 and 66.

[138]Charles Baudelaire. *The Life and Works of Eugène Delacroix* (1863), cited in Jean Seznec. *Literature and the Visual Arts in Nineteenth-Century France.* (Hull: Hull University Publications, 1963), p. 3.

[139]Charles Baudelaire (1863). Cited in Jean Leymarie. *Impressionism: Biographical and Critical Study* Vol. 1. N.Y.: Skira, 1959 (p. 66).

[140]Baudelaire, *Mirror of Art,* trans. and ed. Jonathan Mayne [1955]. (Phaidon, 1956), p. 230. There has been nothing like an adequate full-length study

of literature and photography, although the subject could make an interesting book.   Writers as temperamentally diverse as Ruskin, Henry James, Robbe-Grillet, and Norman Mailer have made abundant use of camera vision in their work.

141Baudelaire. *Mirror,* p. 231.

142Baudelaire.   Cited in Scharf.   *Art and Painting* [1968], (1969), p. 57. Vernet's dates are 1789-1863.

143Baudelaire. *Mirror,* p. 233.

144Baudelaire. *Mirror,* p. 43.

145Baudelaire. *Mirror,* p. 275.

146Mallarmé letter to Henri Cazalis, October 1864, in Stéphane Mallarmé. *Oeuvres Complètes,* ed. Henri Mondor and G. Jean-Aubry.   (Paris:   Gallimard, 1961), p. 1440.

147Baudelaire. *Mirror,* p. 29.

*Chapter Three*

*British and American Literary Influences*
*On Henry James's Impressionism*

## British Authors

Walter Houghton has written that "to look into the Victorian mind is to see some of the primary sources of the modern mind." When we look closely at the work of such Victorians as Ruskin, Whistler, Beardsley, Pater, Wilde, George Moore, Du Maurier, and Arthur Symons, we see the truth of Houghton's statement. These writers, temperamentally disparate though they are, all contributed not only to the development of Modernism in the arts, but also to the development of one of its distinctive art forms—the Impressionist novel. To explain how these Victorians made their contributions to this art form will be the purpose of the first half of Chapter three.

John Ruskin (1819-1900) probably did more than any writer of his time to enhance the prestige of the visual arts in England. After he graduated from Oxford, he began a five-volume defense of the landscape painter J.M.W. Turner (1775-1851) that was published under the title *Modern Painters* (1843-1860). These volumes were instantly well-received and widely talked about in England. With the appearance of *The Seven Lamps of Architecture* (1849) and *The Stones of Venice* (1851-3)—both of which were also phenomenal successes in America—Ruskin's popularity reached unparalleled heights in the art world of his day.

In the United States, the architectural message of *The Seven Lamps of Architecture* and *The Stones of Venice* seems to have appealed at first chiefly to those who were interested in painting.[1]

And this visual appeal undoubtedly accounted for much of James's initial interest in Ruskin's work. James referred often to John Ruskin, and he generally did so with approbation.[2] In 1868 James (in "An English Critic of French Painting") referred to Ruskin as the "single eminent representative" of the profession of art criticsm in England.[3] A year after this, James was introduced to Ruskin by his friend Charles Eliot Norton, during the twenty-six year old author's fourteen-month sojourn in Europe. James was impressed, mentioning in a letter to his mother Ruskin's "fitful flashes of ... beautiful genius."[4] But evidence indicates that James had been familiar with Ruskin's work for over a decade prior to their initial meeting.[5] And a decade after this meeting, James wrote that Ruskin is "the author of some of the most splendid pages in our language"—high praise, coming from the Master of Modern Fiction.[6] But the following passage, from the 1882 essay that I have alluded to above, perhaps best captures the feeling of esteem that James felt for Ruskin. After characterizing Ruskin's prose as "demoralized" with its "want of form," James concluded on a strong and favorable note:

> Among the many strange things that have befallen Venice, she has had the good fortune to become the object of a passion to a man of splendid genius, who has made her his own, and, in doing so, has made her the world's. There is no better reading at Venice, therefore ... , than Ruskin, for every true Venice-lover can separate the wheat from the chaff.[7]

On many visual matters in art, Ruskin's thought ran strikingly parallel to that of the French Impressionists.[8] Perhaps foremost of these parallels were Ruskin's revolutionary pronouncements regarding the use of color in painting: "the purest and most thoughtful minds are those which love colour the most," Ruskin observed.[9] Likewise, he believed that "no amount of expression or invention can redeem an ill-coloured picture ... ."[10]

Moreover, as early as the 1850's, we can see an example of Ruskin formulating in words the technique of juxtaposition which the Impressionists came to use in their work. From *Modern Painters:*

> Light, with reference to the tone it induces on objects, is either to be considered as neutral and white, bringing out local colours with fidelity;

or coloured, and consequently modifying these local tints with its own.[11]

While it seems unlikely that this passage would have influenced the pioneer French Impressionist painters, who were not on the whole very literate individuals, it does seem likely that James, who had probably read *Modern Painters* before 1858, would probably have absorbed Ruskin's message; namely, that objects are continually transformed by their surroundings.

Like his French contemporary Baudelaire, Ruskin also insisted that the artist could render nature more precisely than the camera, and that the artist should use his imagination in order to capture the accurate "impression" that the camera was incapable of:

> For as a photograph is not a work of art, though it requires certain delicate manipulations of paper and acid, and subtle calculations of time, in order to bring out a good result; so, neither would a drawing *like* a photograph, made directly from nature, be a work of art, although it would imply many delicate manipulations of the pencil and subtle calculations of effects of colour and shade.[12]

In depicting a tree, Ruskin moreover observed, "it is more important to give the appearance of energy and elasticity in the limbs which is indicative of growth and life, than any particular character of leaf, or texture of bough.[13]   In a letter to the *Times* (May 5, 1854) regarding Holman Hunt's "The Light of the World," Ruskin furthermore said:

> The true work represents all objects as they would appear in nature in the position and at the distances which the arrangement of the picture supposes. The false work represents them with all their details as if seen through a microscope.[14]

Ruskin's fundamental attitude toward the rendering of nature was probably formulated as early as 1843, in the first volume of *Modern Painters,* wherein he sought to praise the English landscape painters— Turner, chiefly—who were his contemporaries. Ruskin's thesis commences:

> The picture which is looked to for an interpretation of nature is invaluable, but the picture which is taken as a substitute for nature had better be burned.

He then went on to discover in Turner an interpretation of nature as revealing divine majesty, eternal mystery, and breathless infinity. On such matters Ruskin could have cited as an authority the leading British art critic of the generation that preceded him. "A mere copier of nature," Sir Joshua Reynolds declared in his Discourse to Students of the Royal Academy (14 December 1776), "can never produce anything great." In a similar vein, Ruskin wrote in *Modern Painters* that the great landscape painting "must be capable of producing on the far-away beholder's mind precisely the impression which the reality would have produced. . . ."[15]

Furthermore, Ruskin said that the great artist does not merely record the facts of appearance, he treats his subject in such a way as to give "not the actual facts of it, but the impression it made on his mind . . . ."[16] And Ruskin's axiom that "we never see anything clearly" perhaps contributed to the Impressionist method, or paralleled it; in Impressionist novels such as *The Red Badge of Courage, Lord Jim, The Ambassadors,* and *The Good Soldier* the major issues are seldom clearly presented. The critic must not relinquish his task, which is what Ruskin set forth in *The Stones of Venice.* Ruskin herein tells of the way with which, after contemplating the universe, we extricate it from infinity "as one gathers a violet out of grass; one does not improve either violet or grass in gathering it, but one makes the flowering visible; and then the human being has to make its power upon his own heart visible also . . . . And sometimes he may be able to do more than this, and to set it in strange lights, and display it a thousand ways before unknown."[17]

Surely, then, affinities between Ruskin and Impressionism exist. To overlook the ways in which they diverge, however, would be to distort the evidence of Ruskin's writing on art. We must bear in mind that as early as Volume One of *Modern Painters,* for example, Ruskin declared that "the representation of facts . . . is the foundation of all art . . . ."[18] A statement which is, of course, antithetical to Impressionist doctrine. Moreover, toward the end of his career Ruskin became increasingly possessed by what he saw as his mission; namely, to see to it that "the beauty which is to be a joy forever, must be a joy for all."[19] It was this kind of attitude which seemingly gave issue to the notorious quarrel with Whistler—

the quarrel that led to the well-publicized Whistler-Ruskin trial of 1878.

James McNeill Whistler (1834-1903) was one of the many talented Americans who resided in Paris and London during the early Modernist period. Whistler met the Impressionists during the 1860's at the Café Guerbois and exhibited with them in the Salon de Réfusés in 1863 (at which time he was studying art in the French capital). His paintings generally demonstrated the qualities that we have come to associate with Impressionism: the capture of the fleeting moment, the lack of clear outline, and the air of captured motion. Whistler was also seemingly concerned to stress that the subject itself was of little importance; the importance was in the execution of the painting—in the way in which the artist himself made use of color and form. In keeping with this feeling, Whistler gave musical titles to a number of his best paintings: "Arrangement in Black and White," for instance, or "Nocturne in Blue." Quite unlike the later Ruskin, Whistler made it clear that he himself was a member of an artistic elite, that he painted for an elite audience that demanded neither anecdote nor description. The audience that Whistler painted for was one that was concerned not with the factual and descriptive, but with the beautiful and ornamental.

This elitist sense in Whistler, which seemingly manifested itself as a lack of concern for the realistic, largely prompted the public attack by Ruskin that caused Whistler to bring suit for libel. Ruskin was outraged that Whistler had asked such a high price for one of the "impressions" that the American artist had on sale at a London gallery in 1877. The art critic thus declared:

> I have seen, and heard, much of cockney impudence before now; but never expected to hear a coxcomb ask two hundred guineas for flinging a pot of paint in the public's face.[20]

This comment prompted Whistler to bring suite against Ruskin, whose comments Whistler felt were in violation of his character and well-being. The results for Whistler were in one way disastrous: in order to pay the costs of the libel suit, he had to sell his splendid white-brick house in Tite Street, almost as soon as it was finished. Yet in other, more enduring ways, he triumphed;

for the wide press coverage that followed, and the essays and lectures that Whistler wrote about the trial, did a great deal to
spur *art pour l'art* and to lay the foundations for other similarly
inclined artists who were about to move up in the art world
of the day.

Henry James himself covered the Whistler-Ruskin trial (we recall that after his departure from Paris in the autumn of 1876, James
had taken up residence in London). In his report for *The Nation*
(1878) he found the trial reprehensible largely on the grounds of bad
manners. On the entire affair, James's words provide eloquent testimony:

> The case had a two days' hearing, and it was a singular and most regret-
> table exhibition. If it had taken place in some Western American town,
> it would have been called provincial and barbarous; it would have been
> cited as an incident of a low civilization. Beneath the towers of London it
> hardly wore a higher aspect. A British jury of ordinary taxpayers was ap-
> pealed to to decide whether Mr. Whistler's pictures belonged to a high
> order of art, and what degree of 'finish' was required to render a picture
> satisfactory. The painter's singular canvases were handed about in court,
> and the counsel for the defence, holding one of them up, called upon the
> jury to pronounce whether it was an 'accurate representation' of Battersea
> Bridge . . . . [On the whole] the crudity and levity of the whole affair
> were decidedly painful, and few things, I think, have lately done more to
> vulgarize the public sense of the character of artistic production.[21]

Like Ruskin, Walter Pater (1839-1894) made his early reputation largely as a critic of the arts, but Pater was perhaps closer in
method to Henry James than to John Ruskin. Pater's style, for instance, is much "sparer" than the latter's; it contains a great deal of
the element that Saintsbury has referred to as "quietism":

> If there is one thing which, more than another, can be justly urged against
> Ruskin, it is the absence of quiet. If there is one thing, more than another,
> that may be put to the credit of Pater, it is the presence thereof. On this
> apex of English prose, if on no other, there is Rest.[22]

On this point James would probably have agreed, since he stated in
his 1878 report on Whistler and Ruskin that

Mr. Ruskin's language quite transgresses the decencies of criticism, and he has been laying about him for some years past with such promiscuous violence that it gratifies one's sense of justice to see him brought up as a disorderly character.[23]

Pater, on the other hand, admired Flaubert as "the martyr of literary style" and quoted with approbation Maupassant's passage describing Flaubert's quest for the unique word. "To write our English language as the Latins wrote theirs, as the French write, and scholars should write," Pater remarked in the "Postscript" to *Appreciations* (1889), should be the ideal.[23a]

James, who knew Pater's work well, wrote to Edmund Gosse, shortly after Pater's death, that Pater " . . . shines in the uneasy gloom—vaguely, and has a phosphorescence, not a flame. But I quite agree with you that he is not of the little day—but of the longer time."[24] And in James's subsequent remark one finds more than a touch of admiration when he speaks of "the most exquisite literary fortune" of "faint, pale, embarrassed, exquisite Pater."

Both authors moreover felt that art should be a spiritual adventure that could purify life. For them, therefore, art should reflect the awareness of a sensitive observer of life at its most significant level. To Pater, the philosophy of Heraclitus remained always important. He used a line from the Greek philosopher as an epitaph for the "Conclusion" of *The Renaissance.*[25] Much later in life, he opened his lectures on Plato and platonism (1893) with a discussion of Heraclitus's phrase, "all things are in flux."[26] Given his interest in "the philosopher of flux," Pater, not surprisingly, remained always the champion of the relative spirit.

"What is this song or picture, this engaging personality presented in life or in a book, to me?" Pater asks in the Preface to *The Renaissance.*[27] He also implied that subjective impressions of beauty are the only knowable reality. In his essay on Botticelli, for instance, he asks: "What is the peculiar sensation, what is the peculiar quality of pleasure which his work has the property of exciting in us, and which we cannot get elsewhere?"[28]

Of course, in his relativism, Pater may have been reacting to

John Ruskin, whose description of the facade of St. Mark's in *The Stones of Venice* "undertakes," as William Hazlitt maintained, "to formulate a verbal equivalent for the aesthetic effects of the work under consideration"—a notion of the function of art criticism that in the Modern world can be traced from Diderot through Pater, Wilde, and James to Marcel Proust and Ford Madox Ford. As early as Volume 1 of *Modern Painters*, Ruskin moreover stated, "there are no degrees of truth, only degrees of approaches to it."[29] And he remarked in *Modern Painters, IV*, that all men see the world differently, but *"all the differences are there"*[30]—which is but another way of expressing quite the same idea.

At some time in his career, James probably absorbed the lesson that was developed by Diderot and Pater,[31] since he observed in an 1893 essay on Flaubert, "someday or other surely we shall all agree that everything is relative, that facts themselves are often falsifying and that we pay more for some kinds of knowledge than those particular kinds are worth." [32]

Oscar Wilde, who often freely misadapted his sources, stated that Ruskin and Pater treated "the work of art simply as a starting-point for a new creation." Matthew Arnold contended (for the first time in "On Translating Homer,II") that the aim of criticism "is to see the object as in itself it really is." Several years later, Pater implicitly invoked Ruskin by adding that "the first step towards seeing one's object as it really is, is to know one's impression as it really is, to discriminate it, to realize it distinctly."[33] Wilde then amended Arnold and Pater-Ruskin by remarking that "the primary aim of the critic is to see the object as in itself it really is not . . . [!] "[34]

For Pater, what is "real in our life" is that "single, sharp impression, with a sense in it, a relic more or less fleeting, of such moments gone by."[35] Less than a month after James first mentioned having read Pater's *Studies* (see Henry's letter to William, cited above), he wrote to William Dean Howells (on June 22, 1873):

> I have done in all these months since I've been abroad less writing than
> I hoped. Rome, for direct working, was not good—too many distrac-

tions and a languifying atmosphere. But for 'impressions' it was priceless, and I've got a lot duskily garnered away somewhere under my waning. . .*chevelure* which some day may make some figure.[36]

Later in the Conclusion to *The Renaissance* Pater said,

not the fruit of experience, but experience itself, is the end. A counted number of pulses is given to us of a variegated, dramatic life. How may we see in them all that is to be seen in them by the finest senses?[37]

The argument of the "Conclusion" takes an important turn, however, for it is only "the wisest" who attempt to seize these "moments" in art. "Our one chance," Pater concludes, lies in "getting as many pulsations" or moments of heightened awareness into our personal "interval" of life. Mainly artistic enjoyment renders that interval with a "quickened, multiplied consciousness," for it is art which "comes . . . proposing frankly to give nothing but the highest quality to your moments as they pass, and simply for those moments' sake."[38] In keeping with this attitude toward the moment—one that Pater and James shared with the Impressionist painters—Pater recorded the following notion in his essay on the poet Joachim duBellay (in *The Renaissance*):

A sudden light transfigures a trivial thing, a weathervane, a windmill, a winnowing flail, the dust in the barndoor; a moment—and the thing has vanished, because it was pure effect; but it leaves a relish behind it, a longing that the accident may happen again.[39]

Between James and Pater other connections—which *The Renaissance* helps to make clear—exist. For instance, in *Henry James and the Visual Arts*, Viola Hopkins Winner has pointed out that James's description of Botticelli (in "Florentine Notes," 1874) is a virtual paraphrase of a passage on Botticelli by Pater in his essay on the subject in *The Renaissance*. Evidence of this paraphrase serves further notice that James, over a year after he had initially read Pater's book, maintained a strong sense of individual passages in it.[40]

Pater suppressed the "Conclusion" to the second edition of his *Renaissance,* since he evidently feared that some of his disciples were corrupted by his famous dictum: "to burn always with this

hard, gemlike flame, to maintain this ecstasy, is success in life."
But before long, he took up some of the same questions in *Marius
the Epicurean*.[41]

As Maurice Beebe has noted, Marius "is the classic exposition of what Henry James was to describe as 'the free brave personal way'—of the conviction that it is enough to *be* rather than
to *do*."[42]  Early in the novel Marius saw that his goal was to be
"Not pleasure, but fullness of life, and 'insight' as conducting to
that fullness."[43]  The hero thus protects himself by an ironical
manner while he accommodates himself to the demands that society makes:

> He was becoming aware of the possibility of a large dissidence between
> an inward and somewhat exclusive world of vivid personal apprehen-
> sion, and the unimproved, unheightened reality of the life of those
> about him . . . . To move . . . in that outer world of other people, as
> though taking it at their estimate, would be possible only as a kind of
> irony.[44]

After the death of his mother, Marius becomes a sceptic whose
confrontation with ceaseless flux is strengthened by his reading of
Heraclitus, though, unlike Heraclitus, he cannot discern a divine order beneath the flux. He then settles into a modified form of hedonism which consists of an appreciation of beauty in all of its forms, an
appreciation which leads to personal fulfillment. Since the emphasis
in this new philosophy of life is upon personal vision, Marius must
exercise great discipline upon his faculties, in order to allow him the
fullest development:

> As other men are concentrated upon truths of number, for instance, or
> on business, or it may be on the pleasures of appetite, so he is wholly
> bent on living in that full stream of refined sensation. And in the pro-
> secution of this love of beauty, he claims an entire personal liberty of
> heart and mind, liberty, above all from what may seem conventional
> answers to first questions.

Liberty leads to final aloofness. As Marius reflects on the course of
his life he realizes that

> actually, as circumstances had determined, all its movement had been

inward; movement of observation only, or even of pure meditation; in part, perhaps, because throughout it had been something
of a *meditatio mortis,* ever facing towards the act of final detachment.[45]

In the later sections of the novel, Marius tests and discards the
other philosophies of his day. And as he lies dying, a martyr to the
Christianity he refused to embrace, he takes comfort in the realization that his life was not without value:

> Revelation, vision, the discovery of vision, the *seeing* of a perfect hu-
> manity, in a perfect world—through all his alternations of mind, by
> some dominant instance, determined by the original necessities of his
> own nature and character, he had always set that above the *having,* or
> even the *doing,* of anything. For, such vision, if received with due at-
> titude on his part was, in reality, the *being* something, and as such was
> surely a pleasant offering of sacrifice to whatever gods there might be,
> observant of him. And how goodly had the vision been!—one long un-
> folding of beauty and energy in things upon the closing of which he
> might gracefully utter his 'Vixi!'[46]

This Jamesian passage, which could almost be placed intact in the
Conclusion of *The Ambassadors* (which Pater's novel preceded by
over fifteen years) expresses the conviction of a personal ethic that
transcends hedonism—an ethic that is reflected in much of the literature of the Modernist writers from James through Forster and the
Bloomsbury Group. Years before G. E. Moore had published his influential volumes on ethical theory, however, Pater (and James, concurrently) had demonstrated again that good art always precedes
philosophical formulations.47

As Marius's yearning for self-effacement and "final detachment" shows him to be something more than a typical aesthete, the
novel leaves him short of his goal. In "Sebastian van Storck" (1886),
however, Pater clarified what he seems to have meant when he used
the term "final detachment" in *Marius the Epicurean.*

"Sebastian van Storck" is one of the four stories that make up
Pater's *Imaginary Portraits* (1887).[48] But before turning to "Sebas-
tian," let us examine some Impressionist touches in the first of the
*Imaginary Portraits,* "A Prince of Court Painters" (1885). Subtitled

"Extracts from an Old French Journal," this story essentially deals with Watteau and his family, as they are seen from the "framing viewpoint" of another character, Jean-Baptiste Watteau's unnamed sister.

While "The Prince of Court Painters" contains very little "Action" (and still less plot) in the traditional sense in which the word was used before James and Pater, the narrative contains a great deal of spiritual adventure—most of which is related in the form of the vivid impressions that the sister records (apparently for her benefit alone) in the pages of her journal. What we read, then, is a constant series of "impressions" that are regulated, and often seemingly distorted, through the sister's eyes. Needless to say, the technique requires the reader's close and continual participation.[49] Consider, for instance, this *Journal* entry of August 1705:

> I am just retruned from early Mass. I lingered long after the office was ended, watching, pondering how in the world one could help a small bird which had flown into the church but could find no way out again. I suspect it will remain there, fluttering round and round distractedly, far up under the arched roof, till it dies exhausted. I seem to have heard of a writer who likened man's life to a bird passing just once across a cheerfully-lighted hall. The bird, taken captive by the ill-luck of a moment, re-tracing its issueless circle till it expires within the close vaulting of that great stone church:—human life may be like that bird too!

> Antony Watteau returned to Paris yesterday. Yes!—Certainly, great heights of achievement would seem to lie before him; access to regions whither one may find it increasingly hard to follow him even in imagination, and figure to one's self after what manner his life moves therein.[50]

And the following passage seems to reflect the influence of James's *Portrait of a Lady* (1881) while it looks forward to some of the early scenes in *The Ambassadors* (as well as, perhaps, *Swann's Way*):

> With myself, how to get through time becomes sometimes the question, —unavoidably; though it strikes me as a thing unspeakably sad in a life so short as ours. The sullenness of a long wet day is yielding just now to

an outburst of watery sunset, which strikes from the far horizon of this quiet world of ours, over fields and willow-woods, upon the shifty weather-vanes and long-pointed windows of the tower on the square—from which the *Angelus* is sounding—with a momentary promise of a fine night. I prefer the *Salut* at Saint Vaast. The walk thither is a longer one, and I have a fancy always that I may meet Anthony Watteau there again, any time; just as, when a child, having found one day a tiny box in the shape of a silver coin, for long afterwards I used to try every piece of money that came into my hands, expecting it to open.[51]

In line also with this apparent James-Pater-James influence is another passage, in which Jean-Baptiste's sister attempts to persuade herself of the truth of her initial impression of Antony Watteau's paintings of the Paris that is for her a "world so different": "Those coquetries, those vain and perishable graces, can be rendered so perfectly, only through an intimate understanding of them."[52] For an ironic comment such as this, Pater might very well have drawn upon James's "A Bundle of Letters" (1878), an early Impressionist story that we shall consider in Chapter Four. And here is the sister's Stretheresque and Impressionist vision of what is at once the value of Antony's art and "the purpose of the arts":

> The world he sets before us so engagingly has its care for purity, its cleanly preferences, in what one is to *see*—in the outsides of things—and there is something, a sign, a memento, at the least, of what makes life really valuable, even in that.[53]

As most of the rest of her narrative serves to indicate, the signs and mementoes that make life really valuable in Watteau's art are the internal, invisible elements that inform it—the "free brave personal" ones that can only be perceived by an observer who possesses the narrator's sensitivity to the human scene.

"Sebastian van Storck," the third of the stories in the 1887 collection of Pater's *Portraits*, likewise uses the "framing" device that we have referred to in "The Prince of Court Painters." In "Sebastian," however, the framing device is most effectively employed when it is coupled with word paintings that are reminiscent of the "Advice-to-a-Painter" poems.

The "Advice-to-a-Painter" poems comprise a tradition that runs from the Greek *Anacreonta* through Italian and English poetry into the latter half of the nineteenth century.[54]    In her monograph on the subject of such poems, Mary T. Osborne traces the genre from its classical roots in the odes of the Anacreonta through its major practitioners in the British poetic tradition.    Originally, the advice-to-a-painter poem was seemingly intended not to direct an artist, but merely to serve as "an enveloping design, or framework—a structural pattern" which "enabled the author to give pictorial, concrete, and, at times, even dramatic treatment to his subject matter. . . ."[55]    This, too, was the way in which the tradition was used by British poets, such as Shirley, Waller, Maxwell, Matthew Prior, Swift, William Cooper, Elizabeth Barrett Browning, and Charles Dickens, and the way that it was carried forward by Pater in "Sebastian van Storck." While Pater's narrator is neither working within a genre that can be strictly referred to as "poetry," nor giving directions to a specific portrait painter, his style is both poetic and "plastic." In it, in other words, there is the sense that directions are being given *the reader* who himself must imagine (or "paint," as it were) his own picture of the scene that is being presented. Pater, for example, has the narrator present the following passage (which opens the tale). The details of the picture alone are given to us; we must, with difficulty, try to discern the specific scene:

> It was a winter-scene, by Adrian van de Velde, or by Isaac van Ostade. All the delicate poetry together with all the delicate comfort of the frosty season was in the leafless branches turned to silver, the furred dresses of the skaters, the warmth of the red-brick house fronts under the gauze of white fog, the gleams of pale sunlight on the cuirasses of the mounted soldiers as they reached into the distance.[56]

The rest of Pater's tale proceeds in a similarly "plastic" and indefinite manner.

It comes as no surprise to the twentieth-century reader that the author of such evocative, ambiguous, and very often ironic works as the ones that Pater has written should therefore have exerted such a powerful influence on the early Modernist authors whose talents were beginning to develop during the '80's and '90's. As the foregoing discussion perhaps indicates, then, during the latter third of the nineteenth century James and Pater nearly simultaneously discovered some methods in prose which were in many ways analogous to techniques that were used by many of their contemporaries in French Impressionist painting.

Henry James himself was evidently influenced to some extent by Pater's example, and so were many other writers of less substantial talents. Among the more notable of these was Oscar Wilde (1854-1900). Wilde claims especially to have been greatly influenced by Pater's *Renaissance*. In his autobiography, *De Profundis,* Wilde says that he first read *The Renaissance* when he was in his first term at Oxford (at a time when he was very much under the influence of Ruskin). Wilde declared that Pater's book "was to have such strange influence over my life."[57] Elsewhere he spoke of *The Renaissance* as his "golden book; I never travel anywhere without it."[58]

But *The Renaissance* was not the only book by Pater that held great appeal for Wilde who wrote, in "Mr. Pater's Imaginary Portraits" (*Pall Mall Gazette,* 11 June 1887), "to convey ideas through the medium of images has always been the aim of those who are artists as well as thinkers in literature." Wilde was probably also attracted to the "image-making" capacity that runs throughout all of the works of Pater that I have alluded to above.

Henry James, of course, said that Wilde was "never in the smallest degree" of interest to him.[59] Since to my knowledge James nowhere refers to Wilde in his published criticism, we have recourse primarily to the words of Leon Edel in *Henry James: The Treacherous Years.* Edel herein indicates, perhaps correctly, that James was by no means enamoured of Wilde's work. But Edel is incorrect when he says of them that "they had no common bonds of temperament; and they represented two diametrically opposed attitudes toward life and the imagination."[60]

Many passages in the criticism of Wilde may have served to reinforce James's Impressionist inclinations. For instance, in "The Critic as Artist" (which first appeared in book format in 1891 in *Intentions*), Wilde remarked that "all artistic creation is absolutely subjective. The very landscape that Corot looked at was, as he said himself, but a mood of his own mind. . . ."[61] And James would have agreed in essence with Wilde's description of the sense of beauty and its need for authentic atmosphere:

> there is in us a beauty sense, separate from the other senses and above them . . . a sense that leads some to create, and others, the finer spirits, as I think, to contemplate merely. But to be purified and made perfect this sense requires some form of exquisite environment.[62]

In a dialogue in the same essay, Wilde repeated Pater's ideas with some exaggeration. The aesthetic critic, on the basis of his impression, manages to exploit his personality and to make a new work of art which is often better than the object ostensibly being considered. Wilde described the meditation on the Mona Lisa, for instance, as "criticism of the highest kind. It treats the work of art simply as a starting point for a new creation." The beholder "lends the beaubeautiful thing its myriad meanings."

Wilde pursued these ideas more fully in a somewhat less well-known essay that is also collected in *Intentions*. In "Pen, Pencil, and Poison: A Study in Green," Wilde wrote of his ostensible subject, Thomas Griffiths Wainwright:

> As an art critic he concerned himself primarily with the complex impressions produced by a work of art, and certainly the first step in aesthetic criticism is to realise one's own impressions.[63]

As early as 1868, James's view was essentially in accord with most of the aforementioned statements. And from mid-career at least, he concurred with Wilde's remark, from the Preface of *The Picture of Dorian Gray,* that "there is no such thing as a moral or an immoral book. Books are well written or badly written. That is all." While James would not perhaps have gone so far as to agree with Wilde that "Art never expresses anything but itself," much else in Wilde's art-for-art's sake posture James would have found agreeable.

In the previously cited essay, for example, Wilde described the realism of Zola as "the true decadence . . . from which we are now suffering." And the James who wrote to H. G. Wells that "art *makes* life" would probably have concurred with Wilde's ". . .things are because we see them, and what we see, and how we see. . ., depends on the arts that have influenced us." Nor would Wilde's ". . .Life imitates Art far more than Art imitates life,"[65] have gone unnoticed by the Master during his later period.[66]

Like Oscar Wilde, George Moore (1852-1933) was also a disciple of Walter Pater, to whom Moore referred as "the president of the high court of criticism."[67] In Pater, whom Moore first met in Oxford in 1889, Moore seems to have found a principal model and philosopher. Moore acknowledged Pater's eminence as a critic when he stated in his first volume of literary essays, *Impressions and Opinions* (1891): "I understand criticism more as the story of the critic's soul than as an exact science."[68]

During his early career, Moore was himself a painter, and spent his early twenties in Paris where he made the acquaintance of such artists as Manet, Monet, Renoir, and Degas—with all of whom he met frequently in the Nouvelle Athènes in Montmartre during the period of his "café education," from 1877 to 1880. Moore's *Confessions of a Young Man* (1888) seemingly described his life in the Paris of this time and records impressions not only of the Impressionist painters, but also of writers, such as Zola, Verlaine, and Mallermé, who were associated with the Movement.[69]

Over a thirty-year period Moore was influential in spreading knowledge about the Impressionist painters and their work. In addition to *Confessions of a Young Man,* he discussed the Impressionists in *Modern Painting,* a volume of essays first published in 1893, in *Hail and Farewell,* his three-volume autobiography (1911, 1912, and 1914), and even in *Modern Painters,* 1923. Within a year of Whistler's "art-for-art's-sake" document, the "Ten O'clock," a group of young painters under Walter Sickert set about organizing the New English Art Club, a society that was dedicated to a return to nature and which followed the example of the French Impressionist painters. Moore was also friendly with the leading members of this group —Tonks, Steer and Sickert,[70] in particular—and recorded his impressions of them at the end of the "Ave" section, in Volume One of *Hail and Farewell.*[71]

Moore himself claimed that the major influences in his life remained Turgenev and Corot—"they have been and still are," he wrote as an old man, "the holy places where I rested and rest; together they have revealed to me all that I need to know."[72] When John Eglinton asked Moore to write an Irish book on the lines of Turgenev's *Tales of a Sportsman*, Moore warmly responded: "As well ask me to paint like Corot."[73] Of the '90's authors, it deserves to be pointed out, Moore was one of the most famous and influential in America; here his work received consistently favorable reviews in the leading periodicals.[74]

Ties between Moore's foremost Impressionist novel, *A Mummer's Wife* (1885) and Flaubert and Zola, for instance, have already been demonstrated by other scholars.[75] Nevertheless, it seems worth mentioning that in writing *A Mummer's Wife*, George Moore seems to have drawn quite heavily upon Zola. The Irish author translated several of Zola's novels into English, and sometimes even addressed the Frenchman as "Mon cher Maître."[76] Zola, in turn, encouraged Moore in his efforts to find a publisher for *A Mummer's Wife*, a novel that Moore began with the hope of being, as he wrote to the French novelist, "Zola's ricochet in England."[77] Why Zola would have approved of *A Mummer's Wife* is not difficult to see, for Yeats referred to the work as "the first realistic novel in the language." Yet despite the evident approval of Zola and Yeats, Moore had difficulty first in getting the novel published, and then in having it properly circulated.

Not surprisingly, perhaps, Moore's *A Modern Lover* (1883) and *A Mummer's Wife* were refused by Mudie's circulating library. Moore made an unsuccessful attempt to interest Henry James in the cause of having Mudie's accept the latter novel. During the '80's, the Irish author sent James a copy of the novel and requested that James support it for him with Mudie's. James's reply, however, apparently limited itself to problems of technique in the novel.[78] Yet the fact that James did not endorse Moore's request does not rule out the possibility that James, who continually refined his technique by reading other literature, did learn something from Moore's technique —however the Master might have seen fit to criticize it.

On the whole, Moore's novel can best be described as "naturalist" or "realist" (in the sense that if offers a seemingly faithful depiction of contemporary reality within a literary frame). But *A Mummer's Wife* also contains numerous techniques that draw upon the knowledge of Impressionism that Moore had gained during the period of his "café education" in Paris, several years before the novel was published. Early in the narrative, for instance, the description of the heroine's hair makes notable use of the technique of juxtaposition whereby an object is transformed by what surrounds it:

> The lamp at her elbow burned steadily, and the glare glanced along her arm as she raised it with the large movement of sewing. Wherever the light touched it her hair was blue, and it encircled, like a piece of rich black velvet, the white but too prominent temples . . . .[79]

Another novelistic effect seemingly borrowed from the Impressionist painters is the emphasis in the novel upon the importance of the scene as viewed from the standpoint of the individual observer. When Lennox and Kate (the novel's heroine) are viewing the town in which she lives, it is rendered thus:

> All was red—generally red brick turning to purple, and it blazed under a blank blue sky. No spray of green relieved the implacable perspectives, no aesthetic intention broke the frigidity of the remorseless angles.[80]

And the following passage—which presages Stephen Crane's descriptive style—emphasizes, to an even more marked degree, the important role of the observer in the novel:

> The streets were filled with dark masses of people who passed in surging confusion toward Piccadilli. The evening was fine. Streaks of purple and touches of yellow hills rendered insignificant and toylike the unending angles of the town.[81]

The next possible influence upon James's Impressionism is a figure who is possibly even more of an enigma than Moore. George Du Maurier (1834-1896), although intimate with most of the English painters of the time (including the American born Whistler, whose supremacy he gladly acknowledged[82]), remained content with his position on the staff of *Punch,* for which he turned out, during thirty years (dating from his thirtieth year), his weekly stint of two cartoons. Du Maurier, who did illustrations for Henry James's fiction, is also the author of *Trilby* (1894), a novel that was tremendously popular during the 1890's. This sentimental and profusely illustrated novel is a seemingly accurate portrayal of the time that Du Maurier spent as an artist in Paris. *Trilby* is also noteworthy for its rather thinly disguised portrait of Whistler. If Bersot was wrong (and I think that he was) when he said that "it is a mistake to believe. . .that the book that makes the most stir is the most characteristic of its epoch,"[83] then by the nineties the English-speaking world was surely ripe for acceptance of the Impressionist message—in literature, as well as in painting; for while *Trilby* is decidedly not a good Impressionist novel, it nevertheless contains a great deal of detailed description of Bohemian life and art, presented in an atmosphere that seems very like the one in which the Impressionist school of painters originated and thrived.[84]

Du Maurier's *Trilby* is in some ways a classic *roman-à-clef*— with Joe Sibley (whose name was changed to Anthony, a Swiss, after Whistler threatened a suit and demanded that Harper's delete the character of Joe Sibley from the novel) representing Whistler, and Little Billee representing Du Maurier himself. The novel was not only popular; it may have had some effect upon the Impressionist writing of Henry James. Although Du Maurier's social insights as a novelist lack the acuteness of James, the American author nevertheless had a certain admiration for Du Maurier as story-teller. In the Preface to the New York edition of *Daisy Miller,* for instance, James reported that Du Maurier (to whom the Master referred as my "much-loved-friend") suggested to him the Impressionist story for "The Real Thing" (1892). And in an article on Du Maurier in *Harper's New Monthly Magazine* (September, 1897), James wrote:

> No companion of his walks and talks can have failed to be struck with the number of stories that he had, as it were, put by; none either can have failed to urge him to take them down from the shelf . . . . They dazzled me with the note of invention. He had worked them out in such detail that they were ready in many a case to be served as they stood.

In their *Trilbyana* (1895) Joseph B. and Jeannette L. Gilder moreover included some remarks by Du Maurier about a conversation with James. Du Maurier said:

> It was one day while we were walking together on Hampstead Hearth. We were talking about story writing, and I said to him: 'If I were a writer, it seems to me that I should have no difficulty about plots. I have in my head now plots for fifty stories. I'm always working them out for my own amusement.' 'Well,' he said, 'it seems to me that you are a very fortunate person; I wish you'd tell me one of those plots.' Then I told him the story of 'Trilby.' Yes, he praised it very generously. 'Well,' I said, 'you may have the idea and work it out to your own satisfaction.' But he refused to accept it. 'You must write it yourself,' he said: 'I'm sure you can do it, if you'll only try.'[85]

Using the stimulus thus provided by James, Du Maurier tried a hand at his first novel, *Peter Ibbetson* (1891). Although *Trilby* did not appear until January, 1894 (in serialized form in *Harper's Monthly*), or approximately seven years after the conversation on Hampstead Heath, James is nevertheless the one who seems to have provided the initial impulse for the novel.[86] When we therefore see occasional Impressionist word paintings and Impressionist effects in *Trilby*, we realize that James, too, probably read these passages with special care, since it was he who first urged Du Maurier to put his novel of Bohemian life onto paper.

Here, for example, is a passage in which Little Billee sits gazing at the sea, a passage that could almost be a seascape by Boudin or Monet:

> There was a fresh breeze from the west, and the long, slow billows broke into creamier foam than ever, which reflected itself as a tender white gleam in the blue concavities of their shining shoreward curves as they came rolling in. The sky was all of turquoise but for the smoke of a distant steamer—a long thin horizontal streak of dun—and there were little brown or white sails here and there, dotting, and the ships went on . . . .[87]

A year after *Trilby* appeared, James received the celebrated "germ" for *The Ambassadors*. This germ came to him when his friend Jonathan Sturges recollected his meeting with William Dean Howells at Whistler's place in Paris, when the older man told Sturges, in effect: "Oh you are young, you are young—be glad of it: be glad of it and *live*. Live all you can. . . ." In James's novel this "germ" is transformed into art. But as Maurice Beebe has shown (in "Paris Was Where the Twentieth Century Was: Literary Memoirs of the Twenties"),[88] James may have learned something about the truth of Howells's dictum from the *Trilby* that he had not only read, but whose composition he had inspired—and he had done so just before he first received the germ for his greatest Impressionist novel, *The Ambassadors*.

Arthur Symons (1865-1945) is perhaps closer to Walter Pater than any other author heretofore considered. Pater allusions and references can be found throughout Symons's work.[89] In his propensity to act as press agent for Impressionism, however, Symons resembled George Moore perhaps even more than Pater. What is probably Symons's foremost pronouncement in behalf of literary Impressionism was his 1893 article for *Harper's Monthly*, entitled "The Decadent Movement in Literature."[90] Notwithstanding its title, Symons's article is not about Decadence but about Impressionism. " 'The Impressionist Movement in Literature' would have been a far better choice of title," as Tom Gibbons has observed. "Its greatest value is probably to emphasize that Symons equated impressionism not with vagueness but with unprecedented accuracy and immediacy of communication."[91]    Symons remarks, for instance, upon "the ideal of the Decadence, " which he sees to be "to fix the last fine shade, to fix it fleetingly." "The Impressionist, in literature as in painting," the author goes on to say in a passage similar to one by Stephen Crane in "War Memories," "would flash upon you in a new, sudden way so exact an image of what you have just seen, just as you have seen it . . . ."[92]

In his essay on "Impressionistic Writing" Symons more directly champions the cause of Impressionism when he states that of all of the qualities necessary to be an Impressionist writer, "the first thing is to see, and with an eye which sees all, and as if one's only business were to see; and then to write from a selecting memory . . ."

And in an essay on Laforgue, who himself knew well the Impressionist painters and their work, Symons praised the French poet for pursuing to its limit "the theory which demands an instantaneous notation (Whistler, let us say) of the figure or landscape which one has been accustomed to define with such vigorous exactitude."[94] Symons, who was primarily a literary man, nevertheless realized the effect that the Impressionist painters were striving for, since he was far from ignorant regarding matters of technique in painting. In his 1891 review of Moore's *Impressions and Opinions,* for example, Symons especially commended Moore's perceptive study of Degas.[95] And he took special notice of the interest of the Pre-Raphaelites in life's critical moments. According to Symons, it was from Ford Madox Brown that Pre-Raphaelites learned to focus their attention upon capturing the moment on their canvases.[96]

Symons, who as Ruth Z. Temple has shown, was probably the most important link between France and Britain during the *fin de siècle,* seems to have learned a great deal about the Impressionist method during his early sojourns in France. He then applied these lessons in his important literary essays—essays that were well known and widely disseminated during the early Modernist age.[97]

## Possible Impressionist Literary Sources in America

Like Henry James, William Dean Howells (1837-1920) has often been classified as a Realist. Everett Carter, for example, has used the term "limited realists" to describe James and Howells. But these two authors use a great many Impressionist techniques in their work—some of which they may have learned from each other.

Certainly they were familiar with each other's work from a very early period. James's first published comments on Howells were in his 1868 review of *Italian Journeys* for *North American Review.*[99] Howell's first review of James's fiction was an anonymous essay on *A Passionate Pilgrim and Other Tales;* the review was published in *Atlantic* in April, 1875. Yet even by this early date, Howells had developed a strong acquaintance with his budding contemporary. Howells's own statements provide perhaps the best testimony to the impression that James first made upon him. "I came to a knowledge of Mr. Henry James's wonderful workmanship in the first manuscript of his that passed through my hands as sub-editor. I fell in love with it instantly, and I have never ceased to delight in that exquisite artistry," Howells wrote in *My Literary Passions* (1895). Nor did Howells's passion for James's work abate with the passing of time. "I have read all that he has written," Howells continued in the same passage, "and I have never read anything of his without ecstatic pleasure in his unrivalled touch. In literary handling no one who has written fiction in our language can approach him, and his work has shown an ever deepening insight."[100] Howells's acquaintance with James's work, in fact, extended as far back as 1866 when his "kindly chief" J. T. Fields consulted him about accepting James's story "Poor Richard." After reading the story, Howells replied that he desired not only to publish this story but to obtain all the stories he could get from its author.

By the time Howells first came to publish a review of James's fiction, he himself was an established author of considerable reputation; Howells's admiration for James was therefore no mere case of astonished hero worship. By 1875 Howells had already published *Venetian Life* (1866); *Italian Journeys* (1867); *Suburban Sketches* (1871); *Their Wedding Journey* (1872); *A Chance Acquaintance* (1873); *A Foregone Conclusion* (1875); his fortuitous campaign biography of Lincoln, and a great deal of uncollected miscellaneous periodical literature.

Henry James, in turn, was very grateful to Howells for his friendship and assistance. On these matters, James's words perhaps adequately express his indebtedness. On the occasion of Howells's seventy-fifth birthday, the Master wrote from London (on February 10, 1912):

> My debt to you began well-nigh half a century ago, in the most personal way possible, and then kept growing with your own admirable growth—but always rooted in the early intimate benefit. The benefit was that you held out your open editorial hand to me at the time I

began to write—and I allude especially to the summer of 1866—with a frankness and sweetness of hospitality that was really the making of me, the making of the confidence that required help and sympathy and that I should otherwise, I think, have strayed and stumbled about a long time without acquiring. You showed me the way and opened me the door; you wrote to me, and confessed yourself struck with me—I have never forgotten the beautiful thrill of that. You published me at once—and paid me, above all, with a dazzling promptitude; magnificently, I felt, and so that nothing since has ever quite come up to it. More than this even, you cheered me on with a sympathy that was in itself an inspiration. I mean that you talked to me and listened to me—ever so patiently and genially, and suggestively conversed and consorted with me. This won me to you irresistibly and made you the most interesting person I knew—lost as I was in the charming sense that my best friend was an editor, and that such a delicious being as that was a kind of property of my own.[101]

Out of the fruit of their mutual admiration something perhaps of the Impressionist technique developed. It was through James, as Clara Kirk has pointed out (in *W.D. Howells and Art in His Time*), that Howells "grew to know Morris Hunt, John La Farge, George Fuller, and many other artists of the early Impressionist group."[102] These James-inspired friendships, coupled with the fact that Howells had been reading James almost since the latter's first published piece, leads one to suspect that James probably exerted some influence upon Howells's literary Impressionism. That Howells's Impressionist writing may in turn have influenced James, to some extent, is of course a possibility that likewise cannot be discounted.

As early as 1870, Howells praised the ability of Bjonstjerne Björnson who, in tales such as "Arne," represented a situation or character by "a few distinct touches," and made "one expressive particular serve for all introduction and explanation."[103] This shorthand method is the literary device known as "synechdoche"—a device which had been used to great advantage by the comic novelists in English from *Tristram Shandy* through Dickens. But synechdoche is also a favorite device of the Impressionist painters who use only the merest suggestion to elicit the emotional response of the viewer. That Howells pointed out this element in the work of the relatively obscure Scandinavian writer serves as sufficient indication that he might also have been aware of synechdoche as it was so deftly employed by James.

In his imaginative writings, also, Howells seems to have profited by the Impressionists' example. In "A Counterfeit Presentment," a little drama that Howells wrote for *Atlantic* (August, 1877), the author depicted a character named Bartlett, a painter who attempts to catch the impression of the autumn foliage of New Hampshire. The drama opens with the following descriptive passage:

> On a lovely day in September, at that season when the most sentimental of the young maples have begun to redden along the hidden courses of the meadow streams, and the elms, with a sudden impression of despair in their languor, betray flecks of yellow on the green of their pendulous boughs—on such a day at noon, two young men enter the parlor of the Ponkwasset Hotel, and deposit about the legs of the piano the burdens they have been carrying: a campstool, namely, a fieldeasel, a closed box of colors, and a canvas, to which, apparently, some portion of reluctant nature has just been transferred.[104]

Throughout the play, Bartlett seeks to reproduce on canvas his own impressions of the autumn colors of the landscape, but is forced to confess that his painting is but an imitation Corot or Meissonier; his work is, in other words, only "a counterfeit presentment." Eventually Bartlett comes to realize that his brush must have a larger sweep, and he begins to paint landscapes on a much larger scale—six by eight performances after the manner of Bierstadt.[105]

During Howells's six-year tenure at *Harper's Monthly,* he continued to advance the notion of literary Impressionism with the many comments that he made in "The Editor's Study" regarding the necessity for fiction to employ the painter's suggestion, as when he admired a novel because the characters are "vigorously painted and interestingly contrasted where others are merely blocked out."[106] Further, as Kenneth Bidle has pointed out, Howells's *Impressions and Experiences* (1896)—whose ironic echoes of George Moore's volume of essays cannot be overlooked—is likewise important for the development of literary Impressionism in America; for Howell's "impressions" of New York, which originally appeared in *Cosmopolitan* in 1894, are not unlikely the sketches of similar subjects that were being done concurrently by Stephen Crane in his *Bowery Tales* and by Hamlin Garland in "Chicago Studies."[107]

Between Henry and his brother William (1842-1910) there was, undoubtedly, a great deal of unconscious rivalry.[108] Yet rivalry—be it conscious or unconscious—need not preclude respect, and even admiration. Between the two brothers, as Richard A. Hocks has demonstrated, there existed a great deal of professional respect.[109]

Both were men of masterful demeanor[110] and both literary stylists of the highest order.[111] William, like Henry, was a great reader of French literature.[112] William was moreover drawn to the visual arts, in which, as a youth, he evidently showed no small talent.[113]

It is, therefore, understandable that Henry may have learned something of his Impressionist method from his highly regarded older brother. Here, for instance, is a passage from *The Principles of Psychology* (1890): ". . . the charm of conversation is in direct proportion to the possibility of abridgment and elision and in inverse ratio to the need of explicit statement."[114] Elsewhere in the same volume, William presents his general law of perception: *"Whilst part of what we perceive comes through our senses from the object before us, another part* (and it may be the larger part) *always comes . . . out of our own head."*[115] Statements like these from his brother's monumental study would probably have appealed to Henry, whose dictum for the artist was ever to "be one of the people on whom nothing is lost."[116] Henry's dictum, of course, presupposed the kind of conversational awareness that William alluded to so well in his study. Henry and William, then, seemingly appreciated the importance of the viewer or spectator in art—an importance that the Impressionist painters, too, recognized and allowed for in their paintings.

Henry, who has written that nothing was ever his *last word* on any subject, would also have seemingly found congenial the Impressionist attitude expressed in William's 1893 letter to Flourney (written from Florence) where William asserted that the good thing about a work of art was its ability to tell "all sorts of things to different spectators of some of which things the artist never knew a word."[117]

Earlier William touched upon something of the same sentiment when in *The Principles of Psychology* he observed that, "properly speaking, *a man has as many social selves as there are individuals who recognize him* and carry an image of him in their mind."[118]

William develops this question from another angle in his collection entitled *The Will to Believe, and Other Essays in Popular Philosophy* (1897) where he refers to man's ability to conquer the crowding evils of life through his "unconquerable subjectivity."[119] And in "On a Certain Blindness in Human Beings" (in *Talks to Teachers on Psychology*), William declared " . . . neither the whole of truth nor the whole of good is revealed to any single observer, although each gains a partial superiority of insight from the peculiar position in which he stands."[120] This passage (which like many in William's work echoes John Ruskin) implies much of the feeling that we get in viewing an Impressionist painting and in reading an Impressionist novel.

The possibility of course exists that both Henry and William might have learned something of the aforementioned notions from a pair of figures from the Continent. Before William's treatises began to appear, Jules Laforgue (1860-1887) attempted to analyze the creative process of an Impressionist artist: "Object and subject are unapprehending. In the flashes of identity between subject and object lies the nature of genius."[121] During Laforgue's brief lifetime, one of his two sinecures was as secretary to the art critic, Charles Ephrussi. Ephrussi was editor of the *Gazette des Beaux Arts* and an early defender of the Impressionists in his publication. He moreover encouraged the group by purchasing their paintings at a time when their work was in very small demand. In line with his duties as assistant to Charles Ephrussi, Laforgue met most of the Impressionists. That the young French author may therefore have derived his ideas on artistic genius and reality at least partially from them seems altogether likely.[122]

In addition to the important literary figures whom I have heretofore discussed, other American Impressionist writers were working during James's lifetime. While it is unlikely that any of these minor figures exerted a direct influence upon the master, they may have exerted some indirect influence, through some of the major American Impressionists, such as Garland and Crane.

Edgar Saltus (1855-1921) and Stuart Merrill are sometimes referred to as Cosmopolitan Impressionists. This descriptive term seems
accurate for several reasons. Saltus, who was a great admirer of
Henry James (although the admiration was assuredly not mutual),
wrote in an essay entitled "Morality in Fiction" (in *Love and Love.*
1890) that fiction now searches for "a new manifesto," which will
be "the Exact Representation of the Fugitive Impression." "Art in
fiction," Saltus wrote, "consists in the detention of the evanes-
cent."[123]

Stuart Merrill (1863-1915), a Francophile and good friend of
the British Impressionist, Arthur Symons, wrote about literary Impressionism in a widely-circulated article in The New York *Times*
(February 26, 1888), entitled "Thirty Years of Paris," wherein he
pointed out some Impressionist aspects of Daudet's writing, and implied a similarity of approach between the French author and the
school of painting that he has sometimes been associated with.[124]
Merrill, who generally wrote in French, also translated *Pastels in
Prose* (1890) for an American audience. And this group of Impressionist sketches (which was accompanied by an Introduction by
W. D. Howells), seems likewise to have done much to spread the message of Impressionism to the America of the 1890's.

With Hamlin Garland (1860-1940) we come to the first American fiction writer of genuine stature who used the Impressionist
style with any degree of consistency.[125] Although he sometimes declared himself a disciple of Howells in the realist school, Garland
often employed Impressionist techniques. Between 1885 and 1889,
he earned his living primarily as lecturer, and spoke on topics such as
Turgenev and Impressionism. In sketches done as early as 1886, Garland made Impressionist word pictures—a practice which he continued in *Main-Travelled Roads* (1891), "Chicago Studies,"[126] and
*Rose of Dutcher's Coolly* (1899). While Garland occasionally referred to himself as an Impressionist,[127] he more often used the term
"veritist" to describe his style of writing.[128] Yet as Donald Pizer
has pointed out, Garland tended to use the terms *Veritism* (which
was probably first coined by Garland in his June, 1890, *Arena* article on Ibsen) and *Impressionism* synonymously.[129]

Garland (who had great respect for the craftsmanship of Henry James)[130] found in the French Impressionist exhibits at the Chicago Palace of Fine Arts hints that would influence the technique that he came to refer to as veritism or Impressionism. His viewing of these Impressionist paintings in Chicago led him to write the essay on Impressionism[131] that John Rewald terms "probably the first all-out defense of the movement in America."[132] Garland's essay first appeared in May, 1894, six months after Arthur Symons's article in the November 1893 issue of *Harper's*. Garland may well have drawn inspiration, and perhaps even ideas, from Symons, but the former's essay leaves little doubt that Garland clearly understood what the Impressionists were doing: "Impressionists are, above all, colorists," Garland declared. They place colors "fearlessly on the canvas side by side, leaving the eye to mix them, as in nature." By doing so, they achieve "a crispness and brilliance, and a peculiar vibratory quality . . . which is unknown to the old method."[133]

In *Main-Travelled Roads* (1891) Garland set out to prove his understanding of the Impressionist practice in painting, as the following pair of passages, with their search for precision and their use of color and movement, perhaps indicate:

> Over the western wall of the circling amphitheatre the sun was setting. A few scattered clouds were drifting in the west wind, their shadows sliding down the green and purple slopes. The dazzling sunlight flamed along the luscious velvety grass, and shot amid the rounded, distant purple peaks, and streamed in bars of gold and crimson across the blue mist of the narrower upper coollies.
>
> The circling hills were the same, yet not the same, as at night, a cooler, tenderer, more subdued cloak of color lay upon them. Far down the valley a cool, deep, impalpable, blue mist hung, beneath which one divined the river ran, under its elms and basswoods and wild grapevines. On the shaven slopes of the hill cattle and sheep were feeding, their cries and bells coming to the ear with a sweet suggestiveness. There was something immemorial in the sunny slopes dotted with red and brown and gray cattle.[134]

The evidence of *Rose of Dutcher's Cooly* furthermore indicates that Garland learned something else about the Impressionist technique. K. E. Bidle has written especially well about Garland's techniques in *Rose*. As Bidle has remarked, "Rose is not condemned for being vitally aware of her sexuality. She is presented objectively, and it is left to the reader to make a moral decision concerning her." Bidle also remarks of Rose's impressions:

> That Garland has the young lady's mind record constantly changing impressions of the scene is another device of impressionistic writers. All of the impressions are rendered as if Rose were looking at a series of impressionistic paintings of the same scene, comparable, perhaps, to Jongkind's companion paintings of Notre Dame at different times of the day.[135]

But Garland's importance to literary Impressionism probably transcends the contributions that he has made in his own writing, for his contacts with Stephen Crane were seemingly important to a development of the latter's Impressionist techniques. Crane came to know Garland in the early 1890's, after the latter had written "An Ambitious French Novel and a Modest American Short Story" for *Arena* in June, 1893,[136] judged by R. W. Stallman to have been "the first important review of a Crane work, *Maggie*."[137] This review not only brought a small measure of success and a friendship with Garland, but it also helped bring Crane into contact with the influential W. D. Howells.[138] While the exact details of the friendship between Crane and Garland have been somewhat complicated by the various and conflicting accounts that Garland himself has rendered,[139] there is no doubt that, as Donald Pizer and Stanley Wertheim have made clear, Crane was at least partially in Garland's debt for his knowledge of the Impressionist techniques that he employed in his fiction.[140] Crane clearly learned from Garland, and also appreciated what he learned. "I am grateful . . . to Mr. Garland who, as you know, gave me sound advice about 'The Red Badge'," Crane wrote to a friend shortly before his death.[141]

Like Garland, Stephen Crane (1871-1900) may very well have become familiar with the Impressionist movement in painting upon its introduction to America during the eighties. Crane's literary Impressionism could have been an outgrowth of his knowledge of French Impressionism and the work of the minor American Impressionist painters,[142] of his wide reading, or of a combination of the two with his youthful genius.

Of the American writers of the early '90's, Crane seems one of the most likely to have known about the work of the Impressionist painters and art theorists. He was an omnivorous reader and was familiar with the literature (sketchy though it was) on Impressionism that was beginning to come forth in considerable volume in the reviews and magazines of the day. During the summers of the early '90's, moreover, Crane reported upon the activities at the Seaside Assembly, Asbury Park, New Jersey, where his sister taught classes in art. In these articles, "Along the Shark River" (*New York Tribune*, August 15, 1892) and "The Seaside Assembly" (September 6, 1892), Crane wrote about the artistic activities of Madame S. E. LePrince (of New York City) and her summer students.

From 1891 to 1894 Crane lived, for the most part, on New York's 23rd Street, in the building which housed the Art Students' League. In this residence, he had ample opportunity to become familiar with the "new" theories of art which were crossing the Atlantic. Considering Crane's seeming interest in painting, and considering that he lived for so long in the building which housed the Art Students' League, many of Corwin Linson's claims about Crane must be held up for doubt. Linson claimed that he "was the only painter among . . . [Crane's] early intimates."[143] Linson also claims that Crane's color sense was a talent that he was born with, and that he learned little or nothing from the Impressionist painters. Linson goes on to attempt to bolster his argument by stating that the *Sullivan County Sketches* and *Maggie*—both of which were written before Linson met Crane—have as much color as *The Red Badge of Courage* and *The Third Violet*—which were written afterward.[144] Linson's comments imply in part that Crane learned about Impressionism only by the author's association with Linson himself. Yet it is equally likely that Crane learned about Impressionism through many sources, in much the same way that Garland seemingly did.[145]

Other evidence points to the likelihood that Crane knew far more about Impressionist painting than Linson gave Crane credit for. In an 1896 article in *The Illustrated American*, for instance, Herbert P. Williams reported that Stephen Crane had Impressionist landscapes in his room during that year.[146] Even more direct evidence of

Crane's knowledge of Impressionism is that in an 1893 photograph, taken by Corwin Linson, Crane is surrounded by a number of landscape paintings that are seemingly done in the Impressionist style. This 1893 photograph is especially important, since it was taken at approximately the same time that the twenty-two-year-old Crane was composing *The Red Badge of Courage* (1895).

In addition to his early contacts with Garland, painters in the cosmopolitan New York of the 1890's, Impressionist paintings themselves, and the periodical literature of the Impressionist art theories of his day, Crane was also seemingly interested in the work of such writers as Émile Zola and George Moore who were themselves directly influenced by the French Impressionist painters.147

Another possible major influence on Crane was his association with the Impressionist writers of the so-called "James group." Crane's association with "the Group" is a subject that has been much misunderstood by scholars in the past; recent scholarship has indicated that "the Group" may not have been so close-knit as people have heretofore believed. People seize upon literary legends eagerly and part with them reluctantly. Crane scholars in the past have made much of the relationship between Crane and Henry James. Yet in some ways that relationship may not have been so close and long-lasting as people have been led to believe. In *Hail and Farewell* George Moore quotes A. E. as having said that " 'a literary movement consists of five or six people who live in the same town and hate each other cordially.' " While this was not the case with the so-called "James group," still the friendships among its members were at times little more than cordial.

On the surface, it would seem unlikely that Crane and James would have struck up a friendship at all. They first met when Crane was only twenty-seven and James was in his mid-fifties. Their meeting took place after Crane had returned from the Greco-Turkish War (where he saw his first actual combat) and before the Spanish-American War. After Crane's experiences in Cuba and the Puerto Rican campaign, he returned to England and settled all too briefly in a mansion at Brede, eight miles from James's residence at Lamb House, Rye.

Like many men of vigorous and original talent, Stephen Crane had in him an enduring streak of vulgarity that was offensive to some. He was, moreover, a splendid athlete. Although evidently infected by the tubercle bacillus at an early age, he excelled at baseball, boxing, and horseback riding well into his brief decade of literary productivity. In many respects, then, it would not have been surprising if Crane and James would never even have made each other's acquaintance. Leon Edel reports that no correspondence between the two has survived (a judgment likewise shared by R. W. Stallman). And James has nowhere, to my knowledge, alluded to Stephen Crane in print.

As Leon Edel has noted in *Henry James: The Master,* for sometime prior to meeting Crane, however, James had known about the younger man. He knew that Howells had praised *Maggie: A Girl of the Streets* and he had read *The Red Badge of Courage,* seeing in it qualities that he associated with Zola.

In *Henry James: The Master* Leon Edel moreover notes that James gave Crane a copy of *In the Cage,* and that he also inscribed *The Awkward Age* to the younger man. He was quoted as saying: " 'We love Stephen Crane for what he is; and admire him for what he is going to be.' "148 And while it is difficult to ascertain the truth of some of the tales of friendship between James and Crane that Ford Madox Ford relates in his amusing books of memoirs, Leon Edel notes that upon learning that the tuberculous Crane was going to die, James sent a check for 50 pounds (roughly equivalent to $1500 today) to Cora, Crane's common-law wife, suggesting that she cash it without saying a word: "Dedicate it to whatever service it may best render my stricken young friend. It meagrely represents my tender benediction to him."149

In spite of the apparent differences in their personalities, several factors may have attracted these two literary men to each other: they shared a common interest in the craft of fiction, and they used a number of the same themes and techniques. Both drew upon "the initiation theme" for some of their most admirable work in the Impressionist vein. Significantly, perhaps, Crane thought *The Portrait of a Lady* (1881) one of James's masterpieces, and the younger author reportedly argued his point at great length with Julian Ralph when the latter was in Athens with Crane.[150] James's *What Maisie Knew* and Crane's *Whilomville Stories* (1900), moreover, both center on the reactions of children to the events of the adult world. And in an 1898 essay, entitled "Concerning the 'English Academy,' " (published in *The Bookman*), Crane praised *Maisie*, saying that this Impressionist novel "is alive with all the art which is at the command of that great workman."[151]

Although there are similarities between Crane and James, of the major Impressionist authors contemporary with him, Crane is probably closest in style and in temperament to Joseph Conrad. In an 1897 letter to his brother, Crane remarked that a writer needed advice from a fellow author who could gauge the development of his work.[152] To the Crane who had recently left America for the last time, Joseph Conrad was perhaps just such a fellow author.

Crane was impressed by the serial version of *The Nigger of the "Narcissus"* and he arranged to meet Joseph Conrad in London in October, 1897. The two men became friends at once. They saw little of each other, however, after their first meeting in London; Conrad's wife was about to give birth to their first child and could hardly travel to Oxted to visit with the Cranes. Conrad himself, aside from being occupied with his work and with the depression that kept him from working, did not fit easily into the informality that typified the Crane household at Brede. Moreover, Crane spent altogether only about two years in England: from September, 1897 to April, 1898; and from January, 1899 to June, 1900. His days were numbered, and he probably knew it. He wished to devote as much time as he could to his writing, and to the violent activities that sparked his writing; Crane was a Sacred Fount author, and his life had to nourish his art.

Although the relationship between the two men was brief, it was generally typified by sympathy and encouragement.[153] Conrad, who was certainly not in need of money himself, thought so much of Crane that he borrowed a considerable sum of money from his publisher, in order to finance his impecunious young friend's ill-starred venture to Cuba.[154] Of the several tributes that Conrad paid to

Crane, perhaps none can match the remarkably moving and sincere "Introduction" that the former seaman contributed to the first biography of Stephen Crane, Thomas Beer's volume of 1923. Readers of this Conradian tribute, written just a year before Conrad's death, will no doubt sense the personal esteem that Conrad felt for his young comrade in genius.

Conrad's admiration for Crane was by no means totally personal, however, since Conrad admired Crane's writing at least as much as Crane did the older man's. On several occasions Conrad expressed his high regard for Crane's critical opinion. Small wonder, since the two authors show such great similarity in their choice of subject matter, themes, and techniques. In much of their best fiction, they both used techniques that were seemingly borrowed from the Impressionist painters. And, typically, their tales concern a man or men, under great psychological or physical stress.

Moreover, the principles of fiction that Conrad expounded in his Preface to *The Nigger of the "Narcissus"* apply with equal validity to Crane's *oeuvre*. Crane read Conrad's novel as it appeared serially in *New Review* (August 1897). And in 1898 Crane wrote in the *Bookman* that *The Nigger of the "Narcissus"* "is unquestionably the best story of the sea written by a man now alive, and as a matter of fact, one would have to make an extensive search among the tombs before he who has done better could be found . . . ."[155] Even before this, however, he had written to Conrad to praise the sensory and emotional appeal of Conrad's work:

> The simple treatment of the death of Waite [sic] is too good, too terrible. I wanted to forget it at once. It caught me very hard. I felt ill over that red thread lining from the corner of the man's mouth to his chin. It was frightful with the weight of a real and present death. By such small means does the real writer suddenly flash out in the sky above those who are always doing rather well.[156]

These words were certainly not lost upon Conrad, who responded to Crane's letter of appreciation:

I must write to you before I write a single word for a living today . . . .
If I've hit you with the death of Jimmy I don't care if I don't hit
another man . . . . When I feel depressed about it I say to myself
'Crane likes the damned thing'—and am greatly consoled . . . . The
world looks different to me now, since our long powwow . . . . The
memory of it is good.[157]

Conrad was more than likely pleased by the words of compliment from the pen of the author of one of the greatest war novels
ever written, *The Red Badge of Courage* (1895). Conrad read *The
Red Badge* soon after it was published in London by William Heinemann in the week of November 30, 1896. In a letter dated December 1, 1897, Conrad used the following Jamesian diction to express his
appreciation of Conrad's performance: " . . . Your method is fascinating," Conrad wrote. "You are a complete impressionist. The illusions
of life come out of your hand with [sic] a flaw. It is not life—which
nobody wants—it is art . . . ."[158]

Many early critics have referred in a vague way to Crane's Impressionism. And his friends were among the first to refer to him as an
Impressionist. W. D. Howells, in a review of "The Open Boat" (for
*Literature*, May 7, 1898), used the term Impressionist to describe
Crane, but Howells's definition of Impressionism is so amorphous as
to be of little use to the literary historian. Similarly, H. G. Wells
noted Crane's "persistent selection of the elements of an impression."[159] And R. G. Vosbrugh declared that "impressionism was his
[i.e., Crane's] faith."[160] Joseph Conrad and his literary colleague
Edward Garnett came perhaps closest to the mark when they
attempted to describe the method and the effect of Crane's Impressionism. In an 1898 essay in *Academy*, Garnett stated that "the rare
thing about Mr. Crane's art is that he keeps closer to the surface than
any living writer, and, like the great portrait-painters, to a great extent makes the surface portray the depths."[161]

If these definitions seem vague, so also do those offered by later scholars. R. W. Stallman, for instance, in an essay on *The Red
Badge*, referred to Crane's style as *prose pointillism*, composed of
"disconnected images" which have relationships "to each other and
to the whole as do daubs of color in impressionist paintings."[162]

Jay Martin fails to improve upon Stallman when he later remarks that "the world of Stephen Crane is conveyed by general or fragmentary impressions."163 In these above-cited partial definitions, there is little that one can quarrel with, yet the aforementioned critics do not really come to grips with the important questions of technique in Crane's Impressionist work.164

In contrast to the crucial statements made by Conrad, Ford, and James, Crane's silence about his literary techniques seems remarkable. Yet there can be no denying that Impressionist techniques can be found in Crane's work—beginning especially with his novelistic masterpiece, *The Red Badge of Courage.*

This novel Crane had written, or designed, prior to his twenty-second birthday. Although veterans have sworn to the accuracy of the impressions of battle which Crane renders in his book, the Civil War that he described had ended six years before the author was born. Moreover, Crane himself did not experience combat first-hand until Velestino, in 1897, after he had already done his best writing on the subject.

Nor did Crane seemingly receive a great deal of help from his literary predecessors. The possibility exists that he may have learned something of his fundamental technique from Garland and from Henry James. And he may also have drawn upon Zola and Stendhal. In *The Masterpiece*, Zola treated the momentary play of light upon a landscape. And Crane may have learned something about such a technique from a passage such as the following:

> She [Christine] gave a little shriek of terror, dazzled as the lightning flashed again revealing the city once more, lurid this time, baleful and spattered with blood. It was one enormous trench hacked through the glowing embers of a fire, with the river flowing along it from end to end, as far as the eye could see.165

As regards war novels, Crane may have learned from Stendhal's *The Chartreuse of Parma* (1839). In this novel, the battle of Waterloo is observed from the viewpoint of the bewildered young hero; there is no trace of the heroic or the panoramic which often embraced the war fiction of the time. But Stendhal worked in the medium of black and white, and seldom used colors in the way that Crane so brilliantly did.

Scholars have also suggested that Crane may have learned something of his Impressionist technique from having read Cecilia Waern's "much noted clever article,"[166] entitled "Some Notes on French Impressionism" which appeared in *Atlantic Monthly* in 1892. In addition to being a possible source for Crane's famous wafer image at the outset of his novel, Waern's article made the point that "the first sight of a canvas representing sunlight painted in strict pointille suggests nothing whatever to you but an immense surface dotted with a multitude of little purplish or turquoise-blue, vermillion, and greenish-yellow wafers."[167] If Crane read this article, it may have suggested something of the technique that he seemingly used to distance the performance in *The Red Badge of Courage*; by presenting only the bewildering details of the battlefield action, Crane forces the reader to labor to put the scene together himself in much the same way that the Impressionist painter demands a strong effort on the part of his viewer.

This technique is especially effective in *The Red Badge* because Crane seemingly wishes each reader to judge for himself—each time he reads the novel—whether Henry Fleming's red badge is one of heroism or shame. Unquestionably, Henry's actions on the second day of the battle inspired his unit to a resounding victory, but perfect valor may be something more than mere heroism under fire. "Ce n'est que le premier pas qui coûte"—there is probably some truth in this old French saying. La Rochefoucauld has phrased the same sentiment in a slightly different manner. "Perfect valor," La Rochefoucauld said, "is to behave, without witnesses, as one would were all the world watching."

Like Conrad in his best work, Crane does little to prejudice our response to his characters' conduct. He merely renders his effects; the response to the situations that he renders must be primarily that of the reader, who must renew his vision of the action every time that he returns to the fictional performance.

The next Crane novel that we will consider is one that Crane himself admitted is "pretty rotten work. I used myself up in the accursed *Red Badge*."[168] *The Third Violet* is probably more a Realist than an Impressionist novel. But it has for us a two-fold importance. Its main character, Hawker, is an American Impressionist painter who does canvases after the style of Monet and Cézanne. Secondly, Thomas Beer has reported (and some eminent scholars have followed this report) that Crane, at a party in England, had shown the manuscript of his novel to Henry James.

In his biography of Crane, Beer remarked that Crane brought several of his manuscripts—one of which was supposedly *The Third Violet*—to a party that James attended. After Crane allegedly showed the manuscript to James, the Master supposedly remarked that *The Third Violet* represented "the right thing." Of course, nothing would have prevented James from having read Crane's potboiler, yet it seems unlikely that James would have commented favorably upon Crane's hack work. That James would have seen the novel in manuscript is even more unlikely, since Crane worked on this novel during the months between October 1895 and January 1896; and he mailed the manuscript to Ripley Hitchcock of Appleton either on December 27, 1895,[169] or December 30, 1895.[170]

Although *The Third Violet* was not published in book format (by Appleton's) until 1897, it was published serially during 1896 in the following periodicals—any of which James, though living then abroad, might have seen: Philadelphia *Inquirer*, Pittsburgh *Leader*; Portland *Oregonian*; San Francisco *Chronicle*; Chicago *Inter-Ocean*; and New York *Evening World*. Moreover, while the novel thus appeared initially in serial format, Crane's first brief meetings with James did not take place until Crane came to England, nearly a year later. Therefore, while James very likely read *The Third Violet*, and while he possibly learned something about Impressionist painting technique from reading the novel, the likelihood that he would have first seen the novel in manuscript is slender indeed.[171]

In *The Third Violet* (which has occasionally been compared with *Trilby*)[172] Crane makes use of a number of Impressionist techniques, some of which are used in reflexive fashion. One character in the novel, for instance, complains that the Impressionist painters render shoes in a painting as mere dabs of white paint and a pipe as only a "long streak."

Hawker, the hero of the novel, is a landscape painter who did his apprenticeship in Paris. He often uses the kind of simplification of brushwork that is characteristic of such Impressionist work as Cézanne's "Melting Snow, Fontainebleau" (ca. 1879). In the novel Hawker paints many canvases (especially in Chapter 2), and virtually all of them are done in the open-air and in the Impressionist style. For example, "In a wood the light sifted through the foliage and burned with a peculiar reddish lustre on the masses of dead leaves. He [i.e., Hawker] frowned at it for a while from different points. Presently he erected his easel and began to paint."[173] When Grace Fanhall, the woman with whom Hawker is infatuated, says that she admires Hawker's picture " 'with the cows—and things—in the snow—and a haystack,' " Hawker rejoins that the picture is his favorite, too.[174]

On another occasion, Grace Fanhall asks Hawker why his visage is so bearish and sullen. Hawker responds that "it is a fixed scowl from trying to see uproarious pinks, yellows, and blues."[175] Later in the novel, Hawker's writer friend, Hollander, asks him if the shadow from the trees he is painting appears purple. Hawker thereupon rejoins: " 'Certainly it does, or I wouldn't paint it so, duffer.' " Hollander then comes back to his friend's open-air painting: " 'Well, if that shadow is pure purple, my eyes are liars. It looks a kind of slate colour to me. Lord! if what you fellows say in your pictures is true, the whole earth must be blazing and burning and glowing and—' Hawker went into a rage. 'Oh, you don't know anything about colour, Hallie'."[176]

In a letter to John N. Hilliard, dated January 28, 1896, Stephen Crane attempted to reconcile his theoretical commitment to "realism" when he wrote (concerning one of the stories in *The Little Regiment*):

> I understand that a man is born into the world with his own pair of eyes, and he is not at all responsible for his vision—he is merely

responsible for his quality of personal honesty. To keep close to this
personal honesty is my supreme ambition.[177]

Thus Crane indicated that, almost from the first, he seemed to have
understood what Joseph Conrad meant when he cautioned Arnold
Bennett that "realism in art will never approach reality." For Crane's
reiteration of the word *personal* gives indication that, for him, "realism in art" does not mean "the direct rendering of an observed object." Crane's work seldom fits the "realist" label.

Virtually all of his work has a strong visual quality. A great
deal has been written concerning Crane's associations with the Impressionist Hamlin Garland and with the Impressionist writers of the
James Group. And when we consider Crane's artistic performances,
the importance of his Impressionist associations cannot be gainsaid.
Crane's "War Memories" (1899) are termed by James B. Colvert, in
his "Introduction" to Crane's *Tales of War* (for the University Press
of Virginia edition, 1970), "Crane's reflective history of his experience in Cuba."[178] This tale, which was probably written during the
summer of 1899,[179] was published initially in the *Anglo-Saxon Review* (December 1899) where James would no doubt have read it.
Before giving a description of an American surgeon performing a
vital operation on one of the Spanish wounded, Vernall, the war correspondent who seems to speak for the author, remarks: "The flash
of the impression was like light, and for this instant it illumined all
the dark recesses of one's remotest idea of sacrilege, ghastly and wan-
ton."[180] In reflexive fashion, Vernall goes on to describe the operat-
ing room scene he has just witnessed:

> I bring this to you merely as an effect—an effect of mental light and
> shade, if you like; something done in thought similar to that which
> the French Impressionists do in color; something meaningless and at
> the same time overwhelming, crushing, momentous.[181]

Other passages in Crane's *Tales of War* more precisely parallel the vis-
ual effects of the Impressionist painters. How like Sisley's "Misty
Morning" (Louvre, 1874), for instance, is this scene from "The Little
Regiment," in which the image emerges gradually, and from afar:

> The fog made the clothes of the column in the roadway seem of luminous quality. It imparted to the heavy infantry overcoats a new color, a kind of blue which was so pale that a regiment might have been merely a long, low shadow in the mist.[182]

To these passages of description one must add the indication (which Beer has presented as fact) that Crane admired, to the point of quarrelling over their genius, such leading Impressionist novels as *The Portrait of a Lady* (1881) and *The Nigger of the "Narcissus"* (1897).[183]

At his best in the *Tales of War*, as elsewhere in his *œuvre*, Crane emulates the ideal artist, sketched by Conrad in his Preface to *The Nigger of the "Narcissus,"* who snatches "in a moment of courage . . . a passing phase of life." In an 1897 letter to Edward Garnett, Conrad (with his usual percipience regarding Crane) expresses the feeling one has about Crane when he is least successful: "His eye is very ideal and his expression satisfies me artistically. He certainly is *the* impressionist and his temperament is curiously unique." But then Conrad wonders why Crane is not very popular.

> With his strength, with his rapidity of action, with that amazing faculty of vision—why is he not? He has outline, he has colour, he has movement . . . . While one reads . . . he is not to be questioned. He is the master of the reader to the very last line—then—apparently for no reason at all—he seems to let go his hold.[184]

Crane did not live to grow beyond Conrad's accurate perception of him as a writer; he died five months before his 29th birthday, in the Black Forest of Germany, in the Spring of 1900.

Among the English-speaking Impressionists, Conrad's sometime friend and literary companion Ford Madox Ford (1873-1939) was closest to Crane in age, being four months the American author's junior. Like Conrad, Ford had read and admired *The Red Badge of Courage* for its successful use of Impressionism.[185]

In *Return to Yesterday*, one of several of Ford's splendid autobiographies, he recorded that he read *The Red Badge of Courage* while he was in the trenches of France during World War I. Ford registers a sense of surprise upon having stepped out of his bivouac to find that the men around him were wearing khaki, so vivid had been Crane's imagery. In the same book of memoirs, Ford wrote often and affectionately of his friendship with Crane. In "Stevie and Co." (New York *Herald Tribune Book*,January 2, 1927; rpt. *New York Essays*, 1927), Ford also reviewed *The Works of Stephen Crane*, and in doing so he referred to *The Third Violet* as a "gem" and as his favorite of all of the Crane works.[186]

Ford Madox Ford[187] was the principal advocate of the Impressionist movement and the most prolific explicator of its aims and methods. Like James, Crane and Conrad, Ford's background was a very international one. His father was a German musicologist, his mother the daughter of a prominent Pre—Raphaelite painter. His grandfather on the English side was Ford Madox Brown. Like Conrad and James, Ford himself had an especial fondness for France and for French writers. He spent a great deal of time on the continent, he loved French literature of all ages, and, despite his being far beyond the age for conscription at the time, he volunteered for service in France during World War I.

Aside from French authors and the other members of the James Group, Ford's favorite writer probably was George Moore who was, as Ford remarked, "as Parisian of the '70's to '80's as an Anglo-Irishman could be."[188] Ford, on another occasion, referred to Moore as "the father of Anglo-Saxon Impressionism."[189]

Ford's autobiographies, in particular, had many affinities with Moore's *Hail and Farewell*.[190] Moore would surely have congratulated the author of the following comments (from *Return to Yesterday*): "For myself, I disliked virtue, particularly when it was pressed between the leaves of a book,"[191] and "the only human activity that has always been of supreme importance to the world is imaginative literature."[192]

Aside from George Moore and Conrad (to whom we shall return later), the Impressionist writer with whom Ford has most often been associated is Henry James. As Leon Edel and others have recently shown, however, the relationship between James and Ford was never very close. Ford first visited James in 1896, when the former was twenty-three years old and the latter, fifty-three. From this time onward, the pair's relationship can at best be described as cordial. In the late '90's Ford moved to a Winchelsea bungalow that was not far from Conrad and from James (who was then living at Rye).

Although James had little time for Ford, Ford's admiration for James was seemingly a life-long one. The younger man dedicated two of his novels (one of which was *Romance*, a collaborative effort with Conrad) to James, and included references and anecdotes (some of which were surely apocryphal) to James throughout Ford's many volumes of autobiography. And Ford's *Henry James: A Critical Study* (1914) is adjudged by many to be the first really important critical volume on James.[193]

Ford Madox Ford's autobiographies are all singularly *ben trovato*. In the Preface to the English edition of *Return to Yesterday*, the author characteristically remarks that his accounts are not all the time strictly true, but proceeds: "Where it has seemed expedient to me I have altered episodes that I have witnessed but I have been careful never to distort the character of the episode. The accuracies I deal in are the accuracies of my impressions."[194]

One of Joseph Conrad's best biographers, Jocelyn Baines has judged that the meeting of Conrad and Ford was "the most important event in Conrad's literary career"[195] and Baines seems to be correct. Not long before Conrad wrote *Lord Jim*, he met the youthful Ford. Although Conrad was older, Ford was more literate; and the less fluent, Polish-English, seaman-turned-writer went to Ford for help. Ford's first book was published when he was sixteen, and his first novel, *The Shifting of the Fire*, was published in 1892 when he was nineteen. Ford and Conrad began their collaboration in 1898. Prior to the collaboration, Conrad's only novels were *Almayer's Folly* and *An Outcast of the Islands*. Up to that time, Conrad's best imaginative performance probably was *The Nigger of the "Narcissus,"* a tale which, although not lacking Impressionist elements, really is cast in the traditional nineteenth-century narrative mold. Within a few years of the collaboration, however, Conrad had drafted *Lord Jim*, "The Heart of Darkness," and *Nostromo*.

The collaboration between Ford and Conrad can be dated very precisely during October of 1898. In a letter to David S. Meldrum, dated October 12, 1898, Conrad expressed his enthusiasm over the Pent Farm: "I got it from a man called Hueffer, a grandson of Madox Brown and nephew to D. G. Rossetti. He is an exceedingly decent chap who lets me have the thing awfully cheap. Besides the whole place is full of rubbishy relics of Brown's and Rossetti's."[196] Ford claims to have done the "literary dustings and sweepings" for Conrad during the times from 1897 to 1909 that Conrad himself was not equal to it. Although their work together did not begin until 1898,[198] Ford's comments on the collaboration appear on the whole to be correct.

Between them, Ford and Conrad developed a literary technique that they referred to as Impressionism. And Ford was the principal expounder of its aims. As he points out in *The March of Literature,* many art critics now believe that the history of painting can be divided into the periods before and since Cézanne, and a "similar caesura is observable in the aesthetics of creative writing."[199] Ford indeed felt that "the supreme discovery in the literary art of our day is that of Impressionism, . . . the supreme function of Impressionism is selection and . . . Mr. James has carried the power of selection so far that he can create an impression with nothing at all . . . ."[200]

Although Ford felt that James carried Impressionism as far as it could go, he also felt that Conrad is "the greatest of impressionist writers."[201] In Ford's asseverations of the Impressionist method that he developed in collaboration with Conrad, several dicta appear over and again. Firstly, "like the Impressionist painters who recorded what was before their eyes, the Impressionist writer records the impression of a moment . . . not the corrected chronicle."[202] Ford also claims that he and Conrad developed the idea, likewise introduced by the Impressionist painters, that "story" or "plot" is less important than "technique" or "impression." Both writers seemingly recognized, and for the most part desired to show in their art, what Ford observed in *Thus to Revisit* when he remarked that life is not "an affair of bashings of skulls, plots, conspirings." It "is really a matter of 'affairs'; of minute hourly embarrassments; of sympathetic or

unsympathetic personal contacts; of little-marked successes and failures, of queer jealousies, of muted terminations—a tenuous, flutter-
ing, and engrossing fabric. And intangible."[203]

Ford has sometimes come in for criticism because of the messiness of his personal life. Perhaps more than most men, Joseph Conrad (1857-1924) knew that the messiness of a man's life does not dis-
credit the depth or genuineness of his feelings. The former seaman
was therefore not loath to collaborate closely with Ford over a
period of nearly ten literarily fruitful years.

Like the gentleman that he essentially appeared to be, Ford
denies ever having quarrelled with Conrad, although Arthur Mizener,
in his Ford biography, publishes correspondence to show quite clearly that a quarrel and ill-feeling had indeed attended their break.[204]
And yet, when in *Return to Yesterday* Ford remarks that Conrad's
"memory remains the most treasured of my possessions,"[205] one be-
lieves that he sincerely means it. The Ford who wrote of Conrad on
his death bed that "he had the air of a chained eagle waiting for his
old enemy, the sun, to rise and find him no longer there"[206] is the
Ford that the Conrad scholar should wish to remember.

Unlike Ford, Crane, and James, Joseph Conrad began his writing career rather late in life.[207] After he left Poland, Conrad (whose
full name was Josef Teodor Konrad Nalecz Korzeniowski) served for
twenty years as a seaman and officer in the merchant navy, and did
not actually see England until he was twenty-one. His first published
work, *Almayer's Folly*, he began in September, 1889, in London and
finished in first draft on April 1, 1895. Conrad's best writing, however, does not begin to appear until the late '90's—at approximately
the same time that he began to come into contact with the members
of "the James Group."

As is almost certainly true of Ford and James, the primary literary influences on Conrad probably were French. He spent three of
his formative years in France and on French sailing ships, and remained throughout his days very much of a Francophile. In his non-
fictional prose about Conrad, Ford Madox Ford has emphasized that
Conrad's masters in fiction were above all Maupassant and Flau-

bert.209 Guy de Maupassant's Preface to *Pierre et Jean* (1888) was especially influential with Joseph Conrad, who paraphrased certain passages in his Preface to *The Nigger of the "Narcissus"* (it is very likely, of course, that Conrad also learned a great deal from James's *"The Art of the Novel,"* which Maupassant also almost certainly learned from).210

In a letter to Marguerite Poradowska, written in the autumn of 1894, Conrad remarked:

> I am afraid I am too much under the influence of Maupassant. I have studied *Pierre et Jean*—thought, method, and everything—with the deepest discouragement. It seems to be nothing at all, but the mechanics are so complex that they make me want to tear out my hair. You want to weep with rage in reading it. That's a fact.211

As George J. Worth has shown, Conrad's Preface has a great deal in common with Maupassant's "Le Roman," the Preface to *Pierre et Jean*, which we know from the above-cited letter Conrad had been reading with great interest, as late as 1894.

Conrad's Preface to *The Nigger of the "Narcissus,"* the clearest statement of his Impressionist aesthetic, was published in December, 1897, at the conclusion of the serialized edition of the novel which ran for five months in *The New Review* (the novel was published in New York in the same year). In both Prefaces, Conrad and Maupassant insist that the artist-writer should continually attempt to depict the truth, and they agree that this involves a rejection of the transitory and fleeting surfaces of things. Conrad, in fact, defines art as

> a single-minded attempt to render the highest kind of justice to the visible universe, by bringing to light the truth, manifold and one, underlying its every aspect. It is an attempt to find in its forms, in its colors, in its light, in its shadows, in the aspects of matter and in the facts of life, what of each is fundamental, what is enduring and essential—their one illuminating and convincing quality—the very truth of their existence.212

In these thoughts Conrad is very much in agreement with Maupassant's (and Baudelaire's before him) dictum that art, however true to life, must be more than mere photography:

Le réaliste, s'il est un artiste, cherchera, non pas à nous montrer la photographie banale de la vie, mais à nous en donner la vision plus complète, plus saisissante, plus probante que la réalité même.213

The writer must first appeal to his reader's senses—the sense of sight, first of all. Maupassant credits Flaubert for having helped him to develope his visual sense:

Ayant, en outre, posé cette vérité qu'il n'y a pas, de par le monde entier, deux grains de sable, deux mouches, deux mains ou deux nez absolument pareils, il me forçait à exprimer, en quelque phrases, un être ou un objet de maniére à le particulariser nettement, à le distinguer de tous les autres êtres ou de tous les autres objets de même race ou de même espèce.214

To Conrad it is no less important to render sense impressions. "All art . . . appeals primarily to the senses," he remarks, "and the artistic aim when expressing itself in written words must also make its appeal through the senses, if its high desire is to reach the secret spring of responsive emotions."215 In what is perhaps the best known sentence in his criticism, Conrad goes on to emphasize:

My task which I am trying to achieve is, by the power of the written word to make you hear, to make you feel—it is, before all, to make you *see*. That—and no more, and it is everything.216

To Conrad and Maupassant, however, *the written word* was of primary importance, for language was their essential vehicle of communication.

Quelle que soit la chose qu'on veut dire, il n'y a qu'un mot pour l'exprimer, qu'un verbe pour l'animer et qu'un adjectif pour la qualifier. Il faut donc chercher, jusqu'à ce qu'on les ait découverts, ce mot, ce verbe et ce adjectif, et ne jamais se contenter de l'à peu près, ne jamais avoir recours à des supercheries, même heureuses, à des clowneries de langage pour éviter la difficulté'

And it is only through complete, unswerving devotion to the perfect blending of form and substance; it is only through an unremitting never-discouraged care for the shape and ring of sentences that an approach can be made to plasticity, to colour, and that the light of

magic suggestiveness can be brought to play for an evenescent instant
over the commonplace surface of words: of the old, old words, worn
thin, defaced by ages of careless usage.217

As F. R. Karl remarks in his *Reader's Guide to Joseph Conrad,*
"everything [that] Conrad says about Maupassant also applies to
Flaubert, whom the young seaman had read with respectful admiration by 1892."218 Flaubert, dead since 1880, assumed for many of
the '90's writers a mythic stature. Certainly Conrad held the Frenchman in great esteem. "Although he wrote no essay on Flaubert,"
Karl goes on to point out, "Conrad's letters are peppered with allusions to the French writer's major novels."219

Conrad is also often associated with Stephen Crane, of whom
the former has remarked (in an 1897 letter to Edward Garnett),
"he is *the* only impressionist and only an impressionist."220 In Conrad's "Introduction" to Thomas Beer's *Stephen Crane,* he claims that
he knew Crane "from October, 1897, to May, 1900. And out of that
beggarly tale of months must be deducted the time of his absence
from England during the Spanish-American War and of his visit to
the United States shortly before the beginning of his last illness."
And even when Crane was in England, Conrad wrote, "our inter-
course was not so close and frequent as the warmth of our friendship
would have wished it to be."221

It nevertheless seems very likely that Crane exerted a profound
influence on Conrad's literary Impressionism. The latter remarked,
"apart from the imaginative analysis of his own temperament tried
by the emotions of a battlefield [in *Red Badge*], Stephen Crane dealt
in his book with the psychology of the mass—the army; while I—in
mine [i.e., in *"Narcissus"*] had been dealing with the same subject on
a much smaller scale and in more specialized conditions—the crew of
a merchant ship brought to the test of what I may call the moral problem of conduct."222 In this Introduction, Conrad goes on to suggest that he had not read *The Red Badge* until after he had written
*The Nigger of the "Narcissus."* But Bruce Johnson has presented a
convincing argument, based upon chronological evidence and some
of Conrad's own statements, to demonstrate that Conrad had read
*The Red Badge of Courage* either prior to, or during the composition of his tale.223

Since other scholars have documented the seeming influence of *The Red Badge* upon Conrad's tale, and since I do not think that Conrad's tale itself is strictly Impressionist, I shall not dwell upon the possibilities of influence. The important thing to note about Johnson's argument, however, is that it demonstrates fairly convincingly that Conrad had read Crane's novel before he had completed the writing of *The Nigger of the "Narcissus."* And since, as I have indicated above, Conrad wrote his famous Preface *after* he completed his novel in serial form, Crane's Impressionist performance may very well have provided Conrad with additional inspiration in the setting out of his Impressionist principles.

In Conrad's letters there is a great deal to suggest that he was the kind of author who was drawn to Impressionism. "Explicitness is fatal to the glamour of all artistic work," he wrote to Richard Curle, "robbing it of all suggestiveness, destroying all illusion . . . ."[224] In line with Conrad's stated abhorrence of the explicit is James's careful avoidance in his fiction of the description of people, objects, and places. We are at a loss, for instance, to attempt to describe Isabel Archer or to name the *objets d'art* in *The Spoils of Poynton*, for James never once himself provides anything like descriptions of this woman or of these spoils. Like Baudelaire, James evidently saw that imagination is indeed "the queen of truth."[225]

In light of this attitude toward suggestiveness, Conrad's early remark, in an 1895 letter to Edward Noble, seems especially pertinent. Conrad remarked that "everyone must walk in the light of his own heart's gospel. No man's light is good to any of his fellows."[226] And in *A Personal Record* (1925), he wrote:

> the part of the inexplicable should be allowed for in appraising the conduct of men in a world where no explanation is final. No charge of faithlessness ought to be lightly uttered. The appearances of this perishable life are deceptive like everything that falls under the judgment of our imperfect senses.[227]

And in the same year, in the "Author's Note" to *Typhoon and Other Stories*, Conrad spoke tellingly of what he called "the truth of my own sensations."[228]

In keeping with these expressions of the subjective attitude, Conrad, like James, chose to write from a detached and ironic standpoint—one that would allow each reader to judge the truth of the story that is presented. The kind of detached impersonality that is found in James and Conrad, is of course, a trait that typifies much of Modernist literature. "You must preserve an attitude of perfect indifference . . . ," Conrad wrote to John Galsworthy, late in 1901, "You seem . . . to hug your conceptions of right and wrong too closely."229 In his best fiction, Conrad takes to heart the caution that he offered Galsworthy.

In a manner that is not unlike that of James, Conrad was a supreme ironist. The word *irony* is itself a comparatively modern term. It does not appear in English until approximately 1502 and, as D. C. Muecke informs us, "did not come into general use until the eighteenth century."230

As Muecke also points out, the "non-literary arts are not very often ironical . . . ."231 Yet if one accepts the definition of irony that Samuel Hynes provides in *The Pattern of Hardy's Poetry* (1961), then I think that we can say that most Impressionist painting possesses a distinctly ironic touch. Hynes writes that [Irony is] "a view of life which recognizes that experience is open to multiple interpretations, of which no *one* is simply right, and that the co-existence of incongruities is a part of the structure of existence."232 In viewing an Impressionist painting, the viewer must, in a sense, blend the "vibrating" colors as he perceives them. And this blending involves what might be termed "irony of performance." In earlier schools of painting than the Impressionists, all the effort seems to be directed toward presenting the illusion that the surface simply is not there, that the picture frame is simply an aperture through which one observes the scene that is depicted. The Impressionists were the first to remind the viewer that the illusion is produced by daubs of paint on a real surface, and that the surface has an interest of its own. The viewer must stand at the distance from the painting which brings these two principles into balance; if he stands too close, he sees only the surface; if he stands too far away, he sees only the subject. The ironic performance that the Impressionists have provided, therefore, presents for the first time in painting what the Impressionist writers demonstrate for the first time in literature; namely, the ironic principle that Hynes has set forth in his book on Hardy: "a view of life which recognizes that experience is open to multiple interpretations, of which no *one* is simply right. . . ."

In a bibliographical essay which summarizes the critical commentary on Impressionism in Conrad, Bruce E. Teets points out that many critics had called attention to Conrad's Impressionism, even before Ford Madox Ford had begun to do so.[233] This information comes as no especial surprise, since Conrad had begun to write tales of a decidedly Impressionist nature very early in his career. In "Karain: A Memory," published in *Tales of Unrest* during the same year that the Ford-Conrad collaboration started, Conrad provides the following description of the Mindanao presided over by Karain:

> the purple semi-circle of hills, the slim trees leaning over houses, the yellow sands, the streaming green of ravines. All that had the crude and blended colouring, the appropriateness almost excessive, the suspicious immobility of a painted scene . . . .[234]

In keeping with this immobility (which is unlike the earliest Impressionists, but very much like some of the transitional figures, such as Cézanne and Gauguin), is the attitude toward "the moment" in Conrad's tale:

> He spoke at last. It is impossible to convey the effect of his story. It is undying, it is but a memory, and its vividness cannot be made clear to another mind any more than the vivid emotions of a dream. One must have seen his innate splendour, one must have known him before—looked at him then. The wavering gloom of the little cabin; the breathless stillness outside, through which only the lapping of water against the schooner's sides could be heard; Hollis's pale face, with steady dark eyes; the energetic head of Jackson held up between two big palms, and with the long yellow hair of his beard flowing over the strings of the guitar lying on the table; Karain's upright and motionless pose, his tone—all this made an impression that cannot be forgotten. He faced us across the table. His dark head and bronze torso appeared above the tarnished slab of wood, gleaming and still as if cast in metal.[235]

Of Conrad's works, *Lord Jim* probably displays most of Conrad's favorite devices, and it is also usually considered his greatest Impressionist novel.236 *Lord Jim* was serialized in *Blackwood's Magazine* from October 1899 to November 1900 and first published in one edition in 1900. Conrad began the novel during the early summer of 1898, shortly after he wrote "Youth." He started the novel as a sketch called "Tuan Jim" which was originally meant to be a part of the volume of short stories later published as *Youth and Other Stories*, but he put "Tuan Jim" aside to write *Heart of Darkness* which, along with "The End of the Tether," eventually appeared in the volume with "Youth." He then returned to writing the expanded version of "Tuan Jim" which in 1900 he called *Lord Jim*.

*Lord Jim* is a novel whose primary burden is the sense of personal honor. The text itself can be read as an eloquent commentary upon the passages on courage that are found in the *Nicomachean Ethics*. Although the theme of the novel is fairly simple, the manner of presenting it is very complex. In this, Conrad's greatest work, as C. B. Cox has observed of most of Conrad's œuvre, "there is no conclusive resolution of meaning; endlessness is made an end."237

In *Lord Jim*, as in *Nostromo* and Conrad's other major masterpieces, the "facts" are exceedingly difficult to ascertain. As Jim himself remarks, "the trouble was to get to the truth of any thing" in Patusan. The questions of facts and reality—of "knowability," as it were—are questions that loom large also in James and in Ford.

*Lord Jim*, which was written during the period in which Ford and Conrad were collaborating, may have had some influence upon *The Sacred Fount* and *The Ambassadors*, as well as on *The Good Soldier*. There are a number of reasons why James was drawn to Conrad's work. James had always loved seaman's tales and had often referred to himself as a spectator, watching the spectacle of life from a detached viewpoint.238

The two men met when Conrad was thirty-nine and James was fifty-three. On "the professional side," Leon Edel judges, " . . . there was great esteem" between the two men. "In a word," Edel says, "James honored Conrad the craftsman; yet he was uneasy about the man. He spoke of him as 'curious' and 'interesting,' or as 'the interesting and remarkable Conrad.' "[239] On the morning before James's first meeting with Conrad—a luncheon at the DeVere Gardens in February 1897—James had written to Whistler, "with the artist the artist communicates."[240] Although the actual meeting seemingly resulted in no great intimacy between them, James and Conrad struck up some manner of friendship. During the autumn of 1898, Conrad and his family established themselves in a home that was just across the county line from James's Lamb House residence.[241]

Of Conrad's early work, James seems most likely to have been influenced by *Lord Jim*, a subject that has been dealt with at some length by previous scholars.[242] That James, even fairly late in life, was temperamentally akin to the Conrad who wrote *Lord Jim* can be seen in the Master's Preface to *The American:* "The panting pursuit of danger awaits us possibly at every step and faces us at every turn . . . ." But James goes on to say that

> there are immense and flagrant dangers that are but sordid and squalid ones, as we feel, tainting with their quality the very defiances they provoke; while there are common and covert ones, that 'look like nothing' and that can be but inwardly and occultly dealt with, which involve the sharpest hazards to life and honour and the highest instant decisions and interpredities of action.[243]

We recall that *Lord Jim* was written during 1899 and published in hardback in 1900. Henry James dated a 20,000 word synopsis of *The Ambassadors* September 1, 1900; the novel appeared serially in *The North American Review*, January-December, 1903, and was published in book form the same year. As I have indicated previously, the "germ" for the novel was supplied by Du Maurier, several years before the turn of the century, yet we cannot rule out the likelihood that James gathered a great deal of the technical complexity of *The Ambassadors* from his contacts with Conrad and the recently serialized *Lord Jim*. Among Conrad's works, James confessed to having admired this novel second only to *The Nigger of the "Narcissus."*[244]

*Lord Jim* may in turn have been influenced by the Impressionist painters. The following passage from Conrad's novel, for instance, seems to combine elements of Monet's "Terrace Near Le Havre" (1866) and the same artist's "Train in the Snow" (1875):

> And under the sinister splendour of that sky the sea, blue and profound, remained still, without a stir, without a ripple, without a wrinkle-viscuous, stagnant, dead. The *Patna*, which a slight hiss, passed over that plain, luminous and smooth, unrolled a black ribbon of smoke that vanished at once, like the phantom of a track drawn upon a lifeless sea by the phantom of a streamer.[245]

Another feature held in common by the members of "the James Group" is one perhaps first consistently demonstrated in the visual arts by Turner, who claimed that "indistinctness" was his "forte." In the Impressionist literature of James, Crane, Conrad, and Ford this attitude finds its analogue especially in their way of handling characterization. Along with Turner and his Impressionist followers— in painting and in literature—the members of "the James Group," especially, seem to have known what one of T. S. Eliot's characters expresses in *The Confidential Clerk*:

> There's always something one's ignorant of
> About anyone, however well one knows them;
> And that may be something of the greatest importance.

Absolute certainty in interpreting character is something that even the psychologist does not claim to achieve. Among creative artists, the Impressionists were probably the first to demonstrate in their work the truth of this statement. The Impressionist painters do away with character and theme, in their traditional senses, and create a picture out of a system of graded nuances and color vibrations, as in Monet's "Poplars." In a similar way, James, Crane, Conrad, and Ford (in *The Good Soldier*, in particular) work by shifting our perspective on their characters and presenting an effect that is not unlike that which Monet achieves when he "shifts" the light and color on his canvas.

The problem with Conrad's Jim, as with Crane's Henry Fleming, is to determine what we mean when we speak of bravery and heroism. Jim says that he wanted to be like "a hero in a book" of romantic adventure. But in the novel, as in all of the Impressionist works of art, *l'être vrai est l'être intérieur.* With respect to Jim, Oscar Wilde's words seem particularly apposite: "Action takes place in the sunlight, but the soul works in the dark."[246]

Conrad's best critics have recognized what Albert Guerard has formulated when he remarked that

> the . . . central preoccupation of Conrad's technique, the heart of the impressionist aim, is to invite and control [I would have omitted these last two words, were I formulating the statement] the reader's identifications  and so subject him to an intense rather than passive experience . . . . *Lord Jim* is a novel of intellectual and moral suspense, and the mystery to be solved, or conclusion to be reached, lies not in Jim but in ourselves.[247]

In line also with this attitude as it is manifested in the fiction is what Guerard refers to as Conrad's "conjectural method," a method which is useful "where the narrator does not want to report a scene at length, or cannot, and where it is desirable for the reader to do a good deal of active imagining."[248] Conrad's "conjectural method" forms an adjunct to his use of reflexivism in the novel,[249] in which he uses multiple viewpoints, intermediate narrators, and complex time shifts to move the novel back upon itself.[250]

In *Lord Jim*, the character of Marlow contributes perhaps most to the obscurity which surrounds the protagonist. Looking into the mist which surrounds Jim, Marlow observes:

> The mist of his feelings shifted between us, as if disturbed by his struggles, and in the rifts of the immaterial veil he would appear to my staring eyes distinct of form and pregnant with vague appeal like a symbolic figure in a picture.[251]

This passage is reflexive in its style and in its meaning. As throughout *Lord Jim* the syntax is torturously difficult to follow, so too here the diction is—seemingly deliberately—vague. The meaning of the passage can only be understood after several readings; and even then, the meaning perhaps eludes us. The passage is quintessentially reflexive, then, not only because it calls attention to itself by virtue of its difficulty, but also because the reader must work exceedingly hard in order to ascertain the meaning. The passage, like so many others in the novel, lacks determinateness of meaning in some respects, because of its extreme ambiguity.

From at least as far back as the time of Jane Austen, of course, plot and characterization have been rendered by means of context, but seldom has context been so relative and meaning so little dependent upon fixed signposts in the world outside the novel. The Jim that Marlow sees is *"like a symbolic figure in a picture,"* [italics mine], not a realistic fugure. The figure of Jim that appears in the novel is so far removed from reality that the reader can only imagine what Jim is really like by putting himself into his conception of Jim and of the rightness or the wrongness of Jim's actions.

This is the kind of complex effort that Henry James often demands of his reader. Very likely, in their best Impressionist work, the influence between James and Conrad goes back and forth a good deal more than most scholars have realized.252 In several important ways, then, Conrad and James are the earliest and most important Impressionist writers in English. In the foregoing discussions, I have touched upon some of the ways in which Conrad and others may have contributed to the Impressionism of Henry James. In the chapter that follows, I shall demonstrate the way in which Henry James's Impressionism operates. In so doing, I shall attempt to indicate some of ways in which James himself has drawn upon the powerful tradition of Impressionism—in literature and the visual arts—in the formulation of his aesthetic.

## Notes

[1] See Henry-Russell Hitchcock. *Architecture: Nineteenth and Twentieth Centuries.* (Baltimore: Pelican, 1971), p. 271.

[2] A good summary of James's fluctuating opinion of Ruskin can be found in Viola H. Winner. *Henry James and the Visual Arts.* (Univ. Press of Virginia, 1970), pp. 20-22. For the general influence of Ruskin upon James, see Bruce Lowery. *Marcel Proust et Henry James.* (Paris: Plon, 1964), pp. 68-70 and p. 332.

[3] James. "An English Critic of French Painting" (1868). Cited in *The Painter's Eye*, p. 33.

[4] F. W. Dupee. *Henry James.* (William Sloane, 1951), pp. 74-75.

[5] For evidence of James's early familiarity with Ruskin, see T. S. Perry's reminiscences of James in 1858, in *Letters,* Vol. 1, ed. Lubbock (1920), pp. 5-9.

James certainly knew *Modern Painters* and *Stones of Venice,* since he alluded to each of them in print on at least two separate occasions. On *Modern Painters,* see the 1868 essay that I have cited above—which originally appeared in *North American Review,* CVI (April 1868), 716-723. See especially p. 716. See also "Hours of Exercise in the Alps," *Atlantic Monthly,* XXVII (November 1871), 634-636, especially p. 634. James alluded also to *Stones of Venice* in his essay on Gautier and the theater. *North American Review,* CXVI (April 1873), see p. 319; and in "Venice," *Century Magazine,* XXV (November 1882). See especially p. 3 and p. 16.

[6] James. "Ruskin's Collection of Drawings by Turner" (1878) in *The Painter's Eye*, p. 160. These drawings were again exhibited in London in 1900.

[7] Henry James. *Portraits of Places.* (Boston: Houghton, Mifflin and Co., 1897), p. 3.

8Although it should perhaps be noted here that it is unlikely that Ruskin would have known the works of the French Impressionist Masters early enough for them to have had an influence on his writing. On this subject, see George P. Landow. *The Aesthetic and Critical Theories of John Ruskin.* (Princeton University Press, 1971), p. 20.

9John Ruskin, *The Stones of Venice*, Vol. 2, Chpt. 5, para. 30. *The Works*, ed, E. T. Cook and Alexander Wedderburn (London, 1903-1912). Hereafter, unless otherwise indicated, all Ruskin citations will refer to this edition.

10Ruskin. *Stones*, Vol. 3, Chapt. 4, para. xxi. In a passage like the following, Ruskin's attitude toward color symbolism parallels Flaubert's: "I think the first approach to viciousness in any master is commonly indicated chiefly by a prevalence of purple . . . ." *Modern Painters*, Vol. 1, Part II, Sec. II, Chapt. 2, Para. 17. Cited in Joan Evans, ed. *The Lamp of Beauty.* (Phaidon, 1959), p. 29. Compare this passage with Flaubert's statement about the genesis of *Salammbô* (see Chpt. 2). In some of his best publicized comments upon painting, Oscar Wilde followed John Ruskin's precepts. See, for example, Wilde's *"The Critic as Artist," Intentions. The Works of Oscar Wilde.* (Brainerd, 1909), p. 219.

11Ruskin. Modern Painters. Vol. 1, Pt. II, Sec. II, Chapt. 1, Para. 14. Cited in Joan Evans, ed. *The Lamp of Beauty,* p. 27. On the subject of juxtaposition, see p. 6 above, as well as n. 5, Chapter One.

12Ruskin. *Stones of Venice.* Vol. III, Chapt. IV, Para. VI.

13Ruskin. *Modern Painters*, Vol. 1, Pt. II, Sec. I, Chapt. 6, Para. 1, Cited in Evans, ed. *The Lamp of Beauty.* Phaidon, 1959, p. 22.

14On Ruskin's attitude toward camera vision, see Aaron Scharf. *Art and Photography.* (Penguin [1968], 1969), pp. 72-78.

15Ruskin. *Modern Painters.*IV. *Work*, VI, pp. 35-36. On the possibility that Ruskin, through Monet and Pissarro, influenced the Impressionists, see Camille Pissarro. *Letters to His Son Lucien.* (N. Y. Pantheon Books, 1943), p. 335 n, and p. 355 ff.

16Ruskin. *Works.* 6.32, 35-36. Cited in Landow. *Aesthetic and Critical* (p. 63). Ford Madox Ford, of course, repeated Ruskin's dictum on numerous occasions. And Ruskin's comment compares closely with Sisley's. See, for example, Sisley's undated letter in Robert Goldwater and Marco Treves, eds.

*Artists on Art* (Pantheon, 1945), where Sisley writes: "The artist's impression is the life-giving factor, and only this impression can free that of the spectator." (p. 309).

17Ruskin. *Stones of Venice.* Vol. 1, Chapt. 30, para. 5.

The likelihood is of course good that Ruskin's influence carried forth strongly into the twentieth century in the personage of Marcel Proust. Proust (1871-1922) was, as Bruce Lowery has shown, under considerable literary debt to Henry James. But the French author was also greatly indebted to Ruskin, as several scholars have already ably demonstrated. See, for instance, Jean Autret. *L'influence de Ruskin sur la vie, les idées et l'œuvre de Marcel Proust* . . . . Geneva: Droz (2nd ed.), 1961; Philip Kolb. "Proust et Ruskin: Nouvelles Perspectives" [1959] in *Cahiers de L'Association Internationale Des Etudes Françaises.* Paris, 1960. pp. 259-273, also pp. 299-300; and the passages on Proust's indebtedness to Ruskin in George Painter. *Marcel Proust.* 2 Vols. London, 1959.

The influence of the Impressionist painters on Proust is already very well documented. The reader interested in this subject is referred to the items on Proust in the bibliography at the end of the book.

18Ruskin. *Modern Painters.* Vol. 1, Pt. 2, Sec. 1, Chapt. 1, para. 7, cited in Evans, p. 21.

19See, for example, *Sesame and Lilies* (1865). (N. Y.: Ginn and Co., 1927).

20Ruskin. *Fors Clavigera.* July 2, 1877, cited in Whistler. "Whistler v. Ruskin" (1878), *The Gentle Art of Making Enemies.* (N. Y.: Putman's, 1927), p. 1. This volume is dedicated thus: To/the rare Few, who, early in Life/have rid themselves of the Friendship of the Many, these pathetic/Papers are inscribed.

21Henry James. "On Whistler and Ruskin." *The Painter's Eye,* p. 173. James has written of Whistler's prose, as well as his painting, in "On Art-Criticism and Whistler," (1879), in *The Painter's Eye,* pp. 175-177. By 1897, James came to praise Whistler highly. See *Letters,* Vol. 1, ed. Lubbock. 1920, p. 340. See also the intelligent commentary on this letter in Winner. *Henry James and the Visual Arts,* p. 48.

On the trial itself, see Francis L. Fennell. "The Verdict In Whistler v. Ruskin," *Victorian Newsletter*/40 (Fall 1971), 17-21.

22George Saintsbury. *A History of English Prose Rhythm* [1912]. (London: Macmillan, 1922), p. 420.

23In typical fashion, however, James goes on to ameliorate this judgment by considering the other side of Ruskin's reputation. See *The Painter's Eye*, pp. 174-75.

23aIn "Impressionism Limited," Miss Hay observes that Pater's Impressionism is "a necessary supplement to the mainstream of impressionism in France" (p. 60).

24James. Letter to Gosse (1894). *Letters*, Vol. 1. ed. Lubbock. (1920), p. 222.

25Pater. *Studies in the History of the Renaissance.* (London: Macmillan, 1873), p. 205. James, incidentally, had read Pater's volume and had commented upon it shortly after its appearance. See "Old Italian Art," *The Independent* (June 18, 1874), 2-3, rpt. *Transatlantic Sketches.* (Boston: James R. Osgood and Co., 1875), p. 299. On May 31, 1873, James wrote to his brother William: "I saw Pater's *Studies* just after getting your letter, in the English bookseller's window: and was inflamed to think of buying it and trying a notice. But I see it treats of several things I know nothing about." *Henry James: Letters*, Vol.1, 1843-1875, ed. Edel. (The Belknap Press of Harvard University Press, 1974), p. 391. In the same volume of letters, we learn, however, that James subsequently *did* review Pater's *Studies.* See *Henry James: Letters.* Vol 1, ed. Edel. 1974 (pp. 411-412). In a corollary to the letter to William of May 31, 1873, James, almost six months later, wrote to his parents that he had sent T. S. Perry two reviews: Howells' *Poems* and Pater's *Studies* (p. 411). Edel's note tells us that "there is no record of any publication of James's review of Pater's studies, and no manuscript has been found" (p. 412).

26Pater. *Plato and Platonism: A Series of Lectures* (1893) (London: Macmillan, 1901), pp. 5-6.

27Pater. *The Renaissance. Works* (Library edition, 1910), p. viii.

28Pater. *Studies in the History of the Renaissance.* (London: Macmillan, 1873), p. 40. For this reason, perhaps, we can see why A. E. once cynically observed that much of twentieth century literature has been "infected" by "Pater's relative."

29Ruskin. *Modern Painters. Works,* III, p. 106.

30Ruskin. *Modern Painters. Works,* VI, 367-368. Italics mine. As Monroe Beardsley has carefully pointed out, the Ruskin description of St. Mark's emphasizes the importance of describing the experience of the cathedral, as distinct from the cathedral, but this is not relativism in itself.

31To my knowledge James did not refer to Diderot in his published criticism, but since he read so voraciously, we cannot overlook the likelihood that James read the French author.

32James. "Gustave Flaubert" (1893). *Essays in London and Elsewhere.* (London: James R. Osgood, McIlvaine and Co., 1893), p. 131. In "Art Criticism As a Prose Genre" (in *The Art of Victorian Prose,* eds. George Levine and William Madden (Oxford University Press, 1968), G. Robert Stange has credited the art criticism of Ruskin and Pater with opening the way for some of the prose techniques of Modernist fiction. The aforementioned quotations alone should serve to indicate on what bases Stange has made his judgment.

James's observation will assume larger meanings when we examine it in the context of his fiction.

33Pater. Preface to *Renaissance* (N. Y.:Macmillan, 1873), pp. viii-ix.

34Wilde. "The Critic As Artist." *Intentions. Works.* (Brainerd, 1909) p. 160. In the same essay, Wilde says much the same thing on pp. 155-159; and p. 161. In "Pen, Pencil, and Poison," in *Intentions. Works.* Brainerd, 1909, he makes a similar comment about Thomas Griffiths Wainewright (see p. 81). Here Wilde loops Ruskin into his example.

35Pater. *The Renaissance. Works.* (London, 1910), pp. 234-236. Subsequent quotations from *The Renaissance* will cite this volume of the 1910 edition.

The "Conclusion" to *The Renaissance* appeared in four separate versions over a twenty-five year period. The first version appeared not in *The Renaissance,* but in the form of a conclusion to an unsigned review of a book of poems by William Morris. See *Westminster Review* (October 1868), 309-312. Pater neither alluded to this unsigned peice in his subsequent writing, nor acknowledged that he was its author. See Gerald Monsman and Samuel Wright. "Walter Pater: Style and Text," *South Atlantic Quarterly.* 71 (Winter 1972), 106-123.

On the differences between the 1868 "Conclusion" and the 1873 version, see Monsman and Wright, pp. 114-116; between the editions of 1888 and 1893 (the last to be published during Pater's lifetime), see p. 122. I cite from the 1873 edition, however, since this is the version that James certainly read and the one that seems most likely to have influenced him.

36James letter to W. D. Howells in *Henry James: Letters,* p. 397. In typical fashion, James lived to carry out his boast.

37Pater. *Renaissance,* p. 236.

38Pater. *Renaissance,* pp. 238-239.

39Pater. *Renaissance.*

40See "Florentine Notes", *The Independent (May 21, 1874),* 1-2. Moreover, in order to represent fruitful artistic production, James and Pater often employed the metaphor of growth. See, for instance, *Renaissance,* p. 196 and p. 197; for James see, for instance, Preface to the *Portrait of a Lady. The Art of the Novel,* p. 45.

41Pater did not seemingly accord with James's view of the typical English imagination. In "Taine's Notes on England" James remarked that "The French possess that lively aesthetic conscience which, on the whole, is such a simplifier . . . but in English imaginations it is the moral leaven that works most strongly." *Nation,* XIV (January 25, 1874), p. 60.

*Marius* was originally published in two volumes by Macmillan in 1885. But Pater did his work on the novel from 1881-1884. He began research for the novel in the Spring of 1881, very close to the appearance of *The Portrait of a Lady.* See Lawrence Evans' bibliographical essay on Pater in David De Laura, ed. *Victorian Prose.* MLA, 1973, p. 327.

42Maurice Beebe. *Ivory,* p. 151. My discussion of *Marius the Epicurean* is heavily indebted to Beebe. *Ivory Towers,* pp. 151 ff.

43Pater. *Marius the Epicurean* (1885). (The Modern Library, 1921), p. 125.

44Pater. *Marius the Epicurean,* 4th ed. (London: Macmillan, 1898, 1909 rpt., Vol. 1), p. 133.

45Pater. *Marius*. (Modern Library edition). pp. 219-220; and p. 370.

46Pater. *Marius*, p. 378.

47Here, however, it deserves to be said that Pater may have been influenced to some extent by Wordsworth and Arnold. In "Culture and Anarchy" (1867-1868) Matthew Arnold dealt with the Ovidian notion that "est deus in nobis." Arnold argued along similar lines when he judged that "human perfection is an internal condition . . . ." *Selected Poetry and Prose*. (New York: Holt, Rinehart and Winston [1953] , 1964) p. 197.

In Pater's best criticism and fiction, one finds "moments" that are analogous to those that are found in Wordsworth's "Preludes" when he claims to have experienced, though infrequently, his "spots of time." In *Hebrew and Hellene in Victorian England* (University of Texas Press, 1969), David De Laura deals with the Arnoldian echoes in Pater. See also De Laura's "The Wordsworth of Pater and Arnold: 'The Supreme Artistic View of Life,' " *Studies in English Literature, 1500-1900*, VI (Autumn 1966), 651-667.

48Hereafter I shall cite the edition of *Imaginary Portraits* that was published by Macmillan in 1887. These stories originally appeared in *Macmillan's Magazine* from 1885 to 1887. Although James does not refer to either "Sebastian van Storck" or "A Prince of Court Painters" in his published criticism, this does not rule out the likelihood of his having read them. James's only literary contribution to *Macmillan's Magazine* was in December, 1887—not so many months after the appearance in the same periodical of Pater's stories. An experienced journal contributor such as James would more than likely have at least checked the previous few volumes of the *Magazine* before sending in his piece for publication. James's essay was a perceptive piece on "The Life of Emerson."

In "The Critic as Artist," Wilde observed that Pater's *Imaginary Portraits* present "under the guise of fiction, some fine and exquisite piece of criticism . . . " (p. 205), but the *Imaginary Portraits* do much more than that.

Pater used the term Imaginary Portraits to refer not only to the sketches that are collected in the volume of that name, but also to works such as *Marius* and *Gaston de Latour*. See Pater's letter to Violet Paget (Vernon Lee), 22 July, 1883 in *Letters of Walter Pater*, ed. Lawrence Evans. (London: Macmillan, 1970), pp. 51-52.

49Although Pater first takes up this fictional technique in "The Prince of Court Painters," he continued it through *Gaston de Latour* (1896) where, in

Chapter 3 (on "Modernity") he gives an impression of the verse of Ronsard as it appeared to a young Bishop's page and clerk-in-order of the sixteenth century.

50Pater. *Imaginary*, pp. 14-15. The real Antoine Watteau died at the age of 37, in 1721. In 1702 he went to Paris to seek his fortune.

René Huyghe has described Watteau's character as a "mixture of youth and premature weariness." *Watteau* (1968), trans. Barbara Bray. Braziller, 1970, p. 52. If Huyghe's description is accurate, then Watteau's attraction to Pater seems understandable. James, like the Goncourts, was interested in Watteau, and was moved to write about the French genre painter on at least two occasions. See, especially, "The Bethnal Green Museum," *Atlantic Monthly*, XXX (January 1873), p. 74.

51Pater. *Imaginary*, p. 25.

52Pater. *Imaginary*, p. 27.

53Pater. *Imaginary*, p. 33

54On the classical background of the Advice to a Painter tradition in the Anacreontic odes, see Mary T. Osborne. "Advice to a Painter Poems, 1665-1688: with some account of earlier and later Poems of this Type." Univ. of Texas at Austin dissertation, 1947, pp. 9-13. See also Osborne. *Advice-to-a-Painter Poems, 1633-1856: An Annotated Finding List,* with Introduction by Mary T. Osborne. (The University of Texas Press, 1949), Addenda IR-3R.

55Osborne. "Introduction." *Finding List*, p. 9.

56Pater. "Sebastian van Storck, *Imaginary*, p. 81. It should be noted, perhaps, that James also knew the winter scenes done by Isaac Van Ostade (1621-1649), a Dutch landscapist (whose brother Adrian likewise painted genre scenes). James referred to Isaac Van Ostade in at least five separate essays from as early as June 1872 to February 1879—a period in which Dutch landscapists were much exhibited in London and New York.

57Wilde. *The Letters*, ed. Rupert Hart-Davis (New York: Harcourt, Brace, 1962), p. 471.

58Wilde cited in James Nelson. *The Early Nineties*, p. 243.

59James. *Selected Letters*, ed. Edel (New York: 1955), p. 147.

For Wilde's opinion of James, see "The Decay of Lying," *Intentions. The Works of Oscar Wilde* (New York: Brainerd, 1909), pp. 15-16.

[60]Leon Edel. *Henry James: The Treacherous Years.* (Philadelphia: Lippincott, 1969), p. 43.

[61]Wilde. "The Critic as artist," *Intentions. Works,* p. 201.

[62]Oscar Wilde. "The Critic as ARtist," in *The Complete Writings of Oscar Wilde,* Vol. 7 *Intentions* (New York: Brainerd, 1909), p. 200.

[63]Wilde. "Pen, Pencil, and Poison: A Study in Green," *Intentions. Works,* p. 77.

[64]Wilde. "The Decay of Lying," in *The Writings of Oscar Wilde. Intentions. Works,* p. 61.

[65]Wilde. "The Decay of Lying," *Intentions. Works,* p. 38.

[66]This "Art"—"Life" controversy can be traced at least as far back as Book 10 of Plato's *Republic.* For a summary of the issue in ancient Greek aesthetics, see J. J. Pollitt. *The Ancient View of Greek Art.* (Yale University Press, 1974) p. 56.

[67]On Moore's debt to Pater—especially *Marius*—see George Moore. *Avowals* (New York: Boni and Liveright, 1919), p. 92 and p. 215.

[68]Cf. Anatole France's notion of criticism—"the adventures of a sensitive soul among masterpieces." *Impressions and Opinions* seems to have been one of Moore's favorite books—see his Preface to the 2nd edition (1913)—and was a very popular one that did much to enhance his reputation in England and America.

[69]Here, however, we must keep in mind that the glimpses that Moore provides are "impressions" only, as he himself admitted. In *Impressions and Opinions,* for instance, he at one point remarked of *Confessions of a Young Man:* "Don't you see, my dear friend, that book is not my real opinion about life and things, but rather an attempt to reduce to words the fugitive imaginings of my mind, its intimate workings, its shifting colours?" Moore, cited in Derek Stanford, ed. *Critics of the Nineties,* pp. 181-2. In this and in much else, the reminiscences of "Dear audacious Moore" (Pater's words for him) are not unlike those of Ford Madox Ford.

[70]Virginia Woolf, incidentally, has written a revealing book on Fry. (*Roger Fry: A Biography.* N. Y.: Harcourt, Brace and Co., 1940).

[71]Moore refers to the Impressionists throughout *Hail and Farewell.* But see especially pp. 268-282 of the Appleton edition of 1925. In *Confessions of a Young Man* and *Hail and Farewell,* he is a great autobiographer, mentionable even with St. Augustine—although the two authors seemingly differed *toto caelo!* In the Preface to his *Confessions* George Moore observed: "St. Augustine . . . wrote the story of a God-tortured soul; would it not be interesting to write the story of an art-tortured soul?"

[72]Cited by Gilbert Phelps. *The Russian Novel in English Fiction* (London: Hutchinson's University Library, 1956), p. 109.

[73]Cited by Janet Egleson Dunleavy. *George Moore: the Artist's Vision, the Storyteller's Art.* (Bucknell University Press, 1973), p. 119.

[74]On George Moore's American reputation, see Grant Knight. *The Critical Period in American Literature* (University of North Carolina Press, 1951), p. 98. Moore has furthermore been given credit for having first brought Mallarmé to American attention with the publication, on both sides of the Atlantic, of *Impressions and Opinions.* On this book's initial exposure of Mallarmé to America, see J. Patnode. *English and American Literary Relations in the 1880's: The Cosmopolitan Impressionists.* University of Minnesota Dissertation, 1968, p. 196. Mallarmé, we recall, was a good friend of Degas. And so also was Moore, who used many of the painter's pictures in scenes from his novels. Theodore Reff has identified these inter-art borrowings in his article entitled, "Degas and the Literature of His Time," in *Symposium on Literature and Painting in the Nineteenth Century,* ed. Ulrich Finke (Manchester University Press, 1972). See Appendix II and p. 231. On Mallarmé's friendships with the Impressionists, see especially Wallace Fowlie. "Mallarmé and the Painters of His Age," *Southern Review,* (1966), pp. 542-558.

Also perhaps worth noting here is that one leading American literary historian has claimed for Moore "the first considerable reading public that Naturalism had" in America. Oscar Cargill. *Intellectual America: Ideas on the March.* (New York: Macmillan, 1941), p. 82. But on this subject Cargill was wrong, for he overlooked the strong influence of Flaubert and his circle upon America during the 1880's. In *The Victorian Conscience,* (New York: Twayne, 1952), Clarence Decker reported that in the late 1880's " . . . altogether there were nine English publications of Flaubert's works, five translations of the novels of the Goncourts, thirty-five translations of Daudet, twelve of Maupassant [and] forty-five of Zola. . ." p. 32. During the very cosmpolitan period of the '80's, when *important* news travelled at least as rapidly as it does today (and was perhaps more readily absorbed by the members of the literary public), that many of these English editions did not find their way hastily into American Libraries is very unlikely.

75See, for instance, Mary Neale, *Flaubert en Angleterre.* (Bordeaux: Sobodi, 1966), Appendix III, pp. 119-126; and G. Paul Collet. *George Moore et la France* (Geneva: Librairie Droz, 1957). Collet also examines (*passim*) Moore's borrowings from the other members of the Flaubert circle.

76See, for example, Moore's letters to Zola in Auriant. "Un Disciple anglais d'Emile Zola." George Moore, *Mercure de France,* CCXCVII (May 1940), pp. 312-323.

77Zola cited in Jeffares. *George Moore.* (London: British Writers and Their Work, 1965), p. 18.

78See George Moore. *Avowals* (London: Heinemann, 1936), pp. 174-75. In all of his published criticism James, incidentally, mentions Geroge Moore only once. See *The Middle Years. Autobiography* (N. Y.: Criterion, 1956), p. 561.

79George Moore. *A Mummer's Wife,* (N. Y.: Brentano's 1925), p. 2.

80George Moore. *A Mummer's Wife,* pp. 68-69.

81Moore. *A Mummer's Wife,* p. 39.

82See, for example, *The Young George Du Maurier: A Selection of His letters, 1860-67,* ed. Daphne Du Maurier (New York: Doubleday, 1952), *passim.* This volume indicates the frequency with which George Du Maurier and Whistler corresponded and provides some important glimpses of Du Maurier's relationship with Whistler, who was his frequent correspondent and with whom he briefly shared a flat during Du Maurier's early years.

83Bersot cited in André Morize. *Problems and Methods of Literary History: With Special Reference to Modern French Literature.* (Boston: Ginn and Co., 1922).

84On the popularity of *Trilby* on both sides of the Atlantic, see Holbrook Jackson. *The Eighteen Nineties: A Review of Art and Ideas at the Close of the Nineteenth Century.* (New York: Capricorn Books, 1966) p. 39 and

Thomas Beer, who in an essay on American culture in the '90's, discussed the Trilby craze. See Beer. *The Mauve Decade* (N. Y.: A. Knopf, 1926).

85 James and Du Maurier cited from *Henry James: Notebooks,* 1947, p. 98.

86 It deserves mention, however, that James's direct influence upon *Trilby* may otherwise not have been very strong. See *Notebooks,* eds. Matthiessen and Murdock. (New York: Braziller, 1955), p. 98, where the editors qualify the probable extent of the direct influence.

87 Du Maurier. *Trilby: A Novel* (1894). (New York: Harper and Bros., 1895), p. 269.   That James read *Trilby* with great care is more than mere surmis, since he referred to the novel in his criticism on at least four separate occasions from 1894 to 1898. James first refers in print to *Trilby* in *Harper's Weekly,* XXXVIII (April 14, 1894), less than three months after the novel appeared in serialized format in *Harper's Monthly.*

88 Beebe. "Paris," unpublished paper, pp. 8-10.

89 See, for example, Derek Stanford. "Arthur Symons as Literary Critic (1865-1945)" which first appeared in its entirety in *Queens Quarterly.*

90 This article appeared in *Harper's Monthly,* LXXXVII (November 1893), pp. 858-867. Symons's article appeared at a time when Henry James, Hamlin Garland, Stephen Crane, and Joseph Conrad, among the major English speaking Impressionist authors, had ready access to it.

91 Tom Gibbons. *Rooms in the Darwin Hotel.* (University of Western Australia Press, 1973), p. 75. Gibbons goes on to show, however, that "the basic concerns of the essay on the Decadent Movement are already evident in Symon's less well-known, 'Note on Browning and Meredith' of 1885", p. 75.

92 Symons. "Decadence," p. 859. Symons goes on to say that the Impressionists make an "attempt to give sensation, to flash the impressionism of the moment, to preserve the very heat and motion of life." (p. 860).

93 Symons. "Impressionistic Writing," rpt. *Dramatis Personae.* (New York: Bobbs-Merrill, 1923), p. 343.

94 Symons. *The Symbolist Movement in Literature.* (London: Heinemann, 1899), p. 106. One of the first cases of the term "Impressionist" to describe a style of writing in English was in the Review of Swinburne's *Songs and Ballads* in *Scribner's,* October, 1880.

95 See Symons. *"Impressions and Opinions* by George Moore," *The Academy,* XXXIX, No. 985 n.s. (21 March, 1891), p. 294.

96 Symons. *Dante Gabriel Rossetti: L'Art et le Beau.* (Paris: Quatrième année, II, n.d.), p. 10. In Symons's observation there may have been more than a little truth, since the English invention of tin paint tubes in the early 1840's made true outdoor painting possible for the first time. In the development of *plein-air* technique, the importance of this invention cannot be too much emphasized.

97 While James almost certainly knew Symons's essays, the Master's sole reference to Symons in print was his review of Symons's translations of D'Annunzio's *Gioconda and Francesca da Rimini* to which James afforded modest praise. See "Gabriele D'Annunzio," *Quarterly Review,* CXCIX (April 1904), 388.

98 Everett Carter. *Howells and the Age of Realism* (Philadelphia: Lippincott, 1954), see especially pp. 249-263.

99 Henry James. "Italian Journeys," *North American Review,* CVI (January 1868). 336-339.

100 William Dean Howells. "Henry James." *My Literary Passions* (1895), cited in Albert Mordell, comp. and ed. *Discovery of a Genius: William Dean Howells and Henry James,* w. Introduction by Sylvia Bowman. (New York: Twayne, 1961), p. 169.

101 Henry James. Cited in Mordell. *Discovery,* pp. 7-8.

102 Clara Kirk. *W. D. Howells and Art in His Time.* (Rutgers University Press, 1965), p. xvii.

103 W. D. Howells cited in Everett Carter. *Howells and the Age of Realism* [1954] rpt. Hamden, Conn.: Archon Books, 1966. p. 13. Synechdoche is used to good advantage also by Zola and Moore.

104 W. D. Howells. "A Counterfeit Presentment," *Atlantic,* XL (August 1877), p. 148.

105 Albert Bierstadt (1830-1902) was an American landscape painter whose paintings were fairly well known during the '70's. See, for instance, Henry James. "On Some Pictures Lately Exhibited," *The Galaxy,* XX (July 1875),

89-97, p. 96, in particular; and James's essay on The London Exhibitions, *The Nation,* XXVI (June 6, 1878), 371-372.

106Howells. "The Editor's Study," *Harper's Monthly* (October 1887), p. 802.

107Howells's sketches in *Cosmopolitan* appeared in Vol. XVI (January, February, March 1894), pp. 259-277, 415-425, 558-569. For much of the foregoing discussion on Howells and James I am indebted to Clara Kirk's previously cited volume and to Kenneth E. Bidle. *Impressionism in American Literature to the Year 1900.* Northern Illinois University Dissertation, 1969.

108See, for example, Leon Edel. *Henry James: The Conquest of London. (Lippincott, 1962), pp.* 135-151, and pp. 418-420.

109See Hocks. *Henry James and Pragmatistic Thought: A Study in the Relationship Between the Philosophy of William James and the Literary Art of Henry James. (University of North* Carolina Press, 1974). See especially Chapter 2, "The Brothers: On Each Other's Work." This chapter is a good summary evaluation of the general respect that William and Henry had for each other's writing. Hocks also points to a number of ways in which key passages in William's writings "characterize our reading experience of Henry's later manner" (p. 87).

110On William's presence see, for example, Bertrand Russell. *Unpopular Essays.* (New York: Simon and Schuster, 1950), p. 167.

111Which is not to say that William did not, on occasion, find fault with Henry's work. See, for instance, his 1905 letter concerning his younger brother's "method of narration by interminable elaboration of suggestive reference." Cited in Ralph Barton Perry. *The Thought and Character of William James.* (Boston: Little, Brown, 1935), p. 424. See also William's letter to Henry, dated May 4, 1907, in *The Letters of William James,* ed. [William's son] Henry James. (Boston: Atlantic Monthly Press, 1920), Vol. 2, p. 278.

112See, for example, *The Letters of William James,* Vol. 1, ed. Henry James, p. 106.

113See, for example, Royal Cortissoz. *John La Farge,* p. 117.

114William James. *The Principles of Psychology,* 2 Vols. (New York: Henry Holt, 1890), Vol. 2, p. 370.

115William James. *Principles of Psychology,* Vol. 2, p. 103.

116Henry James. *The House of Fiction,* ed. L. Edel. (London: Rupert Hart-Davis, 1957), p. 33.

117William cited in Ralph Barton Perry. *The Thought and Character of William James.* (1935), Vol. 2, p. 256.

118William James. *Principles.* Vol. 1, p. 294. While this question of one man's having multiple existences was among contemporary psychologists perhaps most lucidly introduced by William James, the idea was also notably grappled with by Henri Bergson. Neither William nor Bergson were the first to come to grips with the question, of course. Goethe's *Faust* observed that not two souls, but many souls or selves took root in our person. Before Goethe (1749-1832), Montaigne interestingly entertained the question. See Chapter 25 of the *Essais.* The panoptic James, of course, knew Goethe's work, as well as Montaigne's; and he wrote about these authors on several occasions. James's first published references to *Faust* appeared as early as 1873. See "Dumas and Goethe," *The Nation,* XVII (October 30, 1873), 292-294. James referred to Montaigne (1533-1592) in one of his earliest essays, "The Letters of Eugénie De Guérin," *The Nation,* III (September 13, 1866), 206-207. See p. 206.

119William James. *The Will to Believe, and Other Essays in Popular Philosophy* [1897]. (New York: Dover, 1956). p. 59.

120William James. "On a Certain Blindness in Human Beings," *Talks to Teachers on Psychology: and to Students on Some of Life's Ideals* (New York: Henry Holt and Co., 1912), rpt. *The Writings of William James,* ed. John J. McDermott. (New York: The Modern Library, 1968), p. 645.

121Jules Laforgue. "Impressionism: The Eye and the Poet" (1883), trans. William Jay Smith. *Art News* (May 1956), 44.

122To my knowledge, Henry James has nowhere commented in print upon Laforgue's work.

123Saltus. "Morality in Fiction." *Love and Love* (1890). Cited in Jack Patnode. Dissertation, p. 36 and p. 35.

124See Stuart Merrill. "Thirty Years of Paris," The New York *Times* (February 26, 1888), p. 10.

125I do not strictly consider James under the rubric "American author."

[126]See James B. Stronks. "A Realist Experiments with Impressionism: Hamlin Garland's 'Chicago Studies.' " *American Literature,* XXXVI (March, 1964), 38-52.

[127]See, for instance, the letter cited by E. F. Harkins in *Little Pilgrimages Among the Men Who Have Written Famous Books.* (Boston: Houghton-Mifflin, 1902), p. 259.

[128]See, for example, Garland. "Productive Conditions of American Literature," *The Forum,* XVII (August 1894), 690.

[129]See Donald Pizer. *Hamlin Garland's Early Work and Career.* (University of California Press, 1960), p. 125. In this volume, Pizer also does a commendable job of tracing many of Garland's ideas to the work of the chief representative of the emotionalist aesthetic, Eugène Véron, and to the Spanish novelist, Valdés.

[130]In "Productive Conditions," for instance, Garland stated that James preferred truth to popularity. See also Bruce R. McElderry, Jr., "Hamlin Garland and Henry James." *American Literature,* XXIII (January 1952), 433-446.

[131]This essay was first collected in the *Crumbling Idols* volume of 1894.

[132]Rewald. *The History of Impressionism.* 1946. ed., p. 447.

[133]Garland. *Crumbling Idols: Twelve Essays on Art Dealing Chiefly with Literature, Painting and the Drama,* ed. Jane Johnson. (The Belknap Press of Harvard University Press, 1960).

[134]Hamlin Garland. *Main-Travelled Roads.* (New York and London: New Edition, 1899), pp. 74-75 and pp. 90-91. In the same volume, see also p. 134; p. 172; and p. 322 for similar Impressionist word paintings.

[135]Ken E. Bidle. *Impressionism in American Literature to the Year 1900.* Northern Illinois University Dissertation, 1969, p. 220 and p. 213.

[136]This piece appeared in Vol. 8, pp. xi-xii.

[137]Robert W. Stallman. *Stephen Crane: A Critical Bibliography.* (Iowa State University Press, 1972), p. 239.

[138]See, for instance, Howells's letter to Crane, dated April 8, 1893. Cited in *Stephen Crane: Letters,* ed. Stallman and Lilian Gilkes (N. Y. U. Press, 1960), p. 18.

139On Garland's various asseverations of their friendship, see the following: Corwin K. Linson. *My Stephen Crane,* ed. Edwin H. Cady. (Syracuse University Press, 1958); Donald Pizer. "The Garland-Crane Relationship," *Huntington Library Quarterly,* XXIV (November 1960), 75-82; rpt. in Pizer's *Realism and Naturalism in Nineteenth Century American Literature.* (Southern Illinois University Press, 1966); Robert Mane. "Une recontre littéraire: Hamlin Garland et Stephen Crane," *Etudes Anglaises,* 17 (January-March, 1964), 30-46; and Stanley Wertheim "The Saga of March 23: Garland, Gilder, and Crane." *Stephen Crane Newsletter* (Winter, 1968), 1-3.

140See, for instance, Pizer. "Romantic Individualism in Garland, Norris, and Crane," *Arizona Quarterly.* X (Winter 1958), 463-475; rpt. Pizer. *Realism and Naturalism;* and Stanley Wertheim. "Crane and Garland: The Education of an Impressionist," *North Dakota Quarterly.* 35 (Winter, 1967), 23-28.

141Stephen Crane. *Letters,* ed. Stallman and L. Gilkes. p. 56. Fredson Bowers has recently discovered that Garland read *The Red Badge* in manuscript and made handwritten suggestions for Crane's corrections. See *The Red Badge of Courage: An Episode of the American Civil War,* ed. Fredson Bowers. Vol. II of the Virginia edition of *The Works of Stephen Crane.* (The University Press of Virginia, 1975). To my knowledge James alludes to Garland only once in print. See "American Letter." *Literature,* II (April 9, 1898), 422-423; rpt. *The American Essays* (N. Y.: Vintage Books, 1956), pp. 205-206.

142For speculations on these possibilities, see Joseph J. Kwiat. "Stephen Crane and Painting," *Arizona Quarterly,* 4 (Winter 1952), 331-338.

143Corwin Linson. *My Stephen Crane,* ed. Edwin H. Cady. (Syracuse University Press, 1958). Although this volume was written during the 1920's, it was not published until 1958.

144See Linson. *My Stephen Crane,* pp. 46-47.

145It probably deserves to be pointed out here also that Impressionist paintings were beginning to be reproduced in magazines, but color photography was not sufficiently well-developed by the early 1890's to have allowed the inclusion of color reproductions in the magazines that Crane and Garland would have known.

146Herbert. P. Williams. "Mr. Crane as a Literary Artist," *The Intellectual American,* XX (July 18, 1896), 126.

147The foregoing discussion of Impressionism in Crane owes no small debt to Benjamin Giorgio. *Stephen Crane: American Impressionist.* University of Wisconsin Dissertation, 1969.

148Edel. *Henry James:* The Master, p. 63.

149Edel. *Henry James:* The Master, p. 66.

150See Thomas Beer. *Stephen Crane: Portrait of an American Man of Letters.* (New York: Alfred A. Knopf, 1923), p. 166 and p. 157.

151Stephen Crane. "Concerning the 'English Academy,' " *The Bookman* VII (1898), p. 23. Small wonder that Crane thus praised *Maisie,* for this novel was like so many of the fictional performances of James and Crane in its experimentation with point of view and avoidance of fully detailed plots and completely delineated characters.

152Stephen Crane. Letter to His Brother. 1897. *Stephen Crane: Letters,* p. 146.

153Even here, however, the undercurrent of competition that existed between the two was quite strong.

154On Crane's financial difficulties during this period, see J. C. Levenson. *Tales of Whilomville* (University Press of Virginia, 1969), pp. xxv-xxviii.

155Crane. "Concerning the 'English Academy,' " *Bookman* (1898), p. 23.

156Stephen Crane. Letter to Conrad. *Letters,* ed. Stallman, p. 150.

157Stephen Crane. Letter to Conrad. *Letters,* ed. Stallman, p. 151.

158Conrad. Letter to Crane. *Letters of Stephen Crane,* p. 154.

R. W. Stallman says that "Conrad in writing *The Nigger* (finished by February 19, 1897) was influenced by *Red Badge,* although Conrad denied any such influence." Stallman. *Stephen Crane: Bibliography.* (Iowa State University Press, 1973), p. 295. This suggestion was first made by a contemporary reviewer, as Stallman acknowledges. (See *Stephen Crane: Letters,* 1960, p. 157, no. 139). Stallman further develops this suggestion in the "Introduction" to *The Red Badge of Courage* in his *Stephen Crane: An Omnibus.* (New York: Knopf, 1952), pp. 175-225. See especially pp. 200-1 where Stallman compares *The Red Badge* to *The Nigger of the "Narcissus"* and *Lord Jim.*

159H. G. Wells. Letter in *Stephen Crane: Letters,* ed. R. W. Stallman and Lilian Gilkes, p. 310.

160R. G. Vosbrugh. "The Darkest Hour in the Life of Stephen Crane," *The Book-Lover,* II (Summer, 1901), p. 338.

161Edward Garnett. "Mr. Stephen Crane: An Appreciation," *Academy,* 55 (December 17, 1898), 483-484.

162Stallman. "The Red Badge of Courage," in *The Houses that James Built.* (Michigan State University Press, 1961), p. 83.

163Jay Martin. *Harvests of Change.* (Englewood Cliffs, N. J.: Prentice-Hall, 1967). See Crane section, *passim.*

164To my mind, the best study of Crane's Impressionist technique is that done by Rodney O. Rogers. "Stephen Crane and Impressionism," *Nineteenth Century Fiction,* 24 (December 1969), 292-304. While Rogers' definition of Impressionism seems to me to be likewise too broad, he does do an adequate job of relating Crane's color sense to that of the Impressionists. Other treatments of Crane and Impressionism are too broad: for example, Orm Overland. "The Impressionism of Stephen Crane: A Study in Style and Technique." *Americana Norwegica,* ed. Sigmund Skaard and Henry H. Wasser (University of Pennsylvania Press, 1966), Vol. 1, pp. 239-285; Joseph J. Kwiat. "Stephen Crane and Painting," *Arizona Quarterly,* 4 (Winter 1952), 331-338, or too narrow: for example, Robert L. Hough. "Crane and Goethe: A Forgotten Relationship," *Nineteenth Century Fiction,* XVII (September 1962), 135-148.

165Zola. *Masterpiece,* trans. Walton, (1957), p. 15.

166See Benjamin D. Giorgio. *Stephen Crane.* Dissertation, pp. 250-252.

167Cecilia Waern. "Some Notes on French Impressionism" *Atlantic Monthly,* LXIX (1892), p. 539.

168Stephen Crane. Letter to Curtis Brown, Dec. 31, 1896 [for 1895]. *Letters of Stephen Crane,* eds. Stallman and Gilkes, p. 87.

169*Stephen Crane: Letters,* eds. Stallman and Gilkes. p. 83.

170See *Stephen Crane: Letters,* eds. Stallman and Gilkes. p. 85.

171Beer's biography may not be the most authoritative source on Crane. Although *Stpehen Crane: A Study in American Letters* (New York: Alfred A. Knopf, 1923), appears to catch the essence of Crane's temperament, Beer's biography is undocumented, save for one surviving piece of evidence.

172See, for example, *Bookman* (London) 12, (June 1897): "There is Trilby in the tale—this time Florinda, with fine arms instead of feet; and there are a troop of Trilby—that is, Florinda admirers," p. 72.

173Stephen Crane. *The Third Violet* in *The Work of Stephen Crane,* ed. Wilson Follett. Vol. 3 (New York: Alfred A. Knopf [1897], 1926). Revised, Russell and Russell, 1963, p. 145.

174Stephen Crane. *The Third Violet,* p. 133.

175Stephen Crane. *The Third Violet,* p. 151.

176Stephen Crane. *The Third Violet,* p. 173.

177Stephen Crane. Letter to John N. Hilliard. *Letters,* p. 108.

178Stephen Crane. "War Memories," *Tales of War* (University Press of Virginia, 1970), p. xxx.

179See Letter from Crane to Pinker of August 4, 1899, in *Stephen Crane: Letters,* p. 223.

180Stephen Crane. "War Memories," in *Wounds in the Rain. Tales of War.* p. 254.

181Stephen Crane. "War Memories," p. 254.

182Stephen Crane. "The Little Regiment," *Tales of War.* p. 1.

183It is worth pointing out, I think, that Crane, like James, uses a number of expressionist and surrealist word paintings. Crane's affinities with expressionism have not been lost on the critics. See, for example, Charles C. Walcutt. *American Literary Naturalism, a Divided Stream.* (University of Minnesota Press, 1956), pp. 84-86, in particular; and David R. Weimer. *The City as Metaphor (New York: Random House,* 1966), pp. 55-60. While Walcutt sees Crane as being closer to Expressionism than Impressionism, he rightly, I think, sees Impressionism as being one of the major sources of Expressionism.

In "The Little Regiment," Crane readers see this Expressionist scene: "The waters of the given river curled away in a smile from the ends of the great boats, and slid swiftly beneath the planking. The dark, riddled walls of the town upreared before the troops . . . ." *Tales of War,* pp. 6-7.

In Surrealist manner, Crane describes a burning village at nightfall: "A fiery light was thrown upon some palm trees so that it made them into enormous crimson feathers." *Tales of War,* p. 226. For the foregoing examples I draw upon my "The Art of Stephen Crane," *Modern Age,* 18 (Winter 1974), 105-106.

[184]Conrad. Letter to Edward Garnett. December 5, 1897. Cited in Edward Garnett, ed. *Letters from Joseph Conrad: 1895-1924.* (Indianapolis: Bobbs-Merrill, 1928), p. 326. It is interesting to compare this assessment of Crane with Cézanne's famous statement about Monet: "Monet is only an eye, but, good Lord, what an eye!" Cited in Erle Loran. *Cézanne's Composition* (University of California Press, 1943).

[185]In *Stephen Crane in England* (Ohio State University Press, 1964), Eric Solomon points to several parallels between Ford's war fiction and Crane's *Red Badge of Courage.* Most of these parallels relate to these authors' common interests in Impressionism.

[186]Ford. "Stevie and Co.," New York *Herald Tribune* (Book Supplement) January 2, 1927. Sec. 7, p. 6.

[187]I shall consistently use this appellation, although Ford signed all of his novels prior to 1919 under other surnames. Born Ford Hermann Madox Hueffer, he changed his name by deed poll in 1919. On the question of Ford's personal and professional identity, see especially R. A. Scott-James. "Ford Madox Ford When He was Hueffer," *South Atlantic Quarterly,* LVII (Spring 1958), 236-253.

[188]Ford Madox Ford. *It Was the Nightingale.* (Phila.: J. P. Lippincott, 1933), p. 33.

[189]Ford. *The March of Literature.* (New York: Dial Press, 1938), p. 840. 1947 edition, p. 767. In fairness, however, it should be pointed out that Ford, in judging the qualities of Moore's literary art, sometimes contradicts himself. See, for example, "Literary Portraits—XXVII: Mr. George Moore and 'Vale,' " *Outlook* (London), XXXIII (March 14, 1914), 358-359, wherein Ford expresses distaste for Moore's frigid and mysterious didacticism. Even here, however, Ford concedes that "*Vale* is very good reading and very lovely writing" (p. 359).

In *Experiments in Autobiography* (New York: Macmillan, 1934), H. G. Wells identified Ford's appearance with Moore's, see p. 526.

190In *It Was the Nightingale* (1933), Ford remarked that he liked Moore's reminiscences more than anything else that he ever wrote. Ford also greatly admired *A Modern Lover* and *A Mummer's Wife*. Cf. *The March of Literature, 1947, p. 767.*

191Ford. *Return to Yesterday,* Gollancz, 1931; Liveright, 1932, reissued limited cloth edition, 1972, p. 21.

192Ford. *Return,* p. 178.

193See, for instance, Tony Tanner. Introduction. *Henry James: Modern Judgments.* (New York, Macmillan, 1968), p. 21. Also probably worth mentioning is Ford's *The Panel* (1912), an hilarious spoof of James's popularity among the intelligentsia. On this subject, see especially R. W. Lid. "Ford Madox Ford and His Community of Letters," *Prairie Schooner,* XXXV (Summer 1961), 136.

194On Ford's indifference to facts, see also his "Dedication" to *Ancient Lights.* (London: Chapman and Hall, 1911), p. xv; and Richard M. Ludwig. "The Reputation of Ford Madox Ford," *PMLA,* LXXVI (December 1961), 544-551.

Ford's method of narration is not, after all, very much unlike that of Thucydides. See *History of the Peloponnesian War,* trans. Rex Warner, 1954. Rev. and rpt. (Penguin, 1974), I, 22, p. 47.

195Jocelyn Baines. *Joseph Conrad: A Critical Biography.* (London: Weidenfeld and Nicolson, 1959), pp. 214-215. But this is not to say that the influence did not work both says. On this subject, see, for instance, Ivo Vidan. "Ford's Interpretation of Conrad's Technique" and Thomas Moser. "Conrad and *The Good Soldier,*" both of which are collected in Norman Sherry, ed. *Joseph Conrad: A Commemoration.* Barnes and Noble, 1976. For Vidan, see pp. 183-193; for Moser, pp. 174-182.

196Conrad. *Letters to William Blackwood and David S. Meldrum,* ed. William Blackburn. (Duke University Press, 1958), p. 30.

Ford's grandfather was the Pre-Raphaelite painter Ford Madox Brown, to whom Ford dedicated his first novel.

197Ford. *Return to Yesterday,* p. 187.

198See Conrad's "Letter to John Galsworthy," in G. Jean-Aubry. *Joseph Conrad: Life and Letters*, Vol. 1 (New York: Doubleday, 1927). The October 1898 letter to Galsworthy indicates precisely the date when the collaboration began. In *The Saddest Story* (New York: World Publishing Co., 1971), Arthur Mizener, Ford's biographer, corroborates the October 1898 date.

199Ford. *The March of Literature: From Confucius to the Modern Times* (London: George Allen and Unwin, 1938), p. 731.

200Ford. *Henry James*, p. 152.

201Ford. *Return*, p. 187.

202Ford. "On Impressionism," *Poetry and Drama*, II (June and December, 1914), rpt. Frank MacShane, ed. *Critical Writings of Ford Madox Ford*. (University of Nebraska Press, 1964), p. 41.

203Ford. *Thus to Revisit*. (New York: E. P. Dutton, 1921), p. 36.

204See also Conrad letter to Meldrum, Dec. 31, 1909, in *Letters to William Blackwood and David S. Meldrum*, ed. William Blackburn. (Duke University Press, 1958), p. 191.

205Ford. *Return*, p. 60.

206Ford. *It Was the Nightingale*, p. 311.

207Conrad's wife said that he claimed "The Black Mate" (1886) as his first written work. Of this story, Frederick R. Karl writes, it "is of such inconsequential stature that beyond matters of chronological interest it merits no discussion in its own right." F. R. Karl. *Reader's Guide to Joseph Conrad*. (N. Y.: Noonday Press, 1960), p. 91.

208This information is provided by Conrad in a letter to Poradowska that is cited by Karl in *Reader's Guide*, p. 91.

209Ford. *Joseph Conrad: A Personal Remembrance* (London: Duckworth, 1924), pp. 36, 94, 195; *Southern Review*, 1 (July 1935), p. 25. Conrad has remained quite popular with the French. See Elizabeth Gallagher Von Klemperer. "The Fiction of Henry James and Joseph Conrad in France: A Study in Penetration and Reception," Radcliffe College Thesis, 1958.

210In *A Reader's Guide to Joseph Conrad,* F. R. Karl notes the similarity of spirit between Conrad's Preface and "The Art of Fiction," which was published nine years earlier. See pp. 24-25.

211John A. Gee and Paul J. Sturm, eds. *Letters of Joseph Conrad to Marguerite Poradowska.* (New Haven: Yale University Press, 1940), p. 84.

212Conrad. Preface to *The Nigger of the "Narcissus."* (London: Dent, 1923), pp. vii-viii.

213Maupassant. Preface. *Pierre et Jean,* Paris: Conard, 1909. xiv.

214Maupassant. Preface. Conard edition, p. xxiv.

215Conrad. Preface, p. ix.

216Conrad. Preface, p. x.

217Maupassant. Preface, pp. xxiv-xxv; and Conrad. Preface, p. ix. Much of the foregoing discussion is indebted to George J. Worth. "Conrad's Debt to Maupassant in the Preface *The Nigger of the "Narcissus," Journal of English and Germanic Philology,* LIV (October 1955), 700-704.

218Karl, *Guide,* p. 30.

219Karl. *Guide,* p. 30. In the chapter entitled "The Mantle of Flaubert," in his *Mimesis and Metaphor: An Inquiry into the Genesis and Scope of Conrad's Symbolic Imagery* (The Hague: Mouton, 1969), Donald C. Yelton notes the linguistic echoes from *Madame Bovary* and other Flaubert novels in *The Nigger of the "Narcissus," Lord Jim,* and *Nostromo.*

Also worth noting, I think, is that in 1918 Conrad denied that he had read any of Flaubert's works before he wrote *Almayer's Folly* (1895). See Conrad's letter to Hugh Walpole, 7 June 1918, in Jean-Aubry. *Life and Letters.* Doubleday, 1927. Vol. 2. A letter to Marguerite Poradowska, however, written on 6 April, 1892, proves that, as early as 1892, Conrad had re-read *Madame Bovary.* See *Letters of Joseph Conrad to Marguerite Poradowska, 1890-1920,* trans. and ed. John A. Gee and Paul J. Sturm. (Yale University Press, 1940), p. 44.

220Joseph Conrad. "Letter to Edward Garnett," 5 December 1897 in *Stephen Crane: Letters,* ed. R. W. Stallman and Lillian Gilkes, p. 155.

221Conrad. Introduction. Beer. *Crane,* p. 5.

222Conrad. Introduction. Beer. *Crane*, p. 3.

223See Bruce Johnson. "Joseph Conrad and Crane's *Red Badge*," *Papers of the Michigan Academy of Science, Arts, and Letters*, XLVIII (1963), 649-55. Johnson's article forms what I feel is a healthy corrective to the view proposed by Jocelyn Baines. See the chronology in *Joseph Conrad: A Critical Biography*.

224Joseph Conrad. "Letter to Richard Curle," April 24, 1922, *To a Friend: 150 Selected Letters to Richard Curle*. (London: Sampson, Lowe, Marson, 1928), p. 142.

225This seems true also of Pater—from whom Conrad may likewise have learned something about suggestiveness. See J. J. Duffy. "Conrad and Pater: Suggestive Echoes." *Conradiana*. 1 (1968), 45-47.

226Conrad. "Letter to Edward Noble," Nov. 2, 1895, in Jean-Aubry. *Life and Letters*, I, p. 184.

227Conrad. *A Personal Record* (New York: Doubleday, 1925), pp. 35-6.

228Conrad. "Author's Note," *Typhoon and Other Stories*. (New York: Doubleday, 1925), p. ix.

229Karl is probably right when he remarks that "all of Conrad's artistic devices, if they were to be listed categorically, would perhaps come together under the classification of aesthetic distance or impersonality." *Guide*, p. 18.

230D. C. Muecke. *Irony*. (London: Methuen, 1970), p. 15.

231Muecke. *Irony*. p. 3.

232Samuel Hynes. *The Pattern of Hardy's Poetry*. (University of North Carolina Press, 1961), pp. 41-42. Herbert J. C. Grierson approaches Irony from another angle. Grierson considers the way in which Irony serves to develop the subject: "the effect is an illumination of the speaker's feeling, not by the revelation of his subject in a more vivid or transfiguring light, but by the peculiar angle which is presented between the object and the speaker's mind." *Rhetoric and English Composition*. London: Oliver and Boyd, 1944 (p. 76).

233Bruce E. Teets. "Literary Impressionism: Conrad and Ford," in *Literary Impressionism in Ford Madox Ford, Joseph Conrad and Related Writers. Preliminary Papers*, MLA Seminar 8, ed. Todd Bender. (University of Wisconsin Press, 1975), pp. 35-42.

234Conrad. "Karain: a Memory" (18) in *Tales of Unrest* (1898). (New York: Doubleday, Page and Co., 1922), pp. 10-11.

235Conrad. "Karain." *Tales,* pp. 42-43.

236See F. R. Karl. *Guide,* p. 121 and Bruce Teets's essay, cited above.

237C. B. Cox. *Joseph Conrad and the Modern Imagination.* (London: Rowman and Littlefield, 1974), p. 12. In this regard, R. M. Hare likewise contributes an   observation that is not only, I think, applicable to Jim's decision, but applicable also to most of the Impressionist fiction that I have considered:
" . . . a complete justification of a decision would consist of a complete account of its effects, together with a complete account of the principles which it observed, and the effects of observing those principles—for, of course, it is the effects (what obeying them in fact consists in) which can give content to the principles too. Thus, if pressed to justify a decision completely, we have to give a complete justification of the way of life of which it is a part. This complete specification it is impossible in practice to give . . . ."
R. M. Hare. *Language of Morals* [1955]. Oxford University Press, rev. ed., 1961. (p. 69).

238For similar statements by Conrad see, for example, "Letter to Arthur Symons" in Jean-Aubry. *Life and Letters,* II, p. 83.

239Edel. *The Master,* p. 49.

240James cited in Edel. *The Master,* p. 51.

241It should be pointed out here, perhaps, that the only Jamesian published references to a Conrad work that I have been able to discover are to *Chance.* See *Notes on Novelists with Some Other Notes.* (New York: Charles Scribner's Sons, 1914), pp. 345-355, in particular.

242See, for example, H. A. P. Theimer. *Conrad and Impressionism.* Stanford University Dissertation, 1962. Especially Chapter 6, which contains an extended comparison of *Lord Jim* and *The Ambassadors;* and Walter O'Grady. "On Plot in Modern Fiction: Hardy, James, and Conrad," *Modern Fiction Studies,* XI (Summer 1965), 107-115.

243James. *The Art of the Novel,* ed. Blackmur, pp. 32-33.

244See Edel. *The Master,* p. 53.

245Conrad. *Lord Jim,* ed. Thomas C. Moser. (New York: W. W. Norton and Co., 1968), p. 11.

246Wilde cited by Richard A. Johnson in "Wilde and Impersonation," *The Sewanee Review.* LXXXIV (Winter, 1976), 152. Also perhaps apposite is the following comment by Thucydides: " . . . the man who can most truly be accounted brave is he who best knows the meaning of what is sweet in life and of what is terrible, and then goes out undeterred to meet what is to come." *The Peloponnesian War,* trans. Rex Warner. Penguin [1954] . 1972 (p. 147).

That Conrad had also perhaps read his Montaigne is indicated by his use of "the jump motif." See *The Complete Essays of Montaigne,* trans. Donald M. Frame. Doubleday, 1960. Vol. III (p. 124).

247Cited by Maurice Beebe in " 'A Mirror Carried Along the Roadway of Life,' Reflective and Reflexive Trends in Modern Fiction" [Forthcoming. *The Bucknell Review* (date of publication not set)] .

248Guerard. *Conrad the Novelist* [1958] . (Harvard Univ. Press, rpt. Atheneum, 1970), p. 271.

249Reflexive books are those "that tell how they came to be written." Maurice Beebe. *Ivory Towers and Sacred Founts,* p. 303. On reflexivism in Conrad's fiction, see Albert Cook. *The Meaning of Fiction.* (Wayne State University Press, 1960), p. 287. See also Beebe. " 'A Mirror Carried Along the Roadway of Life,' Reflective and Reflexive Trends in Modern Fiction"; and my paper, "Impressionist Painting and the Reflexive Novel of the Early Twentieth Century" (forthcoming), *The Proceedings of the 8th Congress of the International Comparative Literature Association* (1977).

250On Conrad's use of time, consult F. J. Karl. *Guide,* pp. 72-90; and Adam Abraham Mendilow. *Time and the Novel* (London: Peter Nevil, 1952); rpt. Humanities Press, 1965, pp. 20, 48, 54, 75, 83, 104, 181, 185, and 226.

251Conrad. *Lord Jim,* ed. Thomas C. Moser.

252Of Conrad's novels, *Chance* (1913) is probably one of the most decidedly Impressionist. And it is also, perhaps, the most "Jamesian" of Conrad's works of fiction. See, for example, the passage beginning "A young girl, you know, . . . [*Chance.* Doubleday, Page and Co., 1923 (pp. 311-312)] .

The novel, which first appeared in serial format in the New York *Herald* (January to June 1912), is probably one of Conrad's worst, yet Henry James himself admired it. (See note 241, above). It appeared too late, however, to have influenced the Master's work in any appreciable way.

On the subject of the possible influence of Conrad upon James and vice versa, I can add little to the thorough treatment of the subject which is provided by Elsa Nettels. *James and Conrad.* University of Georgia Press, 1977. *passim.*

*Chapter Four*

*Impressionism in the Work of Henry James*

Before demonstrating the ways in which James's Impressionism operates, I think it worthwhile to summarize briefly the probable
influences upon the author's Impressionism. James seems to have developed his Impressionist technique from the three main sources that
I have discussed in the preceding chapters. From the French painters
and all but two of the French authors that we have reviewed, he
seems to have learned something of the techniques that have come to
be associated primarily with pictorial Impressionism: the rendering
of direct, fleeting impressions, the use of "open-air" effects, the moving around a subject and "painting" it from several different angles,
the use of techniques which require aesthetic distance, the juxtaposition of colors to obtain artistic effects, and the presentation of
scenes in a hazy atmosphere. The French influence, then, seems to
have acted primarily upon James's rendering of external reality. But
from Baudelaire and Mallarmé and from the major British and American Impressionist authors whose work we have examined, James
probably learned something about the *selectivity* of Impression, the
use of suggestion and nuance, and the attitude toward time that
eventually came to be characterized by Bergson as *La durée.* And
James's Impressionism, insofar as it uses the world of the consciousness to demonstrate the drama of man's inner self, seemingly helps
to show the way for the great stream-of-consciousness writers whose
work flourished during the first part of the twentieth century.A

In the development of his style, then, James seems to have
drawn upon most of the work of the artists that we have considered
in the previous chapters. But as we shall see, in some cases he has also
anticipated the possible sources that we have alluded to. Because he
has done this, because he has shown the way for many of the major

twentieth century writers of fiction, and because he has written the most consistently great fiction in the English language, Henry James truly deserves the title of respect by which he was known by his contemporaries—the Master.

Henry James is a novelist frequently considered in his relationship to the visual and plastic arts.[1] This does not seem surprising, since James's *œuvre* comprises not only many stories dealing with the artist and his efforts to create, but also numerous notes, essays, reviews, and travel sketches commenting upon the visual arts.[2] Although it is true that, as Leon Edel and Ilse Dusoir Lind have remarked in their "Introduction" to James's *Parisian Sketches,* "in matters of painting the novelist was essentially an amateur rather than a connoisseur,"[3] still James's powers of observation were considerable.[4] And in his later criticism and travel writings [*The American Scene* (1907), for instance], he displayed a considerably well-developed talent for discussing creative performances in the visual arts.

According to Robert L. Gale, "the largest single category of similes and metaphors from his [i.e., James's] fiction is that of art. Of a total of more than sixteen thousand figures of speech, nearly two thousand derive from art in one or more of its forms . . . ." Of James's figures of speech, "painting accounts for well over four hundred . . . , music over three hundred, sculpture less than two hundred, and the dance and architecture over fifty together."[5] James's evident love of painting is moreover recalled by the title of his first novelistic masterpiece, *The Portrait of a Lady* (1881). In volumes of travel writings, such as *Portraits of Places* (1883) and *Partial Portraits* (1888), the frequent use of images drawn from painting furthermore reminds us of James's interest in the visual arts. The title of *The American Scene* invites us to anticipate a painting, and painting metaphors proliferate throughout.[6]

In his seminal essay, "The Art of Fiction" (1884), written when James had a full life-time of fiction writing ahead of him, James made clear his belief that the painter and the novelist attempt something quite similar when they create:

The only reason for the existence of a novel is that it does attempt to represent life. When it relinquishes this attempt, the same attempt that we see on the canvas of the painter, it will have arrived at a very strange pass. It is not expected of the picture that it will make itself humble in order to be forgiven; and the analogy between the art of the painter and the art of the novelist is, so far as I am able to see, complete. Their inspiration is the same, their process (allowing for the different quality of the vehicle) is the same, their success is the same. They may learn from each other, they may explain and sustain each other. Their cause is the same, and the honour of one is the honour of another.[7]

In his non-fictional writings, James often referred to the writer as a painter. In 1899, he wrote to the students of the Deerfield School who wanted to hear James's last word on the novel, that "there are no tendencies worth any thing but to see the actual or the imaginative, which is just as visible, and to paint it."[8] Ten years later, he wrote that "the novel is of all pictures the most comprehensive and the most elastic. It will stretch any where—it will take in absolutely any thing. All it needs is a subject and a painter. But for its subject, magnificently, it has the whole human consciousness."[9] And very late in life, in his *Autobiography,* James admitted that in fiction "the picture was still  after all in essence one's aim."[10] Thus, his concern for the visual and plastic quality of fiction is one that stayed with him throughout a very long and distinguished career.

Of course, Henry James was first and foremost a writer of fiction. But this is not to say that his theory of fiction should not be of concern to us. "Art lives upon discussion, upon experiment, upon curiosity, upon variety of attempt, upon the exchange of views and the comparison of standpoints," James said. "The successful application of any art is a delightful spectacle, but the theory too is interesting; and though there is a great deal of the latter without the former," James wrote, "I suspect there has never been a genuine success that has not had a latent core of conviction."[11] In the pages that follow, then, I shall sketch the outlines of what I see to be James's "latent core of conviction"—a theory of fiction that I believe to be closer to that of Impressionism than to any other artistic school.

Of the movements in art contemporary with him, James appears to have found the Impressionist school the most fascinating. Moreover, the comments that he makes in several articles and reviews seem to reflect this deep interest.[12] Some of the Master's remarks on these painters are altogether favorable. In his essay "New England: An Autumn Impression" (1905), James writes about a large house on a hilltop in Farmington, Connecticut

> in which an array of 'impressionistic' pictures, mainly French, wondrous examples of Manet, Degas, of Claude Monet, of Whistler, of other rare recent hands, treated us to the momentary effect of a large slippery sweet inserted, without a warning, between the compressed lips of half-conscious inanition . . . no proof of the sovereign power of art could have been, for the moment, sharper . . . it made everything else shrivel and fade: it was like the sudden trill of a nightingale, lord of the hushed evening.[13]

Some thirty years prior to this, James described for the New York *Herald Tribune* a painting that was supposedly done by the Italian painter Jean Boldoni (1842-1931), who settled in Paris around 1872. And James's account of the painting that Boldoni supposedly had done favorably emphasizes the aspects of the Italian artist's performance which are most decidedly Impressionist:

> M. Boldoni's picture represents a corner of the park at Versailles under Louis XVI. A sedan chair containing a fine lady, escorted by several fops and élegantes, had been deposited, while the carriers stand resting, beneath a great wall of horse chestnut trees. Nearby is a fountain and a couple of statues, and where the horse chestnuts stop a broad cedar spreads itself into the brilliant summer light. The figures are very small—they belong to the class of what the French call little bonshommes; but their animation, expressiveness, and grace, the shimmer of their tense silk stockings, the way they hollow their backs and turn out their toes, are all extraordinary and delightful. . . [Boldoni's] great triumph . . . , however, has been his landscape—his great mass of verdure, and his dazzling, almost blinding summer light . . . . As a representation of objects shining and glowing in the open air, and as an almost childishly irreflective piece of fantasy, the work is a singular success. [13a]

That James moreover remained at least partially fascinated by the basic techniques of the Impressionists can be seen in his reactions to the second Post-Impressionist Exhibition (1912) that was arranged by Rogert Fry in London.[14] Yet evidence also indicates that during his early career James held mixed feelings about Impressionism.[15] On one occasion, for example, he referred to the Impressionist group as "the Irreconcilables."[16] In this review, which originally appeared in 1876 as a letter to the New York *Herald Tribune,* [17] James wrote about the 1876 show of Impressionist paintings in Paris. The show contained 252 paintings, pastels, watercolors, drawings, and etchings by 20 exhibitors, including Degas, 24 works; Monet, 18; Berthe Morisot, 17; Renoir, 15; Pissarro and Sisley. In his review, which was dated May 13, 1876, James denounced the Impressionists for what he felt was a failure to impose artistic design upon their material. These "partisans of unadorned reality," James wrote, "abjure virtue altogether . . . send detail to the dogs and concentrate themselves on general expression." He furthermore wrote that these painters were "absolute foes to arrangement, embellishment, selection, to the artist's allowing himself, as he has hitherto, since art began, found his best account in doing, to be preoccupied with the idea of the beautiful."[18] Additionally, he says that "the Impressionist doctrines strike me as incompatible in an artist's mind, with the existence of first-rate talent."[19]

In 1877 James wrote: "to be interesting it seems to me that a picture should have some relation to life as well as to painting."[20] It is therefore not surprising that a year later, while praising the second Grosvenor exhibit, his reactions to the Whistler entries were less than favorable: "Mr. Whistler's productions are pleasant things to have about, so long as one regards them as simple objects—as incidents of furniture or decoration. The spectator's quarrel with them begins when he feels it to be expected to regard them as pictures. His manner is very much that of the French Impressionist."[21] These negative comments notwithstanding, in James's prose writings, especially his lengthy "portraits of places," one detects what appears to represent a movement toward the techniques of the Impressionist painters and a step further toward the literary sophistication of his later years. Numerous hints indicate, furthermore, that James came to embrace

both the philosophy and the technique of the Impressionist movement during his so-called Major Phase.

Although critics have often compared James with the Impressionist painters, previous discussions of this subject have been vague,
fragmentary, or confusing.[22] Chief among the published statements
concerning James's relationship to Impressionism are those by Viola
Hopkins Winner. In her generally valuable and wide-ranging *Henry
James and the Visual Arts* (1970), Winner remarks, "It seems to me
highly probable that James's knowledge of impressionist painting influenced his way of seeing but only indirectly his method of rendering in prose an impressionist scene or any other." She furthermore
judges that "what James had in common with the Impressionist painters was his view of the inter-relatedness of all experience, of consciousness as unified and unstable, and his emphasis on the subjective
aspects of experience." He had much in common with the contemporary impressionists in technique and in thought, Winner observes,
"but crucially differed from them in his formalism and traditional-
ism."[23]

Winner feels that James "was closer in sensibility and in style
to the mannerist Tintoretto, the Italian painter for whom he felt the
deepest affinity."[24] That James's sympathy with the mannerists—
Tintoretto, in particular—  s indeed great, Miss Winner ably documents. In the qualities that i. ʾorm his fiction, as well as his theory of
fiction, however, Henry James 's on the whole much closer to Impressionism than to Mannerism, or to any other artistic school.

Winner states that "the qualities of James's art which make
him a member of the mannerist family should be apparent."[26] And
she lists the qualities as follows:

> the mani. ʾist approached nature subjectively, defying established
> rules of pers ective, proportion, and composition. For the mannerist
> it was not a q stion of creating the object as one might or should or
> does see it, but as, to quote Friedlaender, 'from purely artistic motives,
> one would have it seen.' Not attempting to represent the object ac-
> cording to what would be viewed as natural, the mannerist stretched
> limbs and fingers, broke up symmetry, dissolved figures, in space—all

for the sake of a particularly personal and rhythmic feeling for beauty. As exemplified by the works of Parmigianino, Tintoretto, Bronzino, and the Michelangelo of the Medici Chapel and of the anteroom of the Laurentian Library, mannerist art lacks the repose and stability of the High Renaissance as well as the turbulent struggle and triumphant resolution of the baroque. It is an art of preciosity, of intricate asymmetrical patterns leading to no final solution, of subjects treated from unexpected angles, of 'rigid formality and deliberate disturbance, bareness and over-decoration.'27

Winner sees a relationship between "the mannerist tendency to spiritualize the material world" and James's quest for "the sacramental sensibility" (R. W. B. Lewis's phrase, as cited by Winner). She furthermore observes that "the irresoluteness of James's endings is suggestive of the mannerist style—the struggle for repose which lacks a final triumph."28

As with the mannerist painter, it is not nature as seen by the ordinary person or by the conventions of another art style that was James's concern but rather nature as he would have it seen, hence, the super-intelligence and hyper-sensitivity of James's characters, the probing dialectical conversations which in real life one cannot imagine sustained by even the most perceptive and highly cultivated beings, and the omission except through implication of drives and passions. What James said in an essay of 1892 about Tintoretto's *Marriage at Cana* at the Santa Maria della Salute is applicable here: 'There could be no better example of the roving independence of the painter's vision, a real spirit of adventure for which his subject was always a cluster of accidents; not an obvious order, but a sort of peopled and agitated chapter of life in which the figures are submissive pictorial notes.' For both painter and novelist, the schemata are first; the figures from life are treated as elements in the composition, subordinated to the prevailing artistic rhythm.29

Winner therefore feels that James's late style may be called either mannered or mannerist. She points out, too, that "asymmetry and preciosity in detail is [sic] characteristic of both mannerist architecture and painting." Winner's comments are difficult to dispute in detail, yet they do not get to the center of the Jamesian canon. About the aforementioned list of observations on the mannerist parallels with James's art, I feel not unlike James himself who, after enumerating Mr. Besant's advice to the aspiring writer of fiction, remarked: "I should find it difficult to dissent from any one of these recommendations. At the same time, I should find it difficult positively to assent to them . . . ."[30] Unquestionably Winner's claims for James as a mannerist do provide us with another way of looking at James's immense talent, but assuredly they do not provide us with the only way (as Miss Winner herself would probably admit). Despite James's own generally negative early remarks about the painters of the Impressionist movement, I contend that we get closest to the heart of James's *œuvre* when we consider his work in terms of Impressionism.

Every artist works in a complex and continually changing environment, and an artist of James's sensibility probably did so more than most. Moreover, artists are often either unconscious of their sources, or remain silent about them. And, as T. S. Eliot has said, "Sensibility alters from generation to generation, whether we will it or no." The period in which James was developing his literary craft was shaped by Impressionism.

True, in his art criticism James did not have much to say that was favorable about the Impressionists. But what is much more to the point is that the techniques that were used by the Impressionists were not only used by James in his fiction, but were also enumerated by him in the theory of fiction that emerges from his voluminous literary essays and reviews, letters, critical prefaces, and volumes of autobiography.

There are a number of good reasons why Henry James would have been attracted to the Impressionist painters. For one, their careers followed not dissimilar patterns. James, for example, never really had a large popular following during his lifetime. *Daisy Miller* was his one clear triumph, far out-stripping *The Wings of the Dove,* for instance—a fact that understandably chagrined James in his later years.[31]

He likewise shared with most of the Impressionists a supreme urbanity of temperament. In his youth James enjoyed what are known as advantages. He and his brother William were fortunate in having been given a stimulating if slightly irregular education—one in which eccentricities were readily tolerated and culture freely embraced. "The literal played in our education," Henry wrote, "as small a part as it perhaps ever played in any. And we wholesomely breathed inconsistency and ate and drank contradictions."[32] "What we were to do instead [of seeking a vocation] was just to *be* something...."[33] Significantly, what James appreciated most in his own life was the freedom of self-development that Henry James, Sr., allowed his sons; the "magnanimity" of spirit that make it possible for them "to have all the benefit of his intellectual and spiritual, his philosophic and his social passion, without ever feeling the pressure of it to our direct irritation or discomfort."[34]

Not surprisingly, perhaps, the author in possession of such an admirable up-bringing was also little inclined to political activity; and in this, too, James was temperamentally akin to the Impressionists. James and the Impressionists lived through successive periods of wars and political upheavals, yet these incidents assume little importance in their arts. The Impressionists left to other artists the depiction of the events of the Franco-Prussian War and the Commune that so rent the French nation; they instead painted mostly idyllic glimpses of Paris and of the beautiful countryside that surrounded it. James, meanwhile, for the most part overlooked the Civil War and the violent and rapid westward expansion that took place in his own country; he chose instead to write about spiritual adventures—adventures which, *avec le passage du temps*, speak far more directly to us than do the works of most of James's contemporaries.

Thanks perhaps largely to a liberal education which taught him not to interfere with the rights of others, James chose to be an apolitical writer. He was a supreme believer in the value of the individual, in the right that every individual has to develop his own potential.[35] In an 1865 review of Arnold's *Essays in Criticism*, James quoted with approval Arnold's claim that criticism must be disinterested. Criticism could only be disinterested, said Arnold, "by steadily refusing to lend itself to any of those ulterior political, practical considerations about ideas which plenty of people will be sure to attach to them."[36] James of course did not confine such expressions of distaste for the political to his non-fictional writings. In *The Tragic Muse*, for example, Gabriel Nash urges his friend Nick to give up politics for art, to be "on the side of beauty." When Nick rejoins that there will be little beauty if he produces nothing but daubs, Nash answers: "There will be the beauty of having been disinterested and independent; of having taken the world in the free, brave, personal way."[37] In his biography of William Wetmore Story, James quotes several of Story's poems about painters and comments: "Such passages in an artist's projection of another artist may mostly be taken as the revelation of the former's own emotion."[38] That James in the passage from *The Tragic Muse* was more than likely speaking here also for himself can be seen by comparing Gabriel's answer to that given by James when he declined the chairmanship of the English Association. In a letter that he wrote to John Bailey on November 11, 1912, James remarked: "I am a mere stony, ugly monster of Dissociation and Detachment . . . . I believe only in independent, individual and lonely virtue, and in the serenely unsociable practice of the same . . . ."[39]

Like the Impressionists, too, James depicted the world from the standpoint of a detached observer. In an 1882 entry in his *Notebooks,* he referred to his Parisian experience of the mid-seventies and gave several reasons to explain what proved to be his temporary disenchantment with Paris, but his concluding thought probably summarized them all, for he remarked that he saw that he would be "an eternal outsider."[40] It became increasingly obvious, however, not only that this "on-looker position" had become congenial to James, but also that he had gotten far more out of his Parisian sojourn than he was willing to admit at the time. Further in keeping with James's detached stance[41] is the not infrequent expression in James of the attitude that Art is more real than Life.[42] This attitude is one of the major ones in the Ivory Tower tradition which, as Maurice Beebe has demonstrated, "equates art with religion rather than experience."[43]

Just as we find an absence of traditional religious concerns in the work of the Impressionists, so too do we find a corresponding absence in James. That this should be the case with James is not altogether surprising. In his monumental *The Thought and Character of*

*William James,* Ralph Barton Perry has remarked of Henry, Senior, that "he grew up in a circle in which heresies were more gladly tolerated than orthodoxies."[44] It therefore comes as no surprise that the father evidently transmitted this kind of liberal philosophy to Henry, a son who held a warm and genuine respect for his father. Fairly early in life Henry came to look upon art as a religion. In an early *Notebook* entry, for example, he records that "art is the only thing which makes life supportable."[45] And in his *Autobiography,* when he speaks of the youthful time that he spent working in the Newport studio of William Morris Hunt, James recalls these days with the reverence that a mystic might relate a supernatural experience. He was, he tells us, "at the threshold of a world." "Frankly, intensely—that was the great thing—these were hours of Art."[46]

Elsewhere in his criticism he addresses the subject of art in terms that are redolent of the mystical experience: "It appears to me that no one can ever have made a serious artistic attempt without becoming conscious of an immense increase—a kind of revelation—of freedom. One perceives in that case—by the light of a heavenly ray— that the provence of art is all life, all feeling, all observation, all vision."[47] In like manner, art provides James with a shelter from the chaotic world. "Oh art, art, what difficulties are like thine, but, at the same time, what consolations and encouragements, also are like thine? Without thee, for me, the world would be, indeed, a howling desert."[48] By selection, art imposes order and shape upon "life," which is "all inclusion and confusion." "In the face of the constant force that makes for muddlement," art creates that which is eternal and indestructible.[49]

That to James art was the fundamental religion is a premise that is partially supported by several intriguing images in his fiction. In "Collaboration," a story that concerns two dedicated men of art, we read that "Art protects her children in the long run—she only asks them to trust her. She is like the Catholic Church—she guarantees paradise to the faithful."[50] And in "Mora Montravers," Traffle, an art lover, meets by chance the young heroine Mora while he is visiting what James calls a place "of pilgrimages" to see "the idol in the numbered shrine"; that is, a painting—in one of the Dutch rooms of London's National Gallery.[51] In using religious imagery to describe works of art and the buildings that house them, James was working within a nineteenth-century tradition. For Goethe, the museum was a shrine. Hölderlin moreover called it an "aesthetic church."[52] And during the early part of the century, a Gothic cathedral was planned on the site of the battleground of Leipzig. This cathedral was intended to serve as a sanctuary for the arts, as well as a national monument. Finally we recall Wagner's comment; that "Das Kunstwerk ist die lebendig dargestellte Religion" ("The work of art is the living representation of religion"—from *Das Kunstwerk der Zukunft*).

Although James was working within a well-established tradition in viewing art as a religion, his view of the importance of *consciousness* was a view that seems to have originated with his genius. In a letter to Grace Norton, written in the summer of 1883, James remarked:

> I don't know why we live—the gift of life comes to us from I don't know what source or for what purpose: but I believe we can go on living for the reasons that (always of course up to a certain point) life is the most valuable thing we know anything about, and it is therefore presumptively a great mistake to surrender it while there is any yet left in the cup. In other words consciousness is an illimitable power, and though at times it may seem to be all consciousness of misery, yet in the way it propagates itself from wave to wave, so that we never cease to feel, and though at moments we appear to, try to, pray to, there is something that holds one in one's place, makes it a standpoint in the universe which it is probably good not to forsake.[53]

Additionally, he saw consciousness as the key to whatever immortality man might realize. In an essay entitled "Is There a Life After Death?" written for *Harper's Bazaar* in 1910, James admitted that science was probably right in its view that men—"however nobly thinking and feeling creatures"—are "abjectly and inveterately shut up in our material organs." But then he goes on to ask, "How *can* there be a personal and a differentiated life 'after,' it will then of course be asked, for those for whom there has been so little of one before?—unless indeed it be pronounced conceivable that the possibility may vary from man to man, from human case to human case, and the quantity or the quality of our practice of consciousness may have something to say to it."[54] "The question is of the personal experience, of course, of another existence," James remarked in another passage on the same subject, "of its being I my very self. ..," and James finds it difficult to conceive the "disconnection of a consciousness"[55] that one has spent a lifetime refining and developing.[56]

If we keep in mind James's concern for refining and developing consciousness, then we can readily see why the Impressionist dictum, that the artist must render the impression that objects make on the eye, greatly appealed to James. He often praised the "visual curiosity" of the French realist writers who validated his belief that "in any description of life the description of places and things is half the battle."[57] James moreover conveyed this conviction in several of his most important critical statements on the practice of his fiction. "Any point of view is interesting that is a direct impression of life," he wrote in the late '80's.[58] And in his "Art of Fiction"—which originally appeared in *Longman's Magazine* in September 1884—he said that "a novel is in its broadest definition a personal, a direct impression of life: that, to begin with, constitutes its value, which is greater or less according to the intensity of the impression."[59] Significantly, James's essay pre-dates by four years Maupassant's article which was published as the preface of *Pierre et Jean* in 1888. While James almost certainly read Maupassant's piece (in his *Notebooks,* James refers to *Pierre et Jean* as being "a supremely happy instance of the short novel"),[60] Maupassant in turn almost certainly read James's article, since the Frenchman evidently admired James at least as much as James did Maupassant. We thus have an instance where Conrad demonstrably drew for his famous Preface upon the work of Maupassant, who almost certainly drew upon James. And James, who surely influenced Conrad's statement, was himself, by his contacts with Maupassant's tightly wrought fiction, more than likely influenced in his attempts to render fiction economically.[61] But the situation with regard to these artists becomes more fascinating still when we recall that Maupassant accompanied Monet on several of his expeditions to paint, *en plein air,* the cliffs at Étretat. And James, in Letter 20 to the *Tribune* (done during the mid-1870's), provided a vivid rendering of the same beach area where "the sea is blue as melted sapphires, and the ragged white faces of the bordering cliffs look like a setting of silver."[62]

James's use of the direct impression in his non-fiction was of course not restricted to his literary criticism, literary theory, and *Notebooks,* since his travel writings contain many examples of his ability to render the direct impressions that objects make upon the eye. Perhaps one of the most interesting examples of this technique in James's travel writings can be found in his essay, "London" (1888), wherein he recalls entering London by train: "There is a certain evening that I count as virtually a first impression—the end of a wet, black Sunday, twenty years ago, about the first of March. There had been an earlier version, but it had turned to grey, like faded ink, and the occasion I speak of was a fresh beginning."[63] When we compare this opening passage of James's essay to Ezra Pound's "In a Station of the Metro":

> The apparition of these faces in the crowd
> Petals on a wet, black bough

it is perhaps not difficult to see the ways in which James may have influenced Pound in the latter's writing of his famous Imagist poem.[64]

James's *The American Scene* also is replete with examples of the artist's rendering the impressions that a scene makes upon the eye. In a chapter that was written around 1904, for example (at a time when Philadelphia was the third largest city in the United States!), James referred to Philadelphia as "a goodly village."[65] In another passage from the same volume of travel writings, James remarked upon the "multitudinous skyscrapers" of New York: "They are triumphant payers of dividends; all of which uncontested and unabashed pride, with flash of innumerable windows and flicks of subordinate gilt attributions, is like the flare up and down their long, narrow faces, of the lamps of some general permanent 'celebration.' "[66] And in a passage on Cape Cod, the term "impressionism" reflexively becomes a felicitous element in James's own composition:

> Cape Cod, on this showing, was exactly a pendant, pictured Japanese screen or banner; a delightful little triumph of 'impressionism,' which during my short visit at least, never departed, under any provocation, from its type.[67]

James himself was indeed very sensitive to scene and to weather.[68] Not surprisingly, therefore, he had a sympathy for the Impressionist technique that called for painting open air scenes on the spot. He criticized Thackeray, for instance, for his "extraordinary avoidance of picture" in *Denis Duval*: "the impression of today's reader is that the chapters we possess might really have been written without the author's having stood on the spot."[69]

Yet James also knew that "the difference between the roundabout, faint descriptive tokens of respectable prose and the immediate projections of the figure by pencil"[70] is such that, in competition with the visual artist, the writer is almost always the loser. Of the Goncourt brothers James, for example, remarked:

> The most general stricture to be made on their work is probably that they have not allowed enough for the difference of instrument, have persisted in the effort to render impressions that the plastic artist renders better, neglecting too much those he is unable to render.[71]

James himself preferred to read of places that he knew that he would never see. In writing of Pierre Loti, James remarked that when an author provided him with "the happiest conceivable utterance of feelings about aspects," he never wanted to spoil those impressions by a visit.[72] On the basis of what we know of James's methods of composition, as well as of his fictional theory, we must then conclude that his statement from the Preface to *The American* stands as his general verdict on the second major Impressionist technique:

> I have ever, in general, found it difficult to write of places under too immediate an impression—the impression that prevents standing off and allows neither space nor time for perspective.[73]

Given this apparent feeling toward composition soon after the experience, James's penchant for presenting salient figures, done in a few strokes, seems altogether understandable. In an 1887 essay on Sargent, James judged that " . . . the latent dangers of the impressionist practice . . . [are] the tendency to simplification and the neglect of a certain faculty for lingering reflection."[74] Although he felt the "tendency to simplification" was a latent danger of the Impressionist technique,[75] still he did not himself eschew this principle as a

worthy element in the body of commentary that comprises the heart
of his critical theory. "Working out economically almost any thing is
the very life of the art of representation . . . ,"[76] he said. In writing
about "The Birthplace," moreover, James referred to his "very joy of
the suppressed details."[77]

For James,"Life being all inclusion and confusion, and art
being all discrimination and selection . . . ,"[78] the artist should be
interested in what the Master referred to in the Preface to *The Ambassadors* as the "grace of intensity"; for " . . . life has no direct
sense whatever for the subject and is capable, luckily for us, of nothing but splendid waste. Hence the opportunity for the sublime
economy of art . . . ."[79] In the same Preface James provides a capital
example of what he means by "the sublime economy of art" as it
applies to his method of composition. He relates that *The Spoils of
Poynton* grew out of "an impression" gathered "some years ago . . . ,
one Christmas Eve when I was dining with friends: a lady beside me
made in the course of talk one of those allusions that I have always
found myself recognizing on the spot as 'germs.' The germ, when-
ever gathered has ever been for me the germ of a 'story,' and most of
the stories straining to shape under my hand have sprung from a
single small seed, a seed as minute and wind-blown as that casual hint
for 'The Spoils of Poynton' dropped unwittingly by my neighbor, a
mere floating particle in the stream of talk."[80] "There had been but
ten words," James goes on to say, "yet I had recognized in them, as
in a flash, all the possibilities of the little drama of my 'Spoils,' which
glimmered then and there into life; so that when in the next breath
I began to hear of action taken, on the beautiful ground, by our engaged adversaries, tipped each, from that instant, with the light of
the highest distinction, I saw Clumsy Life again at her stupid work."[81]

Aligned perhaps with this desire of attaining "the grace of intensity" in fiction, James advocated a method of fore-shortening that
was analogous to the Impressionists' avoidance of the use of details
and elaborate finish. Where the Impressionist painters advocated
"summary brush-work," Henry James wished for a fore-shortened
composition. James's clearest and most concise use of the term fore-
shortening occurs in "The Present Literary Situation in France," an
1899 essay in *The North American Review* where he speaks of Emile

Faguet's "admirable piece of fore-shortening" in the Frenchman's commemorative article on the critic Francisque Sarcey: "The portrait, in a few strokes . . . was a little miracle of understanding and expression."[82]

Although it is true that James, in an 1887 essay on J. S. Sargent, said that "the latent dangers of the impressionist practice . . . [are] the tendency to simplification and the neglect of a certain faculty for lingering reflection,"[83] he yet, as I have indicated, generally expressed in his theory of fiction an admiration for the artist who is capable of economically mastering his subject. Partially for this reason, therefore, critics who have labelled James a Realist have failed to get at the heart of his *œuvre*—either critical or fictional. Michael Egan, in *Henry James: The Ibsen Years,* for instance, implies that before 1890, James's goals were "the faithful representation of contemporary reality within a literary frame."[84] And Adeline R. Tintner, one of the most perceptive contemporary critics of the Master, more recently remarked "that James's appetency for 'facts' establishes him once and for all as a realist, for in spite of the linguistic elaborations of his style and the increasing subtlety of his characters, his writing never gives up its dependency on the real world."[85] True, James remarked in "The Art of Fiction" that " . . . the only classification of the novel that I can understand is into that which has life and that which has not." The creation of "the air of reality (solidity of specification)" is, James moreover maintained, "the supreme virtue of a novel—the merit on which all its other merits . . . helplessly and submissively depend."[86] He also maintained a life-long admiration for Balzac and Turgenev—a pair of authors who are often considered the foremost among Continental Realists.[87] Yet he furthermore held that both writers ultimately "sacrificed too much to detail" (James's specific verdict on Turgenev).

While on the one hand James has been incorrectly labelled a Realist, on the other, he has sometimes been negatively criticized by Marxist-oriented critics, because of his lack of realism and absence of adequate treatment of the working classes. Yet Seymour Chatman seems much closer to the truth when he remarks (in *The Later Style of Henry James*) that "thoughts and perceptions in James's world . . .

occupy a space—the mind; though intangible, they are 'things' *in* the mind."[88] In an article entitled " 'Things' and Values in Henry James's Universe," M. A. Goldberg has moreover remarked that "in all of James's novels, the essence is certainly the growing and perceptive consciousness, and 'things,' as such, must take what James might call their 'real' or 'proper' . . . place."[89] Such observations seem to me to serve as a rightful counter to the Marxist/Realist arguments that I have alluded to above.

Even more germane to our present considerations, however, is the fact that James generally espoused these beliefs about "things" as a principle in his critical theory. In his early reviews, for example, he referred to "photographs," in order to point out a writer's literal reproduction of surface detail (a technique that he for the most part deprecated). Trollope's manner, for instance, has the "virtue of a photograph" because he is "true to common life" but fails to be "equally true to nature."[90] And in "The Art of Fiction," James remarks that "the power to guess the unseen from the seen, to trace the implication of things, to judge the whole piece by the pattern, the condition of feeling life in general so completely that you are well on your way to knowing any particular corner of it . . . . If experience consists of impressions, it may be said that impressions *are* experience . . . ."[91] For James, "the moral consciousness of a child is as much of a part of life as the islands of the Spanish Main . . . ."[92] And even special gestures and ways of looking are material for the artist for whom spiritual adventures are of the utmost importance. James supremely recognized, for instance, that the way a woman looks at you across a room can provide far more adventure than a lifetime of wars and political revolutions. "It is an incident," James remarked, "for a woman to stand up with her hand resting on a table and look out at you in a certain way; or if it be not an incident I think it will be hard to say what it is."[93] In his critical theory, then, James realized almost from the outset what André Malraux many years later expressed in *The Temptation of the West* when he said that "Suggestion is the highest technical perfection in art."[94]

Another Impressionist painting technique that finds an analogue in the Jamesian body of fictional theory is the interest in seizing "the moment." In the Preface to *The Ambassadors*, James refers to the supreme importance to the story-teller of "the grace of intensity."[95] Related to this interest is James's method of beginning his stories and novels. For the most part, James says, his stories and novels begin with a sensation, a color, a glimpse—what he himself referred to as a *donnée*. In the Preface to *The Spoils of Poynton,* he speaks on several occasions of his inspiration as coming to him of a sudden, as a "germ" or an air-blown grain.[96] As I have indicated in Chapters One and Two, the Impressionists' concern with time was probably related to a large-scale break-up of a belief in immortality, a belief that James realized in his fiction and in his non-fiction alike. His essay, "Is There a Life After Death?" (1910), for example, sets forth "a religion of consciousness," but concedes that men, "however nobly thinking and feeling creatures," are "abjectly and inveterately shut up in our material organs."[97]

In his critical theory James, like the Impressionists, advocated the artists' continually circling around the same motif. As he notes in his letters, he was ever preoccupied with "framing and encircling" his subjects, "anxious and worried as to . . . getting the effect in the right way."[98] James more than likely held these concerns because he realized that "the *whole* of anything is never told"[99]—a feeling that surely contributes to the open-ended quality in much of Modernist art. On April 29, 1876—two weeks before he had reviewed the second Impressionist exhibit, James wrote about the long time that he spent looking at Chartres Cathedral:

> . . . I revolved around it, like a moth around a candle; I chose twenty different standpoints: I observed it during the different hours of the day, and saw it in the moonlight as well as the sunshine. I gained, in a word, a certain sense of familiarity with it; and yet I despair of giving any very coherent account of it.[100]

With the Impressionist painters, too, James asserted in his criticism and travel writings the importance of the artist's recording a view at only one particular moment and in the particular light present then. This view was also held by the critic Walter Pater, but it is not widely recognized that James himself had emphasized the importance of individual observation, at least concurrently with Pater's similar pronouncements. In this regard see, for example, James's January 1868 review of Howells's *Italian Journeys.*[101]

In the Preface to *The Portrait of a Lady,* James moreover observed that

> the house of fiction has . . . not one window, but a million . . . every one of which has been pierced, or is still pierceable . . . by the individual vision and by the pressure of the individual will . . . at each one of them stands a figure with a fieldglass, which forms . . . a unique instrument, insuring to the person making of it an impression distinct from every other. He and his neighbors are watching the same show, but one seeing more where the other sees less, one seeing black where the other sees white . . . one seeing coarse where the other sees fine . . . . The spreading field, the human scene, is the 'choice of subject'; the pierced aperture . . . the 'literary form'; but they are singly or together as nothing without the posted presence of the watcher. . . .[102]

In another essay, after he described "the little peaceful, lazy Cher," and the way a chateau and the river looked from the opposite side, James wrote: "This was the right perspective; we were looking across the river of time. The whole scene was deliciously mild."[103]

In a work that is often cited as the most authoritative study of the autobiographical genre, Roy Pascal remarks that "autobiography means . . . discrimination and selection in the face of the endless complexity of life . . . . Everything depends on the standpoint chosen."[104] Common sense tells us that Pascal is mostly right. But James, in his critical theory and in his fiction, had demonstrated Pascal's words nearly a century before *Design and Truth in Autobiography* was first published.

Although James and the Impressionists were obviously interested in attaining "the grace of intensity" in their artistic performances, they were concerned also to provide a sense of perpetual movement in their work. James developed this notion in his critical prefaces where he spoke of the donnée for Maisie as "the growth of the 'great oak' from the little acorn."[105] And in the Preface to *Roderick Hudson,* he remarked that in " 'developments' " lie "the very essence of the novelist's process, and it is by their aid, fundamentally, that the idea takes form and lives, . . . the painter's subject consisting ever, obviously, of the related state . . . . To exhibit these relations, once they have all been recognized, is to 'treat' his idea."[106]

James felt that the artist's main duty is to treat " 'developments' " since, as he remarked in "The Art of Fiction," "Experience is never limited, and it is never complete; it is an immense spider-web of the finest silken threads suspended in the chamber of consciousness, and catching every air-borne particle in its tissue."[107] But he also went on to declare that experience "is the very atmosphere of the mind,"[108] and in this he differed somewhat from the Impressionists, who sought to reproduce instantaneous sense perceptions, but did so, seemingly, only for the delight of the visual effects that they produced. Conversely, James most often used his visual images to turn the reader inward, to enlarge the range of his consciousness of the Jamesian characters, and of their situations in life.[109] That this should be so is not especially surprising, especially considering the many critical comments that he makes in support of this view. "Be one of the people on whom nothing is lost"[110]—this was ever James's message for the artist—a dictum that he himself also followed. "I am that queer monster, the artist, an obstinate finality, an inexhaustible sensibility"—thus James described himself in a 1914 letter to Henry Adams.[111]

In viewing himself and the practicing artist in this light, James is writing in the tradition of Hawthorne who, in a passage near the end of *The Blithedale Romance,* observed that Nature's highest purpose for man "is that of conscious intellectual life and sensibility."[112] For James, as for Hawthorne, the true reality does not lie in the inter-play of individuals with their environments, but rather in the consciousness and awareness that individuals possess. This attitude probably is much closer to the truth than is the reality that is portrayed by so many of James's contemporaries in the literary profession. Whatever readers of "Romance Novels" like to think, life does not consist of adventures or actions, per se; it is, rather, to use James's phrase, "our apprehension and our measure of what happens to us."[113] James therefore chose uncommon characters for his protagonists—people who, like the characters of Turgenev, could be placed in a situation drawn from an anecdote—and with their aesthetic ideals and moral sensibilities confront their circumstances and live their lives.

"The novel is of all pictures the most comprehensive and the most elastic," James said. "It will stretch anywhere—it will take in absolutely any thing. All it needs is a subject and a painter. But for its subject, magnificently, it has the whole human consciousness."[114] Small wonder, then, that James commented thus upon *Our Mutual Friend*: "Seldom, we reflected, had we read a book so intensely written, so little seen, known, or felt,"[115] for James sought always "to feel" and "to know," but his sense of these terms differed *toto caelo* from that of a Dickens, or even a D. H. Lawrence.[116] In the 1888 essay on London that I have cited above, James, for instance, uses a glimpse of the physical world in order to turn the thought inward: "A sudden horror of the whole place came over me, like a tiger pounce of homesickness which had been watching its moment."[117]

John Rewald tells us that it was "only the Impressionists" who "pursued the instant for the instant's sake, not as the climax of biblical or historical or mythological events, not as a symbol, not as a distillation of intimate visions, but as the immediate response of their retinas and brushes to their observations of nature."[118] James in his critical theory is pretty much opposed to this Impressionist view of art. In "The Art of Fiction" he observed that "a psychological reason is, to my imagination, an object adorably pictorial; to catch the tint of its complexion—I feel as if that idea might inspire one to Titianesque efforts."[119] In this same relatively early essay, James tellingly remarked (and, as was his habit, went on to demonstrate in his fiction) that "the moral consciousness of a child is as much a part of life as the islands of the Spanish Main," and the one sort of geography is, for an author of James's sensibility, filled with as many surprises as the other.[120]

James remarked that the primary aid for a writer of fiction "is a capacity for receiving straight impressions";[121] he also felt that the only reality that matters is the reality of the individual. This conviction is illustrated at some length in a 1909 letter to G. B. Shaw wherein James remarked, "You surely haven't done all your own so interesting work without learning what it is for the imagination to *play* with an idea—an idea about life—under a happy obsession, for all it is worth. Half the beautiful things that the benefactors of the human species have produced would surely be wiped out if you don't allow this adventurous and speculative imagination its rights."[122] For James, then, the term "experience" carries a new and somewhat revolutionary meaning—one that takes account perhaps more of inner than of outer action, and one that often uses the physical world merely as a starting point:

> The power to guess the unseen from the seen, to trace the implication of things, to judge the whole piece by the pattern, the condition of feeling life in general so completely that you are well on your way to knowing any particular corner of it—this cluster of gifts may almost be said to constitute experience, and they occur in country and in town, and in the most differing stages of education. If experience consists of impressions, it may be said that impressions *are* experience, just as (have we not seen it?) they are the very air we breathe. Therefore, if I should certainly say to a novice, 'Write from experience and experience only,' I should feel that this was rather a tantalizing monition if I were not careful immediately to add, 'Try to be one of the people on whom nothing is lost!'[123]

The Impressionist painters considered light and the exchange of colored reflections as the unifying elements of a picture. This attitude finds its analogue in several important passages in James's critical theory. In the Preface to *The Awkward Age,* for example, James wrote, "In sketching my project . . . I drew upon a sheet of paper . . . the neat figure of a circle consisting of a number of small rounds disposed at equal distance around a central object. The central object was . . . my subject in itself . . . and the small rounds represented so many distinct lamps . . . the function of each of which would be to light with all due intensity one of its aspects"[124] (an image, incidentally, that presages Virginia Woolf's famous "gig lamps" passage).[125] Also in his Preface to *The Portrait of a Lady* James fondly remembered Ivan Turgenev's account of "his own experience of the usual origin of the fictive picture."[126] About Turgenev (the Russian allegedly related to James) hovered some person or persons, as *disponibles*, "subject to the chances, the complications of existence, and [he] saw them vividly, but then had to find for them the right relations, those that would bring them out."[127]

The Impressionists, too, insisted upon sensitive changes of tone on their canvasses—a technique that would have appealed to the

Henry James who wrote that "a man's supreme use in the world is
to master his intellectual instrument and play it in perfection."[128]
James's ideal reader, in other words, was someone who would be supremely capable of appreciating the sensitive changes of tone in an
Impressionist work of art. And in his criticism James himself often
made the kind of fine "tonal" distinctions that he would have hoped
for, from his readers. For example, in remarking that the novel *Emily
Chester* is immoral because it provides a false representation of human behavior, James wrote: "Beasts and idiots act from their instincts: educated men and women, even when they most violate
principle, act from their reason, however perverted, and their affections, however misplaced."[129]

The Impressionists furthermore demonstrated that complementary colors heighten each other's intensity when set close together.
In his "Art of Fiction" essay, James developed a similar notion when
he used the organic metaphor (one that was often used also by Pater):
"A novel is a living thing, all one and continuous, like any other or-
ganism, and in proportion as it lives will it be found, I think, that in
each of the parts there is something of each of the other parts."[130]
In the Preface to *Roderick Hudson* he further elucidates this idea:
"Really, universally," James wrote, "relations stop nowhere, and the
exquisite problem of the artist is but to draw, by a geometry of his
own, the circle within which they shall happily appear to do so."[131]
That James may have drawn these relational metaphors from a pair
of philosophers whose work he knew well is not altogether unlikely.
In a spirit that William James would eventually come to approve,
Edmund Scherer,[132] in an 1861 article on Hegel (in *Revue des Deux
Mondes*), remarked that "It is . . . not enough to say: everything is
only relative; we must add: everything is only relation."[133] At approximately the same time as the Impressionist painters were beginning to paint, the philosophers William James and Edmund Scherer,
as well as Henry James himself, expressed in their work the same fundamental truism: that just as a line or a color that is beautiful in one
picture is not necessarily beautiful in another, so the artist must usually depend upon relations to establish his effect. As is almost always
the case, good art is a matter of relations. This is a principle that the
Impressionist painters demonstrated over and again in their imaginative

works. And James, almost from the start of his career, professed this principle as one of the basic tenets of his critical theory.

He also shared with the Impressionists a concern for color, harmony and nuance at the expense of "story" or "subject." As Viola Hopkins Winner has pointed out in her article on "Pictorialism," James often used the color metaphor in the ordinary sense to convey a feeling of piquancy in writing. Conversely, James, for instance, remarked of Stendhal that he "is never pictorial . . . his style is perversely colorless."[134]

Although it is true that in an 1893 Notebook entry James said that "the great question of subject surges in grey dimness about me. It is everything—it is everything, " it is also true that in the Preface to *The Ambassadors* he remarked that " . . . the Story is just the spoiled child of art . . . ,"[135] a position that he held in most of his writings. For James, "Experience is our apprehension and our measure of what happens to us as social creatures . . . ."[136] "It is, not surprisingly, one of the rudiments of criticism," James furthermore said, "that a human, a personal 'adventure' is no *a priori,* no positive and absolute and inelastic thing, but just a matter of relation and appreciation—a name we conveniently give, after the fact, to any passage, to any situation, that has added the sharp taste of uncertainty to a quickened sense of life. Therefore the thing is, all beautifully, a matter of interpretation and of the particular conditions; without a view of which latter some of the most prodigious adventures, as one has often had occasion to say, may vulgarly show for nothing."[137]

For James, as also for the Impressionists, technique was more important than subject. That this should be so for the writer who remarked upon "the fatal futility of Fact"[138] is not surprising. In an 1873 letter to Grace Norton, James set forth his intention: "To produce some little exemplary works of art is my narrow and lowly dream. They are to have less 'brain' than *Middlemarch,* but (I boldly proclaim it) they are to have more *form.* "[139]

James, of course, was "beset constantly with the sense that the painter of the picture . . . can never be responsible enough, and for every inch of his surface."[140] And in his non-fiction, as well as in his fiction, he continually demonstrated this conviction.[141] He cared a great deal for technique, but "one's subject," as he confessed, "is the merest grain, the speck of truth, of beauty, of reality, scarce visible to the common eye. . . ."[142] This is so partially because "there are some subjects which speak to us and others which do not, but he would be a clever man who should undertake to give a rule—an *index expurgatorius*—by which the story and the no-story should be known apart. It is impossible (to me at least) to imagine any such rule which shall not be altogether arbitrary."[143] James would probably have a-greed with Proust that the great artist "can make as precious discoveries in an advertisement for soap as in the *Pensées de Pascal*."

He therefore eschewed traditional "action" and with a techni-cal virtuosity analogous to the Impressionists pursued such "limited" subjects as he saw fit. In an 1881 letter to T. S. Perry, James referred to a story which "will be the best thing that I have done, in spite of an impudent lack of incident—or of what is commonly understood to be such."[144] In "The Royal Academy" (1878), he castigated the English artists and their audience for a common insensitivity to "the plastic quality" of art:

> At all events, I never go into an exhibition of English pictures without being strongly reminded of M. Taine; I put on his spectacles; I seem to see so well what he meant. With M. Taine's spectacles you immediate-ly see that the exhibition is only in a secondary sense *plastic*; that the plastic quality is not what English spectators look for in a picture, or what the artist has taken the precaution of putting into it. The artist must tell a story or preach a sermon; his picture must not be an image, but, in some fashion or other, a lesson; not a reproduction of form and colour, but of life and experience.[145]

James and the Impressionists also developed a method whereby their art was more "true to life" than the art of the more realistic schools that preceded them. On the whole, he agreed with Flaubert when the Frenchman exhorted his fellow writers: *"soyons exposants et non discutants."* James's theory of fiction is therefore akin to the work of the Impressionists, since he feels that the work of fiction should have little articulation and that the objects that are depicted within the work should have blurred boundaries. Partially for these reasons, there is a need for the ideal viewer's/reader's assistance in "putting the scene together." Just as the viewer must synthesize the colors and supply the missing elements, so the spectator's/reader's collaboration is needed.146 In painting, these kinds of demands first seem to have been made upon the viewer by Corot, whose pupil Pissarro claims to have been. In this regard, see, for example, the extremely sensitive tone changes in "Avignon from the West" (1836). In James's Chapter of *The American Scene*, entitled "New York and the Hudson: A Spring Impression," he describes "the mere blinding radiance of a visit to West Point" in Impressionist terms. And it is interesting to note that he brings Corot into the description:

> . . . both as to essence and as to quantity, its prose seemed washed away, and I shall recall it in the future much less as the sternest the world over, of all the seats of Discipline, than as some great Corot-composition of young, vague, wandering figures in splendidly-classic shades.147

In literature in English, these kinds of demands can perhaps be traced back to Emerson and Whitman. In "The Over-Soul," Emerson wrote that "the act of seeing and the thing seen, the seer and the spectacle, the subject and the object are one."148 James, however, with his ironic stance, rings a change upon Emerson's dictum and upon Whitman's practice.

On the reader-text aspect, James's *theory* is closer to Whitman than to Emerson. "The reader will always have his or her part to do, just as I have mine," Whitman exclaimed. "I seek less to state or display any theme or thought, and more to bring you, reader, into the atmosphere of the theme or thought—there to pursue your own flight."149 Whitman, of course, could have summoned an authoritative ally in Sainte-Beuve, who held that "for us the greatest poet is he who in his works most stimulates the reader's imagination, and reflection . . . . The greatest poet is not he who has done the best; it is he who suggests the most; he, not all of whose meaning is at first obvious, and who leaves you much to desire, to explain, to study, much to complete in your turn."150

Because James, in Impressionist fashion, recognized the need for the reader's assistance, he especially deplored what he saw to be the march of "the high prosperity of fiction . . . with another 'sign of the times,' the demoralization, the vulgarization of literature in general."151 During the Victorian era, James thought, until the 1880's "there was a comfortable good-humoured feeling that a novel is a novel as a pudding is a pudding, and that our only business with it could be to swallow it." In the 1880's, he felt, things were beginning to change—"the era of discussion would appear to have been to a certain extent opened."152 As early as 1866 James wrote: "In every novel the work is divided between the writer and the reader; but the writer makes the reader very much as he makes his characters. When he makes him ill, that is, makes him indifferent, he does not work; the writer does all. When he makes him well, that is, makes him interested, then the reader does quite the labour."153

Since in his critical theory James afforded such an important part to the reader, it is not suprising that he would also have demanded a great deal from him. In the Preface to *The Wings of the Dove* James makes quite clear what his demands are, and why: "Attention of perusal, I thus confess by the way, is what I at every point . . . absolutely invoke and take for granted . . . . The enjoyment of a work of art, the acceptance of an irresistible illusion, constituting, to my sense, our highest experience of 'luxury,' the luxury is not greatest, by my consequent measure, when the work asks for as little attention as possible."154

In the sphere of the visual and plastic arts, I have already alluded to the early Continental example of Corot—a leading Impressionist forerunner whose sensitive changes of tone James evidently admired. But James's inspiration with regard to "the participating spectator" might very well have come from a source much closer to him than Corot. In his study of John LaFarge, Cortissoz relates that William Morris Hunt told John LaFarge that he carried his refinements of tone and color too far, as not even " 'one in a hundred or five hundred artists [were] capable of appreciating such differences of accuracy.' 'So much the better,' LaFarge rejoined, 'if only one man in a thousand could see it; I should then have exactly what I wanted in the appeal to the man who knew and to the mind like mine.' "155 We know that James took LaFarge's attitude to heart, since in the first volume of his *Autobiography,* James wrote the following of LaFarge: "with the implication, a hundred times beneficent and fertilizing, that if one didn't in these connections consistently take one's stand on super-subtlety of taste one was a helpless outsider . . . a doctrine more salutary at that time in our world at large than any other that might be sounded."156

With this LaFargian attitude perhaps in mind, James was able to counter William's criticism of the last paragraph of *Daisy Miller* by remarking to his older brother that "the teller is but a more developed reader," another way of expressing his feeling for the importance of having intelligent readers. In the same passage James goes on to say, "I think you are altogether right in returning always to the import- ance of subject. I hold to this, strongly; and if I don't as yet seem to proceed upon it more, it is because, being 'very artistic,' I have a con- stant impulse to try experiments of form, in which I wish to not run the risk of wasting or gratuitously using big situations."157 When we keep in mind James's relationship to the reader, then we realize that James was not especially condescending about literary critics when he wrote, in an 1868 Review of *Dallas Galbraith* (by Mrs. R. H. Davis), that "the critic is simply a reader like all the others—a reader who prints his impressions."158

James, therefore, recognized the need for "attention of peru- sal" on the part of his readers. He assumed an alert readership and proceeded to develop his experiments with form—exercises in spirit- ual adventure in which he seems to have increasingly employed such favorite expressive devices as qualification, parenthesis, complex met- aphor, and elaborate periodicity.159

In his later period, especially, James declared that he had grown determined to give "not . . . my own personal account of the affair in hand, but . . . my account of somebody's impression of it . . . through the opportunity and the sensibility of some more or less de- tached, some not strictly involved, though thoroughly interested and intelligent witness or reporter."160 This view, as it finds form in the fiction, is analogous to James's use of irony as a distancing feature, which is not altogether unlike the Impressionist technique that re- quires the viewer to maintain a distance from the canvas, in order to appreciate fully the painter's technique.161

Related to this ironic attitude is the open-ended quality that one finds in much Modernist art—from James and the Impressionists until roughly the beginning of World War II (at which time art begins to move in another direction, toward involvement and commitment). Sainte-Beuve was probably right when he said that the function of poetry is not to tell us everything, but to set our imaginations at work: "La Poésie consiste à ne pas tout dire, mais à tout faire rêver." James, who himself much admired Sainte-Beuve, remarked that "there are degrees of feeling—the muffled, the faint, the sufficient, the barely intelligent, as we may say; and the acute, the intense, the complete, in a word—the power to be finely aware and richly responsible. It is those who move in this latter fashion who 'get most' out of all that happens to them and who in so doing enable us, as readers of their record, as participators by a fond attention, also to get most."162

In order, therefore, to allow the reader to "get most" out of a work of art, James, like the Impressionists, chose a method that would force his reader to "step back," in order to allow the sense of disengagement that would enable him to complete the scene. But since the ultimate "action" in Jamesian fiction is mostly internal, the fiction itself must needs be open-ended. James himself, of course, often declared his opposition to the "closed-form" of fiction. And he did so perhaps most amusingly in "The Art of Fiction" where he remarked that "the 'ending' of a novel is, for many persons, like that of a good dinner, a course of dessert and ices, and the artist in fiction is regarded as a sort of meddlesome doctor who forbids agreeable aftertastes."163

As Ethel Cornwell has stated, "because he thinks that no one can completely know another, James presents his characters (to us, and to each other) in such a way as to leave deliberate ambiguities. He acquaints us with his people gradually, by accumulated impressions which lead by degrees toward a further, but never a complete, understanding of his characters."164 "Nothing," Henry James would write in response to a reviewer of *An International Episode* (1879) "is my *last word* about anything"165—a sentiment that would show the way for most of the major Modernist authors who would follow him.

Now that we have seen how closely James's theory of fiction accords with that of the Impressionist methods in painting, let us examine some representative works from James's fictional *œuvre*, in order that we can see in what ways these performances can be said to show James to be a prose fiction writer for whom the term "Impressionist" provides the most accurate descriptive label.

As readers, we cannot allow the statements in the letters and criticism, however useful, to substitute for the experience of the imaginative canon of the author. (In this regard we recall, for instance D. H. Lawrence's famous letter to Edward Garnett, wherein the author expressed his "intentions" in writing *Sons and Lovers,* yet how different from his stated intentions the fictional performance proves itself to be!) Analogously, there is no reliable reason to expect a serious writer such as James to explain in his Prefaces the techniques that are to be found within his novels. An artist's statements in behalf of a theory of art do not hold him to that theory in the practice of his craft, but neither do they mean that he must eschew in his art the theory that he has articulated in his critical writings. James did not say much about the Impressionists in his criticism. But what is much more to the point is that techniques that were used by the Impressionist painters were paramount not only in his theory of art, but also in his fiction. "The form . . . ," James said, "is to be appreciated after the fact: then the author's choice has been made, his standard indicated; then we can follow lines and directions and compare tones and resemblances."166 In the following discussion of representative works of fiction from the Jamesian canon, I shall indicate the manner in which James's "lines and directions . . . tones and resemblances" follow (or parallel) those of Impressionism in the arts. In James's fiction, as I shall demonstrate, Impressionist techniques can be found from the earliest stories through the novels of the so-called Major Phase.

Henry James first uses Impressionist techniques in his third story, " A Landscape Painter." This brief tale first appeared in the *Atlantic Monthly* for February 1866 and was reprinted in Volume Two of James's *Stories Revived,* published by Macmillan in 1885 (the same year in which Zola published *The Masterpiece*). As with most of the work that James republished during his lifetime, "A

Landscape Painter" underwent revision from magazine version to
book publication. And a number of these revisions moved James's
tale further in the direction of Impressionism.

In the magazine version of James's story, the hero is a lately
deceased landscape painter named Locksley, who records his impressions of nature on his canvases and in the last hundred pages of his
diary. These last pages are disclosed by his fiancée, Esther Blunt, in
order to satisfy a friend's curiosity regarding "the great Nemesis of
his [i.e., Locksley's] treatment of [his former fiancée] Miss
Leary."[167] Early in the narrative, Locksley reports his impressions
of the seascape from the cove where he has just dropped anchor. The
1866 version reads thus: "I spent the whole afternoon in wandering
hither and thither over the hills that encircle the little cove in which
I had landed, heedless of the minutes and of my steps, watching the
sailing clouds and the cloudy sails on the horizon, listening to the
musical attrition of the tidal pebbles . . . ."[168] In the 1885 version,
James makes a minor but seemingly significant change in this passage.
In lieu of "cloudy . . . horizon," James substitutes "flitting, gleam-
ing sails," thus lending to his scene a sense that it is in perpetual
movement and that the diarist is reproducing his instantaneous
sense-perceptions, much as the Impressionist painters themselves
were doing at that very time.[169]

Later in the story, James's revisions shed even more direct
light upon his movement toward Impressionism in mid-career. In
Locksley's diary entry for August 14th, for example, he reports upon
his afternoon drive, accompanied by Miss Blunt, over Weston's
Beach. He notes that "the tide was very low; and we had the whole
glittering, weltering strand to ourselves."

> At our left, almost from the lofty zenith of the pale evening sky to
> the high, western horizon of the tumultuous dark-green sea, was sus-
> pended, so to speak, one of those gorgeous vertical sunsets that Turner
> loved so well. It was a splendid confusion of purple and green and
> gold,—the clouds flying and flowing in the wind like the folds of a
> mighty banner borne by some triumphal fleet whose prows were not
> visible above the long chain of mountainous waves. As we reached
> the point where the cliffs plunge down upon the beach, I pulled up,

and we remained for some moments looking out along the low, brown, obstinate barrier at whose feet the impetuous waters were rolling themselves into powder.[170]

In the 1885 version which was prepared for book publication, this passage was heavily revised, James giving especially close scrutiny to the manner in which Locksley has rendered the scene. In the later version, James substitutes "that Turner sometimes painted" for "that Turner loved so well." Moreover, in the final lines of the passage, where in the original version the emphasis is upon "the obstinate barrier," in the later version James emphasizes instead his viewer, Locksley, who records his momentary impressions of the scene. Rather than "we remained for some moments," and so forth, James has the 1885 passage read: "we remained for some time looking at their long, diminishing, crooked perspective, blue and dun as it receded, with the white surge playing at their feet."[171]

Of James's early tales "The Story of a Masterpiece" (1868) illustrates well the young author's inclination to use certain Impressionist methods—even, on this occasion, before the painters themselves used them in their art. "The Story of a Masterpiece" appeared in two parts. The first installment was published in *Galaxy*, Part I in January, 1868 (pages 5-21), Part II in February (pages 133-143).

In this story John Lennox, a wealthy widower, meets Miss Marian Everett in Newport. While travelling in Europe with an invalid widow, Miss Everett met and fell in love with Stephen Baxter, who seemingly fell more deeply in love with her than she with him. After she quarrelled and broke with Baxter, Miss Everett became engaged to Lennox. Thereafter Lennox, through a painter friend, meets Baxter, who is painting a portrait that reminds Lennox of Miss Everett. He commissions Baxter to paint Miss Everett, but finds himself dissatisfied with the portrait which he finds both disarming and disconcerting:

> Was she a creature without faith and without conscience? What else was the meaning of that horrible blankness and deadness that quenched the light in her eyes and stole away the smile from her lips? . . . Had Baxter been a man of marvellous insight—an unparalleled observer; or had he been a mere patient and unflinching painter, building

infinitely better than he knew? Would not a mere painter have been
content to paint Miss Everett in the strong, rich, objective manner of
which the work was so good an example, and to do nothing more?
For it was evident that Baxter had done more. He had painted with
something more than knowledge—with imagination, with feeling.172

Baxter, in short, had seemingly done in his portrait what such
Impressionists as Degas and Van Gogh were to do in theirs; he had
given only the impression of his subject. For Lennox, however, Baxter's impression was enough—or perhaps it was too much—for after
viewing the painting twice (the second time under a dimmer light),
Lennox concludes that "his love was dead, his youth was dead . . . .
His love's vitality has been but small, and since it was to be short-
lived it was better that it should expire before marriage than after. As
for marriage, that should stand, for that was not of necessity a matter of love. He lacked the brutal consistency necessary for taking
away Marian's future."173 Lennox goes ahead with the marriage to
which he has committed himself, but he allows himself the luxury of
vengefully attacking Baxter's portrait of his betrothed: " . . . with a
half-a-dozen strokes, he wantonly hacked it across. The act afforded
him an immense relief."174

Like the art of the Impressionists which treats quotidian subjects that lead to no apparent artistic resolution (by way of contrast, we think of the subjects being dealt with by the Academic
painters who were working concurrently with the Impressionists),
James's story is extremely "open-ended"; that is, it ends, like so
many of James's works of fiction, by leaving the reader to frame the
resolutions of plot and character himself. In a romantic novel, such
as by Jane Austen, we are led to see that after marriage Emma will
live happily "ever after." In a Victorian novel, such as Dickens'
*Bleak House,* we see that after the nuptials the couple emerges into
"a world of light and shade"—symbolic, perhaps, of the way that
married life will be for them. At the conclusion of James's story,
however, the narrator relates of Lennox: "How has he fared—how is
he destined to fare—in matrimony, it is rather too early to determine. He has been married scarcely three months." Just as the Impressionists refused to provide minute details and elaborate finish, so
also does James deliberately refuse to give the reader all the answers
and to provide a plot that is "rounded" in any true sense. I say

*deliberately* here, because of the statement that James made, in his letter dated October 23, 1867, to one of the editors of the *Galaxy*. James wrote:

> . . . As for adding a paragraph I should strongly object to it. It doesn't seem to me necessary. Silence on the subject will prove to the reader, I think, that the marriage *did* come off. I have little fear that the reader will miss a positive statement to that effect and the story closes in a more dramatic manner, to my apprehension, just as I have left it.[175]

Some scholars have claimed for James's late '70's story, "The Diary of a Man of Fifty," the first expression by James of his theme of "too late." In a sense, however, "The Madonna of the Future" (1873) could be said to be James's first treatment of this Jamesian theme. "The Madonna of the Future" is the story of an artist who devotes his life to the creation of a single masterpiece which after his death is exposed as a blank canvas. This story is especially important for our concerns, since in it James seems to have drawn upon Balzac's "Le Chef-d'œuvre inconnu" (we recall that in James's tale the painter Theobald refers to that "horrible little tale by Balzac"). And the indications are that Émile Zola, in drafting plans for his Impressionist novel, *The Masterpiece* (1885), drew his inspiration for Lantier's behavior from Balzac and from James (we recall also that James's story was translated and printed in a popular French periodical, shortly after the story appeared in English in 1873).[176] James himself admitted, of course, that "if a work of imagination, of fiction, interests me at all . . . I always want to write it over in my own way."[177]

In "The Madonna of the Future," the old Yankee painter who has lived out his life in Florence, confesses sadly that American artists "lack the deeper sense" of the European, and are condemned to "live in perpetual exile." To which the young narrator rejoins, speaking perhaps for the young James's hopes: " 'Nothing is so idle as to talk about our want of a nursing air, of a kindly soil, of opportunity, of the things that help. The only thing that helps is to do something fine. There's no law in our glorious Constitution against that. Invent, create, achieve!' " It is not difficult to see how the narrator's words might really have been those of James himself; for he was a writer capable of making a splendid, if horrifying, work of literary creation even out of the consciousness of a failed artist's sensibility. And in the same year in which "The Madonna of the Future" appeared in America, James wrote the following sentence (in an essay on Gautier): "a man's supreme use in the world is to master his intellectual instrument and play it in perfection."[178] Ever the faithful artist, James never hesitated to express his distaste for the slothful artist, the one who pursued only the "cheap and easy" in the realm of art.[179]

The next Jamesian work of fiction that I will examine is anything but "cheap and easy." Written in the summer of 1873, *Madame de Mauves* is the story of the disastrous marriage of an American girl, Euphemia Cleve, to a French aristocrat of questionable morals. In matters of technique, this short novel is in many way James's best effort to date. The story is told in a dramatic fashion, mostly through the impressions of the hero—thus representing a technical advance over "the diary narration" provided, for instance, in "A Landscape Painter" and the omniscient narration of "The Story of a Masterpiece." With this advance comes an increase in narrative complexity, for we as readers must frequently interpret what filters through to us from the consciousness of James's narrator Longmore, a younger, more naive, and less sanguine version of the Lambert Strether of *The Ambassadors.*

James alerts us right away to the Impressionist nature of his narrative. He begins the tale with a marvelous Impressionist word picture of Paris—one that could be drawn from one of Monet's or Pissarro's views-from-a-terrace paintings of the early '70's:

> The view from the terrace at Saint-Germain-en-Laye is immense and famous. Paris lies spread before you in dusky vastness, domed and fortified, glittering here and there through her light vapors, and girdled with her silver Seine. Behind you is a park of stately symmetry, and behind that a forest, where you may lounge through turfy avenues and light-checkered glades, and quite forget that you are within half an hour of the boulevards.

In this scene, which is drawn in a manner not unlike some of the passages in Daudet's *Kings in Exile,* the speaking voice almost immediately enlists the viewer's/reader's participation in the unfolding narrative. James does this by using a form of the direct address: "Behind you is a park . . . where you may lounge . . . , and quite forget . . . ." Right away the reader is not shown the scene, but forced, in a sense, to conjure it—to figure out where he belongs and where the action takes him.

In the early portions of the narrative James produces this effect by use of an authorial voice that speaks ambivalently about Comte Richard de Mauves. De Mauves, for instance, is said to be seen thus by the Jane Eyre-like Euphemia: "M. de Mauves was the hero of the young girl's romance made real, *and so completely accordant with this creature of her imagination* [italics mine], that she felt afraid of him, very much as she would have been of a supernatural apparition." The description of her infatuation with the thirty-five year old Comte continues: "He was perhaps a trifle handsomer than Euphemia's rather grim quixotic ideal, but a very few days reconciled her to his good looks, as they would have reconciled her to his ugliness." Here, as throughout the narrative, we receive little by way of specific characterization of M. de Mauves. He is "perhaps a trifle handsomer than Euphemia's rather quixotic ideal . . . ."—an impression only—and one that is given us by a narrator who is himself very quixotic.[180]

After M. de Mauves, Rochester-like, is temporarily invalided by a fall from "an unruly horse, which Euphemia with shy admiration had watched him mount in the castle yard,"[181] she nurses him back to health. During this period,

> Euphemia studied with noiseless diligence what she supposed to be the 'character' of M. de Mauves, and the more she looked the more fine lights and shades she seemed to behold in this masterpiece of nature. M. de Mauves's character indeed, whether from a sense of being generously scrutinized, or for reasons which bid graceful defiance to analysis, had never been so amiable; it seemed really to reflect the purity of Euphemia's interpretation of it.[182]

In this description we see a number of the important elements that comprise the Impressionist style. In Euphemia's finding in M. de Mauves's "character" the "fine lights and shades" she seems to want to find, we see an analogue to the Impressionists' use of light and colored reflections as the unifying elements of a picture. More importantly, perhaps, is the need for the reader to put this passage together, much as the viewer of the Impressionist painting has to supply the missing elements to the work of art. As in many of James's best works of fiction, the verbs in *Madame de Mauves* reflect this aspect of the author's fundamentally Impressionist style. In the previously quoted passage, for instance, Euphemia "*studied* with noiseless diligence" what "she *seemed to behold*" in her "masterpiece of nature." M. de Mauves' character in short, "really *seemed* to reflect the purity of Euphemia's interpretation of it." In this tale, as in such disparate masterpieces as *Daisy Miller, The Portrait of a Lady, The Turn of the Screw, What Maisie Knew,* and *The Ambassadors,* that which makes James's fiction difficult is also that which makes it enjoyable to reread. Were one to replace all of James's "seems," "perceives," "makes outs," and "appears" with verbs of more specific quality, James's fiction would undoubtedly be less ambivalent, but it would also be considerably less fascinating.

In Part III of the novella, the weight of the narrative is borne increasingly by Longmore, whose impressions of Madame de Mauves (formerly Euphemia) inform this section of the narrative. M. de Mauves urges the young American, who is travelling in Europe, to entertain his wife, in order perhaps to try to bring her "out of herself" and make her less introspective. But Longmore immediately divines that Madame de Mauves "was not sweeping the horizon for a compensation or a consoler; she had suffered a personal deception which had disgusted her with persons."[183] But James, with his ironic sense, also immediately characterized Longmore thus: "Longmore was a man of fine imagination, whose leading-strings had never been slipped." Thus, the reader has the right to be bemusedly skeptical when he learns that Longmore "began to regard his hostess as a figure haunted by a shadow which was somehow her intenser, more authentic self." Longmore then goes so far as to envision "this hovering mystery" itself as a physical presence which he sees to have "delicate beauty," "to his eye" endowed with "the serious cast of certain blank-browed Greek statues . . . ."[184] In this descriptive passage, the irony is multi-dimensional, since this description, the most precise and evocative one in the tale, is Longmore's impression of the "hovering mystery" which he feels to be a physical presence surrounding Madame de Mauves!

Later in this section, on very little evidence Longmore proceeds to "gauge" what he feels to be M. de Mauves' feelings toward his wife: "M. de Mauves was tired of his companion: he relished a higher flavor in female society. She was too modest, too simple, too delicate; she had too few arts, too little coquetry, too much charity. M. de Mauves, someday, lighting a cigar, had probably decided she was stupid. It was the same sort of taste, Longmore moralized, as the taste for Gerôme in painting and for M. Gustave Flaubert in literature."185

Later in the narrative, in compliance with his friend "Mrs. Draper's injunction to give her an account of his impressions of her friend," Longmore writes, "The only time she ever spoke to me of her marriage, . . . she intimated that it had been a perfect love-match." In the manner of James's narrator in *The Sacred Fount,* Longmore then proceeds to give what is for him a typically flustered commentary on such matters: "With all abatements, I suppose most marriages are; but in her case this would mean more, I think, than in that of most women; for her love was an absolute idealization."186 Despite the confusion indicated by the first two parts of his sentence, in the third clause, Longmore seemingly gets closer than before to the heart of Madame de Mauves' original feelings toward her husband.

In a lyric passage about three quarters of the way through the novella, Longmore "wandered into an unfamiliar region," "a perfectly rural scene [that] . . . the still summer day gave . . . a charm for which its meagre elements but half accounted." And this scene is done in a manner which indicates that by 1873 James was equally familiar with Impressionist elements in French literature and in French painting:

> Longmore thought he had never seen anything so characteristically French; all the French novels seemed to have described it, all the French landscapists to have painted it. The fields and trees were of a

cool metallic green; the grass looked as if it might stain your trousers, and the foliage your hands. The clear light had a sort of mild grayness; the sunbeams were of silver rather than gold. A great red-roofed, high-stacked farm-house, with whitewashed walls and a straggling yard, surveyed the high road, on one side, from behind a transparent curtain of poplars . . . . [The scene] was full of light atmosphere and diffused sunshine, and if it was prosaic, it was soothing.[187]

In this lyrical passage we can recognize many elements that are found also in the painting and the literature of the Impressionist era: the rendering of the impressions that objects make on the eye, the open air scene that is "painted" on the spot, the recording of a view in the particular light present at the moment when the subject is rendered, the reproduction of instantaneous sense-perceptions, the capturing of the effects of light, and the depiction of objects whose boundaries are blurred. All of the Impressionist effects are demonstrably present in this passage. But what seems to me to be even more important about this passage is the way its inclusion leads us to feel about Longmore. While he does not yet seem capable of grasping fully the situation with regard to Madame de Mauves and her husband, Longmore's appreciation, two thirds of the way through the narrative, of the Impressionist scene in which he finds himself, leads us to accept more fully the seeming truth of his final comments with regard to the pair whose behavior he judges. After he bears fine witness to the lovely rural scene that I have quoted above, we come to feel that Longmore's judgments regarding the human figures in his scene may not be so confused as we had hitherto believed. In a manner not unlike James's use of Strether's appreciation of the Impressionist elements in his environment (to which I shall return), the author's handling of Longmore's artistic vision prepares us to accept the accuracy of his moral-perceptual one. By the time that we finally learn that M. de Mauves has committed suicide, James has therefore prepared us to accept Longmore's feelings of suspicion. He has prepared us at least in part, I think, by allowing us to witness the sensitive manner in which Longmore responds to the Impressionist scene in which he finds himself—a landscape which, through his sentient observations, Longmore also enables us to see.

The next Jamesian story that we shall consider has received remarkably little critical attention, yet it is perhaps James's most technically brilliant work of short fiction. In "A Bundle of Letters" (1879), James successfully meets what he refers to (in the Preface to *The Tragic Muse*) as "the challenge of economic representation."[188] What is of especial interest for our purposes, however, is that in his story James skillfully utilizes for the first time some important techniques that are at least partially drawn from the Impressionist art.

"A Bundle of Letters" first appeared in serial format in *Parisian,* December 1879 (first book publication came the following year). The story is especially significant, since in it can be found many of the techniques that we have come to associate with the Master's Major Phase: the story is extremely ironic, it places a great deal of emphasis upon manners (indeed, without them there would be no story),[189] and it experiments with point of view in ways that make the story boldly original.

By his own testimony, James wrote "A Bundle of Letters" at one long sitting during several days in which he was snow-bound in a Paris hotel.[190] Since James left Paris for London in 1876, it seems probable that he wrote "A Bundle of Letters" during his autumn vacation visit to Paris in 1877. If the story were written in this year, then this would seem especially appropriate, since James's writing of his story would therefore have coincided with the appearance of the third Impressionist exhibit, which opened in Paris that same year. In this third exhibition there were eighteen participants, among them Monet, Pissarro, Renoir, Sisley, and Cézanne.

1877 is further significant, because in this year *L'Impressionniste,* under the editorship of Georges Rivière, was founded in Paris. When we recall that Henry James had reviewed the second Impressionist exhibit when it opened in Paris the previous year, it would seem very likely that he would also have attended the well-publicized third exhibit. He may even perhaps have read the new organ for the movement, *L'Impressionniste,* whose editor moved in the same Parisian circles that James did when he was on the continent.

"A Bundle of Letters" is done entirely in the epistolary form and contains letters by six correspondents. The letters are dated from September 5, 1879, to October 22 of the same year. The story begins with a letter from Miranda Hope, who writes to her mother who is living in Maine. Miss Hope provides her impressions of the French scene generally, but in particular of the pension of Madame de Maisonrouge, in which the young girl is staying while she tries to learn French. In the meantime, Miss Violet Ray, who is seemingly from a fashionable family in New York, writes from the same pension about the provinciality of Miss Hope. Meanwhile, Louis Leverett, who Miss Ray refers to as "an aesthetic young man, who talks about its being 'a real Corot day,' "191 writes home from the pension Maisonrouge to tell his Boston friend (named Harvard) about the snobbish and conceited Miss Ray and the awkward and unsophisticated Miss Hope. On this occasion, Leverett also mentions a picturesque English girl named Evelyn Vane.

When Miss Hope writes home again, she praises Leverett's urbanity, and charm, remarks upon the aloofness of Miss Ray, and notes Miss Vane's timidity. She also comments at this time upon the intelligence of a certain German boarder in the pension, and remarks upon the fluency of Madame de Maisonrouge's cousin Leon Verdier. Miss Vane then writes of family plans, describes Miss Ray as a pleasant person, Miss Hope as vulgar, Verdier as base, the German as boring, and Leverett as too aesthetic. Verdier in turn writes a friend, telling him what fun it is to observe the delicate English girl, the pretty American (Miss Ray), and the aggressive one (Miss Hope). Then the German, Dr. Rudolph Staub, writes a colleague in condemnation of all decadent Americans, Englishmen, and Frenchmen—particularly those worthless ones who are residing in the pension where he is staying! The final letter comes from Miss Hope, who is blithefully departing for another interesting European country.

As my summary perhaps serves to indicate, "A Bundle of Letters" has something of the final effect of the parlor game in which a sentence is whispered about in a circle; the point of the game is the amusement that comes when the last version is compared with the original. But in James's version we have the double delight in witnessing the manner in which "the message" of the same pension atmosphere is transmitted by six correspondents from four countries.

In "A Bundle of Letters" James uses a number of techniques that he may have learned from the Impressionist painters whose work had been so freshly viewed by him. In 1878 James published *Daisy Miller,* a short novel in which a great deal of the fascination lies in the manner with which Winterbourne's opinion of the young American girl continues to change. But in "A Bundle of Letters" James shows not an individual, but an environment—one which continually changes for us as readers. James moves us around the same subject, the pension, in a manner analogous to the Monet who paints the same subject—a haystack, for example—from different viewpoints and at different times of the year.

Although in the James story the pension atmosphere is described by six letter writers, the sequence with which James has arranged the letters leaves us certain that, while each letter has contributed to our impression of the scene, none of them has been written from an entirely reliable veiwpoint. As with the Impressionist painting which provides little articulation in the whole, so in James's ironic story the atmosphere emerges only gradually, as we read each successive letter. The only final judgment that can be made about the quality of the atmosphere is the one that we, as readers, make, when we finish the last letter. James's ironic humor forces us to step back, in order to appreciate the comedy of manners that he presents us with. And the real "action" in the story consists in the impressions that the various letters make upon the consciousness of the detached reader. Probably because of this Jamesian method of rendering "action," Joseph Conrad many years later referred to the sense of movement and open-endedness in James's fiction—aspects of James's craft from which Conrad himself almost certainly learned a great deal.[192]

In his use of the epistolary form, James of course could also have drawn upon the British and Continental tradition in the novel. In his use of the form, James seems closest to the British novelist, Tobias Smollett. In Smollett's *Humphrey Clinker,* for instance, there are five letter writers who have different personalities and who thus present five different points of view. But James's story differs from Smollett's novel in two major ways. Firstly, James unifies his tale by having all six correspondents write of one atmosphere; namely, that of the pension. Smollett's characters, on the other hand, confront situations that, if more strictly human, are also more understandably diffuse. Secondly, Smollett orders his letters in such a way that the divergent views come together; in the course of the narrative, experience brings the characters to revelations of seemingly unified truths: old Bramble, for example, who cherishes order, comes to see the need for variety; Lydia, who is in love with change and variety, comes to learn the need for order. This ordering of the chaotic is a common strategy in the 18th century epistolary novel, but James goes beyond this in the making of his open-ended fiction (for all of its economic mastery, we recall that "A Bundle of Letters" is even structurally open-ended, since the story ends with another letter from Miss Hope, who is blithefully planning her departure for other lands). The only possible order that one can find in James's story is the temporary order that the reader sees as he finishes James's amusing tale.

Another Impressionist feature in James's story is the use of "the keyhole perspective"—especially in the letters from Louis Leverett. In the plastic arts, Leverett's observations lead us to recall the many nude bathing scenes done by Degas and Renoir. The former's "Le Bain" (ca. 1890), for instance, in which a nude woman is pictured stepping into (or out of—it is difficult to tell which) a bathtub, expresses well the voyeuristic quality of most of Leverett's letters. In Western literary tradition, such 18th century British novelists as Samuel Richardson have produced something of the same effect. We recall, for example, the fleeting seduction scene in *Pamela*. On the whole, of course, James's use of this "keyhole perspective" is much closer to that of the Impressionist painters than to the 18th century novelists, primarily because James has executed his performance with such admirable economy. In his Preface to *The Tragic Muse* James expresses well what he means when he speaks of meeting "the challenge of economic representation":

> To put all that is possible of one's idea into a form and compass that will contain and express it only by delicate adjustments and an exquisite chemistry, so that there will be neither a drop of one's liquor left nor a hair's breadth of the rim of one's glass to spare—every artist will remember how often that sort of necessity has carried with it its particular inspiration. Therein lies the secret of the appeal, to his mind,

of the successfully *foreshortened* thing, where representation is arrived at, as I have already had occasion to urge, not by the addition of items (a light that has for its attendant shadow a possible dryness) but by the art of figuring synthetically, a compactness into which the imagination may cut thick, as into the rich density of wedding-cake.[193]

From the French literary tradition, James may also perhaps have drawn some inspiration from such a minor writer as Gustave Droz. In the early 1870's, Droz had published *Un Paquet de Lettres,* a collection of stories that were similar in tone to James's urbane tale. Although James refers to Droz many times in his critical writings, he nowhere, to my knowledge, mentions *Un Paquet de Lettres.* Of course, this does not mean that he was not familiar with the French author's stories. In a letter to his good friend, Thomas Sergeant Perry, written from the Rue du Luxembourg on February 3, 1876, James mentions having discussed Droz's work with Flaubert. When we keep in mind that this letter was written within weeks of James's review of the second Impressionist exhibit, which James reported upon for the *Tribune,* we can imagine that Impressionism in the arts may at this time have been very much on James's mind. Moreover, from early in his career, T. S. Perry had taken serious interest in Gustave Droz's fiction, which the American author had taken pains to translate for publication. Perry's over-all opinion of the French writer is well-expressed in the following passage: "a keen social satirist, quite free from ill-nature . . . witty, gay, brilliant, and polished . . . . He points out the follies of society with a truth that must convince the most thoughtless . . . ."[194] Such words, of course, can serve to characterize not only the stories in Droz's *Un Paquet,* but also James's "A Bundle of Letters."

Of further interest, perhaps, is that Perry reviewed *Un Paquet* in an article on Droz in *Nation* (February 23, 1871). In her biography of Perry, Virginia Harlow makes the point that, during the period from July 1, 1865 to September, 1880, none of Perry's contributions to the *Nation* was signed.[195] That Perry's piece was unsigned matters little, however, since James, who during this period was a faithful reader of the *Nation* (from which he received his first, very much appreciated honoraria), was also on the best of personal terms with Perry (as the Harlow biography makes abundantly clear), and may possibly have had Perry's essay called to his attention by its author. Interestingly, we do know what Perry's own opinion of James's story was. During the 1880's, Perry wrote of his good companion James to his new friend, the Reverend Hercules Warren Fay: "His greatest failure seems to me to be *The Bostonians,* but how good 'The Pension Beaurepas' and 'A Bundle of Letters' are!"196

One further word about "A Bundle of Letters." It need not be remarked upon in detail how James has used the names in his story to underline his seemingly ironic intent. In Louis Leverett's name, however, James has drawn upon a pair of names from another of his works of fiction; for Louis's name is an amalgam of Marian Everett and John Lennox, the strange couple from "The Story of a Masterpiece," a story whose Impressionist elements I have considered above. With echoes from such a pair of characters in mind, we comprehend the justness of James's characterization of Leverett, who is full of the "French way of looking at life" and who professes to be eager for experience. Although surely there is a great deal of irony in James's characterization of Leverett, there is also probably a great deal of James in Leverett's claim that "the great thing is to *live,* you know—to feel, to be conscious of one's possibilities, not to pass through life mechanically and insensibly, like a letter through a post-office."197 Clearly, then, as this passage perhaps serves to indicate, James put more than his superb knowledge of craft into his exquisitely fashioned tale.

About the time that James was finishing "A Bundle of Letters," he wrote to his brother William, "I rather think I shall become a (sufficiently) great man." Several weeks later he wrote to his mother, whom he promised both monetary success and "reflected glory": "of which latter article I propose to furnish myself with a very considerable amount." James thus figured to be rewarded for a big novel, the outlines of which he had sketched in the year 1878.198

This is the year in which James published *Daisy Miller* and finished "A Bundle of Letters." But for the time being, his attention was focused primarily upon his "big novel," as he referred to it in a letter to William in March of 1879. Henry previously wrote to his mother about the success that his "big novel" would bring. His mother thereupon informed her youngest son, in a letter of 1878, that Henry "is writing a new novel, of the success of which he seems to himself to be very sanguine . . . . He says compared with anything he has yet done 'it will be as wine to water.' " Whereupon the members of the James family gave Henry's untitled work a title: "The wine and water novel." "It will cover you with fame," James promised his mother.[199]

*The Portrait of a Lady* was first published in serial format in *Macmillan's Magazine,* where it ran in fourteen installments, from October 1880 to November 1881 and in *Atlantic Monthly,* from November 1880 to December 1881. In this year the novel was published by Macmillan as a "three-decker" edition which incorporated slight revisions that James made before he sent his manuscript in installments to the printers for Macmillan's.[200]

If a book is well done, it can be read in a number of ways. Of few books could this be more truly said than *The Portrait of a Lady.* The title, first of all, invites the eye to see. And the handling of the novel is often in terms of seeing. And much that is seen of the visible world is portrayed as through the eyes of an Impressionist painter. The first such scene is the light-filled description of Gardencourt. The early scenes at Gardencourt partake of the atmosphere of many Impressionist paintings, such as Camille Pissarro's "Haymaking at Eragny," (The National Gallery of Canada, Ottawa, 1901) in which the atmosphere quivers with suffused light.

In his generally informative article, "Point of View in *The Portrait of a Lady,*" Sheldon Liebman remarks that "in *The Portrait of a Lady* there are two main points of view, Isabel's and James's, which are at times indistinguishable from each other. Even the object to be seen by the reader is in question, for we are not certain . . . what Isabel sees."[201] When we *are* generally sure what Isabel sees, the scenes she glimpses are usually rendered in an Impressionist manner. For example, about mid-way through the novel (and before her marriage to Gilbert Osmond), we read:

> The world lay before her—she could do whatever she chose. There was a deep thrill in it all, but for the present her choice was tolerably discreet; she chose simply to walk back from Euston Square to her hotel.

> The early dusk of a November afternoon had already closed in; the
> street lamps, in the thick, brown air, looked weak and red; our
> heroine was unattended and Euston Square was a long way from Pic-
> cadilly. But Isabel performed the journey with a positive enjoyment
> of its dangers and lost her way almost on purpose, in order to get
> more sensations, so that she was disappointed when an obliging po-
> liceman easily set her right again. She was so fond of the spectacle of
> human life that she enjoyed even the aspect of gathering dusk in the
> London streets—the moving crowds, the hurrying cabs, the lighted
> shops, the flaring stalls, the dark shining dampness of everything.202

And somewhat later in the novel, when after a brief walk with
Pansy among the delicate winter flowers of the Roman Campagna,
Isabel discovers her husband and Madame Merle in the drawing-room:

> The soundlessness of her step gave her time to take in the scene before
> she interrupted it. Madame Merle was there in her bonnet, and Gilbert
> Osmond was talking to her; for a minute they were unaware she had
> come in. Isabel had often seen that before, certainly; but what she had
> not seen, or at least had not noticed, was that their colloquy had for
> the moment converted itself into a sort of familiar silence, from which
> she instantly perceived that her entrance would startle them . . . . The
> thing made an image, lasting only a moment, like a sudden flicker of
> light. Their relative positions, their abosrbed mutual gaze, struck her
> as something detected. But it was all over by the time she had fairly
> seen it. 203

Of the many "impressions" in the novel, however, the major-
ity are internal ones. Some of them—particularly those that pertain
to Isabel and Ralph—are extremely subjective in nature, as for instance, "Isabel had stayed with her grandmother at various seasons,
but somehow all her visits had a flavour of peaches."204 Other impressions are entirely internal, but somewhat less subjective. Here,
for instance, is Ralph's (seemingly accurate) report on Isabel's situation:

> Ralph had listened with great attention, as if everything she said mer-
> ited deep consideration; but in truth he was only half thinking of the
> things she said, he was for the rest simply accommodating himself to
> the weight of his total impression—the impression of her ardent good
> faith. She was wrong, but she believed; she was deluded, but she was
> dismally consistent. It was wonderfully characteristic of her that,

having invented a fine theory about Gilbert Osmond, she loved him not for what he really possessed, but for his poverties dressed out as honours.[205]

With respect to Osmond and Madame Merle, in particular, the narrative contains a number of examples of the "subtle hints and fine distinctions" that we find in many Impressionist paintings. "In the manner and tone of these two persons, on first meeting at any juncture, and especially when they met in the presence of others, was something indirect and circumspect, as if they had approached each other obliquely and addressed each other by implication."[206] And in a passage closely following this one, we read of the same pair: "They stood there knowing each other well and each on the whole willing to accept the satisfaction of knowing as a compensation for the inconvenience—whatever it might be—of being known."[207]

From the standpoint of Impressionism, it is also interesting to note the frequency with which the word "impression" is used in this novel,[208] and particularly the ways in which James uses the word to internalize his characterization. Here, for example, are Isabel's thoughts regarding one of her suitors:

> There was something in the visitor that checked her and held her in suspense—made it more important she should get an impression of him than that she should produce one herself. Besides, she had little skill in producing an impression which she knew to be expected: nothing could be happier, in general, than to seem dazzling, but she had a perverse unwillingness to glitter by arrangement.[209]

James subtly contrasts (partly through Isabel's consciousness and partly through that of his narrator) the kind of impression that she produces with the kind that she is *capable of* producing. And in presenting this contrast, James not only moves his narrative along, but also suggests something very important about his heroine's psychological make-up.

James likewise uses the word "impression" in revelatory ways when he revises from the 1881 edition to the New York edition, published twenty-eight years later. On at least a half dozen occasions, James emends his 1881 text, seemingly in order to place greater emphasis upon the word "impression" in the New York edition. In

Volume I, Chapter 6 of the New York edition, for example, we read
[of Isabel] :

> She was too young, too impatient to live, too unacquainted with pain.
> She always returned to her theory that a young woman whom after all
> every one thought clever should begin by getting a general impression
> of life. This impression was necessary to prevent mistakes, and after it
> should be secured she might make the unfortunate condition of others
> a subject of special attention.

The 1881 edition, on the other hand, reads "This was necessary . . .
etc.," thereby not including the word "impression" which James in-
serted into the later text.

In still other ways James shows his stylistic evolution to Impressionism in his later phase, as when in the New York edition (Volume I, Chapter 13), he substitutes for "Such incongruities were
not . . . ," the following: "The sense of her [i.e., Isabel's] incoher-
ence was not a help to answering Mr. Goodwood's letter, and Isabel
determined to leave it a while unhonoured." In revisions such as
these, James makes his later text more ambiguous than his earlier
version. In the development of his ambiguousness, James demonstrates what W. D. Howells very likely meant when he noted that
among the "concessions" that the reader must make while reading
James is the willingness to be left "to our own conjectures in regard
to the fate of the people in whom he has interested us."[210] What
James manages to do by means of his use of Impressionism, then, is
what Ralph tells Isabel—seemingly in reflexive fashion—early in *The
Portrait*: " 'It's not a romantic old house,' said Ralph . . . 'there's no
romance here but what you may have brought with you.' "[211] Thus
it is in James's own house of fiction, where the romance is primarily
what the reader himself brings with him. The Impressionist manner
in which the author allows his reader the freedom to do so is one of
the supreme virtues of the Jamesian method.

Henry James was a man who knew well "the enduring elegance
of female friendship."[212] And he manages to provide some of his
most interesting Impressionist techniques through the consciousness
of Isabel Archer, who manages to combine an impersonal sense and

a sense of mystery (like most of James's serious chacters, Isabel is surrounded by an air of mystery; his comic characters have a tendency to "tell all"). We learn, for example, that what Isabel liked about Osmond "was not so much what he said and did, but rather what he withheld. . . ."213 And throughout we see her dreaming of abstract trials that she might overcome. For instance, "Sometimes she went so far as to wish that she might find herself some day in a difficult position, so that she should have the pleasure of being as heroic as the occasion demanded." Such abstractness and impersonality are typical of many Impressionist paintings, such as "Le Déjeuner" (ca. 1873; Musée du Louvre). In this painting, neither the child playing beneath the table on the lower left of the canvas nor the strolling woman at the upper right, attracts our attention initially. Perhaps the most striking elements in this picnic scene are the attractively arranged summer luncheon table of fruit and coffee and the colorful woman's hat, flung—by whom we do not know—onto a branch of the tree that overhangs the picnic table.

James's circumspect manner likewise aids in the development of the impersonal tone in his fiction. Sometimes the authorial comments about Isabel are fairly straightforward:

> It was impossible to pretend that she had not acted with her eyes open; if ever a girl was a free agent she had been. A girl in love was doubtless not a free agent; but the sole source of her mistake had been within herself.

At other times, James uses indirection by allowing us a glimpse of Isabel's motives that is half within her consciousness and half outside of it, as when we read that "if she had troubles she must keep them to herself, and if life was difficult, it would not make it easier to confess herself beaten."214 In delineating Isabel's character, James thus calls to mind the Italian saying, "i gran dolori sono muti" (great griefs are silent), a chord which he touches upon continually in this novel and throughout his lengthy career as an author.

In *The Portrait of a Lady,* James also rings an interesting change upon the French saying "il faut souffrir pour être beau" (to be beautiful, it is necessary to suffer). Isabel Archer is beautiful *and* suffers, but only partially because of her beauty. In his rhapsodic

1874 response to Yelena Stakhova's situation in Turgenev's *On the Eve*, James declared:

> The story is all in the portrait of the heroine, who is a heroine in the literal sense of the word; a young girl of a will so calmly ardent and intense that she needs nothing but opportunity to become one of the figures about whom admiring legend clusters . . . . She passes before us toward her mysterious end with the swift, keen movement of a feathered arrow.[215]

In his book on James and Turgenev, Dale E. Peterson judges that James's description of (George Eliot's) Gwendolyn Harleth's fate "prophesies Isabel's final trajectory": "The universe forc[es] itself with a slow, inexorable pressure into a narrow, complacent, yet after all extremely sensitive mind, and mak[es] it ache with the pain of the process."[216] Peterson is only partially right. What James actually seems to have done is to combine the romantic expansiveness of Turgenev's Yelena with the keen sensitiveness of Eliot's Gwendolyn, in order to form the character of Isabel.[217] "Suffering," James's narrator tells us, "with Isabel, was an active condition; it was not a chill, a stupor, a despair; it was a passion of thought, of speculation, of response to every pressure."[218] Like many of James's most memorable heroines and heroes, Isabel Archer possesses what the Germans refer to as *Empfindung*—a word for which there is no precise equivalent in English. The character who has *Empfindung* combines within her or him qualities of feeling, sensitiveness, and perception. Because Isabel has these qualities—whatever we think of her decision not to leave Osmond for Caspar Goodwood—we have to have at least some degree of admiration for James's sentient and fated heroine.

In his *Notebooks* James anticipated "the obvious criticism" of *The Portrait of a Lady:* "Of course [it] will be [said] that it is not finished—that I have not seen the heroine to the end of her situation —that I have left her *en l'air.*—This is both true and false. The *whole* of any thing is never told; you can only take what groups together. What I have done has unity—it groups together. It is complete in itself—and the rest may be taken up or not, later." In his Preface James expressed this idea as it pertains generally to "the exquisite problem of the artist": "Really, universally, relations stop nowhere, and the exquisite probelm of the artist is eternally to draw, by a geometry of his own, the circle in which they shall happily *appear* to do so." And he proceeds to say, "He is in the perpetual predicament that the continuity of things is the whole matter for him, of comedy and tragedy; that this continuity is never broken, and that, to do anything at all, he has at once intensely to consult and intensely to ignore it."[219]

In fiction, bad art often arises from the author's misguided attempt to offer a simple interpretation of life. Yet life is intractable and resists such isolation into a preconceived system. A fiction that aspires to be like life, therefore, should be one in which a rigid pattern is lacking. James's fiction thus often mirrors life in that is succeeds partially because it lacks a rigid pattern.

James was probably right when he remarked (in the Preface to The Portrait of a Lady ) that *The Portrait* was "the most proportioned" of his fictions after *The Ambassadors*. In *The Portrait of a Lady* James resplendently illustrates the truth of his saying about the Novel as a literary form. "The Novel," James said, "remains still, under the right persuasion, the most elastic, most prodigious of literary forms."[220]

The next Jamesian work of fiction that we will consider is in many ways more "pictorial" than any that James has heretofore done. Of "A New England Winter" (1884) James wrote to Howells: "It is not very good—on the contrary; but it will perhaps seem to you to put into form a certain impression of Boston." Howells responds shortly thereafter with a letter which indicates his enthusiasm for the accuracy and vividness of James's "impression."

"A New England Winter" grew out of a *Notebook* sketch that James dated January 18, 1881. The story, however, was not finished until over three years later—in February 1884 (it was first published in *Century Magazine,* August-September 1884). In the transition from *Notebook* sketch to published story, some important changes took place. Most of these changes were seemingly not unaffected by James's conscious attitude toward Impressionism during the 1880's.

"A New England Winter" deals with a mother's elaborate dip-
lomatic efforts to find a wife of her choosing for her son. Mrs. Daintry's son, Florimond, returns from art study in Paris to spend a few
months with his widowed mother. She arranges to have Rachel Tor-
rance come to Boston to entertain him. Rachel comes up from
Brooklyn to stay with her cousin, Mrs. Mesh. Soon after he arrives,
the young man begins to make repeated visits to the Mesh's. To Mrs.
Daintry's chagrin, she eventually learns that Florimond's visits to the
Mesh's are not prompted by a great interest in Rachel, but by his
attachment (seemingly innocent) to the older Mrs. Mesh. As the
story ends, the shocked Mrs. Daintry lures her son Florimond back
to Europe with her—thereby thwarting what she sees to be a poten-
tially dangerous affair.

A comparison of the published story with the *Notebook*
sketch reveals the manner with which James has used his knowledge
of Impressionist painting in order to lighten the tone of the story and
to lend a sense of irony to the tale. In the *Notebook* entry, dated
January 18, 1881, James delineated a story that would have had a
much more serious cast. In this version there was no mention of Florimond's having been an art student who had an interest in Impressionist painting. Nor was there reference to the many lovely Impressionist descriptions of Boston in winter (done mostly through the
consciousness of Florimond, who strolls around Boston in much the
same manner as Zola's Lantier strolled around the Halle district of
Paris in *The Fat and the Thin*). In the *Notebook* entry, James outlines a serious tale—one in which the young man *does* become interested in the young girl. She in turn becomes aware of his interests,
fears that she is being used (by mother and son) and departs. The son
is by now deeply in love. Then, to quote James, Florimond "follows
the girl, leaves his mother alone, and spends the rest of the time that
he is in America in vainly besieging the affections of the young lady—
so that the mother, as a just retribution, loses his society almost altogether. The girl refuses him, and he returns in disgust to Europe,
where he marries [someone else] . . . , while the mother is left lamen-
ting."221

Obviously, then, the story that James outlined became, in several years, much more ironic as it saw its way into print. Apart from

considerations of plot, James lightened his story, at least in part, by making Florimond into a fine comic character. In one of the few critical discussions of this story, Peter Buitenhuis (in *The Grasping Imagination*) refers to the young man as "a kind of Louis Leverett [from "A Bundle of Letters"] with a paint brush."222

Florimond claims to be an Impressionist painter, although James's narrator remarks that "you would never have guessed" this from his "neat and sleek" appearance. Daintry, in short, is a gentlemen's version of the Bohemian Lantier in Zola's *The Fat and the Thin* and *The Masterpiece*. Like Lantier (and like Monet, too, of course), Florimond has what they call in Paris "a great deal of eye." And like Lantier, Florimond renders his landscapes mostly by means of verbal description, eschewing for the most part the hard labor of craft that is required in order to fix his scenes onto canvas.223 Here, for instance, is Florimond's description of "the artificial bosom of the Back Bay" that he traverses in his travels:

> The long straight avenue lay airing its newness in the frosty day, and all its individual facades, with their neat, sharp ornaments, seemed to have been scoured, with a kind of friction, by the hard, salutary light. Their brilliant browns and drabs, their rosy surfaces of brick, made a variety of fresh, violent tones, such as Florimond liked to memorize ....224

In some ways, then, "A New England Winter" was James's most descriptive tale to date. This is not especially surprising, if we keep in mind Leon Edel's remark that as late as 1899, James "barely knew a dahlia from a mignonette."225 James also continually insisted that no illustration to a book of his should have any direct bearing on the story:

> Anything that relieves responsible prose of the duty of being, while placed before us, good enough, interesting enough, and, if the question be of picture, pictorial enough, above all *in itself*, does it the worst of services, and may well inspire in the lover of literature certain lively questions as to the future of that institution.226

Yet in his fiction and his criticism, James had for a long time demonstrated his ability to use the pictorial image and to comprehend the pictorial spirit when it was presented by painters—especially those who made use of the techniques that we have come to associate with Impressionism. "At Isella," for example, (a story which first appeared in *Galaxy* in August, 1871), contains the following image: " . . . the sounding torrent gushed beneath us, flashing in the light of the few stars which sparkled in our strip of sky, like diamonds tacked upon a band of velvet."[227] And in 1875 James wrote that Homer's "vacant lots of meadows" and "pie nurtured maidens" were redeemed only by his ability to see "everything at one with its envelope of light and air. He sees not in lines, but in masses, in gross, broad masses."[228]

As Peter Buitenhuis has moreover remarked, James's story was written at approximately the same time as "The Art of Fiction," the famous essay in which the Master defined good fiction as "a direct impression of life" (a statement that is itself, of course, at least at one remove from life). Not surprisingly, then, from the *Notebook* entry to the finished story he distances his narrative, mostly by use of Impressionist elements in his tale. And in typically reflexive fashion, James (through the medium of his narrator) tells us why he has done so. At the outset of Chapter 5 (Chapter 4, we recall, contains the Impressionist description by Florimond that I have cited above), James's narrator says:

> It may seem that I have assumed on the part of the reader too great a curiosity about the impressions of this young man, who was not very remarkable, and who has not even the recommendation of being the hero of our perhaps too descriptive tale. The reader will already have discovered that a hero fails us here . . . ."[229]

Here, as so often in James, the author tells us what he has done and why.

Like James's painter in the next story that we shall consider and like the painter in "The Story of a Masterpiece," Florimond Daintry found that "it was not important . . . that things should be beautiful; what he sought to discover was their identity, —the signs by which he should know them."[230]

Like James's portrait painter in "The Story of a Masterpiece," Oliver Lyon in "The Liar" (1888) has his portrait painting slashed.

"The Liar" first appeared in *Century Magazine,* May-June 1888 and was first published in a hardbound edition in *A London Life* (1889). In the story, James presents the case of a portrait painter, named Lyon, who meets at a dinner party a minor teller of "tall" tales, Colonel Capadose. The "action" in James's story derives from Lyon's discovery that the Colonel is married to Everina, a woman with whom the painter was once in love. The egotistical Lyon cannot bear the thought that this Everina, for whom he once cared, is not only married to Colonel Capadose, but that she also actually loves her husband. The painter sets out to discover whether Everina is a woman made blind to her husband's flaws or whether she is his captive. When she tells a mild lie in the Colonel's defense (she tells the painter that it was not her husband, but an unemployed model who slashed the portrait of the Capadose's daughter which was painted by Lyon), Lyon, who watched as the Colonel slashed Amy's portrait, concludes that Mrs. Capadose's "surrender" to her spouse is the result of the moral debasement that she has undergone. The painter fails to understand the seemingly evident fact; namely, that Everina loves her husband, in spite of—perhaps partially because of—his minor vice of telling amusingly prevaricating stories about his exploits. At the end of the story, Lyon vainly (and naively) laments:

> . . . why had she treated him as if he were a dear old friend; why had she let him for months suppose certain things—or almost; why had she come to his studio day after day to sit near him on the pretext of her child's portrait, as if she liked to think what might have been? Why had she come so near a tacit confession, in a word, if she was not willing to go an inch further?[231]

As with many of his other stories, James seems to have drawn his inspiration for "The Liar" at least partially from his voluminous reading. As Richard J. Kane and Edward Rosenberg have pointed out, James more than likely derived at least part of his idea for the story from a novel by Daudet and a story by Hawthorne.[232] But James also seemingly drew upon his knowledge of Impressionism for his splendid characterizations of the dinner party guests, as seen through the eyes of Lyon. Here, for instance, is Lyon's "reading" of Arthur Ashmore, the son of Sir David (whose portrait Lyon has been recently commissioned to paint) and his wife:

> Arthur Ashmore was a fresh-coloured, thick-necked English gentleman,
> but he was just not a subject; he might have been a farmer and he
> might have been a banker: you could scarcely paint him in characters.
> His wife did not make up the amount; she was a large, bright, nega-
> tive woman, who had the same air as her husband of being somehow
> tremendously new; a sort of appearance of fresh varnish (Lyon could
> scarcely tell whether it came from her complexion or from her clothes),
> so that one felt she ought to sit in a gilt frame, suggesting reference
> to a catalogue or a price-list.[233]

As with many Impressionist works of art, the reader here must supply the missing elements, must imagine for himself how James's characters look; for James himself provides only the salient features as
they strike the eye of his narrator.

And in the setting of the same dinner party, James introduces
Colonel Capadose with a brief description (again by Lyon) which is a
masterful piece of Impressionism—one which employs all of the subtle hints and fine distinctions that we see in some of the best of the
Impressionist paintings:

> The gentleman might still be called young, and his features were regu-
> lar: he had a plentiful, flair moustache that curled up at the ends, a
> brilliant, gallant, almost adventurous air, and a big shining breastpin in
> the middle of his shirt. He appeared a fine satisfied soul, and Lyon
> perceived that wherever he rested his friendly eye there fell an influ-
> ence as pleasant as the September sun—as if he could make grapes and
> pears or even human affection ripen by looking at them. What was
> odd in him was a certain mixture of the correct and the extravagant:
> as if he were an adventurer imitating a gentleman with rare perfection
> or a gentleman who had taken a fancy to go about with hidden arms.
> He might have been a dethroned prince or the war-correspondent of
> a newspaper; he represented both enterprise and tradition, good
> manners and bad taste.[234]

In this description we notice above all Lyon's hesitations and under-
cuttings of the Colonel's character and appearance (which latter
Lyon afterward frankly admits women find attractive). The Colonel's
looks *might still be called young* and his air was *almost adventurous.*
He is at once "correct and extravagant," like "an adventurer imitat-
ing a gentleman . . . or a gentleman who had taken a fancy to go

about with hidden arms." In this brief passage, moreover, we notice the relatively prominent use of the subjunctive and of such verbs as "appeared" and "perceived"—verb forms and verbs which James seems to use with increasing frequency as he moves toward his so-called Major Phase.[235]

In the Preface to *The Spoils of Poynton* James indicates the choices that he sees for the writer of the short story. The short story "has to choose between being an anecdote or a picture and can but play its part strictly according to its kind. I rejoice in the anecdote," he relates, "but I revel in the picture . . . ." For James "picture" aims "at those richly summarised and foreshortened effects . . . that refer their terms of production, for which the magician has ever to don his best cap and gown, to the inner compartment of our box of tricks."[236] In "The Real Thing" (1892) Henry James provides a story about a picture that seemingly demonstrates something of the inner workings of his "box of tricks," and in so doing also reveals something about his Impressionist method.[237]

Unlike most of Henry James's short stories, "The Real Thing" has given rise to a great deal of worthwhile critical commentary. That much of this commentary has touched upon "art versus life" questions seems particularly surprising, especially in light of James's own comments concerning the genesis of his story. On the evidence provided in his Prefaces, James's story is one of the least "imaginative" of his tales—provided that by *imaginative* we mean that the author has had to fill in a great deal of the anecdote himself. Of "The Real Thing" we might say what Proust's biographer, George Painter, says of his subject: "he invented nothing, he altered everything."

In the Preface to *Daisy Miller,* James relates how his

> much-loved friend George du Maurier had spoken to [him] . . . of a call from a strange and striking couple desirous to propose themselves as artist's models for his weekly 'social' illustrations to *Punch,* and the acceptance of whose services would have entailed the dismissal of an undistinguished but highly expert pair, also husband and wife, who had come to him from far back on the irregular day and whom,

> thanks to a happy, and to that extent lucrative, appearance of 'type'
> on the part of each, he had reproduced, to the best effect, in a thou-
> sand drawing-room combinations.[238]

In the remainder of his lengthy paragraph, James proceeds to fill in
many more of the details (that will eventually find issue in the story)
that Du Maurier related to him on that day in the early '90's. James's
artist-writer friend's anecdote struck James at that time as being
"exquisite," and, as he himself relates, "out of a momentary fond
consideration of it 'The Real Thing' sprang at a bound."[239]

In James's story the Major and Mrs. Monarch are the striking
couple desirous of serving as models for the book illustrations that
the un-named painter-narrator does. Shortly after they arrive at his
studio (whence they go to seek employment), he observes that he
"was disappointed; for in the pictorial sense I had immediately *seen*
them. I had seized their type—I had already settled what I would do
with it."[240] Regarding the Monarchs, he moreover relates, "it was
odd how quickly I was sure of everything that concerned them."[241]

One furthermore soon comes to feel that James's narrator has
captured well the character of the Monarchs in "the real life" of the
story. Of the Major, for example, the narrator relates:

> To listen to him was to combine the excitement of going out with the
> economy of staying at home . . . . When he couldn't talk about greater
> things he could talk cheerfully about smaller, and since I couldn't ac-
> company him into reminiscences of the fashionable world he could
> lower the conversation without a visible effort to my level.
>
> So earnest a desire to please was touching in a man who could so
> easily have knocked one down.[242]

And of Mrs. Monarch the painter remarks, "She was always a lady
certainly, and into the bargain was always the same lady. She was the
real thing, but always the same real thing."[243]

Nevertheless, the narrator confesses that he liked them, he

> felt, quite as their friends must have done . . . . But somehow with all
> their perfections I didn't easily believe in them [because they were

amateurs] . . . . Combined with this was another perversity—an innate preference for the represented subject over the real one: the defect of the real one was so apt to be a lack of representation. I like things that appeared; then one was sure. Whether they *were* or not was a subordinate and almost a profitless question.244

In James's tale, the pair that represents "the appearance" that the artist needs is the "meagre little Miss Churm" and the "sallow but fair" Oronte. Miss Churm "was only a freckled cockney, but she could represent everything from a fine lady to a sheperdess; she had the faculty as she might have had a fine voice or long hair."245 While Major Monarch "became useful only for the representation of brawny giants," Miss Churm on the other hand "was greatly in demand, never in want of employment . . . ."246 And of Oronte, the narrator's initial description seems quite apt:

> He was sallow but fair, and when I put him into some old clothes of mine he looked like an Englishman. He was as good as Miss Churm, who could look, when requested, like an Italian.247

Concerning James's story, Viola Hopkins Winner sagely remarks:

> the 'ideal' is clearly discarded in favor of the 'actual,' (the Monarchs are superseded by Oronte and Miss Churm): however, the 'actual' is not literal fact but what the artist perceives, what the fact stimulates him to see.248

In "The Real Thing," then, what James's artist renders are his impressions of the figures that model for him. Like most good artists working in representational media, James's artist uses his models in the way that they are perhaps best used; namely, as plastic figures to be fixed in whatever manner the artist chooses.

The next James story that we will consider is one of which its author was exceedingly proud. "Greville Fane" (1892) first appeared in *Illustrated London News* (17 and 24 September 1892) and was first published in book format during the following year in the *The Real Thing*. James was particularly pleased with the manner in which he achieved "economic mastery" of his subject—one which he felt lent itself well to the craftsman's "space-cunning," the secret of his " 'foreshortening.' "

James wrote of "Greville Fane": "the subject, in this little composition, is 'developmental' enough, while the form has to make the anecdotic concession; and yet who shall say that for the right effect of a small harmony the fusion has failed?"[249] In his story James evidently prides himself primarily in his arrangement of commentary and detail which, he seems to feel, produces a force and economy that lends to the " 'rich' " effect that he seemingly wished to achieve. This effect is achieved with great mastery in a number of Impressionist paintings by such artists as Cézanne and Seurat (the latter especially on the occasions when he uses large, bold strokes, as in "The Canoe"). We see this effect, for example, in Cézanne's "Melting Snow, Fontainebleau" (ca. 1879; Museum of Modern Art, New York), which was probably painted in the very year that James first conceived the idea for "Greville Fane."[250] In Cézanne's painting, as Van Deren Coke has shown in his study of Modern painting and photography, the over-all arrangement of trees and rocks in the canvas coincides with the photographic source which Cézanne evidently drew upon, yet the painter has unmistakeably simplified the form of his work, in order to achieve his admirable artistic cohesion.[251] This element in Cézanne is also apparently what attracted Van Gogh (and perhaps James, also) to the work of Seurat, after whom the Dutch artist wished to execute his work: "d'une simplicité à la Seurat," as Van Gogh remarked.[252]

"Greville Fane" was finally composed in the late 1880's and early '90's, at a time when James was in the midst of a struggle to keep down the length of *The Tragic Muse*, which had begun to appear in installments in the *Atlantic Monthly* for January, 1889 (we recall James's semi-humorous invocation at this time of "the spirit of Maupassant"). During this period James often alludes to Maupassant's brevity as a model. "*A la Maupassant* must be my motto," he remarks, for example, in a *Notebook* entry for February 2, 1889.[253]

I mention James's struggles with length and his concomitant homage to Maupassant, because the American author seems to have over-estimated the worth of his story. And this is perhaps largely because James was unduly proud of "Greville Fane's" brevity (the story is almost certainly one of James's shortest).

Moreover, while the *Notebook* entries (which date from February 28, 1889) indicate that James intended the story to be a humorous satire on the best-selling author, Greville Fane (whose real name was Mrs. Stormer), the published version is surely less humorous (and to my mind less successful) than his "writer stories" of the mid-'90's. To me, most of the apparently intended satire of Miss Fane has the effect of being a serious intrusion into the narrative flow of the story, in much the same way that Hemingway's writing about literature in *The Green Hills of Africa* virtually "kills" that novel *as novel*. Here, for instance, is James's author-narrator's comment upon Greville's literary performances:

> She had a shrewd perception that form, in prose at least, never recommended any one to the public we were condemned to address; according to which she lost nothing (her private humiliation not counted) by having none to show.

Passages like this go on for pages in James's brief story.[254]

If there is any humorous satire in the story, it is directed at Greville's son and daughter Leolin Stormer and Lady Ethel Luard. After their mother passes away, the narrator observes:

> But she never saw; she had never seen anything, and she passed away with her fine blindness unimpaired. Her son published every scrap of scribbled paper that could be extracted from her table-drawers, and his sister quarrelled with him mortally about the proceeds.[255]

If James does show technical advance in "Greville Fane," it is in his precise characterizations—done in the kind of bold strokes which he uses with increasing success through the remainder of his Middle Phase and into the novels of the Later period. Here, for instance, is the narrator's glimpse of Mrs. Stormer's "little mottled servant": She "flattened herself against the wall of the narrow passage and tried to look detached without looking indifferent." And here his penetrating glimpse of Mrs. Stormer: "She was very expert and vulgar and snobbish, and never so intensely British as when she was particularly foreign." And he describes Lady Ethel thus:

> She was long-necked and near-sighted and striking, and I thought I
> had never seen sweet seventeen in a form so hard and high and dry.
> She was cold and affected and ambitious, and she carried an eyeglass
> with a long handle, which she put up whenever she wanted not to
> see.256

Such precise impressions serve James well in the novels of the Middle
Phase which directly followed the work that he did in the short form
during the early '90's. The first of the novels from this "middle period" that we will consider is one of James's pictorial masterpieces,
and one that uses an important Impressionist technique in the course
of its sad but fascinating narrative.

The heroine of *What Maisie Knew* comes to learn the truth of
Abraham Cowley's lines:

> The world's a scene of changes,
>     and to be
> Constant, in Nature were in
>     constancy.

Maisie, the protagonist of the novel, is the daughter of Beale and Ida
Farange, a quite handsome though not very wealthy couple. After a
stormy marriage with much quarreling, the pair obtains a divorce
with part of the terms providing that the girl live six months at the
residence of each parent, alternately ("She was divided in two and
the portions tossed impartially to the disputants").257 Then Beale
Farange takes on a Miss Overmore to be Maisie's governess. Beale
falls for the handsome governess and makes her Mrs. Beale.

Meanwhile, Ida marries a certain wealthy Sir Claude. These
two then hire Mrs. Wix, a widowed governess, to care for Maisie on
her six-month stay with them. During her shuffling back and forth,
Maisie assumes her role as narrator. With the aid of deeply penetrating
authorial observations, Maisie and the reader come to learn a number
of profound truths. Plato believed that preventing people from
knowing which children's parents they are will inspire them with par-
ental feelings toward all younger people. As is so often true, however,
Aristotle's observations on the same subject show him to have been

Plato's master; for Aristotle saw that if Plato's belief were actualized, the result would be rather that all parents would be equally indifferent to all children: "That which is common to the greatest number has the least care bestowed upon it," Aristotle remarked in his *Politics*.258 In *What Maisie Knew* James provides abundant artistic testimony to the sagacity of Aristotle's observation.

In the course of the narrative, Maisie learns that Ida is running about with at least two other men. She knows two of the suitors personally—the handsome, blue-eyed Count and the chunky millionaire, Mr. Perriam. She also knows that Beale, her father, is seeing a dark American Countess. Of all this, Sir Claude and Mrs. Beale are unaware, but they do not much care because they are having their own affair together. Even at her tender age, the little girl realizes the moral implications of such deceptions. She pleads with Sir Claude to give up Mrs. Beale in order to make possible a complete reversal of the intended double divorce. Her pleas fall on indifferent ears. The novel comes to a close with a loud scene in which Mrs. Wix refuses to permit Maisie to stay with the irresponsible lovers, Claude and Mrs. Beale, who wish to act as the child's real legal father and mother.

Mrs. Wix goes off with the girl and assumes the responsibility for raising her. That the governess decides to take the girl seems just, since with the exception of Maisie herself, Mrs. Wix is the only character in the novel who has any common sense or morality (although the novel leaves us feeling that Mrs. Wix's actions are not altogether unselfish).

Throughout his narrative, James uses a clever change on the Impressionist technique of presenting the same view from different viewpoints, in different seasons, and at different times of the day. As I have indicated above, James uses one aspect of this Impressionist technique in "Madame de Mauves," *Daisy Miller,* and "A Bundle of Letters." In "Madame de Mauves" we witness the narrator's changing responses to a situation (the marriage of the de Mauves) that is presented to us as being comparatively static. In *Daisy Miller* we witness Winterbourne's changing attitudes toward Daisy (although here, too, what she *does* seems consistent throughout the novella, so that Winterbourne can be said to be presenting a fundamentally static picture from shifting perspectives). And in "A Bundle of Letters" the scene (that is, the *pension* wherein the correspondents reside) is fixed, but the various epistolary reports of the scene provide a whirling effect which does not cease until we finish reading the last letter.

*Maisie,* however, represents an important technical advance, for in this novel James presents a shifting scene (namely, the couples involved in the young girl's life) from the veiwpoint of the protagonist who herself continues to change as the novel advances. As Maisie matures, her sensitivity grows also, with the result that her observations and thoughts become increasingly more analytic and perceptive. Largely through Maisie's consciousness, James has developed his quiet, articulate masterpiece—and in doing so, fulfilled, fourteen years after the fact, the prophecy that he made in "The Art of Fiction," that to the sentient artist the consciousness of a child ("the active, contributive close-circling wonder," as James calls it)[259] can provide as much adventure as the islands of the Spanish Main.[260]

What could be more adventuresome than the following image, expressed through the consciousness of a child who "was able at the age for which all stories are true and all conceptions are stories": "Crudely as they had calculated they were at first justified by the event: she was the little feathered shuttlecock. they could fiercely keep flying between them."[261] An adventure which becomes almost too horrible to follow by about one-third of the way through the narrative when, to one of the couples, Maisie says—with a note of perhaps understandable desperation—" 'You're both very lovely; you can't get out of it!'—Maisie felt the need of carrying her point. 'And it's beautiful to see you side by side.' "[262]

In his *Notebooks* James provides a great deal of information on the genesis and development from a literary standpoint of *What Maisie Knew.*[263] But he does not mention some possible sources from Impressionist painting, such as Claude Monet's "A Corner of an Apartment" (1875, Musée du Louvre). In this picture, which James may very well have seen, Monet pictures a lonely boy standing in a corner of his apartment. While the painting is not mentioned specifically by James in his criticism (to my knowledge James's only published non-fictional reference to Monet is the one from *The American*

*Scene* that I have alluded to previously), it seems not unlikely that such a scene may have done something to inspire James's frighteningly accurate portrait. That James, about the time that he began to write *Maisie,* was thinking along Impressionist lines in painting can be seen moreover by his *Notebook* reference to "The Coxon Fund," where he said that:

> the formula is . . . to make it an impression—as one of Sargent's pictures is an impression. That is, I must do it from my own point of view—that of an imaginative observer, participator, chronicler. I must picture it, summarize it, impressionize it, in a word—compress and confine it by making it the picture of what I see. [264]

In *What Maisie Knew,* James shows us what his heroine sees, and much more. And in so doing, he provides us with one of his most magnificent Impressionist performances. In the next Impressionist novel that we will consider, the title notwithstanding, the magnificence lies mostly in its presentation of "inner space." In *The Spoils of Poynton* this mainly consists of the consciousness of its valorous heroine, Fleda.[265]

James's extensive *Notebook* entries for *The Spoils of Poynton* cover a period of over two years' duration—from late 1893 until shortly before first periodical publication in mid-1896. But James makes a major change in moving from *Notebooks* to fiction, insofar as in the fictional version of the narrative, Fleda emerges as the novel's protagonist and center of consciousness. As James himself phrases it (in his Preface to *The Spoils*), appreciation "lives in Fleda," making everyone else in the novel "show as stupid."[266]

James's use of Fleda as a center of consciousness becomes especially interesting when we keep in mind his personal situation at the time that he was mentally composing his novel. The mid-1890's was the time of the traumatic *Guy Domville* incident—shortly after which James wrote to Howells (on January 22, 1895):

> I mean to do far better work than ever I have done before. I have, potentially, improved immensely and am bursting with ideas and subjects—though the act of composition is with me more and more slow, painful and difficult.

He then set down with courage the following challenge to himself: "Proceed again—produce; produce better than ever, and all will yet be well."267 In his *Notebooks* on the following day, James moreover wrote (from De Vere Gardens, January 23, 1895):

> I take up my *own* old pen again—the pen of all my old unforgettable efforts and sacred struggles. To myself—today—I need say no more. Large and full and high the future still opens. It is now indeed that I may do the work of my life. And I will xxxxx I have only to *face* my problems. xxxxx. But all that is of the ineffable—too deep and pure for any utterance. Shrouded in sacred silence let it rest.268

Not succumbing to his sense of personal failure and public embarrassment, James, like Fleda Vetch, made the difficult personal decision to go on and to live his life without compromise. Fleda decides that she will not accept Owen unless he is "free." Analogously, she will not be bribed by Mrs. Gereth for "the Spoils." In thus refusing to compromise on these points, she rings an interesting change on the French saying, "grande fortune, grande servitude." Fleda renounces fortune and Owen, and is left at the end with nothing but the most important of possessions—her self-respect. Her possession of this, it seems to me, finally makes James's novel the shining achievment that it is. And James himself seems to have felt likewise when he remarked of Fleda (in his *Notebooks*) that "her distinguishing herself to the reader by means of her imagination was *almost* all that has made the little anecdote worth telling at all."269 And the primary way in which Fleda distinguishes "herself . . . by means of her imagination" is through the impressions that she provides throughout the narrative. She is determined to paint, "but," we are told, "her impressions, or somebody else's were as yet her only material."270 At the beginning of the novel, she possesses but one half of the material necessary for the novelist. As James himself stated in "The Art of Fiction," "a novel is in its broadest definition a personal, a direct impression of life."

Throughout the novel Fleda's impressions are by far the most vivid when she attempts to capture the feelings which Owen arouses in her. Here, for example, is how she captures his presence when she sees him for the first time "in London form":

There had been days when he struck her as all potent nature in one pair of boots. It didn't make him now another person that he was delicately dressed, shining and splendid, that he had a higher hat and light gloves with black seams and an umbrella as fine as a lance; but it made him, she soon decided, really handsomer, and this in turn gave him—for she never could think of him, or indeed of some other things, without the aid of his vocabulary—a tremendous pull. Yes, that was for the moment, as he looked at her, the great fact of their situation—his pull was tremendous. She tried to keep the acknowledgement of it from trembling in her voice as she said to him with more surprise than she really felt: 'You've then reopened relations with her?'[271]

A passage like this provides a capital example of what Richard Hocks [in *Henry James and Pragmatistic Thought* (1974)] probably means when he refers to the "tumbling" effect of Fleda's impressions. The Owen that she now sees is different—yet at the same time inseparable —from the one whom she knew only when he was "heated with the chase and splashed with the mire."[272] The manner in which she knew him in the country, however, makes his quite different presence in London all the more appealing. His appeal to her is always strong, and "the composite impressions" which she continually provides lead to her sense of bewilderment a feeling that she really is presenting "a personal, a direct impression of life."

In keeping with the "internalizing" British and American Impressionist tradition in literature, James also stubbornly refuses to yield to the pressure of "the external world" in his novel. In Fleda's case, James's refusal lends itself to some interesting metaphors and similes. For example, after she reflects that she had just had to get away from Ricks. "She had neither a home nor an outlook—nothing in all the wide world but a feeling of suspense. It was, morally speaking, like figuring in society with a wardrobe of one garment."[273] Here Fleda notes her loss of material security (the residence at Ricks), which she then shades ambiguously into a moral stance ("an outlook," in this context could mean either "material security to look forward to" or "a moral stance with which to face the world"). In the second sentence, James leads us to believe that the latter meaning is the preferred one, since in it he provides a simile which refers to Fleda's situation, "morally speaking." Here, however, it is important to note that James's garment metaphor *turns on its relationship to the outer world,* but, in doing so, it furthermore brings with it suggestions of denial: "like figuring in society with a wardrobe of one garment." All of this is very much in keeping with the internalizing aspect of James's Impressionism. He seems to have wished to avoid at all costs what he once aptly referred to as "the naive Dutch realism of Balzac."274 James moreover found exceedingly vulgar H. G. Wells's works, which are "so very much more attestations of the presence of material than attestations of an interest in the use of it." Thus it is not surprising that in *The Spoils of Poynton* we learn almost nothing about the actual contents of Waterbath. By the end of the novel, all that we really know about it is that Waterbath was big, rural, and decorated. In the novel, what we mainly learn is how James's characters behave in their relationship to Waterbath and to each other.

By way of gauging the kind of Impressionism that James thus provides, we should probably try to imagine what Balzac, the Goncourts, or Daudet would have done with such a setting as Waterbath. These writers would almost certainly have become enmeshed in the sensory details of the place, but would just as certainly have, to that extent, more than likely blurred the human drama which James manages so clearly to present.

In illustrating James's use of Impressionism in his fiction, it seems particularly important to consider the work of the mature novelist of the later phase. From 1900 onward, James continued to publish a great deal of important work. And much of what he published during this period makes interesting use of techniques that were seemingly drawn primarily from Impressionism. According to Robert L. Gale's count, for example, in *The Ambassadors, The Wings of the Dove,* and *The Golden Bowl* alone, the word "light" appears more than two hundred and fifty times in imagistic or at least highly imaginative contexts. Moreover, in the next novel that we will consider— *The Sacred Fount* (1901)—James uses images of "light" with extreme frequency—over seventy times in a novel that is only slightly more than novella length.275

*The Sacred Fount* comes late in the canon of Henry James, and is frequently considered to be his most vexing novel.276 It is

James's only full-length novel with a first-person narrator. And he seemingly envisioned *The Sacred Fount* as an experimental piece[277] which he used to develop and perfect the Impressionist technique in the novels of the so-called "major phase" which employ so well James's "center of consciousness" technique.[278]

William York Tindall characterizes the Impressionism of Henry James as "a method whereby an observer's mind is the stage upon which all action occurs."[279] Bruce Lowery says much the same thing of James and Proust when he observes ". . .chez James et Proust, le personnage central n'est pas situé objectivement dans le récit, il *est* le récit."[280] Neither Tindall nor Lowery is altogether right, of course. But with respect to *The Sacred Fount,* in particular, their comments are wholly acceptable; for the unnamed narrator of this novel is the reason for its fascination. To illustrate, about midway through the novel Lady John, one of the main characters in the narrative, says to the narrator, " 'You can't be a providence and not be a bore. A real providence *knows,* whereas you . . . .' "[281] While the real meaning of this speech seems obvious, the tone appears to suggest James's ironic treatment of the narrator. Indeed, by allowing one to see the narrator with the distance this irony seems to require, James is writing in a manner typical of the Impressionists. In *Social History of Art,* Vol. IV, Arnold Hauser notes that "nothing is more typical of an impressionist painting than that it must be looked at from a certain distance and that it describes things with the omissions inevitable in them when seen from a distance."[282]

But before discussing the novel in the light of its relationship to Impressionism, I should first outline briefly the complicated plot of *The Sacred Fount.*[283] On a weekend visit to a country home, the narrator notices that Grace Brissenden seems to have grown suddenly much younger, while her husband appears unrecognisably old and fatigued. The narrator furthermore notices that the usually stupid Gilbert Long has attained a considerable amount of wit and suavity. From these observations the narrator deduces that someone must be "paying." He looks for someone, and considers the possibility that it might be Mrs. Server. Moreover, for a time the narrator sees Gilbert Long first as the lover of Briss's wife and then of Mrs. Server. Other possibilities entertained by the speaker are that Mrs. Server is the one who gives of "the sacred fount" to Brissenden (who sparks his wife) and that Brissenden is actually Lady John's lover. Another possibility is that Brissenden is being used by Mrs. Server to deflect attention from her interest in Long.

Toward the end of the novel, when the narrator discloses some of his ideas to Mrs. Brissenden, she tells him he is insane and mocks his attempts to expose Mrs. Server. As Mrs. Brissenden sees it, Lady John is the real interest of Gilbert Long and " 'Mrs. Server isn't in it' " (*S. F.*, p. 455). It turns out that Brissenden himself has told his wife about the attachment—presumably innocent—for Mrs. Server. Thus, the narrator's "palace of thought," as he himself remarks, is reduced to "a house of cards." Yet, although he has been exposed as a character who has tried to violate the personal freedoms of other people within the novel (by playing the artist who must investigate the most personal of subjects), the narrator finally returns to his room—seemingly unflustered and apparently undiscouraged—looking forward to "escape to other air."

Like any novel worthy of serious consideration, *The Sacred Fount* can be viewed prismatically. One approach therefore might be to see the novel as an ironic story about how life intrudes upon art.[284] This kind of reading seems valid partially because the voyeuristic narrator so often speaks as an artist or sculptor. At the end of Chapter VII, for instance after the narrator reveals what he has " 'divined . . . as the tie' " (*S. F.*, p. 386) between Brissenden and Mrs. Server, he says, "I felt as if he [Brissenden] were now, intellectually speaking, plastic wax in my hand" (*S. F.*, p. 386). And just previous to this, the narrator remarks: "I felt I really knew what I was about, for to draw him on Mrs. Server was in truth to draw him indirectly on himself" (*S. F.*, p. 378).[285] Indeed, to consider the narrator as an ironically presented artist-voyeur can be seen not only as a Jamesian attempt to mock the "retinal doctrine" of the Impressionist, but also as a humorous twist upon the necessity for the viewer to maintain distance from the canvas so that the painting may be properly appreciated. It is an Impressionist technique, for example, to disengage the scene from the artist's feelings by using broken brushwork. In this way the atmosphere of the canvas emerges from afar, and gradually.[286]

In passages such as the ones that I have quoted, James may have also been offering an extended parody of certain passages in Ruskin's *Modern Painters*. Ruskin, for example, herein seemingly implies that modern man is too unreliable to be trusted to seek inspiration in nature:

> Examine the nature of your own emotion (if you feel it) at the sight of the Alp, and you find all the brightness of that emotion hanging, like dew on gossamer, on a curious web of subtle fancy and imperfect knowledge.[287]

When we read such a passage, we realize that the author of *The Sacred Fount* and of *The Ambassadors* had read not only his Pater, but also his Ruskin—and that he probably learned a great deal from both.

Another possible approach to *The Sacred Fount* is to view it as an attempt to unravel the problems posed by an egomaniac who attempts to pass judgment on other people. This reading can be justified, since there is a great deal of egotism in the narrator as artist. He shows no inclination to help or to comfort anyone. And he reveals no sympathy for any of the characters (although, on one occasion, he *expresses* pity for Mrs. Server. *S. F.*, p. 359). The narrator furthermore thinks Mrs. Brissenden sees him as "an observer to be squared" (*S. F.*, p. 467), because of his knowledge of her "relationship" to Gilbert Long. At the outset, however, the narrator insists that Lady John and Long are simulating a relationship as a sort of "diversionary action." And when the speaker relates:

> Lady John didn't want a lover; this would have been, as people say, a larger order than, given the other complications of her existence, she could meet; but she wanted, in a high degree, the appearance of carrying on a passion that imposed alike fearless realizations and conscious renouncements (*S. F.*, p. 375).

the effect seems puzzling in a way similar to the effect of many of Dowell's statements in *The Good Soldier: A Tale of Passion*.

In Ford Madox Ford's book, often considered an exemplary Impressionist novel, when Dowell, the passive narrator, remarks about the twenty-two year old romantic Ashburnham, "It is odd how a boy can have his virgin intelligence untouched in this world,"[288] Ford appears to have been directly attempting to top his good friend Henry James in dazzling the reader. And toward the end of Ford's novel, when Dowell says, "It is, at any rate, certain that Edward's actions were perfectly—were monstrously, were cruelly—correct,"[289] Ford's narrator thus seems as confused as at the outset of *The Sacred Fount,* when the narrator's tone and style suggest that he, too, is flustered to the point of confusion.[290] For instance, while spying on Lady John and Guy Brissenden in the arbor, they "were together, that is, because they were scarce a foot apart, and they were thinking, I inferred, because they were doing nothing else" (*S. F.,* p. 372). Like the Dowell of *The Good Soldier* (whose comments often echo those of James's narrator in *The Sacred Fount*), James's narrator feels he is seeing clearly: "I could mark these emotions, and what determined them, as behind clear glass" (*S. F.,* pp. 372-373).

Another indication that James's narrator is quite perplexed comes shortly before this, when he mistakenly refers to "Gilbert Obert" (*S. F.,* p. 368, top line), a name which represents an amalgam of Gilbert Long and Ford Obert (the latter being the very sensible artist in the novel). Keeping the other ironic parallels with Impressionist painting in mind, one might surmise that these observations by James's seemingly unreliable narrator represent the Master's ironic equivalent to the accurate perceptions of the Impressionist painters. The narrator/artist in *The Sacred Fount* who feels he is seeing clearly—"I could mark these emotions, and what determined them, as behind clear glass" (*S. F.,* pp. 372-3)—can be seen thus to mock the kind of accurate visual sensations which the Impressionists attempt to capture on canvas.

Yet, as seems most often true of the realtionship between the Impressionist canvas and its viewer, James's narrator actively solicits the reader's involvement in the interpretation of the appearance and meaning of the various character groupings. For instance, as the narrator considers Lady John and Brissenden, he says:

> That he bored her to death I might have gathered by the way they sat
> there, and she would trust me to believe—couldn't she?—that she was

only musing as to how she might most humanly get rid of him (*S. F.,* p. 373).

After seven chapters of dizzying, yet somehow fascinating, speculation—the narrator states, "I had been right then, and I knew where I stood" (*S. F.,* p. 378). Coming after much confusion, this seemingly confident assertion tends to puzzle the reader, whose assistance in establishing the system of graded nuances within the novel has already been actively solicited by the narrator.

As is the viewer of an Impressionist canvas, the reader of *The Sacred Fount* is invited to make art out of his observations of the labyrinthine mind of the narrator. Within the novel, therefore, to quote Stephen Spender, once again, "the mode of perceiving itself becomes an object of perception, and is included as part of the thing perceived."[291] By using this peculiarly Modernist literary method, there appears a sense in which James allows the reader to become the protagonist, for it is the reader's view of the narrator's judgments and observations which lends articulation to the whole novelistic performance. In a Modern world where the belief in immortality is no longer a certainty, James not only absorbs us in the spatial qualities of the novel, but he permits the reader to play the part of God by observing, and passing judgment upon, the ever-changing character of the narrator and the action this speaker relates.

Other Impressionist techniques utilized in *The Sacred Fount,* while perhaps less subtle, appear none the less successful. James, for instance, seems to have learned from the Impressionists that complementary colors heighten each other when set close together, and that each "object presents to the eye a scheme of color derived from its proper color, from its surroundings and from atmospheric conditions."[292] For example, in a scene describing characters gathered around the piano:

> while our pianist played, my wandering vision played and played as well. It took in again, while it went from one of them to the other, the delicate light that each had shed on the other (*S. F.,* p. 409).

In the visual arts, a comparable scene might be observed in canvases such as Renoir's "Concert at the Tuileries," or Monet's "Mrs. Monet

Under Tree" (National Gallery, Washington, D. C.). Both paintings represent color transitions. In the latter, for example, one notices the way that the pinks throw reverberations into the green colors.

Just as Monet moves around the subjects in his series of canvases, such as those depicting the "Train at St. Lazare" and "Haystacks," so James's egotistical narrator moves around many of his subjects of speculation. For instance, one notes the manner in which the speaker circles about May Server, attempting to divine (or to justify) his "thin idea of the line of feeling in her that had led her so to spare me" (*S. F.,* p. 372).293

Another characteristic Impressionist technique is to arrange the scene on a canvas in an attempt to develop the "real truth" of a landscape or a character grouping, as in Degas' "Absinthe Drinkers" (Louvre, Paris).294 James's narrator, likewise, constantly shifts scenes in his mind to try to get at the real truth (or what he sees it to be, through his seemingly flawed vision):

> I had created nothing but a clue or two to the larger comprehension I still needed, yet I positively found myself overtaken by a mild artistic glow. What had occurred was that, by the same stroke, I became sure I should certainly get him by temporising a little (*S. F.,* p. 374).

After congratulating himself for having informed May Server that "Poor Briss" was always in the "clutches" (*S. F.,* p. 396) of Lady John, the narrator experiences the kind of quick perception characteristic of some of the best Impressionist paintings:

> I quickly saw in it, from the moment I had got my point of view, more fine things than ever. I saw for instance that, magnificently, she wished not to incriminate him (*S. F.,* p. 396).295

Ironically, however, this quick perception on his part seems once again to represent the illusion-filled vision of "the tale of passion" that James's speaker narrates.

On the other hand, not all of what James evidently learned from the method of the Impressionists is utilized in an ironic fashion. For example, in addition to symbolizing what happens to "ideas" in a work of art and to reinforcing the "dazzled" view of the narrator which James seems to be developing, the following sentence contains a great deal that resembles the techniques of the Impressionists:

> I shall never forget the impressions of that evening, nor the way, in particular, the immediate effect of some of them was to merge the light of my extravagant perceptions in a glamour much more diffused (*S. F.*, p. 402).

Here, as in a Pissarro landscape or a Monet canvas, such as "Mrs. Monet Under Tree" (cited above), one notes the lack of specific substance in the description of the scene, and the absence of precise contours.

At other places in the narrative, moreover, the narrator speaks of himself as an artist awaiting a shift in light (see, for instance, *S. F.*, p. 374), and many of these passages seem to recall the Monet who painted "Poplars" (Boston), "waiting for the sun."

More profoundly Impressionist, perhaps, is the conveyed notion that the narrator is observing a world of change and chance. With regard to the various possible combinations of couples, for example, he writes:

> If *he* [Long] 'changed back' wouldn't Grace Brissenden change by the same law? And if Grace Brissenden did, wouldn't her husband? Wouldn't the miracle take the form of rejuvenation of that husband? (*S. F.*, p. 422)[296]

Of course, the very title of James's novel is ironic, because the human relationships that the narrator guesses at in the novel do not partake of the kind of loving that most of us probably experience. In life, most of us seemingly find that loving augments, rather than diminishes, lover and beloved. In James's fiction, on the other hand, it is almost always true to say that loving diminishes, rather than augments. "Amor gignit amorem" (love begets love), the Romans say. But the writers of the Ivory Tower tradition—of which James surely is one of the foremost—would always have it otherwise.

James himself seemingly realized the extent of this fascination with *The Sacred Fount* theme. As late as 1902, for example, he wrote to Howells that the material of *The Sacred Fount* exerted upon him "a rank force of its own"[297]—a strange statement, perhaps, but perhaps not so unusual, coming as it does from the writer who said that by the act of writing "we open the door to the Devil himself."[298]

In *The Sacred Fount,* the narrator's style moreover appears to convey an inherent uncertainty regarding the world that he observes and attempts to arrange into a kind of meaningful composition. In contemplating Mrs. Server, for instance, he says:

> Everything conceivable—or perhaps rather inconceivable—had passed between us before dinner, but her face was exquisite again in its repudiation of any reference (*S. F.,* p. 425).

One further parallel between *The Sacred Fount* and Impressionism lies in "the keyhole perspective" found in both. In James's handling of his narrator, there is a great deal of the voyeuristic example of Degas, for example, who painted many nude bathing scenes during the '90's—see, for instance, "After the Bath, Woman Wiping Her Neck" [1898, Louvre (Jeu de Paume)]—at the very time that James was composing his novel.

As most of the quoted passages from this novel seem to indicate, then, James appears to handle the narrator of *The Sacred Fount* with considerable irony throughout. Indeed, one agrees with Professor Maurice Beebe when he writes (regarding the narrator of *The Sacred Fount*), "that we are intended to see him as deluded, if not villainous, may be seen by comparing him with Lambert Strether of *The Ambassadors.*"[299] While James seemingly handles with ironic detachment the narrator of *The Sacred Fount,* his treatment of Lambert Strether manifests itself in a nearly consistent employment of dramatic irony. In similar fashion to the ironic tone of the earlier novel, the dramatic irony in *The Ambassadors* aligns it with French Impressionism. Like the narrator in *The Sacred Fount,* too, Lambert Strether is a Jamesian center-of-consciousness, an intelligent central observer who has actually become "the drama of his awareness in conflict with the world around him."[300]

As the Impressionist painter, who reproduces the subjective act itself,[301] James provides us with Strether's fascinating thoughts about characters such as Waymarsh, Chad, Maria Gostrey, Madame de Vionnet and the other "ambassadors" in the novel. James's technique seems a particularly apt one to render manifold comparisons of attitudes within the novel; so many of the Impressionist canvases succeed through their fashion both of presenting the surface of a painting as a sequence of graded nuances and of comparing color values on the canvas.

As has been already remarked, both novels make considerable use of irony. In *The Sacred Fount* this device reveals itself in a tone of detachment. This kind of irony, moreover, seems perfectly in keeping with what the Impressionist painters were doing in their heyday—only a few decades before the composition of *The Ambassadors.* Arnold Hauser has written that "nothing is more typical of an impressionist painting than that it must be looked at from a certain distance and that it describes things with the omissions inevitable in them when seen from a distance."[302] Although seemingly true that the treatment of Strether is not ironic in the same way as with *The Sacred Fount* narrator, James does provide a considerable amount of dramatic irony (which provides distance) in the later novel. To illustrate, throughout the first two-thirds of *The Ambassadors,* Strether—in the manner of an Impressionist painter—reports a number of sudden (and seemingly revelatory) glimpses of Chad's appearance and situation in life. On a few occasions one gets remarks about the young man, such as:

> He saw him [Chad], in short, in a flash, as the young man marked out by women; and for a concentrated minute the dignity, the comparative austerity, as he finally fancied it, of this character, affected him almost with awe.[303]

In reading this novel, we come to realize, however, that Strether has been misled by Chad's appearance, for nowhere does the younger man's character show itself to have "the dignity" alluded to by the austere Strether. While there are other examples of the protagonist's naiveté, for our purposes what seems so remarkable is the frequency with which these naive assumptions are expressed in the manner of an Impressionist, working in the open air,[304] who is able to seize an instant of "truth" and transmit it onto his canvas. One recalls Strether's suddenly grasping what he sees to be "the virtuous attachment" (*A.*, p. 136) between Jeanne and Chad, "It was the click of a spring— he saw the truth" (*A.*, p. 136). Yet unlike the successful Impressionist painter working *en plein-air*, Strether's quick apprehension (one soon realizes) is a false one. The irony is this instance is dramatic, then, since the reader immediately suspects that Strether's "revelation" is in fact not true.

But James also includes the kind of irony as a distancing feature which can be found in *The Sacred Fount*. Shortly after telling Little Bilham to " 'Live all you can; it's a mistake not to' " (*A.*, p. 134), Strether goes on to say, " 'I see it now. I haven't done so enough before—and now I'm old; too old at any rate for what I see' " (*A.*, p. 134). This speech appears ironic partially because, once again, Strether does not really "see" the situation with Chad; but perhaps more importantly because James has Strether continue to provide a plethora of metamorphosing impressions (the really delightful aspect of the novel, it seems to me).

According to the evidence in James's *Notebooks* [see entry for October 31, 1895 (p. 226)], the above-cited passage was the seminal one in the Master's composition of *The Ambassadors*. But we also know that W. D. Howells supplied at least something of "the germ" for James's composition. James records that at Torquay he heard how his friend Howells had mentioned to Jonathan Sturges in Whistler's garden that, really, one should "live all one can." And this adjuration caused James to write his long *Notebook* entry on *The Ambassadors*.

The utterance that James overheard in Whistler's garden is a theme that runs throughout his work.[305] Running throughout James's work, we find the same passion for experience that we find in the Conclusion to *The Renaissance*. It is, of course, difficult to discover where the Paterian aspect of James's prose is due to imitation and where to similarity of temperament, a common intellectual climate, and similar education and breeding.

We do know, however, that James had a long-standing interest in Walter Pater. And James, like Pater, insisted "that fiction is one of the *fine* arts."[306] Both Strether and James subscribed to much of Pater's exhortation—particularly to the sentence in Pater which urges that one's passion should "yield this fruit of a quickened, multiplied consciousness."

Like Pater, James often uses the analogy of plant growth to describe modes of composing within his novels. Sometimes these metaphors are used ironically, as when we read of the narrator of *The Sacred Fount* "cherishing the fruit of the seed dropped" (Chapter 6), picking "the full-blown flower of my theory" (Chapter 9) and making a "woven wreath" (Chapter 12) of it. But often, as in the second half of *The Portrait of a Lady* and in Chapter 1, Book 10 of *The Ambassadors,* the garden images are not so ironic when seen in their context.

We recall, too, that Pater's *The Renaissance,* which James had read—and seemingly reviewed—was published in 1873. Less than eighteen months after James read Pater's book, he wrote "The Madonna of the Future" (1875), which contains the elaborately Impressionist description of the Raphael Madonna.[307] And in *Partial Portraits,* in which "The Art of Fiction" first appeared in book format, James preached concentration "upon the moments of life that is itself [sic] but a moment" and remarked upon the "Botticelli women, with wan cheeks and weary eyes, enveloped in mystical crumpled robes," speaking "in strange accents, with melancholy murmurs and cadences."[308]

Between Pater and James there are, however, important differences, some of which some James scholars have already aptly identified. In *Henry James and Pragmatistic Thought* Richard Hocks has remarked upon

> . . . the way Pater often tends to end his fictions like a mind which has closed down shop for the day [I would have used a more graceful phrase, but we understand, I think, what Hocks means here], whereas the stories of the later Henry James have a quality of being projected beyond their conslusions; we often speak of what Lambert Strether

will or will not do after he returns to America, as well as of Isabel Archer's future.309

And in *"The Still Point,"* Ethel Cornwell has observed that "in Pater
there is always the suggestion that the chief value of the aesthetic
sensibility is its extension of consciousness, whereas in James, the
emphasis is reversed and the 'practice of consciousnesss' serves an
aesthetic purpose."310

In the scene in *The Ambassadors* where Strether recognizes
Chad and Madame de Vionnet together on the river, the sketchy
quality of "the picture" is reminiscent of many of Boudin's landscapes—"The Beach at Trouville" (1863, Ittleson Collection, N. Y.),
for example. In Strether's description, the method allows for a grad-
ual revelation from afar, as in Sisley's "Misty Morning" (1874):

> The oblong gilt frame disposed its enclosing lines; the poplars and
> willows, the reeds and river—a river of which he didn't know, and
> didn't want to know, the name—fell into a composition, full of feli-
> city, within them; the sky was silver and turquoise and varnish; the
> village on the left was white and the church on the right was grey; it
> was all there, in short—it was what he wanted: it was Tremont Street,
> it was France, it was Lambinet. Moreover he was freely walking about
> in it.311

What leads Strether to decide upon a day in the country is his distant
memory "of a certain small Lambinet" that had years before called
itself to his attention in a Boston art dealer's. As F. O. Mattiessen has
pointed out, "This nearly forgotten painter of scenes along the Seine
was of the era of Rousseau and Daubigny, all of whom James noted
as having been first shown to him in the early days by Hunt."312
And we recall that it was in Hunt's studio that Henry and William
were perhaps first introduced to Impressionist painting techniques;
for it was here that William, in particular, studied under the tutelage
of John LaFarge (whose work Henry, too, of course, knew and admired).

Another interesting aspect of the previously cited passage is
James's last sentence. In it the author calls attention to the "art-life"
question, since he has the narrator report that Lambert was moving

around in the artistic scene that he is observing—and in doing so, James again calls attention to his novel *as artifact*. In *Partial Portraits* James laments Trollope's "suicidal satisfaction in reminding the reader that the story . . . was only . . . make-believe."313 But James himself seldom hesitates to do that which he castigates in Trollope.314

James, of course, felt nothing but slightly amused contempt for the "many people who read novels as an exercise in skipping."315 And he felt that his reader must "work" in reading a James novel, in much the same way that the viewer of an Impressionist painting frequently must work in order to discover the elements of a scene. On James's part, this feeling probably contributes to the reflexive quality that one often finds in his fiction. In the later fiction, this reflexivism manifests itself especially in James's complex style. In the later style, as Seymour Chatman has pointed out in *The Later Style of Henry James*, "the reader is supposed to figure things out on his own. It is a kind of prose that insists upon selecting its own audience . . . ."316

The reflexive aspects of James's later style are perhaps underscored by Chatman, when he remarks

> in a sense, . . . all fiction is concerned with relationships among characters and situations; what makes the later style of James special is the extent to which it struggles to *name* them, by ransacking grammar and lexicon and, beyond, the far realms of metaphor, and its exquisite ability to find, along the scale of generality, terms to fit the case.317

As Chatman furthermore points out, "James's later fiction characterizes the mental process more frequently as the reception of impressions than as an active performance."318 And it is perhaps this kind of characterization which lends to James's search for exactness of diction and syntax.319 James may, of course, have learned something of his reflexivism from the Impressionist painters, whose paintings also assuredly partake of this quality. That James's practice of dictating his fiction was begun in the 'nineties also more than likely had something to do with the increasing complexity of his style—but this is merely conjecture, since in reading James chronologically I have little sense of a sudden stylistic "break"—rather, James's style seems to *evolve* into complexity. And this feeling is likewise corroborated by several respected colleagues who have, over the years, read James's fiction chronologically.

Strether's enchantment with Paris furthermore recalls the optical splendors of the pictures of Argenteuil by Renoir and Monet, painted between 1871 and 1874. For Strether:

> [Paris] hung before him in the morning, like some huge iridescent object, a jewel brilliant and hard, in which parts were not to be discriminated nor differences comfortably marked. It twinkled and trembled and melted together; and what seemed all surface one moment seemed all depth the next (*A.*, p. 57).

The bold manner of this description combines with the sense of an exquisite and uncritical felt joy in the visible world to suggest Impressionist canvases such as Renoir's "Monet Working in his Garden" (1873), or Monet's earlier "The Breakwater at Honfleur" (1869).

And in an early meeting with Strether, Maria Gostrey is observed across ". . . the small smooth lawn and in the *watery* [italics mine] English sunshine . . . ." (p. 8). Here James's technique recalls to the reader the Impressionist interest in the actual light of day, beautifully presented on many Monet canvases, such as "Flower Garden" (1866) or "Regatta at Argenteuil" (1874).

As is true of the fleeting light of day that the Impressionists attempted to seize in their "plein-air" work, within *The Ambassadors* the moods and morals seem as difficult to fix as the item manufactured in Woollett. Indeed, Lambert Strether's environment constantly forces him to reject certainty of any kind. For example, while sitting with Mrs. Newsome's letters in the Gardens: "What he [Strether] wanted most was some idea that would simplify, and nothing would do that so much as the fact that he was done for and finished" (*A.*, p. 53). Moreover, after Waymarsh poses a question to Strether regarding Chad's opinion of Madame de Vionnet, the protagonist rejoins, " 'You can't make out over here what people do know' " (*A.*, p. 69). These early statements seem typical of Strether's feelings toward Chad and the other "ambassadors" throughout most of the novel; for it is not until we have received almost all of Strether's brilliant impressions that we finally feel that the protagonist pronounces a correct (a realistic) judgment upon Chad.

What furthermore appears in line with Impressionist theory is the use James makes of subtle shifts and fine distinctions in the delineation of Strether's character. About the protagonist one reads, for instance, that "he was Lambert Strether because he was on the cover [of the review], whereas it should have been, for anything like glory, that he was on the cover because he was Lambert Strether" (*A.*, p. 54). Moreover Strether's attitude toward Chad continually shifts as the narrative unfolds: "What it came to was that, with an absolutely *new* quantity to deal with, one could simply not know. The new quantity was represented by the fact that Chad had been made over" (*A.*, p. 93). This constantly altering attitude toward his environment places Strether in a line of Impressionist painters—such as Monet, Sisley, and Pissarro—who studied the shifts in aspect, coloring, and form that winter and summer bring to the same motif. In Pissarro's different canvases of "The Church of Saint Jacques of Dieppe," done from similar veiwpoints in different weathers, and at different times of the year, one sees noteworthy examples of this Impressionist propensity.

After Strether receives a flurry of cables from Woollett, he contemplates visiting Chartres. And in a fashion quite similar to many landscapes by Pissarro, or to Manet's inspiring "River at Argenteuil" (1874), Strether's thoughts render a "word painting" which provides an exhilaratingly shimmering and fleeting sense:

> The early summer brushed the picture over and blurred everything but the near. It made a vast, warm, fragrant medium, in which the elements floated together on the best of terms, in which rewards were immediate and reckonings postponed (*A.*, p. 212).

As with the French painters from whom Henry James seems to have learned so much, *The Ambassadors* gives evidence of a belief that the artifact's world is one where change and chance predominate, and where "the moment" of optical splendor and precious truth is cherished for its own sake. Perhaps this is what Ford Madox Ford means when he refers to "the impression that his [James's] books give us of vibrating reality."[320] Strether, for instance, remarks that:

> He liked Gloriani, but should never see him again; of that he was sufficiently sure. Chad, accordingly, who was wonderful with both of them, was a kind of link for hopeless fancy, an implication of possibilities (*A.*, p. 122).

And after a refreshing conversation with Mamie, Lambert Strether observes: "Mamie would be fat, too fat at thirty; but she would always be the person who, at the present sharp hour, had been disinterestedly tender" (*A.*, p. 271).

In fiction, James, of course, is not the first to have used "the moment" in this fashion. In *White Jacket,* for example, Herman Melville provides the illusion that time stands still when in his last chapter, "The Last of the Jacket," he gives an extended description of the jacket falling into the sea. But James seems to have been the first writer to experiment so successfully with "time's vagaries" (even as the Impressionists seemingly were the first to do so in the visual and plastic arts). Experiments with "the moment" are found not only throughout *The Sacred Fount* and the three novels of the so-called Major Phase, but also in abundance in *The Portrait of a Lady* and in the very late novels, such as *The Sense of the Past* (1917). In the former novel, for instance, in the midst of a penetrating conversation with Ralph Touchett, we read: "There was a moment's silence; the warm noontide seemed to listen. 'I trust you, but I don't trust him,' said Ralph."[321] During such dramatic moments, as James evidently realized, lives are made and broken. And in *The Sense of the Past,* an uncompleted novel, first begun in 1899, James continually plays tricks with time, as when the narrator reflexively refers to the moments "which I can make as long or as short, for intensity, as I like."[322]

While it takes Strether a long time to come to realize the truth of the situation between Chad and the older woman, it does not take him quite so long to come to grips with Chad's true nature. Prior to the recognition scene on the river, in fact, Strether tells Chad face to face that he had " 'no imagination. You've other qualities. But no imagination—don't you see?—at all.' " (*A.*, p. 313). And Strether's last assessment of the charming Madame de Vionnet seems likewise correct, for when she tells him he must now detest her for her actions, he rejoins only: " 'You're wonderful' " (*A.*, p. 352).

Similarly, in his final interview with Chad, Strether shows himself to have the power of seeing truly, in the most perspicuous Impressionist fashion:

> Chad gave a sharper look, as if to sound a suspicion, 'I don't know what should make you think I'm tired of her.' Strether didn't quite know either and such impressions, for the sensitive spirit, were always too fine, too fleeting, to produce on the spot their warrant. There was none the less for him, in the very manner of his host's allusion to satiety as a possible motive, a slight breath of the ominous (*A.*, p. 366).

Strether's realization of the situation with respect to Chad and Madame de Vionnet is but the last of his insights in *The Ambassadors.* In "The Courage of the Artist," Yeats remarks: "Why should we honor those that die upon the field of battle, a man may show as reckless a courage in entering into the abyss of himself."[323] In James's novel, Strether, who speaks of the "wreck of hopes and ambitions, the refuse-heap of disappointments and failures"[324] that his life has been, illustrates something of the truth of Yeats's comment. Strether, for instance

> . . . had again and again made out for himself that he might have kept his little boy, his dull little boy who had died at school of rapid diphtheria, if he had not in those years so insanely given himself to merely missing the mother. It was the soreness of his remorse that the child had in all likelihood not really been dull—had been dull, as he had been banished and neglected, mainly because the father had been unwittingly selfish.[325]

Such comments make clear why, by the time the action of the novel takes place, Lambert Strether has already learned that the superior person considers the feelings of others before he reflects upon the impression that he makes himself. And James, in revealing Strether's impressions, manages also to reveal his protagonist's superiority as a person—a superiority which serves to render Strether's wonderful impressions all the more enjoyable.

What this novel mainly seems to reveal, then, is what the narrator at the outset discursively states to be Strether's unfortunate condition; namely, a "double consciousness" which contains simultaneously "detachment in . . . zeal and curiosity in . . . indifference" (*A.*, p.6). But what comes to interest us most is the way in which this double consciousness is revealed. As Percy Lubbock remarks about James's handling of Strether:

> To bring his mind into view at the different moments, one after another, when it is brushed by new experience—to make a little scene of it, withoug breaking into hidden depths where the change of purpose is proceeding—to multiply these glimpses until the silent change is apparent . . . this is James's way . . . it finally produces the direct impression, for the reader has seen.[326]

It seems quite fitting, therefore, that James concludes this delightful Impressionist novel on a quiet note—the interview with Maria Gostrey. Here Lambert Strether tells her that his " 'only logic is not out of the whole affair, to have got anything for myself.' " Maria Gostrey replies, " 'But with your wonderful impressions, you'll have got a great deal' " (*A.*, p. 375). He has, indeed.

It does not seem surprising, then, that Henry James apparently learned a great deal from the plastic art of the painter. For it is neither as a poet, nor as one with an ear gifted for music, but primarily as a writer of fiction and as a critic of literature and of the plastic arts that James is remembered and discussed. He seems one of the first to have been successful in making of his art a religion, and a way of life (one recalls James's rejoinder to the journalistically disposed H. G. Wells that "art *makes* life. . ."). It therefore appears only fitting that this first truly modern writer should have embraced in his art the complex techniques and forward-looking philosophy of Impressionism—a movement that seemingly did a great deal to shape James's artistic sensibility, and that James himself—primarily through the example that he has provided in his fiction—did a great deal to transform into the style that predominates in all of the arts in the latter third of the nineteenth century.

## *Notes*

AIn his book on the subject, Shiv Kumar points to the use of "psychological time" as "the distinguishing feature of the stream-of-consciousness novel," *Bergson and the Stream of Consciousness Novel.* New York University Press, 1963 (p. 7).

1See, for example, F. O. Matthiessen, "James and the Plastic Arts," *Kenyon Review,* V (Autumn, 1943), 533-50; Giorgio Melchiori, "Two Mannerists: Henry James and Hopkins," in his *The Tightrope Walkers: Studies in Modern English Literature* (London, 1956), pp. 13-33; Percy Lubbock, *The Craft of Fiction* (New York: Viking Compass Paperbook [1921], (1957), p. 185; and Leon Edel and Ilse Dusoir Lind, "Introduction," *Henry James's Parisian Sketches: Letters to the New York Tribune, 1875-1876* (New York: Collier Books [1957] (1961), p. 17.

2John L. Sweeney has selected and edited James's writings on art in *The Painter's Eye: Notes and Essays on the Pictorial Arts* (Cambridge, Mass.: Harvard Univ. Press, 1956). In this useful volume Sweeney has included in "Appendix B" James's lengthy list of "stories and novels concerning the artist and the work of art" and in "Appendix C" the Master's "Travel sketches with comments on art."

3*Parisian Sketches,* p. 17. See also C. Hartley Grattan, *The Three Jameses.* (Longman, Green and Co., 1932, reissued N. Y. U. Press, 1962), p. 229. But this description fit well most art historians of the nineteenth century, since art history is one of the newest disciplines in the Humanities. Erwin Panofsky and others have dated the beginnings of Art History, as the discipline that we know today, to Winckelmann's pioneering study of 1764.

James, however, had the advantage over most who were writing in the late nineteenth century of at least realizing how little his contemporaries knew about the subject. See, for example, Henry James. "An English Critic of French Painting" (1868). Cited in *The Painter's Eye,* p. 34.

[4]On "The Art of Seeing" in James, see, for instance, Leon Edel. *Henry James: The Conquest of London: 1870-1881* (Philadelphia: Lippincott, 1962), p. 53-58.

[5]Robert L. Gale. "Art Imagery in Hnery James's Fiction," *American Literature,* XXIX (March, 1957), 47.

[6]Although it probably deserves notice that James who, in *Picture and Text,* wrote that he had often "illustrated the illustration" (New York: Harper and Row, 1893), p. 2, had a disdain for presenting his own work in an illustrated format. See, for instance, Preface to *The Golden Bowl* in *The Art of the Novel,* ed. R. P. Blackmur (New York: Scribner's 1962), pp. 331-35. See also the letter to Howells, dated January 22, 1895, cited in *The Portable Henry James,* ed. Morton Dauwen Zabel (New York: Viking, 1956), p. 655.

[7]Henry James. "The Art of Fiction" (1884), Edel, ed. *Henry James: The Future of the Novel,* p. 5.

[8]Henry James. *The Selected Letters,* ed. Leon Edel (New York: Farrar, Straus and Cudahy, 1955), p. 93. James's use of the word "paint" in this context may be "a slip," but if it is, it is probably no less revealing a one than that which D. H. Lawrence made when he had Paul Morel "writing" at the easel.

[9]Henry James. "The Future of the Novel: Essays in the Art of Fiction," in Edel, ed. *Future,* p. 33.

[10]Henry James. *Autobiography,* p. 150.

[11]Henry James. "The Art of Fiction," in Edel, ed. *Henry James: The Future of the Novel,* p. 4.

[12]As far as I can discover, James's only specific published remarks concerning the Impressionists can be found in "John S. Sargent," *The Painter's Eye,* ed. Sweeney, pp. 217, 218, and 221; "The Impressionists," ed. Sweeney, pp. 114-115, printed also in *Parisian Sketches,* eds. Edel and Lind, pp. 109-110; and *Henry James, The American Scene* (Bloomington, Ind.: Indiana University Press [1907], Midland Book, 1968), pp. 45-46.

[13]Henry James. *The American Scene,* pp. 45-46.

13AHenry James. *Parisian Sketches: Letters to the New York Herald Tribune, 1875-1876,* eds. Leon Edel and Ilse Dusoir Lind. New York University Press, 1957. pp. 111-112. Now it probably deserves to be pointed out that my check of *L'opera completa di Boldoni* (Milano: Rizzoli, 1970) fails to uncover any such painting as James has described (although several resemble it in differeny ways), but that he should have rendered such an "impression" as though it were actually painted by Boldoni seems to me to be more indicative of James's attitude toward Impressionism than if he were describing an existent artefact in very precise terms.

14See, for example, Virginia Woolf. *Roger Fry: A Biography.* (New York: Harcourt, Brace, and Co., 1940), p. 180. Woolf also records the shock that was shown by most of the visitors to this exhibit, which included paintings by Van Gogh, Cézanne and others.

15In this regard consult Viola Hopkins Winner. *Henry James and the Visual Arts,* pp. 49-51.

16Henry James. "Parisian Festivity," in *Parisian Sketches,* ed. Edel and Lind, p. 109. For commentary on James's remarks, see also note 2, pp. 182-83.

17This series of letters constituted James's only writing for the newspapers in a career of over fifty years devoted to the literary profession.

18Henry James. "Parisian Festivity," *Parisian Sketches,* p. 109.

19Parisian Festivity," *Parisian Sketches,* p. 110.

20Henry James. *The Painter's Eye,* p. 143.

21Henry James. *The Painter's Eye,* pp. 164-65.

22A sample of the commentary on this topic follows: Bruce R. McElderry, in *Henry James* (New York: Twayne, 1965), says that ". . . James's impressionism was not derived from French impressionistic painting, which did not interest him" (p. 163); in *Henry James: The Major Phase* (New York: Oxford Press Galaxy Book 1963), pp. 33-4, F. O. Matthiessen mentions James in relation to the Impressionist movement—Renoir, especially; yet his brief remarks on the subject seem far from thorough; in "The Impressionism of Henry James," *Faculty Papers of Union College,* II (January, 1931), 3-17, Edward H. Hale points out James's affinity of sensibility with the Impressionists, but the scholar neglects to analyze what he considers specifically Impressionist traits of the novelist's work.

23Winner. *Henry James and the Visual Arts,* pp. 88, 89, and VIII.

24Winner. *Visual,* p. VIII.

25See, for example, Winner. *Visual,* pp. 40-44.

26On the entire subject of Mannerism, Winner fails to take account of the manifold problems involved in using the term as a label for a literary style. On this question, confer Branimir Anzulovic. "Mannerism in Literature: A Review of Research," *Yearbook of Comparative and General Literature.* No. 23 (1974), 54-66.

She moreover fails to quote the following, seemingly very revelatory letter from James to W. E. Henley, wherein James sets out to indicate George Meredith's inferiority to Turgenieff:

> "George Meredith strikes me as a capital example of the sort of writer the Turgenieff is most absolutely opposite to—the unrealistic—the *literary* story-teller. T. Doesn't care a straw for an epigram or a phrase—his inspiration is not a whit literary, but purely and simply moral. G. M. cares, I should say, enormously for epigrams and phrases. He is a mannerist; a *coquette,* in a word: vide that pitiful prostitute, Victor Cher [probably Cherbuliez, the French author]. Turgenieff hasn't a grain of coquetry!" Henry James letter to W. E. Henley, 28 August 1878. A. L. S. 18. W. E. Henley Collection. Pierpont Morgan Library.

27Winner, *Visual,* p. 90.

28Winner. *Visual,* p. 91.

29Winner, *Visual,* p. 92.

30James. "The Art of Fiction," Edel, p. 11.

31See Appendix I, "James's Sales," in Roger Gard. *Henry James: The Critical Heritage.* (New York: Barnes and Noble, 1968). James, however, seldom expressed unqualified despair over his lack of an audience. In an 1888 letter to Howells, for instance, he lamented that the demand for his works had been reduced to zero, but he was yet able to express optimism for the future: "Very likely . . . some day, all my buried prose will kick off its various tombstones at once." *The Letters of Henry James,* Vol. 1, ed. Lubbock, p. 135. Two years later, Henry wrote to William these admirable words: "One has always a public enough if one has an audible vibration—even if it should only come from one's self." *The Letters.* Vol. 1, ed. Lubbock. 1920 (p. 170).

32Henry James. Cited in Kenneth Burke. *Attitudes Toward History*. Vol. 1. (N. Y.: The New Republic, 1937), p. 8.

33Henry James. *Notes of a Son and Brother* (1914), *Autobiography*. (1956), p. 268. See also, p. 126 and pp. 253-4 of *A Small Boy and Others (1913)*, *Autobiography*, 1956, where James speaks of "going in for impressions" in his youth—a comment, incidentally, which echoes John Stuart Mill's *Autobiography*, not to mention *Ecclesiasticus* (for the latter, see p. 38:25, Knox translation).

34Henry James. *Notes of a Son and Brother*, pp. 156-7.

35This belief is underscored by Lyall H. Powers in his Introduction to *Henry James's Major Novels: Essays in Criticism*. (Michigan State University Press, 1973), pp. XIII-XL.

36Henry James. Review of Matthew Arnold's *Essays in Criticism. North American Review*, CI (July 1865), 209.

37Henry James. *The Tragic Muse*. N. Y. ed., p. 144.

38Henry James. *William Wetmore Story and His Friends*. (London: Blackwood, 1903), p. 242.

39Henry James. *Letters*, ed. Lubbock, Vol, II, pp. 269-70.

40Henry James. *The Notebooks*, p. 26.

41On James's love of solitude, see also *Notebooks*, p. 43.

42On this subject, see Mark Kanzer. "The Figure in the Carpet." *American Imago*, XVII (Winter, 1960), 339-348; and Milton Mays, "Henry James, or, The Beast in the Palace of Art," *American Literature*, 39 (January, 1968), 467-487.

43Maurice Beebe. *Ivory Towers and Sacred Founts*, p. 13. On the Ivory Tower tendency in the personality of Henry James, see also Bruce Lowery. *Marcel Proust et Henry James*, (Paris: Plon, 1964), pp. 48-9, and the Introduction to *The Letters*, ed. Lubbock, Vol. 1 (XV). Needless to say, James's view of art was diametrically opposed to that of someone like H. G. Wells, of whom James's precise judgment was: "So much talent with so little art."

44Perry, Ralph Barton. *The Thought and Character of William James*.

2 Vols. Boston: Little, Brown and Co., 1935. The first half of volume one provides ample evidence of the truth of this statement.

45Henry James, *Notebooks,* p. 51.

46Henry James. *Autobiography,* p. 285.

47Henry James. *Art of Fiction and Other Essays,* ed. Morris Roberts, p. 17.

48Henry James. *Notebooks,* p. 68.

49See Henry James. *Art of the Novel,* pp. 119-20; and p. 149. For the previous few passages I am especially indebted to Ethel Cornwell, who cites some of these examples in her chapter, "The Jamesian Moment of Experience," in *"The Still Point."* Rutgers University Press, 1962.

50Henry James. "Collaboration," *Collected Tales,* Vol. XXVII, p. 158.

51Henry James. "Mora Montravers," *Collected Tales.* Vol. XXVIII, p. 287. For more on James's view of art as a religion, see the discussion (whose examples I have by and large cited) in Robert L. Gale. *Caught Image,* pp. 164-66. See also Bruce Lowery, *Marcel Proust et Henry James,* p. 56.

52Hölderin. Cited in Werner Hoffman. *The Earthly Paradise, Art in the Nineteenth Century,* trans. Brian Battershaw (N. Y.: Braziller, 1961), p. 136.

53*Letters of Henry James,* Vol. 1, ed. Lubbock, p. 100.

54Henry James. "Is There a Life After Death?" rpt. Matthiessen. *The James Family: Including Selections from the Writings of Henry James, Senior, William, Henry, and Alice James.* (New York: Alfred A. Knopf, 1947), pp. 602-14. This essay is discussed by Matthiessen in *Henry James: The Major Phase* (Galaxy Book), pp. 145-48.

55It is perhaps significant that the notion of "consciousness" is included in one of the two main meanings of the French term *conscience*—a linguistic nuance that would not have been overlooked by James in his discussions of "consciousness" in the non-fictional prose. In *The Unknown Distance: From Consciousness to Conscience: Goethe to Camus.* (Harvard University Press, 1972), Edward Engelberg deals with the way these words and concepts have gradually separated.

56In an interesting passage from his travel writings, James described a woman's moral consciousness as a physical presence. In a March, 1876, letter to the *Tribune* James records the following incident: " 'No French people,' she added in a moment, 'are Republicans—at least no one that any one sees.' This seemed to me in its way quite sublime, and it was certainly excusable to desire to pass an hour in a place so warm and snug and free from uncomfortable drafts as this lady's moral consciousness." Henry James. "Paris in Election Time," *Henry James: Parisian Sketches*, p. 76.

It is not difficult to see how James might have moved from a descriptive passage such as this to his center of consciousness technique. On this subject, see Joseph Warren Beach. *The Method of Henry James.* Yale Univ. Press, 1918.

57Henry James. "Alphonse Daudet," *Literary Reviews and Essays on American, English, and French Literature*, ed. Albert Mordell, p. 184.

58Henry James. "The Great Form" (1889). *The Future of the Novel*, p. 29.

59Henry James. "The Art of Fiction," *Future*, pp. 9-10.

60Henry James. *Notebooks*, p. 135.

61See, for example, James's apostrophe to Maupassant in his *Notebook* entry at the time that he was writing *The Tragic Muse.*

62James's "commemoration of the superb cliffs" (which can be found on pp. 154-55 of *Parisian Sketches*) I think rivals Monet's depiction of the same beautiful scene on canvas.

63Henry James. "London" (1888). Cited in Morton Dauwen Zabel. *The Portable Henry James*, p. 517.

64In *Fortnightly Review* (September 1, 1914), Pound explained that the genesis of his poem was his exit from a "metro" train at La Concorde in Paris. Pound goes on to say that "in a poem of this sort one is trying to record the precise instant when a thing outward and objective transforms itself, darts into a thing inward and subjective.

This particular sort of consciousness has not been identified with impressionist art. I think it is worthy of attention" (p. 465, p. 467). See also *T. P. Weekly* (June 6, 1913), p. 707, where Pound says essentially the same thing, in somewhat abbreviated fashion. Of course, the possibility still exists that Pound may have also drawn upon James for "In a Station of the Metro," for the poet on several occasions expressed great admiration for James's work.

In his brief "London" essay, James uses techniques that are associated with several other schools of painting. The "smeared face and stony heart" of London, p. 522, for example, are Goyaesque descriptive terms. More interesting, perhaps, is the fact that James, like his young compatriot Crane, anticipated surrealist, expressionist, and even dadaist effects nearly two decades before these schools in painting had come to fruition. Compare, for example, James's picture of Maisie, for whom life is "like a long, long corridor with rows of closed doors" at which it is not wise for her to knock, (*What Maisie Knew* [first published 1897], Doubleday, 1954, p. 41) to De Chirico's "The Melancholy and Mystery of a Street," which was not painted until seventeen years after *Maisie* first appeared. The image of the sinister beast that recurs in James's *œuvre* likewise presages beast passages in many surrealist paintings. And the expressionist image of Spencer Brydon's hideous "double" in "The Jolly Corner" (1909)—see Henry James. *Selected Short Stories,* rev. and enl. (New York: Rinehart, 1957), p. 350 —precedes by a decade the full flowering of expressionist art on the Continent.

65Henry James. *The American Scene* (Indiana University Press, A Midland Book, 1968), p. 279.

66Henry James. "New York Revisited," from Chapter 2 of *The American Scene.* Cited in Zabel. *Portable,* p. 541.

67Henry James. *The American Scene,* p. 34.

68See, for instance, Marius Bewley, Introduction to James's *English Hours.* (New York: Horizon Press, 1968).

69Henry James. *English Hours.* (Boston: Houghton-Mifflin, 1905), p. 294.

70Henry James. *Picture and Text.* (New York: Harper and Brothers, 1893), p. 16.

71Henry James. "The Journal of the Brothers Goncourt," *Essays in London and Elsewhere.* (London: Harper and Brothers, 1893), pp. 196-97.

72It deserves mention also, however, that in his 1888 essay on Loti, James referred to the vulture on the back of Impressionism—a reference that in its context is denigratory, but in what specific way it is not easy to determine.

73Henry James. Preface to *The American* in *The Art of the Novel*, p. 27. In his evident lack of spontaneity, James is comparable to Degas who seldom worked *en plein air.*

It is perhaps worth noting here that, as he told W. D. Howells, James envisioned his prefaces as forming "a sort of comprehensive manual . . . for aspirants in our arduous profession." James. *Letters,* Vol. II, ed. Lubbock (p. 99).

James's prefaces, in truth, seem to have hardly served that function, but they do seem to provide a reasonably good indication of James's intentions, insofar as I am able to discern them.

74Henry James. "John S. Sargent," *Harper's New Monthly Magazine,* LXXV (October 1887), in *The Painter's Eye.* Adeline Tintner, incidentally, has shown that in *The Reverberator* James's artist is painting in Sargent's studio. See "Sargent in the Fiction of Henry James." *Apollo.* CII (August 1975), 128-132.

75We recall here Manet's comment that "conciseness in art is a necessity and an elegance . . . . Always move in the direction of conciseness . . . ." Cited in Paul Jamot and Georges Wildenstein. *Manet.* (Paris: Les Beaux Arts, 1932), Vol. 1, p. 71.

76Henry James. Preface to "The Lesson of the Master," *The Art of the Novel,* p. 224.

77Henry James. Preface to "The Altar of the Dead," *The Art of the Novel,* p. 248.

78Preface. *The Spoils. Art of the Novel,* p. 120.

79Preface. *Spoils. Art of the Novel,* p. 120.

80Preface. *Spoils. Art of the Novel,* p. 121. James's example of course remains valid—is perhaps even more precisely validated—when we realize that, as S. P. Rosenbaum has pointed out, "The original notebook entry on the *Spoils* shows that James considerably oversimplified the sources and nature of his inspiration for the novel. Many more words than ten were needed to record the 'inveterate minuteness' of the germ; James took some three hundred just to note down the bare story." See "Henry James and Creativity: The Logic of the Particular case," *Criticism* 8 (Winter 1966), 44-52. I quote from p. 46. That James was willing to go so far as to contradict the evidence of his Notebooks seems to me to indicate how far he was willing to go in the direction of Impressionism in the development of his *theory* of fiction.

82Henry James. "The Present Literary Situation in France," *The North American Review* CLXIX (October 1899), p. 493. James uses the term foreshortening in "The Lesson of Balzac," *Future*, p. 111, and in the following instances in his critical prefaces: *The Art of the Novel*, pp. 87-88; 262-63, 278; and 302. Viola Hopkins Winner probably best defines the term as it is used by James: "the representation of the lines of an object as shorter than they are in actuality in order to give the illusion of relative size, according to the laws of perspective," "Pictorialism," *Criticism*, p. 12. An interesting discussion of the term in James is also to be found in an unpublished essay by Susan Overath, entitled "Show and Tell: The Visual Arts Metaphor in the Criticism of Henry James," pp. 21-26. I am grateful to Miss Overath for allowing me to see her essay in typescript. Critical commentary on James's use of the term foreshortening can also be found in Joseph Warren Beach. *The Method of Henry James*. (Phil.a: Lippincott, 1954), p. 33; Morris Roberts, "Henry James and the Art of Foreshortening," *Review of English Studies*, XXII (July 1946), 207-214; and Philip Grover. *Henry James and the French Novel*. (New York: Barnes and Noble, 1973), pp. 41-49.

83Henry James. "Sargent" (1887). In *The Painter's Eye*.

84Egan. *Henry James: The Ibsen Years*. (New York: Barnes and Noble, 1973), p. 22.

85Adeline R. Tintner. Review of first two volumes of *Henry James: Letters*, ed. Edel, in *American Literary Realism*. 8 (Autumn 1975), 353-359.

86Henry James. "The Art of the Novel," *Future*, p. 16 and p. 14.

87On James's admiration of Balzac, see Henry James. "The Lesson of Balzac" (1905) in *Future*, p. 104. See also Leon Edel. "The Architecture of James's 'New York Edition,' " *New England Quarterly*, XXIV (June 1951), 169-178; Percy G. Adams. "Young Henry James and the Lesson of His Master Balzac," *Revue de Littérature Comparée*, XXXV (July-September 1961), 458-467, and "The Lesson of Balzac," the first part of Philip Grover's *Henry James and the French Novel*, pp. 15-68.

88Chatman. *The Later Style of Henry James*. (New York: Barnes and Noble, 1972), p. 22.

89Goldberg. " 'Things' and Values in Henry James's Universe." *Western Humanities Review*, XI (Autumn 1957), p. 377. In his book on James, Joseph Wiesenfarth makes much the same point.

90James. *Notes and Reviews,* ed. Pierre de Chaignon la Rose. (Harvard University Press, 1921), pp. 70-74.

91Henry James. "The Art of Fiction," *Future,* p. 13 In *A Small Boy and Others* James significantly commented thus upon his early childhood education: ". . . just to *be* somewhere—almost anywhere would do—and somehow receive an impression or an accession, feel a sensation or a vibration." James. *A Small Boy and Others.* Charles Scribner's Sons, 1913 (p. 25).

92Henry James. "The Art of Fiction," *Future,* p. 23.

93Henry James. "The Art of Fiction," *Future,* p. 16.

94André Malraux. *The Temptation of the West* (Paris, 1926), trans. Robert Hollander. (Vintage Books, 1961), p. 65. This is not to say, however, that James was not capable of painting the explicit scene when he wished to do so. See, for instance, the detail in the description of the restaurant scene at the conclusion of "Chartres Portrayed," Letter 12 to the *Tribune* (April 29, 1876), *Parisian Sketches,* pp. 105-6.

95James. Preface to *The Ambassadors. The Art of the Novel,* p. 318.

96In *Longinus and English Criticism* (Cambridge University Press, 1934), T. R. Henn traces the Longinian tradition which emphasizes the sudden single flash, as well as the quality and power of intensity in the artistic work. There is probably more than a little truth to this emphasis upon "the moment of creation," whether it be in literature or in the visual and plastic arts.

97Henry James. "Is There a Life After Death?" (1910), rpt. *The James Family,* ed. F. O. Matthiessen (Oxford University Press, 1947). For more on James's personal philosophy, see Maurice Beebe. *Ivory Towers,* pp. 226-29.

98Henry James. *Letters,* ed. P. Lubbock, p. 347 and p. 362.

99James's answer to "the obvious criticism" that he anticipated of *The Portrait of a Lady. Notebooks,* p. 18.

100*Henry James: Parisian Sketches,* p. 101.

101Henry James. "Italian Journeys by W. D. Howells," *North American Review*, CVI (January 1868), 337-38.

102Henry James. *The Art of the Novel*, p. 46.

103Henry James. *A Little Tour in France*. (Boston: Osgood, 1885), p. 60.

104Roy Pascal. *Design and Truth in Autobiography* (Harvard University Press, 1960), p. 10.

105Henry James. Preface to *Maisie, Art of the Novel*, 1962, pp. 140-1.

106Henry James. Preface to *Roderick Hudson. Art of the Novel*, pp. 4-5.

107Henry James. "The Art of Fiction," *Future*, p. 12.

108Henry James. "Art of Fiction," *Future*, p. 12. On this subject, see also the chapter of "Felt Life" in Naomi Lebowitz. *The Imagination of Loving: Henry James's Legacy to the Novel* (Wayne State University Press, 1965), pp. 21-53.

109James, however, understood well what the Impressionists were seemingly attempting: "to give a vivid picture of how a thing happened to look," he wrote in his 1876 letter to the *Tribune*, cited in *Henry James: Parisian Sketches*, p. 110.

110Henry James. *The House of Fiction*, ed. Edel, Rupert Hart-Davis, 1957, p. 33.

111Henry James. Letter to Henry Adams. March 21, 1914. Cited in Morton Dauwen Zabel, *Portable Henry James*, p. 675.

112James's fascination with Hawthorne is partially revealed by the frequency with which Hawthorne references occur in his criticism. See William T. Stafford's *A Name, Title, and Place Index to the Critical Writings of Henry James*. (Microcard Editions Books, 1975), pp. 135-37. I am much indebted to Stafford for his book which I have consulted often in revising this manuscript. If I had had Stafford's *Index* on hand through my first draft, I would have finished it much more quickly.

113Henry James. *The Art of the Novel*, p. 64.

114Henry James. "The Future of the Novel," in *The Universal Anthology*, Vol. 28 (1899). Cited in *Future*, p. 33.

115Henry James. "The Limitations of Dickens" (1865). Cited in Zabel, ed. *Portable*, pp. 433-40. Commenting upon *Our Mutual Friend*, the young Henry James remarked: "Seldom, we reflected, had we read a book so intensely *written*, so little seen, known, or felt" (p. 434).

116For a rather illustrative contrast between James and Lawrence as critics of the visual arts and of literature, cf. for example, Lawrence's "Art and the Dread of Instincts," in *The Nature of Art*, ed. John Gassner and Sidney Thomas. (New York: Crown Publishers, 1964), p. 97.

117Henry James. "London" (1888), Cited in Zabel, ed. *Portable*, p. 522.

118John Rewald. *The Impressionist Brush*. (Metropolitan Museum of Art, 1974), p. 54.

119Henry James. "The Art of Fiction," *Future*, p. 23.

120Henry James. "The Art of Fiction," *Future*, p. 23.

121Henry James. "The Art of Fiction," *Future*, p. 21.

122Henry James. Letter to G. B. Shaw, January 20, 1909, in *Selected Letters of Henry James*, ed. Leon Edel. (Farrar, Strauss and Cudahy, 1956), pp. 34-35. See also the Preface to "The Altar of the Dead," *Art of the Novel*. *passim*.

123Henry James. "The Art of Fiction," *Future*, p. 13. This being the case, it is not difficult to see some of the important ways that James's view of experience may have anticipated that of such Modernist art movements as Expressionism and Dadaism (where inner and outer worlds are seemingly at war with each other) and Surrealism (where the art world is very often primarily the depiction of the dream landscape of the mind). In the notes to *Henry James and the Dramatic Analogy: A Study of the Major Novels of the Middle Period* (Fordham University Press, 1963), Joseph Wiesenfarth underlines the important point that James does not usually mean "plot" when he says "action," as most of the action in James's books goes on internally.

124Henry James. Preface to *The Awkward Age, The Art of the Novel*, pp. 109-110.

125In *The Modern Psychological Novel*, Leon Edel, however, has pointed out that Woolf's image seemingly owes a great deal to a passage in Benjamin Constant's work (although James, I should add, nowhere alludes to the French author in his published criticism). Since it is nevertheless unlikely that James did not know Constant's work, the progression should probably be from Constant to James to Woolf.

126Henry James. Preface to *The Portrait of a Lady. Art of the Novel*, p. 42.

127Henry James. Preface to *Portrait. Art*, p. 43.

128Henry James. *French Poets and Novelists* (New York: 1964), p. 32.

129Henry James. Review of *Emily Chester. The North American Review*, p. 282.

130Henry James. "The Art of Fiction," *Future*, p. 15.

131Henry James. "The Art of Fiction," *Future*, p. 15.

132On James's opinion of Scherer see the young author's tribute to the philosopher in *The Nation* (12 October 1865), rpt. "A French Critic," in *Notes and Reviews*. (Harvard University Press, 1921), p. 104.

133Scherer. Cited in Irving Babbitt. *The Masters of Modern French Criticism.* (Harvard University Press, 1912), p. 194. In *Contributions to the Analysis of Sensations*, tr. C. M. Williams (Open Court, 1897), the psychologist Ernst Mach extends Scherer's ideas. See p. 6 and 26. Mach expresses his indebtedness to Fechner (see p. viii) and to Thomas Young's optical discoveries (p. 33). And we recall that the work of both of these authors may likewise have influenced to some extent the founders of the Impressionist movement on the continent (See above, Chapter One, p. 6). To my knowledge, in James's published criticism he does not allude to Mach, Fechner or Young, but James was a voracious reader, and may very well have known their work also. Moreover, Henry's brother William knew Mach and Fechner well, and he may have spoken to Henry about them.

134Henry James. *A Little Tour in France.* (Boston: James P. Osgood and Co., 1885), p. 221.

135Henry James. Preface to *The Ambassadors*. Cited in Norton Critical Edition, ed. S. P. Rosenbaum, p. 6.

136Henry James. *The Art of the Novel*, pp. 64-65.

137Henry James. *Art*, p. 286. James clarifies himself somewhat further when he remarks that "the panting pursuit of danger is the pursuit of life itself, in which danger awaits us possibly at every step and faces us at every turn . . . . There are immense and flagrant dangers that are but sordid and squalid ones, as we feel, tainting with their quality the very defiances they provoke, while there are common and covert ones, that 'look like nothing' and that can be but inwardly and occultly dealt with, which involve the sharpest hazards to life and honour and the highest instant decisions and intrepidities of action." *The Art of the Novel* (pp. 32-33). In the attitude to danger as thus expressed, James seems to me to be very close to Conrad.

138Henry James. Preface. *Spoils. Art*, p. 122.

139Henry James. Letter to Grace Norton, Spring 1873. Cited in Leon Edel. *Henry James: The Conquest of London, 1870-1881.* (Phila.: Lippincott, 1962), pp. 128-29.

140Henry James. Preface. *Golden Bowl. Art*, p. 328.

141See, for instance, Henry James. *Autobiography*. (Criterion, 1956), p. 544 and p. 569, and "Is There a Life After Death?" in *The James Family*, p. 613.

142Henry James. Preface to *Spoils. Art*, p. 119.

143Henry James. "The Art of Fiction," *Future*, p. 22.

144Henry James. Letter to T. S. Perry, January 24, 1881, in *Henry James: Letters*, ed. L. Edel. Vol. 2 (1875-1883). (The Belknap Press of Harvard University, 1975), p. 334.

145Henry James. "The Royal Academy" (1878), *The Painter's Eye*, pp. 167-8. On Taine and James, see Jeremiah S. Sullivan. "Henry James and Hippolyte Taine: The Historical and Scientific Method in Literature," *Comparative Literature Studies* 10 (1973), 25-50. See also William T. Stafford's illuminating commentary on this article in *American Literary Scholarship: An Annual/ 1973* (Durham, N. C.: Duke University Press, 1975).

146On the subject of artistic collaboration in James's fiction, see E. Duncan Aswell. "James's Treatment of Artistic Collaboration," *Criticism* 8 (Spring 1966), 180-195.

147Henry James. *The American Scene,* p. 151.

148On this essay and its place in the literary tradition, see especially Frederick Ives Carpenter. *Emerson and Asia* (Harvard University Press, 1930). On the relationship between author and reader in general in the nineteenth century, see Robert A. Colby. *Fiction with a Purpose: Major and Minor Nineteenth Century Novels.* (Indiana University Press, 1967).

149Walt Whitman. *Complete Poetry and Selected Prose,* ed. James E. Miller, Jr. (Riverside edition, 1959), p. 451.

150Sainte-Beuve cited in F. O. Matthiessen. *American Renaissance* (Galaxy, 1968), p. 543. James, of course, had written often, and generally admiringly, of Sainte-Beuve's criticism.

James's overall opinion of Whitman is perhaps best expressed in an 1865 review of *Drum-Taps,* a review that seemingly also tells us a great deal about James's theory of artistic impersonality:

> To sing aright our battles and our glories it is not enough to have served in a hospital (however praiseworthy the task in itself), to be aggressively careless and inelegant, and ignorant, and to be constantly preoccupied with oneself. It is not enough to be rude, lugubrious, and grim. You must also be serious. You must forget yourself in your ideas. Your personal qualities—the vigour of your temperament, the manly independence of your nature, the tenderness of your heart —these facts are impertinent. You must be *possessed,* and you must thrive to possess your possession.

Review of Whitman's *Drum-Taps* (1865). Cited in Zabel, *Portable.* (1956), p. 433.

151Henry James. "The Future of the Novel," in *The Universal Anthology,* Vol. 28 (1899). Cited in Leon Edel. *Future,* p. 34.

152Henry James. "The Art of Fiction," *Future,* p. 4.

153Henry James. "The Novels of George Eliot," *Atlantic Monthly,* XVIII (October, 1866), p. 485.

154Henry James. Preface to *Wings, Art,* p. 304.

155Royal Cortissoz. *John La Farge: A Memoir and a Study.* (1911), pp. 114-115.

156James. *Notes of a Son and Brother,* pp. 97-98.

157Henry James. *Letters,* ed. Edel, p. 193.

158Henry James. Review of *Dallas Galbraith* (by Mrs. R. H. Davis) in *Nation,* VII (October 22, 1868), 330-31. On the other hand, in "Criticism" (1891), James's comments regarding the critic, the artist, and the critical function are salutary indeed: "Just in proportion as he is sentient and restless, just in proportion as he reacts and reciprocates and penetrates, is the critic a valuable instrument; for in literature assuredly criticism *is* the critic, just as art is the artist; it being assuredly the artist who invented art and the critic who invented criticism, and not the other way round," Henry James. "Criticism," *Essays in London and Elsewhere* (New York: Harper and Brothers,1893), pp. 264-65.

159I say *seems to have* here, since this is the sense I get from reading James chronologically. To date, there has been no full-scale study of James's style. Seymour Chatman's *The Later Style of Henry James* (New York: Barnes and Noble, 1972) comes closest to satisfying this demand. But an elaborate stylistic study—one that would take account of representative works from all of James's periods—has yet to be done.

160Henry James. Preface to *The Golden Bowl. Art,* p. 327.

161It is worth noting here, I think, that James mentions "irony" over twenty times in his Prefaces alone. I am grateful to Rosemary Franklin's Index to the *Prefaces of Henry James* (1966) for this tabulation.

162Henry James. Preface to *The Princess Casamassima, Art,* p. 62. On James's opinion of Sainte-Beuve, see especially the comments in *The Nation,* (18 February 1875), p. 118.

163Henry James. "The Art of Fiction," *Future,* p. 8. In writing about *The Golden Bowl,* Quentin Anderson comments wisely on this attitude as it is expressed in James's fiction (an attitude which aligns James very closely with Conrad): See Anderson. *The Imperial Self.* Knopf, 1971 (p. 171).

164Ethel Cornwell. *"The Still Point,"* p. 139.

165Henry James. Cited in Leon Edel. *Henry James: The Conquest of London.* (Philadelphia: Lippincott, 1962), p. 316.

166Henry James. "The Art of Fiction," ed. Edel. *Future,* 1956, p. 10.
And a comparison is precisely what I am attempting in this study, since any
comparison implies affinity and divergence. Just as few of the Impressionist
painters always used Impressionist techniques in their paintings or, to put it
another way, used Impressionist techniques exclusively in those paintings that
are considered Impressionist, so too did James show an aversion to using the
same techniques always in his fiction. What I am concerned to provide in *Henry
James and Impressionism,* then, is a new way of viewing James's *œuvre*—one that
shows it to be more properly akin to Impressionism than to any other school or
movement.

Between Henry James and Impressionism there are, as I hope I demonstrate, many similarities and specific correlations, but what I attempt to reveal
in depth is rather more what Jean Weisgerber has admirably referred to as *con-
fluences* than influences, as such. See Weisgerber. Concluding chapter to *Faulkner et Dostoievski.* Brussels: Presses Universitaires de Bruxelles, 1968 (p. 304,
especially).

167Henry James. "A Landscape Painter" (1866). *The Tales of Henry
James,* Vol. 1, 1864-1869, ed. Maqbool Aziz. Oxford: Clarendon Press, 1973
(p. 58). Subsequent references to this story will cite page references from this
volume.

168James. "Landscape," p. 60.

169In Locksley's description we see evidence of what James himself probably meant when he remarked that he had often "illustrated the illustration."
*Picture and Text.* Harper and Row, 1893, p. 2.

In "An English Critic of French Painting," (1868), James moreover observed that "painters, as a general thing, are much less able to take the literary
point of veiw, when it is needed, than writers are to take the pictorial . . . ."
*The Painter's Eye,* p. 35.

170James, "Landscape," p. 77.

171Textual variants for this story are cited from Aziz, ed. Vol. 1.

172James, "The Story of a Masterpiece," Aziz, ed. *Stories.* Vol. 1, p. 201.

173James, "Masterpiece," Aziz, ed., Vol. 1. p. 208.

174James. "Masterpiece," Aziz, ed., Vol. 1, p. 209. A painting is similarly mutilated in "The Liar" (1888), a tale which I shall discuss later. Strangely enough, John Singer Sargent's portrait of James was knifed in 1914 at the Royal Academy. Here again we see that Art *makes* Life! On these "tomahawked" paintings, see especially G. Hartley Grattan. *The Three Jameses: A Family of Minds: Henry James, Sr., William James, Henry James.* New York: Longmans, Green and Co., 1932, p. 352; and Barbara Martineau. "Portraits are Murdered in the Short Fiction of Henry James." *Journal of Narrative Technique,* 2 (January 1972), 16-25.

175James cited by M. Aziz in *Stories,* Vol. 1, footnote, p. 209. On this subject, see also Charles K. Fish, "Indirection, Irony, and the Two Endings of 'The Story of a Masterpiece,'" *Modern Philology,* 62 (February 1965), 241-243.

176With regard to these three works of fiction, Robert J. Niess has sketched the possible (I would go so far as to say probable) lines of literary apparentation. See "Henry James and Émile Zola: A Parallel." *Revue de Littérature Comparée, XXX (January-March 1956), 93-98.*

177James. *The Letters,* ed. Percy Lubbock, Vol. 1, p. 396.

178Henry James. *French Poets and Novelists.* New York: 1964, p. 32.

179See, for example, James. Preface, Volume XV. New York edition, 1909, p. x.

180The previous quotations are from *Madame de Mauves* in *The Great Short Novels of Henry James,* ed., Philip Rahv. Dial Press, 1965, p. 18. Subsequent quotations likewise refer to this edition.

In *Madame de Mauves,* as in *The Ambassadors,* James sometimes uses limited omniscient narration. The former work of fiction, however, is mainly related through the consciousness of Longmore.

181James, *Madame* p. 18.

182James, *Madame,* p. 19.

183James, *Madame,* p. 27.

184James, *Madame,* p. 27.

185James, *Madame,* p. 33.

186James, *Madame*, p. 41.

187James, *Madame,* p. 62.

188James. Preface to *The Tragic Muse.* Scribner's, 1962, p. 87.

189In this, as in much else in James, we can see how revolutionary was his art. As Marius Bewley has pointed out, "the American novelist before James, in his most successful work, turns his back on manners and society as such." *The Eccentric Design: Form in the Classic American Novel,* Columbia University Press, 1959, p. 15.

190See James. *The Art of the Novel,* p. 212. For other references to this story in the Prefaces, see p. 206 and p. 213.

191James. "A Bundle of Letters," (1879), *The Complete Tales of Henry James,* ed. Edel. Vol. *4, 1962, p. 438.*

192See, For example, Joseph Conrad. "An Appreciation." *Henry James: A Collection of Critical Essays,* ed. Edel. Prentice-Hall, 1963, p. 17.

193James. Preface to *The Tragic Muse. Art of the Novel.* Scribner's, 1962, pp. 87-88.

194Perry cited in Virginia Harlow. *Thomas Sergeant Perry: A Biography.* Duke University Press, 1950, p. 76.

195For Harlow's authorities for attributing this essay to Perry, see her footnotes, p. 360.

196Harlow. *Perry,* p. 101.

197James. "Bundle" (1879), *Complete Tales.* Vol. 4, p. 439.

198According to Leon Edel. "Introduction." *The Portrait of A Lady.* Riverside edition, 1963, (p. VII).

199The passages quoted from the letters are cited by Leon Edel in his Introduction to the Riverside edition of *The Portrait.* 1963 Impression (p. vi). As is often the case with James, he made true his boast. His receipts from the novel's serial versions alone (which he sold to *Macmillan's Magazine* and to *Atlantic*) amounted to over $6000—a great sum of money in 1880.

200Here the situation with regard to James's revisions becomes exceedingly complex. The reader who wishes to trace these revisions should consult the following: Sydney J. Krause, "James's Revisions of the Style of *The Portrait of a Lady*," *American Literature*, XXX (March 1958), 67-88. See especially 68-81; Simon Nowell-Smith, "Texts of *The Portrait of a Lady*, 1881:1882: The Bibliographical Evidence." *Publications of the Bibliographical Society of America*, 63 (1969), 304-310. See especially 305-307. Nowell-Smith's article is especially important because he corrects Krause's mistaken assertion (on p. 68) that the New York edition is set from the revised text that James did between magazine and book publication. As Nowell-Smith points out, when Macmillan's reset *The Portrait* in three volumes for their collected edition of *Novels and Tales of Henry James*, they corrected most of the errors in their copytext, the London one-volume edition that appeared in 1882 (which James, of course, had already revised). While Nowell-Smith corrects Krause on several important points, he shows no evidence, either in text or in footnotes, of having read Krause's 1958 article.

For other treatments of the complicated question of the revisions, see especially the critical material assembled by Robert D. Bamberg for the Norton Critical Edition (1975) of *The Portrait of a Lady*—an indispensible volume for the study of James's novel. Bamberg also helpfully includes James's own major statements concerning the genesis and "desired effect" of his novel.

As Leon Edel indicates, the manuscript notes to the New York edition (these notes are in the Houghton Library) reveal that James "worked over the novel . . . as if it were a first draft." Edel. *Henry James: The Master: 1901-1916.* Vol. 5. Lippincott, 1972 (pp. 324-333).

In the discussion that follows, I cite the Laurel paperback edition of *The Portrait of a Lady*, ed. R. P. Blackmur, 1961. Although Blackmur indicates that he uses the 1881 edition, a close inspection of his text reveals that he in fact uses the text of the New York edition! [since James's death, the 1881 text has been used only once—for the Signet Classic edition, edited by Oscar Cargill (New York: New American Library, 1964)]. In using the New York edition as my basic text, I underscore the fact that, by late career, Henry James was working squarely in the Impressionist tradition that he himself did so much, during the previous forty years, to develop and enhance.

201Sheldon Liebman, "Point of View in *The Portrait of a Lady." English Studies.* 52 (No. 2, 1971), p. 136. In this statement there is only a kernel of truth. I wholeheartedly agree with Monroe C. Beardsley when he argues " . . . the speaker of a literary work cannot be identified with the author—and therefore the character and condition of the speaker cannot be known by internal evidence alone—unless the author has provided a pragmatic context or a claim of one, that connects the speaker with himself." Monroe C. Beardsley, *Aesthetics.* Harcourt, Brace and World, 1958 (p. 24). I therefore cannot assent wholeheartedly to Liebman's claims about "point of view" in the novel, since he too closely identifies James with Isabel.

202Henry James, *Portrait of a Lady.* Laurel (pp. 298-299). Interestingly, James gives us a good idea of when the novel takes place, since Edward Rosier's infatuation with Pansy begins during the summer of 1876, a mere four months from the date of James's Paris letters to the *Tribune,* concerning the Impressionist painters.

As a new suitor, Rosier is described as "an ornament of the American circle in Paris." James, *Portrait.* Laurel ed., 1961 (p. 330).

203James. *Portrait* (p. 376).

204James. *Portrait* (p. 30). For similar uses of this technique in the travel writings, see *A Little Tour in France* [1885]. Farrar, Straus and Co., 1950 (p. 240 and p. 39).

205James. *Portrait* (p. 322).

206James. *Portrait* (p. 225).

207James. *Portrait* (p. 226).

208I stopped counting at twenty-five—roughly halfway through Volume 1.

209James. *Portrait of a Lady* (p. 231).

210W. D. Howells. "Henry James, Jr." *Century*, XXV (November 1882), p. 26.

211James. *Portrait of a Lady* (p. 51).

212Cf. Samuel Johnson. *Rasselas.* Chapter 45, in particular. In a 1902 article in *Harper's Bazaar* W. D. Howells has remarked that "no other novelist has approached Mr. James in his appreciation of women, and in his ability to suggest the charm which is never wholly absent from women . . . ." Howells. "Mr. James's *Daisy Miller,* " *Harper's Bazaar* (January 1902); published also in *Heroines of Fiction.* 1901 (p. 184; Harper's citation).

213James. *Portrait of a Lady* (p. 244).

214James. *Portrait of a Lady.* Laurel. The preceding pair of quotations is found on p. 374 and p. 371.

215James. *French Poets and Novelists,* ed. L. Edel. N. Y.: 1964 (pp. 224-225; 225-226).

216James. *French Poets and Novelists* cited in Peterson. *One Much Embracing Echo.* Kennikat Press, 1975 (p. 114).

217For Isabel's "Yelena-side," see, for instance, *Portrait.* Laurel ed. p. 55; for her "Gwendolyn-nature," see, for example, pp. 52-53.

218James. *Portrait of a Lady.* Laurel (p. 391).

219James. Preface to *Roderick Hudson. The Art of the Novel.* (pp. 4-5).

220James. Preface to *The Ambassadors* in *The Art of the Novel.* ed. R. P. Blackmur, 1962 (p. 326).

221James. *Notebooks* (p. 21).

222Peter Buitenhuis. *The Grasping Imagination: The American Writings of Henry James.* Univ. of Toronto Press, 1970 (p. 134).

223See, for example, Henry James. "A New England Winter" (1884): *The American Novels and Stories of Henry James,* ed. and with an Introduction by F. O. Matthiessen, Knopf, 1947 (pp. 354-356).

In his treatment of the story, Buitenhuis also connects it to Daudet's fiction—a just enough comparison, although the critic might have been more specific, since a great deal of Daudet's fiction is demonstrably not Impressionist.

224James. "A New England Winter." *American Novels and Stories* (p. 355).

225Edel. *Henry James: The Master* (p. 30).

226James. Preface. *The Golden Bowl. The Art of the Novel.* Scribner's 1962 (p. 332). Coming as it does in the early twentieth century, James's salutary remark was an admirably conservative one.

227James. "At Isella" (1871). N. Y.: Scribner's, 1907-1917 (p. 252).

228James. "On Some Pictures, Lately Exhibited" (1875). *The Painter's Eye* (p. 97). James herein uses almost the exact words that Zola used several years before in praising the Impressionist painters.

As I have indicated with my few previous remarks in the text, James's powers of observation were considerable. That this was so is partially indicated by the appearance of his penetrating eyes. On this subject, see Alice Broughton. "A Note by His Photographer," *Hound and Horn*, VII (April-May, 1934), 478; and *The Legend of the Master*, comp. by Simon Nowell-Smith. Charles Scribner's Sons, 1948. See pp. 2, 5, 6, and 8. On James's powers of observation, see Leon Edel. "The Art of Seeing," in *Henry James: The Conquest of London, 1870-1881*. J. B. Lippincott, 1962 (pp. 53-58).

229James. "A New England Winter." *American Novels and Stories* (p. 356).

230James. "A New England Winter." *American Novels and Stories* (p. 355). In this, I might add, James's painters pursue a problem which is analogous to that which he presents to the reader in "The Real Thing" (1892), the story that we will consider after "The Liar."

231James. "The Liar." (1888). *The Complete Tales of Henry James*, Vol. 6, 1884-1888, ed. Leon Edel. Rupert Hart-Davis, 1963 (p. 44). Edel uses the 1889 text that was published in *A London Life*. Since only a year passed between first serial publication and first book publication, and since, as Edel notes, James's tale "had the benefit of revision from magazine to volume" (p. 443), the choice of the book edition is defensible here. From the late '80's onward James would have made few new technical discoveries about Impressionism, an artistic phenomenon with which he had been personally familiar for over a dozen years.

232See Richard J. Kane. "Hawthorne's 'The Prophetic Pictures' and James's 'The Liar.' " *Modern Language Notes*, LXV (April 1950), 257-258. Among the handful of other worthwhile discussions of the story, see especially Wayne Booth. *The Rhetoric of Fiction*. Univ. of Chicago Press, 1961 (pp. 347-354). Booth pays especial attention to the role of James's narrator. On the narrator's role as villain in James's story, see especially Marius Bewley. *The Complex Fate: Hawthorne, Henry James, and Some Other American Writers*. London: Chatto and Winders, 1952 (pp. 84-87).

233James. "The Liar." *Complete Tales,* ed. Edel (p. 385).

234James. "The Liar." *Complete Tales* (pp. 386-387).

235It is worth pointing out, too, I think, that even here, at the dinner party, in the midst of several passages filled with indirection James provides the most direct of visual images, as when he relates that Lyon "was so prepared with a greeting" that when Mrs. Capadose turned to him, "he instantly smiled, as a shaken jug overflows." "The Liar" (p. 389). This sentence also provides a happy example of the way that James moves slightly out of Lyon's consciousness. Throughout the story he does so just briefly enough to supply the sufficient number of ironic touches to the delineation of his protagonist's character.

236James. Preface to *The Spoils of Poynton. The Art of the Novel* (p. 139).

237The connections between some Impressionist elements of this story and of "The Liar," the preceding one in our discussion, have already been well-made by Lyall H. Powers in "Henry James and the Ethics of the Artist: 'The Real Thing' and 'The Liar,' " *Texas Studies in Literature and Language,* III (Autumn 1961), 360-368. Since Powers has covered so well the territory that he has staked out, I will not herein make the same connections.

238James. Preface. *Daisy Miller. The Art of the Novel* (p. 283).

239James. Preface to *Daisy Miller. The Art of the Novel* (p. 284).

240James. "The Real Thing." *The Portable Henry James* ed. Morton D. Zabel. Viking paperback, 1956 (p. 146). Subsequent references will be to this edition. "The Real Thing" was first published in *Black and White,* 16 April 1892. It first appeared in a hard-bound edition as the title piece to James's collection of stories which was published in London and New York in 1893. This edition also includes the first book publication of "Greville Fane" (1892), the next Jamesian story that we will consider.

241James. "The Real Thing" (p. 150).

242James. "The Real Thing." *Portable.* ed. Zabel 1956 (p. 158).

243James. "The Real Thing" (p. 159). Of Mrs. Monarch, James's narrator makes this fine attitudinal distinction: "She wished it to remain clear that she and the Major were employed, not cultivated, and if she approved of me as a superior, who could be kept in his place, she never thought me quite good enough for an equal" (p. 159).

244James. "The Real Thing" (p. 152).

245James. "The Real Thing" (p. 155).

246James. "The Real Thing" (pp. 158-159).

247James. "The Real Thing" (p. 165).

248Viola Hopkins Winner. *Henry James and the Visual Arts.* Univ. Press of Va., 1970 (pp. 108-109).

249James. Preface to "The Author of Beltraffio," in *The Art of the Novel* (p. 234). This story, like so many of James's, has attracted surprisingly little critical attention. One of the few, relatively extended critical discussions of "Greville Fane" can be found in Krishna Baldev Vaid. *Technique in the Tales of Henry James.* Harvard University Press, 1964 (pp. 54-60).

250See entry for January 22, 1879, in James. *Notebooks* (pp. 10-11). In his *Notebooks,* James two years later returned to this initial idea for the development of his story. The story was not finished until several years later. See *Notebooks* (pp. 94-95).

251See Van Deren Coke. *Painting and Photography.* 1972 (p. 207).

252Van Gogh. Cited in Loevgren. *The Genesis of Modernism* (p. 171).

253See James. *Notebooks* (p. 92). We recall one character's comment in *The Tragic Muse:* " 'The book of life's padded, ah but padded—a deplorable want of editing!' "

On the question of "real-life" spokesmen in *The Tragic Muse,* see Oscar Cargill. "Mr. James's Aesthetic Mr. Nash." *Nineteenth Century Fiction,* 12 (December 1957), 177-187; Dorothea Krook. *The Ordeal of Consciousness in Henry James.* See especially p. 83; Leon Edel. *Henry James: The Conquest of London.* Lippincott, 1962, p. 170; and Robert S. Baker. "Gabriel Nash's 'House of Strange Idols' Aestheticism in *The Tragic Muse.*" *Texas Studies in Literature and Language.* XV (Spring 1973), 149-166.

254See, for example, James. "Greville Fane." *Portable Henry James.* ed. Zabel. 1956 (pp. 126-128).

In his collection, Zabel mis-arranges "The Real Thing" and "Greville Fane." Both stories were published in 1892, but the latter one was published later than "The Real Thing" (over which it seemingly represents no technical advance).

255 James. "Greville Fane." *Portable.* 1956 (p. 142).

The kind of cannibalism herein displayed toward Greville's manuscripts represents an ironic twist on the kind of literary cannibalism shown by the protagonist of *The Aspern Papers,* which James published originally in *Atlantic Monthly,* March-May 1888 (and reprinted with subtle but important revisions) in *The Aspern Papers. Louisa Pallant, The Modern Warning.* London: Macmillan, 1888.

256 James. "Greville Fane." *Portable.* p. 122; p. 126; and p. 129.

257 James. *What Maisie Knew* (1897). Doubleday Anchor Book, 1954 (p. 18).

258 See Aristotle. *Politics.* Bk. 2, Chapter 3 in *The Basic Works of Aristotle,* ed. Richard McKeon, N. Y.: Modern Library, 1945 (p. 1148f).

259 James. *Maisie.* Anchor, 1954 (p. 14).

260 James's narrator, of course, enters here and there, in Trollopian fashion, as the following sentence, for example, serves to indicate: "Maisie had a sense of her launching the question with effect; yet our young lady was also conscious of hoping that Sir Claude would declare that preference." James's narrative intrusion—his use of the word "our" in the second part of the sentence—distances the situation just enough to make it bearable. Later in the novel James uses his omniscient narrator in the first person, but to much the same effect. See, for example, pp. 136-137, beginning with the first full paragraph, p. 136.

A word here about my selection of the text for *What Maisie Knew:* the Anchor edition is set from the New York edition of 1908. The publication history of the novel is exceedingly complex. *What Maisie Knew* appeared first in serial format in the *New Review,* February-September 1897. (We recall that Conrad's *The Nigger of the "Narcissus"* began to run in the *New Review* in December of 1897). Beginning with the July issue of this monthly, however, large excisions were made. These excisions were so extensive that they reduced the novel the equivalent of 55 pages from the first British book edition, containing 304 pages altogether.

Moreover, *Maisie* appeared, without these cuts, almost concurrently in *Chap Book*, a bi-weekly American periodical. The novel ran here from January 15 to August 1, 1897.

Because the two periodical versions differ so radically in texture, in narrative pace, and even in diction, and because it is difficult to say which version James definitely preferred, I have cited the N. Y. edition, which represents James's final standard. Moreover, even as early as 1897 James would have learned little that was new about Impressionist painting—to which he had been exposed since the mid-'70's, at the latest. On the complicated textual questions concerning *Maisie* see, in particular, Ward S. Worden, "A Cut Version of *What Maisie Knew." American Literature.* 24 (January 1953), 493-504.

261 James. *Maisie.* Anchor, 1954 (p. 27).

262 James. *Maisie.* Anchor, 1954 (p. 113).

263 James's *Notebook* entries are intelligently compared with the finished novel by Ward S. Worden. "*What Maisie Knew: A* Comparison with *The Notebooks." PMLA* (June, 1953), 371-383.

264 James. *Notebooks* (p. 160).

265 Like *Maisie, The Spoils of Poynton* has an extraordinarliy complicated publishing history. The novel was published in four different versions in James's lifetime. It originally appeared in serial format, under the title, *The Old Things* in *Atlantic Monthly,* from April to October 1896. A year later, the novel appeared, as *The Spoils of Poynton,* in book editions in England and America. These editions were published a week apart, in February, 1897 (a matter of several months from the appearance of *What Maisie Knew). The Spoils* was again published during James's lifetime in the New York Edition of 1908.

As S. P. Rosenbaum has pointed out in his article, "*The Spoils of Poynton:* Revisions and Editions," James's typescript of "The Old Things" was apparently destroyed by the *Atlantic* after the serial was set. Since in all likelihood no copy exists of James's manuscript, it is not possible to tell how closely the *Atlantic* followed James's copy. But since, as Rosenbaum notes, "James did not consider serial publication a permanent form for his work," and since Rosenbaum cites an unpublished letter to the editor of the *Atlantic,* indicating that James did not even read proof for the serial version, then this version can be disregarded for our purposes. See S. P. Rosenbaum. "*The Spoils of Poynton:* Revisions and Editions." *Studies in Bibliography.* 19 (1966), 165.

As Rosenbaum moreover reports, the Boston and London first editions have in common more than twelve hundred revisions from *The Old Things.* For these reasons and for the reasons cited for my textual choices for *Maisie,* I have chosen to cite the New York edition. Beyond the mid-'80's, James works so consistently in the Impressionist vein in his fiction that from this period onward it is difficult to speak of a progression, since most of the fiction from the middle period onward is fundamentally Impressionist.

266James. Preface. *Spoils.* N. Y. edition. Scribner's, 1908 (p. XIV). For James, who believed that art is primarily expression, Mona Brigstock represents a prime contrast to Fleda. Mona was "without a look in her eye or any perceptible intention of any sort in any other feature . . . . Her expression would probably have been beautiful if she had had one." James. *Spoils* (p. 9).

267James. Cited in *Notebooks* (p. 179).

268James. *Notebooks* (p. 179).

269James. *Notebooks* (p. 215). Italics mine.

270James. *Spoils.* N. Y. ed. 1908 (p. 14).

271James. *Spoils.* N. Y. ed. (p. 150).

272James. *Spoils.* (p. 150).

273James. *Spoils.* N. Y. ed. (pp. 145-146).

274James. *Literary Reviews and Essays.* Grove Press, 1957 (p. 151). Although in fairness it should be pointed out that he admired this aspect of Balzac—when he encountered it in the French author's work. See, for instance, James. *The Complete Tales of Henry James,* Vol. 4, ed. Edel. 1962 (p. 441).

275Gale's tabulation can be found in *The Caught Image* (p. 27).

276Ezra Pound counselled that "you would do well to read *The Sacred Fount* when you have read James's prefaces and 20 of his other novels." *ABC of Reading.* London: Faber and Faber, 1951 (p. 90). Whether Pound realized that James only wrote 20 novels, we can only conjecture!

277This is a presumption anticipated by W. D. Howells, as far back as 1903. See W. D. Howells. "Mr. Henry James's Later Work," *The North American Review* (January 1903), cited in Mordell. *The Discovery of a Genius: William Dean Howells and Henry James.* Twayne, 1961 (p. 204).

278On the "center of consciousness" in James, see especially Maurice Beebe. *Ivory Towers.* 1964 (p. 198) and J. W. Beach. *The Method of Henry James.* 1918 *(passim).*

279William York Tindall. *Forces in Modern British Literature, 1885-1956* Rev. ed.; N. Y.: Vintage Bk., 1957 (p. 191).

280Lowery. *Marcel Proust et Henry James* (p. 95).

281James. *The Sacred Fount.* Harper and Row, Perennial Classic [1901], 1968 (p. 414). Hereafter this edition will be cited as *S. F.*, along with the page number, within the text. Neither *The Sacred Fount* nor *The Wings of the Dove* (1902) was serialized.

The exposition which follows is a revised version of my discussion of *The Sacred Fount* in "Henry James's Use of Impressionist Painting Techniques in *The Sacred Fount* and *The Ambassadors.*" *Studies in the Twentieth Century.* 13 (Spring 1974), 83-116.

282Hauser. *Social History of Art,* Vol. 4 (p. 171).

283At this time I should like to acknowledge the assistance of a very useful reference tool—Robert L. Gale. *Plots and Characters in the Fiction of Henry James* [1965]. M. I. T. Press, 1972.

I have read all of James's fiction with especial care. And I have used my own words in summarizing the plots of the fiction that I have considered. I have nevertheless had constant recourse to Gale's helpful reference guide. It proved to be of invaluable assistance to me in attempting to unravel some of James's more complicated novels and stories.

284One recalls, here, James's prefatory comments for *The Spoils of Poynton,* where he expresses a desire to shut out "clumsy life again at her stupid work." (p. 1). Henry James, "Preface," *Collected Edition,* Vol. X (New York, 1909).

285For other examples of this kind of reporting, see, for instance, *S. F.,* p. 368, p. 416, and p. 417.

286I owe this suggestion about the Impressionist method to Sypher, *Rococo,* p. 180, whose thoughts on this matter I have paraphrased.

287John Ruskin. *Modern Painters. Works,* ed. E. T. Cook and Alexander Wedderburn. London: George Allen, 1903-1912 (Vol. 5, p. 177).

288Ford Madox Ford, *The Good Soldier: A Tale of Passion* (New York: Vintage Books, 1955), p. 137.

289Ford. *The Good Soldier* (p. 246). Ford's narrator not only sees the world as an Impressionist, but also, on occasion, as a *pointilliste* (see p. 14).

290See also, the long bottom paragraph of p. 379, for an example of a confused tone, and p. 372 for an example of what seems a deliberately confusing style.

291Spender. *Struggle* (p. 134).

292Rewald. *History of Impressionism.* 1962 (p. 196). A good illustration of Rewald's words is Camille Pissarro's "The Orchard" (1877; Musée du Louvre). In this painting Pissarro's homes in a sense give up their identity to the whole natural landscape of which they are a part.

293See also *S. F.* (p. 371) for similar "maneuvering."

294Note the strong contrast between this Impressionist technique and that of the French Realists who preceded them.

295Regarding his work "on a series of different effects [haystacks]" (p. 34), Monet wrote to his friend, Gustave Geffrey, "what I am seeking to convey is: 'instantaneity' . . . ." "Letter to Gustave Geffrey," in Nochlin, *Sources and Documents of Impressionism.* (p. 34).

296This passage goes on in the same vein for nearly a page, and represents what Maurice Beebe refers to as "the vampire effect" in his chapter on Henry James in *Ivory Towers and Sacred Founts,* p. 422. In a similar vein (a proper word to use in this context!) Osborne Andreas has termed James's view of lovers' relationships "Emotional Cannibalism." See Chapter 1, *passim,* of *Henry James and the Expanding Horizon.* Univ. of Washington Press, 1948. On "the vampire theme" in *The Sacred Fount,* see also especially Norma Phillips. *"The Sacred Fount:* The Narrator and the Vampires," *PMLA,* LXXVI, (September 1961), 407-412. In *The Sacred Fount,* James uses elements of the vampire donnée throughout Chapter 5.

297James. Letter to Howells. Dec. 11, 1902. *Letters,* Vol. 1, ed. Lubbock. 1920 (p. 408).

298James's letter cited in Edel. *Henry James: The Treacherous Years* (p. 355). For a survey of the sacred fount motif in James's fiction, see Edel. "Introduction" to *The Sacred Fount.* Grove Press, 1953 (pp. xxv-xxix).

James entertained the idea for *The Sacred Fount* for an extended period. His first *Notebook* entry touching upon the subject was done as early as February 17, 1894. He returned to the idea in his *Notebooks* several years later. See *Notebooks* (pp. 150-151; and p. 275).

299Beebe. *Ivory Towers* (p. 214). There is even a sense in which in *The Sacred Fount* James is handling one of his own themes with irony. In "The Private Life " (1892), one of James's characters, though a master of all the social graces, has no private life; he ceases to exist altogether when he is not in society, when he is no longer an object of the admiring attention of others. In contrast, *The Sacred Fount* narrator seems to have *little more than* his "private life" to sustain him. In this sense, he aligns himself with Rousseau's savage who is "savent être heureux et contents d'eux-mêmes sur le témoignage d'autrui plutôt que de leur propre" (The savage has his life within himself; social man outside himself, in the opinion of others)—an ironic twist, if ever James has done one!

300Beebe. *Ivory Towers* (p. 198).

301Hauser. *Social.* Vol. IV (p. 169).

302Hauser. *Social.* IV (p. 171).

303Henry James, *The Ambassadors* (New York: [A Signet Classic] The New American Library [1903], 1960), p. 95. Hereafter, unless otherwise indicated, this edition will be cited as *A.* with the page number within the text of the paper.

In 1890 Henry James told William that *The Tragic Muse* was to be his last long novel. James, of course, was wrong. For *The Ambassadors,* his prospectus (intended to attract editors for the serial publication of his novel) alone ran to over 20,000 words (or roughly the same length as "The Coxon Fund"). James accomplished the writing of *The Ambassadors* in about eight months (although he apparently received "the germ" for the novel many years before). The novel appeared in twelve numbers of *The North American Review* for 1903 and was published as a whole during the same year. Although James's novel was not published until 1903, it was written in 1901 (before *The Wings of the Dove,* which first saw publication in 1902).

*The Ambassadors* was James's last novel to appear in serial form prior to publication as a book. Before being accepted by *The North American Review,* the novel was rejected by Harper's.

Like much of James's fiction, the situation with regard to the text of *The Ambassadors* is exceedingly complicated. In the section of the Norton Critical Edition of *The Ambassadors* entitled "Editions and Revisions" (pp. 353-364), S. P. Rosenbaum sets forth a summary of the editorial complexities in the novel. The other major scholarly items of interest on the text of the novel can be found in my bibliography.

Like the discussion of *The Sacred Fount,* the discussion of *The Ambassadors* is a revised and extended version of my *STTC* article, cited above.

304As Renoir, for example, does so well in "Le Moulin de la Galette" (1876, Louvre). Here the brilliant hues and the filtered sunlight lend to the sense of the gaiety of the moment.

305Incidentally, Theodora Bosanquet, who was James's typist over the last twenty years of his career, has pointed out that the only words of advice James would ever give his young companions is to "let your soul live!"

306Henry James. "The Art of Fiction."

307For having called this to my attention, I am indebted to Alwayn Berland. "Henry James and the Aesthetic Tradition." *Journal of the History of Ideas,* 23 (July-September !962), 412.

308James. *Partial Portraits* (p. 369).

309Hocks. *Henry James and Pragmatistic Thought* (p. 67).

310Ethel Cornwell. *"The Still Point"* (p. 10).

311James. *Ambassadors.* N. Y. ed., Vol. 2 (p. 247).

312Matthiessen. *Henry James: The Major Phase.* Oxford Univ. Press (Galaxy Book), 1961 (p. 35).

313James. *Partial Portraits.* Macmillan, 1899 (p. 116).

314On this technique in *The Ambassadors,* see especially John E. Tilford, Jr. "James, the Old Intruder," *Modern Fiction Studies,* 4 (Summer 1958), 157-164.

Tilford's article is a healthy corrective to Percy Lubbock's otherwise worthwhile *The Craft of Fiction* (Viking Compass Paperback ed., 1957). Lubbock judges that in Henry James "the intervention of a seeing eye and a recording hand, between the reader and the subject, is practically avoided altogether" (p. 185). I would say that this is hardly ever true of James.

315Henry James. "The Art of Fiction" (1884). *Henry James: The Future of the Novel.* Vintage, 1956 (See pp. 7-8).

316Seymour Chatman. *The Later Style of Henry James.* Barnes and Noble, 1972 (p. 40). At a number   of points in his fascinating little book, Chatman makes clear what he means by his statement. See, for example, p. 7, p. 21, p. 23, and pp. 56-60. See also  R. W. Short. "The Sentence Structure of Henry James." *American Literature,* XVIII (Spring 1946), 71-88, but especially p. 81.

317Chatman. *Later Style* (p. 78).

318Chatman. *Later Style* (pp. 61, 120).

319See, for example, *The Sacred Fount.* Grove Press, 1953 (p. 128); and *The Ambassadors* on virtually any page.

In his *Autobiography* James makes especial use of the reflexive quality that likewise informs his fiction (upon which Proust seemingly drew for the reflexivism in his fiction). Throughout the *Autobiography*, one can find "false" timidity and poses of modesty in James's selection of vocabulary. See, for instance, p. 209, p. 359, and p. 441. As Bruce Lowery has noted, Proust uses the same technique to especially good effect in *Sodom et Gommorhe.* And Ford Madox Ford (in *The Good Soldier*) and Hemingway (in *The Sun Also Rises*) follow suit.

320Ford Madox Ford. *Henry James.* [1913]. rpt. Octagon Books, 1964 (p. 153).

321James. *The Portrait of a Lady.* Laurel, 1961 (p. 317).

322James. *The Sense of the Past.* Charles Scribner's Sons, 1917 (p. 235). It is not difficult to see how such novelists like Proust, Virginia Woolf, and James Joyce—and with a lesser degree of success, Dorothy Richardson—have used James's suggestions about time in the making of their fiction.

323W. B. Yeats. "The Courage of the Artist." Cited in Richard Ellmann. *Yeats: The Man and the Masks.* N. Y.: Macmillan, 1948 (p. 6).

324James. *Ambassadors.* N. Y. ed. Vol. 1, p. 65.

325James. *Ambassadors.* N. Y. ed. Vol. 1. Scribner's 1909 (p. 84).

326Lubbock. "The Point of View" [of *The Ambassadors*], in ed. Leon Edel. *Henry James: A Collection of Critical Essays,* Prentice-Hall, 1963 (p. 42).

# SELECTED BIBLIOGRAPHY

The following bibliography contains full particulars of books or articles which have been mentioned with shortened titles in the text or notes. In addition, a selection of titles has been included which may be useful for reference, although there has not been occasion to mention them in the course of the work. The bibliography omits books and articles which have been fully cited in the text or the notes.

Abraham, D. J. "L'Héritage de J. Laforgue," *La Revue de littérature comparée*, 43 (January-March 1969), 56-68.

Ahnebrink, Lars. *The Beginnings of Naturalism in American Fiction.* New York: Russell and Russell, 1961.

Alonso, Amado and Raimonda Lida, eds. and trans. *El Impresionismo en el Lenguaje.* Buenos Aires: University of Buenos Aires Press [1936, 1942], 1956.

Baldwin, Carl. *The Impressionist Epoch.* New York: Museum of Modern Art, 1974.

Baron, Wendy. *Sickert.* London: Phaidon, 1973.

Beach, Joseph Warren. *The Twentieth Century Novel: Studies in Techniques.* New York: The Century Co., 1932.

Beebe, Maurice. *A Critical Study Guide to Conrad's* Lord Jim. Totowa, New Jersey: Littlefield Adams, 1968.

—. "The Masks of Conrad." *Bucknell Review,* XI (December 1963), 35-53.

—.      *"Ulysses* and the Age of Modernism." *James Joyce Quarterly,* X (Fall 1972), 172-187.

—.      "What Modernism Was." *Journal of Modern Literature.* 3 (July 1974), 1065-1084.

Beja, Morris. *Epiphany in the Modern Novel.* Seattle: University of Washington Press, 1971.

Benamou, Michel, and others. "Symposium on Literary Impressionism." *Yearbook of Comparative and General Literature,* 17 (1968), 40-72.

Bergson, Henri. *Durée et Simultanéité: A Propos de la Théorie d'Einstein.* Paris: Librairie Félix Alcan, 1922.

Bloom, Harold. "Walter Pater: The Intoxication of Belatedness." *Yale French Studies,* No. 50 (1974), 163-189.

Bowers, David, ed. *Foreign Influences in American Life.* Princeton, New Jersey: Princeton University Press, 1944.

Bowie, Theodore. *Les Rapports entre la littérature et la peinture en France de 1840-1880.* Berkeley, California: University of California Press, 1935.

Boyle, Richard J. *American Impressionism.* New York: Graphic Society of America, 1974.

Brady, Patrick. *L'œuvre d'Émile Zola: Roman sur les Arts, Manifeste, Autobiographie, Roman à Clef.* Geneva: Libraire Droz, 1967.

Briganti, Giuliano. *Italian Mannerism,* trans. Margaret Kunzle. Leipzig: VEB edition, 1962.

Browse, Lillian. *Sickert.* London: Rupert Hart-Davis, 1960.

Burdett, Osbert. *The Beardsley Period: An Essay in Perspective.* New York: Boni and Liveright, 1925.

Busch, Frieder. *Erzahler-, Figuren- und Leserperspektive in Henry James's Roman* The Ambassadors. Munich: Max Hueber, 1967.

Butler, R. "Zola's Art Criticism (1865-1868)." *Forum for Modern Language Studies,* 10 (October 1974), 334-347.

Champa, Kermit Swiler. *Studies in Early Impressionism.* New Haven, Conn.: Yale University Press, 1972.

Chatman, Seymour. *The Later Style of Henry James.* New York: Barnes and Noble, 1972.

Chernowitz, Maurice. *Proust and Painting.* International University Press, 1945.

Child, Ruth C. *The Aesthetic of Walter Pater.* New York: Macmillan, 1940.

Cogniat, Raymond. *The Century of the Impressionists,* trans. Graham Snell. New York: Crown Publishers, Inc., 1959.

Conn, Peter J. "Roderick Hudson: The Role of the Observer." *Nineteenth Century Fiction,* 26 (1971), 65-82.

Conrad, Jessie. *Joseph Conrad as I Knew Him.* London: Heinemann, 1926.

Conrad, Joseph. *Complete Works.* Kent Edition. New York: Doubleday, 1925.

—. *Lettres Françaises.* 5th edition. Paris: Gallimard, 1929.

Cook, David A. "James and Flaubert: The Evolution of Perception." *Comparative Literature,* XXV (Fall 1973), 289-307.

Crane, Stephen. *Stephen Crane: An Omnibus,* ed. with an Introduction by R. W. Stallman. New York: Knopf, 1952.

—. *Bowery Tales,* Volume I of *The Work of Stephen Crane.* Charlottesville, Va.: University Press of Virginia, 1969.

—. *Tales, Sketches, and Reports. Work.* University Press of Virginia, 1973.

Daudet, Alphonse. *L 'Evangéliste.* Paris: Ernest Flammarion, n.d.

—. *Kings in Exile* (1879), trans. Laura Ensor and E. Bartow. London: J. M. Dent and Co., 1902.

—. *Lettres de mon moulin.* Paris: Bibliothèque-Charpentier, n. d.

—. *Le Nabob: Mœurs Parisiennes* (1877). Pairs: G. Charpentier, 1887.

—. *Notes sur la Vie.* Paris: Bibliothèque-Charpentier, 1899.

—. *Le Petit Chose* in *Oeuvres Complètes, Edition Définitive.* Paris: Houssieaux, 1899.

—. *Les Rois en Exil (Oeuvres Complètes illustrées).* Paris: Librairie de France, 1929.

—. *Tartarin de Tarascon.* Paris: C. Marpon et E. Flammarion, 1890.

Da Vinci, Leonardo. *The Notebooks,* ed. Robert N. Linscott. New York: The Modern Library, 1957.

—. *The Notebooks,* ed. and trans. Edward MacCurdy. New York: Braziller [1939], 1955.

Dayez, Anne, ed. *Impressionism: A Centenary Exhibition.* New York: The Metropolitan Museum of Art, 1974.

Demorest, D. L. *L'Expression figurée et symbolique dans l'œuvre de Gustave Flaubert.* Paris: L. Conard, 1931.

Dent, R. W. *John Webster's Borrowing.* Berkeley, California: University of California Press, 1960.

Desprez, Louis. *L'Evolution Naturaliste.* Paris: Tresse, 1884.

Dunstan, Bernard. *Painting Methods of the Impressionists.* Watson-Guptill, 1976.

Edel, Leon and Dan H. Laurence. *A Bibliography of Henry James.* rev. ed. London: Rupert Hart-Davis (Soho Series), 1961.

Edel, Leon. "The Architecture of James's 'New York Edition.' " *New England Quarterly,* XXIV (June 1951), 169-178.

—. ed. *Henry James's* Guy Domville. Philadelphia: Lippincott (Keystone Books), 1960.

—. *Henry James.* University of Minnesota Press, 1960.

—. "Henry James: The American-European Legend," *University of Toronto Quarterly,* XXXVI (July 1967), 321-334.

—. *The Modern Psychological Novel.* New York: 1955 [rev. 1961]. Universal Library Edition, Grosset and Dunlap, 1964.

Ehrsam, Theodore G. *A Bibliography of Joseph Conrad.* Metuchen, N. J. :Scarecrow Press, 1969.

Fabris, Alberta. *Henry James e la Francia.* Rome: Edizioni di Storia Letterature, Biblioteca di Studi Americani, Vol. 18, 1969.

Fardwell, Frances Virginia. *Landscape in the Works of Marcel Proust.* Catholic University Press, 1948.

Fernandez, Ramon. *Messages.* Harcourt, Brace, 1927.

Ferran, André. *L'esthétique de Baudelaire.* Paris: Hachette, 1933.

Firkins, O. W. *Ralph Waldo Emerson* [1915]. New York: Russell and Russell, 1965.

Flaubert, Gustave. *Oeuvres complètes.* Paris: Conard edition, 1910-1939.

Fleming, William. *Arts and Ideas,* 3rd edition. New York: Holt, Rinehart and Winston, 1968.

Ford, Ford Madox. *Joseph Conrad: A Personal Remembrance.* Boston: Little, Brown, and Co., 1924.

—. *Critical Writings,* ed. Frank MacShane. Lincoln, Nabraska: University of Nebraska Press, 1964.

—. *The English Novel from the Earliest Days to the Death of Joseph Conrad.* Philadelphia: J. P. Lippincott, 1929.

—. *Letters,* ed. Richard M. Ludwig. Princeton, N. J.: Princeton University Press, 1965.

—. "Techniques." *Southern Review,* I (July 1935), 20-35.

Fosca, Françoise (pseudonym for Georges de Traz). *Edmond et Jules de Goncourt.* Paris: Albin Michel, 1941.

Franklin, Rosemary F. *An Index to Henry James's Prefaces to the New York Edition.* Charlottesville, Va.: Bibliographical Society of the University of Virginia, 1966.

Friedman, Melvin. "Passages on Aesthetics from Flaubert's Correspondence." *Quarterly Review of Literature.* IV (1949), 390-400.

Frierson, William C. *The English Novel in Transition, 1885-1940.* Norman, Okla.: University of Oklahoma Press, 1942.

Fryer, W. R. "The War of 1870 in the Pattern of Franco-German Relations." *Renaissance and Modern Studies,* XVIII (1974), 77-125.

Gale, Robert L. "Henry James and Italy." *Nineteenth Century Fiction,* XIV (September 1959), 157-170.

Gargano, James W. "Henry James and Baudelaire." *Modern Language Notes,* LXXV (November 1960), 559-561.

Garland, Hamlin. *Crumbling Idols: Twelve Essays on Art and Literature.* Gainesville, Fla.: Scholars' Facsimiles and Rpts., 1952.

Garnett, Edward. "An Appreciation of Stephen Crane's Art." Address to the London Academy, Dec. 17, 1898. Rev. and republished in his *Friday Nights.* New York: Alfred A. Knopf, 1922.

—, ed. *Letters from Joseph Conrad, 1895-1924.* Indianapolis, Indiana and New York: Bobbs-Merrill, 1962.

Garnier, Marie-Reine. *Henry James et la France.* Paris: Librairie Ancienne Honoré Champion, 1927.

Geffroy, Gustave. *Claude Monet: Sa Vie, son œuvre.*2nd. ed., 2 Vols. Paris: G. Crés, 1924.

—. "French Art at Chicago," *Cosmopolitan,* XVI (January 1894), 371-372.

Gerber, Helmut E. *Book Collector,* XXI (Autumn 1972), 422, 425-426.

Gettmann, Royal A. *Turgenev in England and America.* Illinois Studies in Language and Literature 27. 1941.

Gibbons, Tom. "Modernism in Poetry: The Debt to Arthur Symons." *The British Journal of Aesthetics,* 13 (Winter 1973), 47-60.

Gibson, J. J. *The Perception of the Visual World.* New York: Houghton-Mifflin, 1950.

Gilcher, Edwin. *A Bibliography of George Moore.* DeKalb, Illinois: Northern Illinois University Press, 1970.

Gill, Richard. *Happy Rural Seat: the English Country House and the Literary Imagination.* New Haven, Conn.: Yale University Press, 1972.

Glasser, Richard. *Time in French Life and Thought* (1936), trans. C. G. Pearson. Manchester University Press, 1972.

Goldring, Douglas. *Trained for Genius.* New York: Dutton, 1949.

Gombrich, E. H., Julian Hockberg and Max Black. *Art, Perception, and Reality.* Baltimore: Johns Hopkins University Press, 1972.

Goncourt, Edmond and Jules de, ed. *Journal des Goncourt.* Vols. 3 and 5. Paris: Bibliothèque-Charpentier, 1891.

—. *Madame Gervaisais.* Nouvelle Edition. Paris: Bibliothèque-Charpentier, 1919.

—. *Manette Salomon* [1866]. Nouvelle Edition. Paris: Bibliothèque-Charpentier, 1910.

—. *Renée Mauperin* [1864]. Nouvelle Edition. Paris: Bibliothèque-Charpentier, 1920.

Gordan, John D. "The Ghost at Brede Place." *Bulletin of the New York Public Library,* LVI (December 1952), 591-596.

Gross, Theodore L. and Stanley Wertheim. *Hawthorne, Melville, Stephen Crane: A Critical Bibliography.* New York: The Free Press, 1971.

Guillen, Claudio. *Literature as System: Essays Toward the Theory of Literary History.* Princeton, N. J.: Princeton University Press, 1971.

Hamilton, George Heard. *19th and 20th Century Art.* N. Y.: Abrams, 1970.

—. *Painting and Sculpture in Europe 1880-1940.* Hammondsworth, England: Pelican History of Art, 1967.

Harding, F. W. J. "Notes on Aesthetic Theory in France in the Nineteenth Century." *The British Journal of Aesthetics,* 13 (Summer 1973), 251-270.

Harvey, David Dow. *Ford Madox Ford, 1873-1939; A Bibliography of Works and Criticism.* Princeton, N. J.: Princeton University Press, 1962.

Hay, Eloise K. *"Lord Jim:* From Sketch to Novel." *Comparative Literature,* XII (Fall 1960), 289-309.

Hemmings, F. W. J. *Culture and Society in France 1848-1898: Dissidents and Philistines.* New York: Charles Scribner's, 1971.

Herbert, Robert L. *Neo-Impressionism* (catalogue). New York: The Solomon R. Guggenheim Museum, 1968.

Hermerén, Gören. *Influence in Art and Literature.* Princeton, N.J.: Princeton University Press, 1975.

Hoffman, Anastasia Carlos. *Outer and Inner Perspectives in the Impressionist Novels of Crane, Conrad and Ford.* University of Wisconsin Dissertation, 1968.

Holder, Alan. "The Lesson of the Master: Ezra Pound and Henry James." *American Literature,* XXXV (March 1963), 71-79.

Holland, Laurence Bedwell. *The Expense of Vision: Essays on the Craft of Henry James.* Princeton, N. J. : Princeton University Press, 1964.

Holt, Elizabeth Gilmore, ed. *From the Classicists to the Impressionists: a Documentary History of Art and Architecture in the 19th Century.* New York University Press, 1966.

Hone, Joseph. *The Life of George Moore.* London: V. Gollancz, 1936.

Houghton, Walter E. *The Victorian Frame of Mind.* New Haven, Conn.: Yale University Press, 1957.

Hughes, H. Stuart. *Consciousness and Society: The Reorientation of European Thought 1890-1930.* New York: Knopf, 1958.

Humphrey, Robert. *Stream of Consciousness in the Modern Novel.* Berkeley, California: University of California Press [1954], 1st paperback edition, 1958.

Huth, Hans. "Impressionism Comes to America." *Gazette des Beaux Arts,* XXIX (April 1946), 225-252.

Hynes, Samuel. "Two Rye Revolutionaries." *Sewanee Review,* LXXIII (Winter 1965), 151-158.

Ingarden, Roman. "Phenomenological Aesthetics: An Attempt at Defining Its Range." *Journal of Aesthetics and Art Criticism,* XXXIII (1975), 257-269.

Jacobs, Robert Glenn. *Psychology, Setting and Impressionism in the Major Novels of Joseph Conrad.* University of Iowa Dissertation, 1965.

James, Henry. *The Art of Travel: Scenes and Journeys in America, England, France and Italy from the Travel Writings of Henry James,* ed. Morton Dauwen Zabel. Garden City, New York: Doubleday, 1958.

—. *The Complete Tales,* ed. Leon Edel. London: Rupert Hart-Davis, 1962-1964.

—. *French Poets and Novelists,* ed. Leon Edel. New York: Grosset and Dunlap, 1964.

—. *Letters,* ed. Leon Edel. 2 Vols. Cambridge, Mass.: The Belknap Press of Harvard University Press, 1973-1975.

—. *The Ivory Tower.* London: W. Collins Sons, 1917.

—. *Literary Reviews and Essays,* ed. Albert Mordell. New York: Grove Press, 1957.

—. *Novels.* The New York Edition, Scribner's 1907-1909.

—. *Notes and Reviews,* ed. Pierre de Chaignon La Rose. Cambridge, Mass.: Harvard University Press, 1921.

—. *The Question of Our Speech and the Lesson of Balzac: Two Lectures.* Folcroft, Pa.: The Folcroft Press, 1969.

—. *The Reverberator.* London: Macmillan, 1888.

—. *The Sacred Fount.* New York: Charles Scribner's Sons, 1901.

—. *The Sacred Fount.* New York: Grove Press, 1953.

—. *Selected Literary Criticism,* ed. Morris Shapira. New York: Horizon Press, 1964.

James, William. *The Principles of Psychology.* Chicago: Encyclopedia Brittanica, 1952.

Jean-Aubrey, G. *The Sea-Dreamer: A Definitive Biography of Joseph Conrad,* trans. Helen Sebba. Garden City, New York: Doubleday, 1957.

Jeffares, A. Norman. *George Moore.* London: British Council (Writers and Their Work Series), 1965.

Jernigan, E. Jay. "The Bibliographical and Textual Complexities of George Moore's *A Mummer's Wife." Bulletin of the New York Public Library.* 74 (1970), 396-410.

Johnson, J. Theodore, Jr. "Literary Impressionism in France: A Survey of Criticism." *L'Esprit Créateur* (Winter 1973), 271-297.

Jones, Edith R. "Stephen Crane at Brede." *Atlantic Monthly,* CXCIV (July 1954), 57-61.

Karl, Frederick R. "Joseph Conrad's Literary Theory." *Criticism,* II (Fall 1960), 317-335.

Katz, Joseph. "Afterword: Resources for the Study of Stephen Crane." *Stephen Crane in Transition: Centenary Essays,* ed. Joseph Katz. DeKalb, Illinois: Northern Illinois University Press, 1972.

—. "Stephen Crane 'Bibliographed': A Review." *Proof: The Yearbook of American Bibliographical and Textual Studies.* Vol. 3. University of South Carolina Press, 1973.

Kelley, Cornelia P. *The Early Development of Henry James.* Urbana, Illinois [1930]. University of Illinois Press, 1965.

Kermode, Frank. *The Romantic Image* [1957]. Vintage Books, 1964.

Kibler, James E., Jr. "The Library of Stephen and Cora Crane." in Joseph Katz, ed. *Proof: The Yearbook of American Bibliographical and Textual Studies,* I. University of South Carolina Press, 1971. pp. 199-246.

Knox, Norman. *The Word IRONY and Its Context, 1500-1755.* Durham, N. C.: Duke University Press, 1961.

Krauss, Rosalind. "Impressionism: The Narcissism of Light." *Partisan Review,* 1 (1976), 102-113.

Kumar, Shiv. *Bergson and the Stream of Consciousness Novel.* New York: New York University Press, 1962.

Laforgue, Jules, *Oeuvres complètes de Jules Laforgue: Mélanges posthumes* . 6th ed. Paris: Mercure de France, 1919.

—. *Selected Writings,* ed. and trans. William Jay Smith. New York: New York University Press, 1956.

Landow, George P. "Ruskin and Baudelaire on Art and the Artist." *University of Toronto Quarterly.* 37 (April 1968), 295-308.

Langer, Susanne K. *Feeling and Form.* New York: Charles Scribner's Sons, 1953.

Lassaigne, Jacques. *Impressionism* [1966]. London: Heron Books, 1969.

Laughton, Bruce. *Philip Wilson Steer, 1860-1942.* Oxford: Clarendon Press, 1972.

Lehrman, Edgar H., ed and trans. *Turgenev's Letters: A Selection.* Knopf, 1961.

Lerner, Daniel. "The Influence of Turgenev on Henry James." *Slavonic and East European Studies Yearbook,* XX (December 1941), 28-54.

Lethève, Jacques. *Impressionnistes et Symbolistes devant la presse.* Paris: Armand Colin, 1959.

Levin, Harry. *The Gates of Horn: A Study of Five French Realists.* New York: Oxford University Press, 1963.

Levine, Steven Z. *Monet and His Critics.* New York: Garland Publishing Co., 1976.

Lid, R. W. *Ford Madox Ford: The Essence of His Art.* University of California Press, 1964.

Lilly, Marjorie. *Sickert: The Painter and His World.* London: Elek, 1971.

Loesch, Georg. *Die impressionistische Syntax der Goncourt.* Nurenberg: Erlanger Dissertation, 1919 [not seen].

Lytle, Andrew. "Impressionism, the Ego, and the First Person." *Daedalus,* XCII (Spring 1963), 281-296.

Mc Fate, Patricia and Bruce Golden. "*The Good Soldier:* A Tragedy of Self Deception." *Modern Fiction Studies,* 9 (Spring 1963), 50-60.

Martin-Chauffier, Louis. "Proust and the Double I," *Partisan Review* (October 1949), 1011-1026.

Matthews, J. H. "L'Impressionnisme chez Zola: *Le Ventre de Paris. Le Français moderne* (July 1961), 199-205 [not seen].

Maupassant, Guy de. *Contes et nouvelles,* ed. Albert-Marie Schmidt. 2 Vols. Paris: A. Michel, 1957-59.

—. *Romans,* ed. Albert-Marie Schmidt. Paris: A. Michel, 1959.

—.   *Works.* The Conard Edition. 29 Vols., 1908-1910.

Maurois, André. *The World of Marcel Proust.* Harper, 1974.

Mayer, Ralph. *Artist's Handbook of Materials and Techniques.* New York: Viking, 1957.

Meixner, John A. *Ford Madox Ford's Novels: A Critical Study.* University of Minnesota Press, 1962.

Melchiori, Barbara. "Feelings about Aspects: Henry James on Pierre Loti." *Studi Americani.* 15 (1969), 169-199.

Meyers, Jeffrey. *Painting and the Novel.* Manchester University Press, 1975.

Moore, George. *Collected Works.* New York: The Carra Edition. 21 Vols., 1922-1924.

—.   *Confessions of a Young Man,* ed. Susan Dick. Montreal: McGill-Queen's University Press, 1972.

—.   *Conversations in Ebury Street* [1924]. Rev. ed. New York: Boni and Liveright, 1930.

—.   *Impressions and Opinions.* New York: Brentano's [1891], n.d.

—.   *Modern Painting* [London, 1893]. Enl. ed. [New York: Scribner's, 1898], Walter Scott, 1913.

—.   *A Mummer's Wife.* Brantano's, 1885.

Muller, Herbert J. "Impressionism in Fiction." *American Scholar,* 7 (Autumn 1938), 355-367.

Narmann, Rolf. "The Concerted Screws of Henry James." *Neuphilologische Mitteilungen,* LXXVI (1975), 317-337.

Nelson, James G. *The Early Nineties: A View from the Bodley Head.* Cambridge, Mass: Harvard University Press, 1971.

Nochlin, Linda, ed. *Realism and Tradition in Art, 1848-1900: Sources and Documents.* Englewood, N. J.: Prentice-Hall, 1966.

Novotny, Fritz. *Painting and Sculpture in Europe 1780-1880.* Pelican History of Art, 1960.

Nuhn, Ferner. *The Wind Blew From the East: A Study in the Orientation of American Culture.* New York: Harper and Row, 1942.

Pacey, W. C. D. "Henry James and His French Contemporaries." *American Literature,* XIII (November 1941), 240-256.

Pevsner, Nikolaus. *Pioneers of Modern Design from William Morris to Walter Gropius* [1936]. Baltimore: Penguin, 1960.

Pirenne, M. H. *Optics, Painting and Photography.* London: Cambridge University Press, 1970.

Pissarro, Camille. *Lettres à son fils Lucien,* ed. John Rewald. Paris: Albin Michel, 1950.

Price, Larkin B. ed. *Marcel Proust: A Critical Panorama.* University of Illinois Press, 1973.

Prideaux, Tom. *The World of Whistler: 1834-1903.* New York: Time-Life Books, 1970.

Proust, Marcel. *The Guermantes Way,* trans. Scott Moncrieff, Part 1. London: Chatto and Windus, 1925.

—. *Le Temps Retrouvé.* Paris: Livre de Poche, 1954.

—. *Time Regained,* trans. Andreas Mayor. London: Chatto and Windus, 1970.

Reff, Theodore. *"Césanne's Constructive Stroke."* *The Art Quarterly,* 25 (Autumn 1962), 224-227.

Reutersvard, Oscar. "The Accentuated Brush Stroke of the Impressionists." *Journal of Aesthetics and Art Criticism,* X (1952), 273-278.

Rewald, John. *The History of Impressionism.* 1946; 4th rev. ed. Museum of Modern Art, 1973.

Robinson, F. W. and S. G. Nichols, eds. *The Meaning of Mannerism.* Hanover, N. H.: University Press of New England, 1972.

Rogers, B. G. *Proust's Narrative Techniques.* Geneva: Droz, 1965.

Sansom, William. *Proust and His World.* Scribner's, 1974.

Santayana, George. *Character and Opinion in the United States with Reminiscences of William James and Josiah Royce and Academic Life in America.* N. Y.: Charles Scribner's Sons, 1920.

Schniedau, Herbert N. *The Image and the Real.* Louisiana State University Press, 1969.

Sears, Sallie. *The Negative Imagination: Form and Perspective in the Novels of Henry James.* Cornell University Press, 1968.

Sedgewick, G. G. *Of Irony, Especially in Drama* [1935]. Toronto: University of Toronto Press, 1948.

Seitz, William C. *Claude Monet: Seasons and Moments.* Museum of Modern Art, 1960.

Seznec, Jean. "Flaubert and the Graphic Arts," *Journal of the Warburg and Courtauld Institutes,* 8 and 9 (1945), 175-190.

Shearman, John. *Mannerism.* Penguin, 1967.

Sherard, Robert Harborough. *Émile Zola: A Biographical and Critical Study.* London: Chatto and Windus, 1893.

Stafford, William T., ed. *James's* Daisy Miller: *The Story, the Play, the Critics.* Scribner Research Anthologies. N. Y.: Scribner's, 1963.

—. ed. *Perspectives on* The Portrait of a Lady: *A Collection of Critical Essays.* New York University Press, 1966.

—. "William James as Critic of His Brother Henry," *The Personalist,* XL (Autumn 1959), 341-353.

Stallman, Robert Wooster. *Stephen Crane: A Biography.* George Braziller, 1968.

Stallnecht, Newton P., and Horst Frenz, eds. *Comparative Literature: Method and Perspective* [1961], Rev. ed. Carbondale, Ill.: Southern Illinois University Press, 1971.

Stanford, Derek. *Critics of the Nineties.* London: John Baker, 1970.

Steegmuller, Francis, ed. and trans. *Flaubert in Egypt: A Sensibility on Tour.* Boston: Little Brown, 1972.

—, ed. and trans. *The Selected Letters of Gustave Flaubert.* N. Y.: Farrar, Straus and Young, 1953.

Stein, Roger B. *John Ruskin and Aesthetic Thought in America, 1840-1900.* Cambridge, Mass.: Harvard University Press, 1967.

Stone, Donald David. *Novelists in a Changing World: Meredith, James, and the Transformation of English Fiction in the 1880's.* Cambridge, Mass.: Harvard University Press, 1972.

Stronks, James B. "Stephen Crane's English Years" The Legend Corrected," *Papers of the Bibliographical Society of America,* LVII (1962), 340-349.

Sutter, J., ed. *The Heo-Impressionists,* trans. Chantal Deliss. Greenwich, Conn.: Graphic Society, 1970.

Symons, Arthur. "Whistler," *Studies in Seven Arts.* N. Y.: E. P. Dutton, n.d.

—. *Silhouettes.* London: Bodley Head, 1892.

Tanner, Jimmie E. *The Twentieth Century Impressionistic Novel: Conrad and Faulkner.* University of Oklahoma Dissertation, 1964.

Tanner, Tony, ed.  *Henry James: Modern Judgements.*   Bristol: Macmillan, 1968.

Teets, Bruce E., and Helmut E. Gerber, comps. and eds.  *Joseph Conrad: An Annotated Bibliography of Writings About Him.* DeKalb, Illinois: Northern Illinois University Press, 1971.

Teets, Bruce E. "Literary Impressionism: Conrad and Ford," *Literary Impressionism in Ford Madox Ford, Joseph Conrad and Related. Preliminary Papers, MLA Seminar 8,* ed. Todd Bender. University of Wisconsin Press, 1975.

Thibaudet, Albert. *Gustave Flaubert.* Paris: Gallimard, 1935.

Tompkins, Jane P. "The Redemption of Time in *Notes of a Son and a Son and Brother," Texas Studies in Literature and Language.* XIV (Winter 1973), 681-690.

Townsend, Francis G.  *Ruskin and the Landscape Feeling: A Critical Analysis of His Thought During the Crucial Years of His Life, 1843-56.* University of Illinois Press, 1951.

Trevor-Roper, P. D.  *The World through Blunted Sight.*   London: Thames and Hudson, 1970.

Turgenev, Ivan.  *Letters: A Selection,*   ed. and trans. Edgar H. Lehrman. N. Y.: Knopf, 1961.

Tuttleton, James W.  *The Novel of Manners in America.*  University of North Carolina Press, 1972.

Valery, Paul.  *Degas, Manet, Morisot.*  N. Y.: Pantheon Books, 1960.

Vasari, Giorgio.  *Le vite,*   ed. Gaetano Milanesi. 9 Vols. Florence, 1878-1885.

Veeder, William.  "Strether and the Transcendance of Language," *Modern Philology.*  69 (November 1971), 116-132.

—. *Impressionists and Symbolists.* N. Y.: Scribners, 1950.

Viljoen, Helen Gill. *Ruskin's Scottish Heritage: A Prelude.* Urbana, Illinois: University of Illinois Press, 1956.

Ward, J. A. *The Imagination of Disaster: Evil in the Fiction of Henry James.* Lincoln, Nebraska: University of Nebraska Press. 1961.

Weber, Eugen, ed. *Paths to the Present: Aspects of European Thought from Romanticism to Existentialism.* N. Y.: Dodd, Mead, 1962.

Wegelin, Christof. *The Image of Europe in Henry James.* Dallas, Texas: S. M. U. Press, 1958.

Wegener, Alphons. *Impressionismus und Klassizimus im Werke Marcel Prousts.* Franckfort, 1930 [Not seen].

Weingart, Seymour L. *The Form and Meaning of the Impressionist Novel.* University of California Dissertation, 1964.

Weinstein, Philip M. *Henry James and the Requirements of the Imagination.* Cambridge, Mass.: Harvard University Press, 1971.

Weisstein, Ulrich. *Comparative Literature and Literary Theory: Survey and Introduction* [1968], trans. William Riggan in collab. with the author. Bloomington, Ind.: Indiana University Press, 1973.

Wellek, René. *A History of Modern Criticism, Vol. 4. 1750-1950.* New Haven, Conn.: Yale University Press, 1965.

Wenger, Jared. "The Art of the Flashlight: Violent Technique in *Les Rougon-Macquart*," *PMLA*, LVII (Autumn 1942), 1137-1159.

Wiener, Philip P., ed. in chief. *Dictionary of the History of Ideas,* Volume II. N. Y.: Charles Scribner's Sons, 1973.

Wiesenfarth, Joseph. *"The Good Soldier:* A Symposium," *Modern Fiction Studies,* 9 (Spring 1963), 39-49.

Wilenski, R. H. *The Modern Movement in Art.* 5th American ed. N. Y.: Thomas Yoseloff, 1957.

Wolf, Jack C. "Henry James and Impressionist Painting," *The CEA Critic.* XXXVIII (March 1976), 14-16.

Wright, William C. "Hazlitt, Ruskin, and Nineteenth Century Art Criticism," *Journal of Aesthetics and Art Criticism.* XXXII (Summer 1974), 509-523.

Yeazell, Ruth. "The New 'Arithmetic' of Henry James," *Criticism.* XVI (Spring 1974), 109-119.

Zaniello, Thomas. *The Moments of Perception in Nineteenth and Twentieth Century Literature.* Stanford University Dissertation, 1972.

Zola, Émile. *Germinal* (1885), trans. L. W. Tancock. Baltimore: Penguin Books (1954), 1969.

—. *Le Roman Expérimental.* Paris: Charpentier, 1880.

—. *Les Rougon-Macquart,* eds. Armand Lanoux and Henri Mitterand. Paris: Bibliothèque de la Pléiade, 1960-1967.

[Anon.] "Fathers of Literary Impressionism in England," *Littel's Living Age.* 213 (May 1, 1897) 290-303; rpt. from *Quarterly Review.* 185 (January 1897), 173-194.

# INDEX

Adams, Henry 202
A. E. 127, 156
Angrand, Charles 19
Aristotle 244, 245; *Nicomachean Ethics* 148; *Politics* 245, 295
Arnold, Matthew 102, 159, 189; *Essays and Criticism* 189
Austen, Jane 151, 214

Bailey, John 190
Balzac, Honore de 23, 54, 91, 197, 250, 278, 297; "Le Chef-d'oeuvre inconnu" 215
Baudelaire, Charles 16, 29, 32, 75, 76, 77, 93, 94, 97, 145, 181; *Mirror of Art* 93-94
Bazille, Frederic 3, 4, 7, 13, 14, 29, 36, 65
Beardsley, Aubrey 41, 95
Bennett, Arnold 136
Bergson, Henri 36, 167, 181
Besant, Walter 188
Bierstadt, Albert 165
Björnson, Bjonstjerne 119
Blanc, Charles 39
Blanqui, Louis A. 14
Boime, Albert 13
Boldoni, Jean 184, 271
Bosanquet, Theodora 301
Boudin, Eugène-Louis 3, 26, 28, 35, 40, 262
Bouguereau, William A. 20
Bourget, Paul 59, 60, 87

Braquemond, Felix 29
Bronzino, Angelo 187
Brown, Ford Madox 26, 28-29, 117, 138, 140, 174
Brown, Fred 40
Browning, Elizabeth Barrett 108
Brunetière, Ferdinand 60, 61, 62, 87

Caillebotte, Gustave 15
Cassatt, Mary 5, 21, 24
Cézanne, Paul 16, 38, 47, 48, 65, 67, 89-91, 134, 135, 140, 147, 242, 271
Chevreul, M. 8, 17, 38, 39
Chirico, Giorgio de 276
Conrad, Joseph 55-56, 73, 87, 129-133, 136, 138, 140-141, 143-144, 146-147, 150, 152, 164, 177, 180, 193, 223, 283, 285; *Almayer's Folly* 139, 141, 176; "An Appreciation" 288; *Chance* 178-179; "The End of the Tether" 148; "The Heart of Darkness" 139, 148; "Karain: A Memory" 147, 178; *Letters* 173-174, 176-178; *Lord Jim* 98, 139, 148-152, 171, 176, 178-179; *The Nigger of the "Narcissus"* 75, 130, 137, 139, 142, 144-145, 149, 170-171, 176, 295; *Nostromo* 139, 148, 176; *An Outcast of the Islands* 139; *A Personal Record*

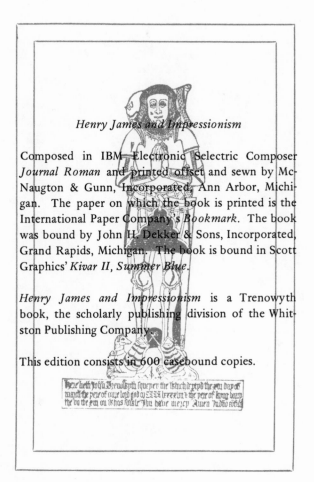

*Henry James and Impressionism*

Composed in IBM Electronic Selectric Composer *Journal Roman* and printed offset and sewn by Mc-Naugton & Gunn, Incorporated, Ann Arbor, Michigan. The paper on which the book is printed is the International Paper Company's *Bookmark*. The book was bound by John H. Dekker & Sons, Incorporated, Grand Rapids, Michigan. The book is bound in Scott Graphics' *Kivar II, Summer Blue*.

*Henry James and Impressionism* is a Trenowyth book, the scholarly publishing division of the Whitston Publishing Company.

This edition consists in 600 casebound copies.